Humana Festival 2013
The Complete Plays

About the Humana Foundation

The Humana Foundation was established in 1981 as the philanthropic arm of Humana Inc., one of the nation's leading health care companies. Located in Louisville, Ky., the site of Humana's corporate headquarters, the Foundation's mission is to promote healthy lives and healthy communities. The Foundation's key funding priorities are childhood health, intergenerational health, and active lifestyles. For more information, visit www.humanafoundation.org.

Humana and the Humana Foundation are dedicated to Corporate Social Responsibility. Our goal is to ensure that every business decision we make reflects our commitment to improving the health and well-being of our members, our associates, the communities we serve, and our planet.

Humana Festival 2013
The Complete Plays

Edited by
Amy Wegener and Sarah Lunnie

New York, NY

Published by Playscripts, Inc.
450 Seventh Avenue, Suite 809
New York, New York, 10123
www.playscripts.com

Cover Design by Andy Perez
Cover Image by Penelope Dullaghan
Text Design and Layout by Erin Salvi

First Edition: April 2014
10 9 8 7 6 5 4 3 2 1

LCCN: 95650734
ISSN: 1935-4452

ISBN-13: 978-1-62384-002-0

Contents

Acknowledgments

The editors wish to thank the following persons for their invaluable assistance in compiling this volume:

Jennifer Bielstein
Sara Durham
Meg Fister
Kirsty Gaukel
Kory Kelly
Danielle Manley
Hannah Rae Montgomery
Steve Moulds
Andy Perez
Jessica Reese
Jeffrey S. Rodgers
Erin Salvi
Zan Sawyer-Dailey
Naomi Shafer
Stephanie Spalding
Les Waters
Sam Weiner
Eric Werner
Kathryn Zukaitis

Jessica Amato
Val Day
Leah Hamos
Mark Orsini
Bruce Ostler
Mark Subias
Chris Till
Rachel Viola
Derek Zasky

Actors Theatre of Louisville Staff
Humana Festival 2013

ARTISTIC DIRECTOR, Les Waters
MANAGING DIRECTOR, Jennifer Bielstein

ARTISTIC

Associate Artistic Director . . . . Meredith McDonough
Associate Director . . . . Zan Sawyer-Dailey
Arts Management Executive Assistant . . . . Meg Fister
Company Manager . . . . Dot King
Arts Administration Intern . . . . Lizzy Thomas

Literary

Literary Director . . . . Amy Wegener
Literary Manager . . . . Sarah Lunnie
Literary Associate . . . . Hannah Rae Montgomery
Humana Festival Literary Assistant . . . . Jessica Reese
Dramaturgy/Literary Management Interns . . . . . . Naomi Shafer, Kathryn Zukaitis

Education

Director . . . . Steven Rahe
Associate Director . . . . Jacob Stoebel
Education Associate . . . . Jane B. Jones
Education/Teaching Artist Interns . . . . Gabriel Garcia,
LeShawn Darnell Holcomb, Lori Pitts
Teaching Artists . . . . Liz Fentress, Keith McGill
University of Louisville
Teaching Artist Partnership . . . . Jody-Ann P. Henry, Ashley Smith

Apprentice/Intern Company

Director . . . . Michael Legg
Associate Director . . . . Amy Attaway
A/I Administration Intern . . . . Michael Whatley
Directing Interns . . . . Kate Eminger, Rachel Karp
Apprentices . . . . Noelia Antweiler, Samantha Beach,
Tamara Del Rosso, Ethan Dubin, Conor Eifler,
Laura Engels, Kim Fischer, Bobby Johnson,
Chalia La Tour, Joseph Metcalfe, Derek Nelson,
Liz Ramos, Andy Reinhardt, Angeliea Stark, Ben
Vigus, Kimberly Weinkle, Sarah Grace Welbourn,
Madison Welterlen, Jeff White, Ian Whitt,
Christa Wroblewski, Michael Zuccola

ADMINISTRATION

General Manager . . . . Jeffrey S. Rodgers
Human Resources Manager . . . . Cora Brown
Systems Manager . . . . Dottie Krebs
Leasing Manager . . . . .John Lepping
Executive Assistant . . . . Janelle Baker
Administrative Services Coordinator . . . . Alan Meyer

AUDIENCES SERVICES AND SALES

Ticket Sales Director . . . . Kim McKercher
Senior Box Office Manager . . . . Saundra Blakeney
Training Manager . . . . .Steve Clark
Season Tickets Manager . . . . Julie Gallegos
Customer Service & Special Projects Manager . . . . Kristy Kannapell
Customer Service Representatives . . . . Cheryl Anderson, Sean Espinal,
Tony Hammons, Melissa Ratliff,
Lizzy Thomas, Kae Thompson

Volunteer and Audience Relations

Director . . . . .Allison Hammons
House Managers . . . . Elizabeth Cooley, Evan McMahon
Amanda Simmons, Michael Whatley
Lobby Manager . . . . Tiffany Walton
Coat Check Supervisor . . . . Cory Vaughn
Coat Check Attendants . . . . .LeShawn Darnell Holcomb, Tanisha Johnson

DEVELOPMENT

Director . . . . Josef Krebs
Associate Director, Individual Giving. . . . . .Kate Chandler
Associate Director, Institutional Partnerships . . . . Danielle Manley
Annual Fund Manager . . . . .Gretchen James
Grant Writer. . . . . .Katie McCandless
Development Coordinator . . . . .Elizabeth Magee
Development Intern . . . . Jessica Angima

FINANCE

Finance Director . . . . .Peggy Shake
Accounting Coordinator. . . . . Jason Acree
Accounting Assistant. . . . . .Dara Tiller

MARKETING & COMMUNICATIONS

Director . . . . .Kory P. Kelly
Public Relations Manager. . . . . Kirsty Gaukel
Public Relations Intern . . . . .Lacy Mudd
Marketing and Sales Manager. . . . . .Olivia Pedolzky
Marketing Intern . . . . Sean Espinal

Audience Development and Special Events Manager . . . . Stephanie Spalding
Audience Development/Festival Management Intern. . . . . Claire Jones
Communications Coordinator . . . . Sara E. Durham
Graphic Designer . . . . Andy Perez
Graphic Design Fellow. . . . . Keith LaRue
Group Sales Manager . . . . .Sarah Peters
Group Sales Associate. . . . . Chris O'Leary

OPERATIONS

Director . . . . Mike Schüssler-Williams
Operations Manager . . . . Barry Witt
Maintenance. . . . . .Ricky Baldon, John Voyles
Building Services. . . . . .Patricia Duncan, Hank Hunter,
Kenny Winfield, Cindy Woodward
Receptionist . . . . Griffin Falvey

PRODUCTION

Production Manager . . . . .Kathleen Kronauer
Assistant Production Manager . . . . .Paul Werner
Production Management Intern. . . . . Megan Lamasney
Production Stage Manager . . . . .Paul Mills Holmes
Resident Stage Manager . . . . .Stephen Horton
Production Assistants . . . . .Jessica Potter, Katie Shade
Stage Management Interns . . . . Hannah Barnes, Alex Lucci,
Jacob Halpern Weitzman

Scenic

Technical Director. . . . . .Jason Grant
Assistant Technical Director . . . . .Alexis Tucker
Shop Foreman . . . . Javan Roy-Bachman
Drafter/Rigger. . . . . Braden Blauser
Carpenters . . . . Alexia Hall, Patrick Jump, Joen Pallesen,
Andrew Patton, Pierre Vendette
Pamela Brown Deck Carpenter . . . . .Peter Regalbuto
Bingham Theatre Deck Carpenter. . . . . Mathew Krell
Scenic Charge. . . . . Kieran Wathen
Scenic Art Intern. . . . . .Caitlin Thompson
Scenic Journeyman . . . . Aaron O'Neill*

Costumes

Costume Director . . . . Kristopher Castle
Costume Administrator . . . . .Lisa Weber
Resident Costume Designer . . . . Lorraine Venberg
Wig and Makeup Supervisor. . . . . Jehann Gilman
Crafts Master . . . . Shari Cochran
Draper/Tailor . . . . Jeffery Park

First Hand . . . . Natalie Maynard
Stitcher Captain . . . . .Elizabeth Hahn
Stitchers . . . . Wesley Jenkins, Justin Collings
Pamela Brown Wardrobe Supervisor . . . . .Jacob Freund
Bingham Wardrobe Supervisor . . . . Megan Shuey
Costume Design Journeymen . . . . .Rhianna Reardon*, Beatrice Vena*
Costume Construction Intern . . . . Shane Hall

Lighting
Supervisor . . . . Nick Dent
Assistant Lighting Supervisor . . . . Christine Ferriter
First Electrician . . . . .John Newman
Lighting Technicians . . . . Jesse AlFord, Ashley Beck,
Kathleen Dieckmann, Alan Pleiman
Lighting Intern . . . . .John Allerheiligen

Sound
Supervisor . . . . .Paul Doyle
Assistant Sound Supervisor . . . . Jessica Collins
Sound Technicians . . . . .Jack Audet, Amanda Neild, Amanda Werre

Properties
Director . . . . Mark Walston
Properties Master . . . . .Joe Cunningham
Carpenter Artisan . . . . Karl Anderson
Soft Goods Artisan . . . . Heather Lindert
General Artisans . . . . .Noah Johnson, Aimee Plant, Jay Tollefsen
Artisan/Shopper . . . . .Jessie Combest

VIDEO
Media Technologist . . . . .Philip Allgeier
Media Specialist . . . . Tim Gooch

USHER CAPTAINS

Dolly Adams, Marie Allen, Katherine Austin, June Blair, Libba & Chuck Bonifer,
Tanya Briley, Maleva Chamberlain, Donna Conlon, Terry Conway, Laurie Eiden,
Doris Elder, Reese Fisher, Joyce French, Carol Halbleib, Sandy Kissling, Nickie
Langdon, Barbara Nichols, Cathy Nooning, Teresa Nusz, Judy Pearson, Nancy
Rankin, Bob Rosedale, Jenna Thomas, Tim Unruh, David Wallace, Megg Ward

Denotes Paul Owen Fellow

Foreword

With every one of its plays receiving a full production, and the national visibility afforded these world premieres, the Humana Festival has the opportunity to place a vibrant mix of voices in the limelight each spring. This year, I had the privilege of curating the Festival plays for the first time, inviting writers whose work I love—from the renowned to the then-unknown—to come and make something remarkable here at Actors Theatre of Louisville.

Among these wonderful playwrights were longtime collaborators of mine like Will Eno (new to Louisville audiences), Sarah Ruhl, and Anne Washburn—but the other end of the spectrum included relative newcomers Mallery Avidon and Jeff Augustin, the latter receiving his first professional production in the Festival while still in graduate school. Perhaps even more important than this variety of career milestones was the diversity of life and cultural perspectives that the writers brought to the stage. From Branden Jacobs-Jenkins' unsettling drama set on an Arkansas plantation to Avidon's tale of growing up in and out of an ashram, from Sam Marks' dissection of failing friends and fathers to Augustin's story of survival in his family's homeland of Haiti—these plays gave voice to a range of experiences and histories, even those originating generations ago, or outside this country's borders.

Here at Actors Theatre, the artistic staff is often asked if the Humana Festival plays are chosen with a theme in mind, and the answer is that they *never* are—in fact, we try to juxtapose very different tales and aesthetics, to honor contrasts rather than commonalities. Looking back in retrospect, though, patterns can sometimes emerge, and it's striking to me how much these plays do speak to one another after all. It's fascinating to detect a running meditation on how elusive happiness seems to be, and our fumbling, sometimes ridiculous attempts to chase after it. These protagonists wander in search of the Self, and are so lost that they even look to celebrities like Julia Roberts and Laurence Fishburne for some kind of sign that they're okay. As the authors of the triptych *Sleep Rock Thy Brain* show us, even the simple act of drifting off at night is fraught with complication. What's happened to our sense of security, and how should we navigate this age of uncertainty? Perhaps it can be said that this year's plays—in ways both comical and deeply tragic—show characters grasping for belonging and some measure of contentment, in the face of troubled histories and a befuddling present. But there's really no roadmap these days, no easy way to find "soup and a blanket, and everything's all right" (to borrow a phrase from Eno's *Gnit*).

As I sit down to write this introductory note, we're embarking on rehearsals for the 2014 Humana Festival, and wondering what the next slate of plays will reveal about the moment we're living through. And looking beyond, Actors Theatre is already cultivating the knowledge and relationships that will lead to future discoveries about what American playwrights and ensembles creating new work can tell us about our time. We're doing this by building our commissioning program, offering encouragement that can span several years of getting to know a playwright's body of work, and through good old-fashioned rigor in reading many voices we don't yet know. Whatever common obsessions or divergent worldviews the selections ultimately reveal, it is a joy to help launch these pieces—and sometimes, writers' careers—into a national conversation each year.

—Les Waters
Artistic Director
Actors Theatre of Louisville

Editors' Note

There's no one left in this family who might have told me about the whole me.
> —Toni in Branden Jacobs-Jenkins' *Appropriate*

It's nice to have someone else plan your life for you.
I don't know if I've been doing the best job of it on my own.
> —Lila in Mallery Avidon's *O Guru Guru Guru,*
> *or why I don't want to go to yoga class with you*

PETER. I'm on a journey to discover, to uncover, the authentic self.
MOTHER. Yeah? Get some milk, while you're out.
> —Will Eno's *Gnit*

In assembling the wonderfully diverse plays of the 2013 Humana Festival between the covers of one compact volume, it's intriguing to see patterns emerge from the composite image that they create. Though the eleven tales collected here depict worlds as varied as an ashram, an Arkansan plantation, "Papa Doc" Duvalier's Haiti, and the vastness of outer space, placing them side by side produces a portrait of souls adrift and searching. In pieces whose tones range from comical to tragic (and sometimes both at once), characters wander without a sure compass, hoping to map some definable identity that might help chart their course forward. But to borrow a phrase from Branden Jacobs-Jenkins' beleaguered Toni in *Appropriate*, we discover instead that they may be "lost, lost, lost, lost, lost." From a man looking for his authentic self to an artist who's tried to disappear, from friends at odds to siblings estranged from one another and their history, the characters in this year's plays find that figuring out who you're supposed to be is a constant struggle. Even gauging one's identity in relationship to family, spiritual practice, or work is really no guarantee that stable footing can be found.

If there's a lesson to be taken from these stories' collective insights, perhaps it's that life just keeps changing in ways we can't control—and yet, we have to find a way to keep living in the world and learning what we can from so much confusion. Whether it's because of the repressive regime that robs a Haitian painter of his creative identity in Jeff Augustin's *Cry Old Kingdom*, the alienation born from an unusual childhood in Mallery Avidon's *O Guru Guru Guru*, or the grief that haunts insomniac and sleeping minds in Rinne Groff's *Comfort Inn* and Anne Washburn's *Dreamerwake,* the people in these plays must actively metabolize loss and a good deal of existential anxiety. The choices they make in order to keep going are never simple, and sometimes they're even ethically murky—for instance, the astronauts in Lucas Hnath's *nightnight* won't be chosen for a high-stakes spacewalk without telling a few big lies. And some protagonists will learn too late (as does *Gnit*'s anti-hero) that it's the small steps along the journey that actually give a life meaning and integrity.

The decisions we face in the present moment aren't the only dilemmas to contend with, though. Many of the plays suggest that history is always with us, and that we fail to understand or to reconcile the past at our own—and perhaps the next generation's—peril. Sam Marks compellingly draws old writer friends recounting former slights and debts in front of their daughters in *The Delling Shore*, making a literary battleground of their professional jealousies and personal failures. The woman trying to rebuild her life in Emily Schwend's *Halfway* is caught between the sins of her past and an uncertain future. And *Appropriate* suggests that it's a white, plantation-owning family's blindness to its own history that breeds dysfunction. Here, conflicts rage not only because of the aggregated betrayals between siblings, but because of the troubled legacy of the generations that came before. It's not enough to think we can forge some kind of new identity for ourselves from scratch; we must first contend with the ancestors and forces that have shaped us.

While the implications of these plays' varied meditations on identity hold difficult truths, there is plenty of light that cuts through the darkness here. Confusion can manifest as hilarity or wistful humor, and conflict can fuel biting comedy, so there are many laughs to be found in the pages of this anthology as well. It's striking, too, that self-knowledge and even a little peace can come from the oddest places (and often from strangers) in these plays. Talking with the person next to you on a plane, as in Sarah Ruhl's *Two Conversations Overheard on Airplanes*, may result in unexpected intimacy. Or an encounter with a celebrity, as experienced by the protagonists of *O Guru Guru Guru* and Jonathan Josephson's *27 Ways I Didn't Say "Hi" to Laurence Fishburne*, may unlock new insights. Yes, it's awfully hard to be a person in the world. But sometimes grace and comfort are nearby, albeit in the weirdest and most fantastical guises.

With vivid imagination, the playwrights in this collection use all the resources at their disposal to tell their stories, and a conscious attempt to experiment in the many orbits of theatrical form and style animates the plays of the 2013 Festival. *Appropriate* (as its title hints) does this by taking the obsessions of American family drama and unleashing them for its own entirely original ends, and *Gnit* reimagines a classic of Western drama with a distinctively contemporary philosophical voice and sense of humor. Elsewhere on the structural spectrum, *O Guru Guru Guru* involves its audience in the action in highly unexpected ways, and the three one-act pieces that comprise *Sleep Rock*

Thy Brain explore how aerial choreography can shape storytelling, launching actors into the air to fly, spin and float.

If they happen to share some preoccupations and questions, the plays that premiered in the 2013 Humana Festival pose those questions in thrilling, surprising, marvelously varied ways. A great pleasure of editing this volume has been not only revisiting the work of these talented playwrights and their diverse aesthetics, but also noting how these scripts, considered together, might speak about a time and culture. Now we have the privilege of sharing these extraordinary new plays with an even wider audience, knowing that the reader will draw her own conclusions and connections.

—Amy Wegener and Sarah Lunnie

CRY OLD KINGDOM
by Jeff Augustin

ABOUT *CRY OLD KINGDOM*

This article first ran in the January/February 2013 issue of Inside Actors, *Actors Theatre of Louisville's subscriber newsletter, and is based on conversations with the playwright before rehearsals for the Humana Festival production began.*

Haiti, 1964. Beneath the watchful eyes of François "Papa Doc" Duvalier's government, revolution is brewing. Words of rebellion against his repressive regime flood the nation's radio waves, even as the Tonton Macoutes death squads prowl the villages, killing or imprisoning anyone who speaks ill of the dictator. The people of Haiti face a stark choice: to join the fight, or to flee. For the characters in *Cry Old Kingdom*, Jeff Augustin's lyrical portrait of a painful moment in Haitian history, the death of the life they once knew forces impossible decisions.

Officially, Edwin's been dead for years; his safety depends on Duvalier's government believing him long-buried. Unfortunately, with the feigned death of his body, his work as a painter has suffered a real demise. An artist once welcomed in high-ranking political circles, Edwin now hides from the world in an underground studio, surrounded by half-finished canvases he's unable to complete. Even his wife Judith, once the seductive muse who danced through the streets during Carnival, can't ignite his inspiration. After all, marriage to a man who doesn't exist hasn't been kind to her. Because she now toils in the open market all day, the sun has baked her bones dry and creaking clumsiness has crept into her every movement. But the calls for revolution rekindle Judith's old vivacity. Ignoring her husband's warnings, she speaks passionately of joining the insurgents.

Edwin will also feel alive again, but for a very different reason. One evening while walking on the beach, he encounters a scarred but beautiful young man, Henri Marx, gathering wood. Like many others longing for freedom and opportunity, Henri Marx plans to construct a plantain boat and escape on this precarious vessel to Miami. Captivated, Edwin proposes an exchange. He'll allow Henri Marx to build the boat in his studio, safe from hostile eyes. In return, Henri Marx will let Edwin paint him as he builds. Edwin's interactions with Henri Marx bring sudden heat to his blood, sparking fresh visions of the future. But while Edwin begins gazing into the horizon toward life beyond Haiti, Judith's determined to maintain her ties to tradition at any cost. And, as Henri Marx declares, "Being alive is having to choose."

Haiti has always been a subject close to Jeff Augustin's heart—as has the conflict between remaining devoted to one's roots and deciding to cast off for strange shores. That conflict is familiar to Augustin from his own experience. His mother emigrated to the U.S. from Haiti in 1979 (eight years after "Papa Doc" died and his equally corrupt son, Jean-Claude "Baby Doc" Duvalier, replaced him as "President for Life"). The youngest of seven, Augustin is one of just two siblings born in America. He remembers watching his brothers and sisters struggle to connect with their new country—even as he envied their innate identification with the family's native land. "I felt like I was constantly searching to know the history of Haiti, like I had to learn a culture," he comments. Writing *Cry Old Kingdom* allowed Augustin to access part of that cultural past, by exploring the era in which his mother came of age. A tension between past and present—and the ways in which national identity and personal identity inextricably intertwine—permeates the play. Judith, with her nostalgia for Carnival and belief that Haiti can still be saved, represents the impulse to hold onto the past. Meanwhile, Augustin explains, "the future is embodied in Henri Marx's idea of beyond." In Edwin resides the problem of the present: the struggle to resolve where one's loyalties should lie.

That isn't the only dilemma Edwin faces. Through his painter protagonist, Augustin poses resonant questions about an artist's responsibilities in times of political turmoil. "I'm interested in why you create art in regimes," Augustin reflects. "To tell the truth, or to promote the government?" For Edwin, it's neither; he tells Henri Marx that he prefers to remain "immune" from the disease of politics, observing events rather than participating in them. But indifference can't be maintained forever. Augustin elaborates, "There are artists who can do what Edwin does: distance himself. But there are artists who actually do push with their work against these kinds of regimes, and I think that's because an artist at some point has to choose."

With *Cry Old Kingdom*, Augustin chooses to tackle what it means to try to dream and survive, and he brings these big questions to the stage in an undeniably visceral way. Before our eyes, Henri Marx hammers his boat together. Before our eyes, Edwin covers a blank canvas with color. Before our eyes, Judith tries to bend her body into the dances of her youth. "I've always been fascinated with movement, and text in relation to movement," says Augustin. "The language that's coming out of the mouth doesn't always match what the body's capable of doing." In *Cry Old Kingdom*, we get both lines that ring with poetic simplicity, and a physicality by turns graceful and brutal to watch. Augustin's play is a sensual, raw call for us to consider the impact of the choices we make, as citizens and as individuals—and to ponder what else might be possible.

—Hannah Rae Montgomery

BIOGRAPHY

Jeff Augustin's play *Cry Old Kingdom* received its world premiere at the 2013 Humana Festival of New American Plays. His work has been developed at the O'Neill National Playwrights Conference (*Little Children Dream of God*), The Ground Floor at Berkeley Repertory Theatre (*The Last Tiger in Haiti*), and American Conservatory Theater (*in the crowding darkness*). Augustin's play *The Imaginary Life of Millo St. Jean* was developed and produced by Snapdragon in New York. He is the winner of the 2011 Lorraine Hansberry Playwriting Award. He is currently an M.F.A. Playwriting Candidate at University of California, San Diego and graduated from Boston College with a B.A. in Theatre Arts. Augustin is a member of the Dramatists Guild.

ACKNOWLEDGMENTS

Cry Old Kingdom premiered at the Humana Festival of New American Plays in March 2013. It was directed by Tom Dugdale with the following cast:

HENRI MARX	Jonathan Majors
EDWIN	Andy Lucien
JUDITH	Natalie Paul

and the following production staff:

Scenic Designer	Daniel Zimmerman
Costume Designer	Lorraine Venberg
Co-Lighting Designers	Russell H. Champa, Dani Clifford
Sound Designer	Benjamin Marcum
Stage Manager	Stephen Horton
Dramaturg	Hannah Rae Montgomery
Casting	Harriet Bass
Directing Assistant	Michael Whatley
Dialect Coach	Rinda Frye
Production Assistant	Suzanne Spicer
Assistant Dramaturg	Kathryn Zukaitis

CHARACTERS

EDWIN, early- to mid-30s Haitian man
HENRI MARX, early 20s Haitian man
JUDITH, late 20s/early 30s Haitian woman

SETTING

Haiti, 1964. A home in a small village and a remote section of the beach. Both are a couple of hours from Port-au-Prince.

NOTE

——   A silent moment when a character reveals or holds back a truth. A time when language is too much or not enough.

For the flag,
For our country
To die is a fine thing!
Our past cries out to us:
Have a strong soul!
To die is a fine thing,
For the flag,
For our country.

—*Final refrain of* La Dessalinienne, *the Haitian National Anthem*

For my mom

Jonathan Majors and Andy Lucien
in *Cry Old Kingdom*

37th Humana Festival of New American Plays
Actors Theatre of Louisville, 2013
Photo by Alan Simons

CRY OLD KINGDOM

Scene One

The beach near sunset. HENRI MARX *is checking the sturdiness, weight capacity and floatability of different types of wood. He is sculpted. His body is agile and regal, his movement fluid, yet weighted/heavy. A moment.* EDWIN *enters unnoticed. He watches* HENRI MARX. *He seems hypnotized by* HENRI MARX's *figure and movement. A few moments.*

EDWIN. There are easier ways to die

> (HENRI MARX, *startled, spins around.* EDWIN *smiles at him.* HENRI MARX *takes him in a beat.*)

HENRI MARX. Macoutes don't come to this part of the beach

EDWIN. But there are eyes. And eyes speak because eyes get threatened. Eyes get hungry

HENRI MARX. And your eyes?

EDWIN. My eyes. My eyes are silent. They see and wonder. Nothing more.

> (*A slight beat.*)

And your eyes?

HENRI MARX. They are focused only on me

EDWIN. They seem gentle

HENRI MARX. They are to most

EDWIN. To new friends?

HENRI MARX. I don't make many

EDWIN. To family friends?

HENRI MARX. Do you know my family?

EDWIN. Your face is familiar

HENRI MARX. It's the young we all make the same nasty faces

EDWIN. You're not that much younger than me

HENRI MARX. The young are getting older

> (EDWIN *smiles/chuckles.*)

EDWIN. Going somewhere?

HENRI MARX. No

EDWIN. The wood?

HENRI MARX. Collecting debris

EDWIN. Ah, I didn't realize you worked for the regime. You're not wearing the uniform

HENRI MARX. I didn't say I worked for the regime

EDWIN. So collecting trash is a hobby?

HENRI MARX. Excuse me the sun will set soon, don't want to worry my mother

> (HENRI MARX *is leaving without the wood.*)

EDWIN. You're forgetting your wood

HENRI MARX. It's not mine

EDWIN. People Anse-a-Foleur

HENRI MARX. Excuse me?

EDWIN. Your family is from Anse-a-Foleur

HENRI MARX. ——

EDWIN. It's your face. The wide slight uneven angles of your nostrils. The weight of your cheeks. The bruised melon shape of your head. The roughness of your skin. Like mine. Although, my cheeks have lost their weight

> (*A beat.*)

What's your family name?

HENRI MARX. ——

EDWIN. It's okay. My family is from Anse-a-Foleur. Maybe you know my great aunt. Dominique. Idline Marie Dominique. She runs the grammar school

HENRI MARX. Yes

EDWIN. We used to try to get her down to Port-au-Prince, but she loves her people too much. It's been twelve, thirteen years since I've seen her, your age I think. Picked her up for my mother's funeral. Took two days. Was she your teacher?

HENRI MARX. Yes, fourth and fifth year

EDWIN. She's strict, quick to strike if you're not prepared. But maybe you were better than I

HENRI MARX. Mostly

EDWIN. You look like you were. What's your family name?

HENRI MARX. Pierre

EDWIN. (*Smiling.*) Arlan's brother?

HENRI MARX. Yes

EDWIN. You I don't remember, but Arlan I do. Before my mother and I left we were schoolmates. He used to stutter. My great aunt tried to beat it out of him

HENRI MARX. She did

EDWIN. How is he?

HENRI MARX. Dead

EDWIN. Sorry

HENRI MARX. It's not your fault

EDWIN. And your mother and father, how are they doing?

HENRI MARX. Papa died, it's just me and my mother

EDWIN. That's hard

HENRI MARX. Yes

EDWIN. What's your name?

HENRI MARX. I'll tell your aunt you said hello

EDWIN. No name, your parents are smart. My parents were foolish. I have the name of a fool, Edwin Jean Dominique.

HENRI MARX. Her famous painter

EDWIN. Ah, she talks about me. Only good things I hope

HENRI MARX. Aren't you dead?

EDWIN. It's a good death

HENRI MARX. Is there such a thing?

EDWIN. Yes. I am still breathing and yet the rest of the world believes I am dead, buried six feet beneath the earth.

HENRI MARX. How is that possible?

EDWIN. Journalists, politicians you know. Faces everywhere. But artists' faces no one knows. Artists can sneak into small villages in the night and live mostly underground. They can escape during sunset through backwood paths, to remote locations, when everyone is too busy paying attention to the sun and looking out for the Macoutes, the boogeymen, to pay attention to everyday figures. But you seem to understand that

HENRI MARX. I don't understand why you don't leave

EDWIN. I can't dream inspiration. I like to paint my people.

(*A beat.*)

Let me paint you

HENRI MARX. (*A bit of confusion/intrigue.*) ——

(*A beat.*)

My mother can't be alone at night.

EDWIN. Does it not still take two days to get back?

HENRI MARX. I don't want to be a part of your politics

EDWIN. I don't have politics

HENRI MARX. Isn't that why you're dead?

EDWIN. No. Misinterpretation is why I'm dead

HENRI MARX. I'm honored, but I can't

EDWIN. Where will you stay?

HENRI MARX. With a friend

EDWIN. A lover?

HENRI MARX. I don't have a lover

EDWIN. So you have nowhere to build your boat?

HENRI MARX. I'm not building a boat

EDWIN. It's fine. You can build your boat in my studio

> (HENRI MARX *turns to exit.*)

I found you this time. What will happen when those other eyes do? You're a brute, young, and bitter. Eyes find those things

HENRI MARX. And if those eyes find you with me?

EDWIN. Your boat would be the least of my worries

> (*A beat.*)

You know my name. What's yours?

> (*A moment.*)

HENRI MARX. Henri Marx

EDWIN. A good name

> (*A moment.*)

HENRI MARX. You can't draw my face

EDWIN. I'm not interested in your face

> (*A beat.*)

HENRI MARX. Alright, we're in agreement

EDWIN. Good. We'll start tonight

Scene Two

> *Evening. A small one-room home with a tin roof.* EDWIN *is sharpening, cleaning his tools.* JUDITH *tosses a sack of groceries on the table. She is a beautiful woman, once elegant.*

JUDITH. It was a beautiful day today

EDWIN. Good

> (*She leans in for a kiss, he kisses her on the cheek.*)

JUDITH. No, it was more than good. It was like Port-au-Prince at the height of Carnival

> (*Throughout this beat,* JUDITH *playfully moves her body in a flirtatious, seductive manner. But her bones have aged in a way that they shouldn't have. It's awkward.*)

EDWIN. I'm glad you had a nice day in the market

JUDITH. I couldn't stop smiling

EDWIN. Smiling is not a bad thing

JUDITH. I had a lot of male customers today

EDWIN. You did?

JUDITH. I did

    (*She leans into his body.*)

EDWIN. ——

JUDITH. Does it make you jealous? Me in the market smiling, flirting, moving my body the way I did during Carnival

EDWIN. A man learns how to get rid of certain vices

JUDITH. There are certain vices a woman never wants her man to get rid of

EDWIN. She says now

JUDITH. And she'll say later

    (JUDITH *rubs her body against his. It's even more awkward. She presses her body even harder against his and kisses him.* EDWIN *hesitates then shyly pulls away.*)

It's been some time since my name slipped off your tongue

EDWIN. What's gotten into you?

JUDITH. The same thing that's gotten to us all

EDWIN. And what's that?

    (*Not giving up on her seduction/her movement.*)

JUDITH. Revolution. Re-vo-luu-tioonnnn

EDWIN. Revolution?

JUDITH. No

    (*Loudly.*)

Revolution

EDWIN. Shhhh…

JUDITH. Let them hear. They can't hurt us, not anymore

EDWIN. Have we become bulletproof?

JUDITH. You don't know

EDWIN. Know what?

JUDITH. The miracle

EDWIN. I've missed the Rapture?

JUDITH. Better. How have you missed this?

EDWIN. I've been working all day

JUDITH. You've got to rise from under the earth sometimes and listen to God's music

(JUDITH *turns on the radio.*)

RADIO. We are not dogs, fed scraps, beaten then slaughtered for the nutriment of the earth. We are not peasants, intellectuals, dark skins, mulattos. We are Haitian. The proud descendants of Toussaint L'Ouverture, Dutty Boukman, and Georges Biassou. Their proud, honorable, and just blood runs through all our veins. All of our bodies. In this nation there is only one people. The people of the Union. And as a people we must unite against oppression as our fathers did before us. This is the beginning. The beginning of freedom. They will not quiet us any longer. Unity makes strength. Unity makes strength.

(*Brief dead time. The sound of a tape running. A beat.*)

We are not dogs, fed scraps, beaten…

(JUDITH *lowers the volume. It plays softly throughout the scene.*)

EDWIN. How long has it been going?

JUDITH. It's been playing since noon. Running on loop all day

EDWIN. No interruption?

JUDITH. No, they took over the airwave

EDWIN. How?

JUDITH. Does it matter? In the market you could smell it. Goat shit and revolution. Tonight everyone will be silently toasting. But we

(*She pulls from the sack a bottle of rum.*)

We will be celebrating loudly

(JUDITH *pours them drinks.*)

EDWIN. Cheri—

JUDITH. Shh…

(*She hands him a drink.*)

Salute

EDWIN. To what?

JUDITH. To Jean-Louis. To the end of death and the birth of a new nation. Salute

(*She drinks, he does not. She sits on his lap.*)

EDWIN. I have to go work

JUDITH. Not tonight

EDWIN. It's cooler at night

JUDITH. Cheri

EDWIN. I'm inspired and I haven't been in a while

JUDITH. I used to be enough inspiration

EDWIN. I won't be long

JUDITH. It'll still be there in the morning

EDWIN. Inspiration lasts as long as dreams

JUDITH. He's back. Everyone Duvalier exiled from his first cabinet promised to return, to fight against his laws. But Jean-Louis is the only one who has. He said he would be back "to rid his people of the devil, of Francois 'Papa Doc' Duvalier. And bring God back to his nation." His words. A man who keeps his word is worth celebrating

EDWIN. You don't even know if it's him

JUDITH. I know his cadence. You worked for the man, you know his cadence

EDWIN. He commissioned me. I painted a painting for him that once hung in his office in the palace. But I chose the subject of the painting. I work only for myself

JUDITH. But you've spoken to the man a number of times. That's his voice. It's him

EDWIN. Zombies can do amazing things with their voices

JUDITH. You can't work tonight. I'm preparing a feast. More than a feast, more than two feasts

    (She pulls each item out as she speaks.)

Mango, avocado, okra, beef. It'll be like being back in Port-au-Prince

EDWIN. The meat and fruits of the rich

JUDITH. Of the people

EDWIN. Where did we get the foods of the people?

JUDITH. Jean-Louis' men came through the market handing them out like they once poured ripe from trees

EDWIN. The food of the people given to them by the elite. I'm going to go work

JUDITH. It's the first time since I've started in the market that the sun has not left me tired

EDWIN. Let me just start it

JUDITH. You've been down there all day

EDWIN. Thinking and planning

JUDITH. The process of an artist

EDWIN. Familiar to you still I hope

JUDITH. Stay with me

JUDITH. ——   **EDWIN.** ——

JUDITH. Soon you'll be able to walk around and be inspired all the time. We both will. Let's live in that tonight.

EDWIN. A voice does not make for a revolution

JUDITH. Michelet spoke to him. Saw him. Touched him

EDWIN. Where did you see Michelet?

JUDITH. He's one of Jean-Louis' men. He gave me the food in the market. He's the one that recorded Jean-Louis and broadcasted him over the airwave

EDWIN. Now I know it is lies

JUDITH. It's not

EDWIN. No one would trust that ignorant fool

JUDITH. He's the only one who's been speaking against the regime

>   (EDWIN *sucks his teeth.*)

EDWIN. The only one walking free. All those young journalists are fleeing, or have been imprisoned or executed. And he's walking around in the middle of markets

JUDITH. He's the journalist of the people. Many are willing and have hidden him

EDWIN. More like the regime's journalist

JUDITH. They killed his wife and daughter

EDWIN. They supposedly killed me too

JUDITH. They're having a demonstration. In three days, at Le Plaza, Jean-Louis will make his first appearance

EDWIN. People like to die

JUDITH. They're calling for us, the intellectuals the artists, to lead. To help get the people heated.

EDWIN. Most of the people can't read

JUDITH. They can see, they can hear

EDWIN. Hopefully, they can see the Macoutes waiting with their guns and machetes. You're not going

JUDITH. Michelet asked for you personally. Spoke of all the beautiful times we had. You, me, him and Tatiana. The four of us getting into trouble at the university. Our weddings. All the parties we had at our house that ended in late night political debates. You being a great host.

EDWIN. And what did you tell him about me?

JUDITH. What do you mean?

EDWIN. Did you seem mournful, sad Judith? Like your husband is dead.

JUDITH. No

EDWIN. You're supposed to deny my existence. Weep. Cry. That's what wives do for their husbands. Are you not a woman?

JUDITH. (*Fights back her anger/hurt.*) ——

(*A beat.*)

Look where we are, in the middle of nowhere. No one around. Soon the electricity will go out and all we'll have are little candles, that don't provide enough light for me to read my bible. And after standing, sweating in the sun all day, to make sure we have enough food to eat, to survive. I can't even clean myself properly. A lesser woman, a lesser woman would have left you

JUDITH. ——   **EDWIN.** ——

EDWIN. I should go work

JUDITH. Go

(EDWIN *grabs his tools, exits.* JUDITH *finishes her drink and pours herself another. She quietly sips.*)

Scene Three

EDWIN's *studio underground.* HENRI MARX *is standing holding a number of tools and wood, waiting for* EDWIN *to direct him.* EDWIN *watches him.*

EDWIN. ——   **HENRI MARX.** ——

EDWIN. ——   **HENRI MARX.** ——

HENRI MARX. How does this work?

EDWIN. You can build right over there

HENRI MARX. Thank you

(HENRI MARX *places the wood down.*)

But where do you want me for the painting? Should I be standing a certain way? Or do you want me sitting?

EDWIN. I just want you to build your boat

HENRI MARX. You should get what you need from me now. Once I'm done, I'm leaving

EDWIN. I know. I want to paint you while you're building the boat. I'm not interested in stillness. If I were I'd paint a bowl of fruits. What interests me is the story the body tells while it's moving. If you want to know who someone is, watch them as they complete a task. Everything you need to know will be in their body

HENRI MARX. Everything?

EDWIN. Yes. Does that frighten you?

HENRI MARX. No, I just never heard that before

    (HENRI MARX *still unsure.*)

EDWIN. ——   **HENRI MARX.** ——

HENRI MARX. You always bring your—what do you call me?

EDWIN. Figure

HENRI MARX. You always bring your figure down here, like this?

EDWIN. You're my first

HENRI MARX. I'm special

EDWIN. No. They usually don't know I'm watching. I prefer it that way. They're more natural in their habitats. But times call for a new approach

    (*A moment.*)

Are you uncomfortable with this? Do you no longer agree with our arrangement?

HENRI MARX. No, I'm fine

EDWIN. Alright, then you can go ahead

    (*A slight moment.* HENRI MARX *lays out his supplies and tools and begins to build.* HENRI MARX *is uncomfortable, but is trying to be natural.* EDWIN *watches him, but does not begin to paint. We should watch him build for a while, for however long it holds dramatic interest. A moment.*)

Relax. You're nervous. You're paying more attention to me than what you're doing

HENRI MARX. No, I'm not

EDWIN. Yes you are. Your body is stiff, but your head moves like a rabid dog ready to strike

    (EDWIN *pours a drink.*)

Here

    (*Hands* HENRI MARX *the drink.*)

You've forgotten who's chasing you

    (HENRI MARX *doesn't take the drink.*)

I don't kill dogs. I prefer to watch them play

HENRI MARX. I'm not a dog

EDWIN. Then what beast are you?

HENRI MARX. I'm human

EDWIN. Humans don't exist here

HENRI MARX. They are rare, but there are many

EDWIN. Drink

HENRI MARX. You're not drinking

EDWIN. I need my senses

HENRI MARX. ——

(EDWIN *takes a sip. Hands the cup to* HENRI MARX. *He takes a sip.*)

EDWIN. All at once

HENRI MARX. What beast are you?

EDWIN. Like you don't know. A vulture

(HENRI MARX *smiles.*)

Go ahead

(HENRI MARX *gulps the drink. He clears his throat.*)

It's strong, heated

(EDWIN *pours him another drink.*)

Take your time with this one

HENRI MARX. I can't build drunk

EDWIN. I'm not sure you can build it sober

HENRI MARX. I've built many homes in Anse-a-Foleur

EDWIN. Is that what you do?

HENRI MARX. No, field work. But I helped my father build many homes in the village

EDWIN. Land is more tranquil than the sea. It doesn't move. It doesn't split open and swallow itself

HENRI MARX. It's a simple foundation. I've seen it done

EDWIN. Seeing is not the same as doing

HENRI MARX. No one taught me how to build a house. I watched it being done, then started myself. They're all still standing

EDWIN. You are a true Anse-a-Foleur man. You believe that life should be simple. My father had the same sensibility

HENRI MARX. And you don't?

EDWIN. I wasn't there long enough to learn it. My father died when I was young, when I still knew your brother. My mother and I moved to Port-au-Prince to live with my uncle

HENRI MARX. So that's why you look down on it all

EDWIN. I don't

HENRI MARX. You don't need to spare my feelings

EDWIN. I have no need to. It's not a place for artists. But it is sweet in all its simplicity, a rich and beautiful valley. The days are rough, but soothing. The dry white dust, hot like the sun, covers everything. Children playing with donkeys, mothers outside scrubbing clothes, picking herbs. Men working in fields singing like little larks. Their raw, tender voices echoing through the valley. And the nights are tranquil. No worries of being robbed, of loud noises. Whispers of Krik? Krak

>   (*He smiles to himself.*)

There was a woman—long dead now. She was nearly 100 years old when I was a child

HENRI MARX. She's not dead

EDWIN. Madame Gerald?

HENRI MARX. Yes, Angelere. Still alive

EDWIN. Her stories spun in me throughout my childhood

HENRI MARX. They still do in me

EDWIN. (*Imitating her.*) Krik?

>   (*Both men laugh.*)

HENRI MARX. Krak. She really should have died a long time ago

EDWIN. They say the shriek in her voice is an undigested child screaming for help

HENRI MARX. I never heard that

EDWIN. Yeah. They say she must eat one every year to stay alive

HENRI MARX. Now when she's ready to tell a story, she stands in the middle of the road and yells Krik over and over again, waiting for someone to say Krak. But we don't want to hear her stories anymore so one says Krak. So after a while she'll tell the story anyways. What's even the point of asking Krik?

EDWIN. She's old. Me I can't wait to be old, not that old, but old. To be able to do whatever I want and no one will say a thing

HENRI MARX. I want to be able to not speak to anyone for days or months. And go walking all night

EDWIN. I want to be able to pee on people I don't like for saying hello

HENRI MARX. I like that

EDWIN. You can have it

HENRI MARX. Thank you

>   (*A beat.*)

I must admit, I've never seen your work

EDWIN. These are all that's left. Mostly unfinished, the little I could grab

>   (HENRI MARX *gestures, asking if he could look.*)

If you want

>   (HENRI MARX *uncovers a couple of the canvases. He studies each one.*)

HENRI MARX. Were all your paintings like these?

EDWIN. Mostly

HENRI MARX. They don't seem political

EDWIN. They hung in the wrong homes. And they aren't bright enough for the regime. The people aren't happy enough

HENRI MARX. How could they tell? Everyone is so dark. Can barely see their faces

EDWIN. It's easy to conceal emotion. Most of our people's faces are blank, their minds are distant. Descendants of slaves do that so easily. But the body we have less control of

HENRI MARX. The face goes blank, but eyes never rest

(*He picks up a different painting.*)

Except maybe hers, they're so dead

(HENRI MARX *shows* EDWIN *the canvas.*)

EDWIN. That's my wife

HENRI MARX. Oh, sorry. I didn't—

EDWIN. No, I agree

HENRI MARX. Her body is elegant

EDWIN. She was a dancer. Her face is the only face I've attempted to paint

HENRI MARX. Not your children

EDWIN. We don't have children

HENRI MARX. Because you don't want—

EDWIN. God has not felt it appropriate for us. For many reasons

HENRI MARX. I'm sorry

EDWIN. It's not your fault

(*A beat.*)

And you? You're hardy and handsome. You must want many children with many women

HENRI MARX. No, I don't want children

EDWIN. One day you will

HENRI MARX. Today, I want a different kind of life for myself

EDWIN. So you're going to America to live a dream

HENRI MARX. No, I'm going there to live. It's not possible to do that here anymore

EDWIN. And it is in America?

HENRI MARX. There, I'll be able to get a job and buy a home. Come in and out of my home whenever I wish. In Miami, people walk around at all times of the night

EDWIN. There's violence there too

HENRI MARX. Not like here. The government isn't inflicting it

EDWIN. But it's about to change here, haven't you heard? A revolution is brewing

HENRI MARX. I thought you weren't interested in politics?

EDWIN. I'm interested in other people's politics

HENRI MARX. A revolution won't change my situation

EDWIN. It's the people's revolution. It will change for us all

HENRI MARX. There will always be regimes, some worse, some better. Each one will benefit a particular group. And those who are left out have three choices. They can suffer, fight, or leave—by force or silently

EDWIN. And then there are the immune. Those who can watch and not participate

HENRI MARX. Is that what you do with your paintings?

EDWIN. There's a reason I don't paint everyone. Most people in society go about living. Because they understand that it's just life. And then there are the others, the infected ones. Their bodies are diseased by politics. The beauty in that is worth capturing

HENRI MARX. Everyone is infected. Some just don't know they are. But when they do, they will have to make a choice

EDWIN. And you've just made that choice

HENRI MARX. And you're afraid to

(HENRI MARX *goes for the bottle of rum.* EDWIN *grabs his hand.*)

EDWIN. You don't need this anymore. Go ahead build

Scene Four

The next morning. JUDITH *has made breakfast, eggs and plantain. She places* EDWIN's *plate in front of him. She cuts him a piece of avocado. She sits with her plate. They eat in silence for a few moments.*

EDWIN. You remember that family we saw when we were leaving Port-au-Prince? They were from Gonaïves, the husband, wife and son. They had a boat.

(EDWIN *stabs his fork into the plantain. Lifts it up like a display.*)

A little plantain boat, similar to this but oddly shaped. Like it was fried. Their own little fried plantain boat

JUDITH. Yes, what about them?

EDWIN. When we were climbing the hill, I kept looking back and watching them creep down to the water. And when they finally jumped into the boat and began drifting towards the sunset all I could imagine was what was ahead of them, the other side of the horizon. You ever think about that, what it would be like to be in America?

JUDITH. I did once

EDWIN. And?

JUDITH. Every day on the radio, they mention some plantain boat sinking, tons of them all the time

EDWIN. What about the ones that don't?

JUDITH. It's not a place for everyone

EDWIN. Is it not for you?

JUDITH. I would have no roots. Without roots, I wouldn't know my function, my place. America is a large country. It spreads endlessly. I wouldn't survive in such a place with no function.

(*A moment.*)

Where is this coming from?

EDWIN. I was just thinking

JUDITH. Is that why you didn't come to bed last night?

EDWIN. I was working. I lost track of time

JUDITH. It's been a while since you've spent all night working. It must be special

EDWIN. Everything I work on is special

JUDITH. Some more than others.

(*A slight beat.*)

Is it one of the unfinished ones?

EDWIN. No, it's something new

JUDITH. There was a time when you wouldn't have been able to drop something you were working on to start something new

EDWIN. I needed to clear my head and step away from the others

JUDITH. What's it about?

EDWIN. It's not a narrative

JUDITH. What are you painting?

EDWIN. A man building a boat

JUDITH. What kind of boat?

EDWIN. Do you know a lot about boats?

JUDITH. As much as you would need to know to paint one

EDWIN. It's a fried plantain boat

JUDITH. What are you trying to say?

EDWIN. Say?

JUDITH. By having this man build a boat?

EDWIN. That's he's going somewhere

JUDITH. Who does this man look like? The one building the boat.

> (*A slight beat.*)

Is it you?

EDWIN. Why do you care so much about what I'm painting and why?

JUDITH. I'm trying to understand what is keeping you out of our bed

EDWIN. You never cared about it before

JUDITH. In the past, it was charming to have a husband with a passion that kept him away. It loses its charm when he is your only physical connection in the world

EDWIN. I'm sorry. It's hard to have a sense of time when you're underground

JUDITH. You said you'd come back up

EDWIN. Next time I say I will. I will

JUDITH. Am I really that awful?

EDWIN. No, that's a stupid question to ask. I didn't mean to upset you

JUDITH. It's different at night here. You can hear all the beasts, things moving out there. Even the shadows of trees move unnaturally. As a girl I was never afraid of the monsters in the dark. But now the boogeyman can be anywhere. And what they do to women who are alone now is a lot more brutal than the monsters we made up as children

EDWIN. I'm sorry

JUDITH. Last night, there was this pounding sound, a constant thump like a hammer hitting against the door

EDWIN. It must've been your heart beating

JUDITH. You didn't hear it?

EDWIN. No

JUDITH. Just come to bed at night

EDWIN. I'll do most of my work in the afternoon

JUDITH. Thank you.

> (*A moment.*)

There's only us. Our roots are deeper here, together.

> (JUDITH *looks at him.* EDWIN *understands. They return to eating in silence.*)

Scene Five

EDWIN's studio a few hours later. HENRI MARX is working on his boat diligently. EDWIN continues to watch him, not painting, a bit frustrated. A moment.

HENRI MARX. You're still not painting

EDWIN. It's a process. I'm trying to figure out how to tell your story

HENRI MARX. But you can see it

EDWIN. Of course

(*A beat.*)

Tell me

HENRI MARX. What?

EDWIN. We know more about the sky and beyond than we know of the ocean. Yet, you're going to put your body on something unstable to cross it. Why?

HENRI MARX. Do you have any water?

EDWIN. What?

HENRI MARX. Water. To drink. It's hot down here.

(*EDWIN grabs a jug of water from the corner of the room. The water is weirdly foggy and slightly colored.*)

You drink that?

EDWIN. Yes

(*HENRI MARX looks at it again then pushes the jug back to him.*)

HENRI MARX. No thank you

EDWIN. When you're in the fields, are there fresh flowing springs of water?

HENRI MARX. No, but drinkable water

EDWIN. Are you not a man?

HENRI MARX. Drinking that will make me a man?

EDWIN. It'll put hair on your face

HENRI MARX. I have enough hair other places

EDWIN. That doesn't make you a man

HENRI MARX. Nor does hair on your face

EDWIN. You don't think I'm a man?

HENRI MARX. I don't know you well enough to have an opinion

EDWIN. How well do you need to know me?

HENRI MARX. We need to be more familiar than we are now

EDWIN. How do we become more familiar?

(*A beat.* HENRI MARX *walks over and gets face to face with* EDWIN. *A longer beat.*)

HENRI MARX. Who's your favorite futbol team?

EDWIN. Ah, yes, the pivotal test. The same team my father loved and every great man, Zenith

(HENRI MARX *sucks his teeth.*)

What?

HENRI MARX. Everyone likes that team, women *love* that team

EDWIN. 'Cause they're good, *manly*

HENRI MARX. Because you don't know the sport. You've probably seen them play once, twice maybe. And since everyone says they're good and they win all the time, you like them

EDWIN. Fuck you, who's your favorite team?

HENRI MARX. Racine. They are sportsmen. Patient, tactful, strike without the aggression, the spectacle. They play with respect and elegance

EDWIN. And that's a man?

HENRI MARX. A desirable man in society

EDWIN. And you're that?

HENRI MARX. I'm trying to be

EDWIN. Well if that's why you're risking your life, I have disappointing news, American men aren't that

HENRI MARX. I'm not going there to learn how to be a man. It's the opportunity to start new, to create a life. To be in a place, a land where you have no history, so you can't feel ashamed or pulled down into its darkness. In America you can be poor and if you educate yourself and work hard, you have the opportunity to create a life that suits you.

EDWIN. It won't be that easy

HENRI MARX. I don't think it will be, but it's worth giving it a try. Look where you are. You can't tell me that your art, inspiration is why you don't leave.

EDWIN. In America opportunity is limitless. And that can be dangerous. Here, with fewer options, you know between the good and bad.

HENRI MARX. There is no such thing as too much opportunity. In America you can take what you need and leave what you don't

EDWIN. Don't be stupid, that's a peasant way of thinking

HENRI MARX. Not only peasants, many of your intellectuals feel the same

EDWIN. And how many intellectuals do you know?

HENRI MARX. A few

EDWIN. Name them

HENRI MARX. I know you

> (EDWIN *sucks his teeth.*)

EDWIN. You know no one. How could you?

HENRI MARX. I know a young journalist, a schoolmate from our village. He has also died the good death.

EDWIN. Why isn't he leaving?

HENRI MARX. He is, with me. In two days. At the spot on the beach where we met. And if the boat's not ready, we'll set another date and another date until it is. 'Cause he believes in the opportunities in America, believes in them so much that he is sure they will help him help our country.

EDWIN. That is one man

HENRI MARX. There are two other journalists joining us. So you see, it's not merely us peasants who believe in America.

> (*A beat.*)

And you never know, I could make a new friend who isn't afraid of opportunity. And he may want to join us.

> (HENRI MARX *returns to building.* EDWIN *watches him. A beat. He begins to paint.* HENRI MARX's *movements are sweeping, powerful, regal.* EDWIN *moves with a staccato precision and fluidity. It is a dance of sorts. It's rhythmic and sensual, almost hypnotizing. And for a while, a good while, we just watch the two men work in silence.*)

Scene Six

The living room. The next evening. JUDITH *is sweeping their home.* EDWIN *is sitting lost in his thoughts. The radio softly plays in the background. Perhaps it is the daily evening news or Duvalier propaganda. Whatever it is, it is very faint.*

JUDITH. Maybe I'll be able to make the legume on Sunday. I know I've been saying that for a while. I tried bartering today with Lucy for the eggplant, but she said she's had enough corn mill to feed her past and future lives. But I'll ask on Sunday. She's usually in a good mood after church.

It's a waste of time for her though. She isn't going to save her soul. She told the Macoutes, the boogeymen, that Madame Lucner put magic on her daughter-in-law and caused her to lose her baby. So they arrested Madame Lucner. Lucy only did it because Madame Lucner was doing better than her in the market. Sometimes you can see the guilt in her eyes, but it's too late.

It's the worst thing you could do to a woman, imprison her. Madame Lucner is locked up somewhere, her head shaved and bound to the ground. The boogeymen think God didn't build women to die in prison. They fear we'll use magic to turn into birds. Transform our hair into feathers and wings and fly out. And they can't have that.

I'd rather be lined up and have holes fired into my body, then spend the rest of my life bald-headed and bound to the ground.

(*A moment.*)

EDWIN. Come cheri, sit with me

JUDITH. Is there something wrong?

EDWIN. Let's talk

JUDITH. That's what we're doing

EDWIN. Let's talk seriously

JUDITH. I'm not making any jokes.

EDWIN. You work hard, relax with me

JUDITH. If I sit, I'll fall asleep

(*A moment.*)

EDWIN. Do you remember what time of year it is?

JUDITH. No

EDWIN. Carnival is in three weeks.

(*A slight beat.*)

Have your cravings started?

JUDITH. What cravings?

EDWIN. Ah, it's easy for you to forget, you weren't the one running around. Sweating, legs cramping, kidneys drying up. It's easier to purchase a gun in Haiti than ice cream

(JUDITH *smiles.*)

JUDITH. Look at what you remember. I lost that a long time ago

EDWIN. Running around two, three times a day in search for ice cream is all I remember about Carnival

JUDITH. It's not my fault. It was the only time when I was a child we were allowed the luxury of ice cream

EDWIN. I don't think you actually ate a meal during Carnival

JUDITH. I spent the entire day dancing. I deserved a treat, and you needed the exercise. You refused to dance with me

EDWIN. I was miserable at it

JUDITH. That's not true

EDWIN. Donkeys dance better than me

JUDITH. I didn't care how you danced

EDWIN. It was embarrassing

JUDITH. It was sweet

EDWIN. Yes, there were times when it was sweet

> (*Holding on to the sweetness…*)

Soon all the radio stations will be playing music, even radio regime. We should buy you some ice cream, have our own little Carnival here.

JUDITH. Would you dance with me?

EDWIN. If it made you happy, I want you to be happy

JUDITH. We were happy

EDWIN. We were. I was your artist and you were my muse

> (*As* JUDITH *speaks we get a glimpse of the mover she was, without her really even trying, without her even moving.*)

JUDITH. You were more than that. You were my education. I was a peasant village girl afraid of the big city and you taught me how to survive. Taught me about elite society, art, and philosophy. You loved teaching me

EDWIN. I did.

JUDITH. And I was more than your muse. I was the first body you painted. After that it was easy for you to give up painting pastorals

EDWIN. You taught me how to see

JUDITH. No. It was the revolutionary in you. You knew there was no beauty in nature. You had such a passion for our people, our country. Before Duvalier, you used to paint on walls, cars, trees, even pigs protesting against mulatto elitism

EDWIN. What did all the revolution get us? Duvalier. A man worse than all the others.

JUDITH. But we were happy

EDWIN. That was a long time ago. But we can be happy again. Start new, create our own opportunities now

JUDITH. We can't. You're dead. And I work, so I can't create, can't be your muse. At least not like this. But with the revolution—

EDWIN. Let's talk about something else

JUDITH. You wanted to talk seriously

EDWIN. About anything else

JUDITH. Well you should go paint, 'cause any other kind of talk will make me more tired.

> (JUDITH *resumes sweeping.* EDWIN *watches her for a moment. A beat. He exits.*)

Scene Seven

EDWIN's *studio. A couple of hours later.* EDWIN *is painting.* HENRI MARX *is building the boat.*

HENRI MARX. This is looking good. It's coming together a lot faster than I thought. And it's sturdy

EDWIN. ——

HENRI MARX. You don't think so?

EDWIN. It looks good

HENRI MARX. Are you surprised by my abilities?

EDWIN. You barely sleep

HENRI MARX. I'll have plenty of time to do that in America

EDWIN. ——

HENRI MARX. What's wrong?

EDWIN. Nothing

HENRI MARX. Am I boring you? Where's the conversation?

EDWIN. I need to focus. I need to get a good foundation before you leave, before I must work from memory. Memory is a very irrational thing

HENRI MARX. How am I looking?

EDWIN. Like you do

HENRI MARX. Not like a beast?

EDWIN. I thought you weren't a beast?

HENRI MARX. I don't think I am, but you do

EDWIN. I think everyone is a beast

HENRI MARX. Then what kind of beast am I?

EDWIN. It doesn't matter

HENRI MARX. Come on

(*A moment.*)

EDWIN. A flamingo

HENRI MARX. A flamingo?

EDWIN. You asked

HENRI MARX. Why?

EDWIN. I don't have to give a reason

HENRI MARX. But there is one?

EDWIN. Yes

HENRI MARX. Well, if I'm a flamingo, then you're not a vulture

EDWIN. You can't see clearly

HENRI MARX. I can see. Maybe you're the one who can't

EDWIN. Do you not like flamingos?

HENRI MARX. I've never really thought about them

EDWIN. You should

HENRI MARX. I can't see myself as a flamingo. They don't do anything. They just wade in the water to be hunted

EDWIN. Every beast is hunted

HENRI MARX. They're pink

EDWIN. They used to fly high, far, and often. Did you know that? Centuries ago. These long elegant birds. Their pink feathers against the blue sky and white sun made them look like balls of fire. When they landed to rest, to drink water, to feed. They would be captured. A few for nutriment, others to be sacrificed to the lwas, the deities. But most were caged and worshipped. They were seen as a good omen

HENRI MARX. I've never heard that

EDWIN. It's another Madame Gerald story

HENRI MARX. Have you ever painted one?

EDWIN. No

HENRI MARX. Then paint one on the boat with me, bring me luck

EDWIN. I have no interest in painting beasts. I'm not a naturalist

HENRI MARX. The brightness of the bird against the darkness of my skin would be interesting

EDWIN. It won't

HENRI MARX. Let me show you

EDWIN. I don't like my figures seeing the work before it's finished

HENRI MARX. They usually don't know you're painting them

EDWIN. Exactly

HENRI MARX. I know what looks good

EDWIN. A flamingo doesn't look good

HENRI MARX. Aren't I a flamingo?

EDWIN. I'll show it to you when I'm done

HENRI MARX. I won't be here

EDWIN. Too bad

> (HENRI MARX *goes to pour himself a cup of water.*)

Now you want my water?

> (He *runs over and looks at the canvas before* EDWIN *can stop him. A moment. He stares at it; the image looking back at him is not what he expected. He's afraid of it.*)

HENRI MARX. Destroy it

EDWIN. No

HENRI MARX. Destroy it.

EDWIN. You're not going to be here

HENRI MARX. You said you weren't interested in my face, any face. You can't have my face

EDWIN. What have you done?

HENRI MARX. It's not what I've done. They can't forget what they've done to me.

EDWIN. You must be involved in politics

HENRI MARX. No, I'm not.

EDWIN. You're lying

HENRI MARX. They can get to my mother. They'll realize I'm gone and think I'm saying things

EDWIN. Why would they care about a peasant boy and his peasant mother?

HENRI MARX. They care as much what peasants have to say as they do artists. My father and my brother were on the porch playing cards, I was watching. No one else. No assembly of people. My father made a joke about how Duvalier thinks he's a voodoo deity. The joke was so bad, that I don't even remember it. But someone's eyes did. And between late night and early morning, the boogeymen crept into our house. Pounded on my brother and father's heads until they were black holes connected to limp bodies.

But before that display of mercy. As the youngest man—*boy*—in the house, they had me climb my mother. Force myself into her. Laughing and taunting. At first I refused, so they started slicing me. I would've died, but my mom begged me. Said they would kill us both. And now, now she walks around, her body in the present and her eyes frozen in the past. And she can never look at me.

> (HENRI MARX *removes his shirt. His body is littered in scars.*)

It's not my face you're interested in. Come touch.

> (EDWIN *doesn't move.*)

You got it wrong. You can't see it.

> (HENRI MARX *goes to* EDWIN. *Places* EDWIN's *hands on his scars.*)

This is what you wanted to paint. This is what's beautiful. What you love.

> (HENRI MARX *guides* EDWIN's *hand over the scars.* HENRI MARX *continues guiding until* EDWIN *no longer needs his guidance and is running his hands freely over his scarred body.* EDWIN *is excited and afraid.*)

Scene Eight

Living room. Early morning the next day. EDWIN *stumbles in from the bedroom. There is no breakfast.* JUDITH *is fully dressed ready for the day, but not in her typical market clothing. She resembles a woman of society, a fragment of what she once was.*

JUDITH. When was the last time you touched me?

EDWIN. (*Exhausted, trying to ground himself.*) ——
What?

JUDITH. A year ago, nearly two years after we went into hiding. The third time my body betrayed me. It was our second move, five months before here

EDWIN. Judith

JUDITH. Oh there it is, my name slips off your tongue so easily now.

EDWIN. Let's not do this

JUDITH. Last night before you came—

EDWIN. I'm sorry it was late, but I did come to bed

JUDITH. I felt your warmth. But the heat off your body was different

EDWIN. I didn't want to wake you

JUDITH. You didn't, I was already awake. Before you came to bed last night, I heard that pounding sound again. But this time all the beasts were silent and the shadows of the trees stood still. So I thought maybe you were right, that this entire time it was the pounding of my heart in my head. But as I listened closely it didn't follow the beat of my pulse. And something in my body told me to go seek it, find it. So I followed the sound and it led me down to your studio. And I saw him. His strength, his elegance. His body. He moves so beautifully. I moved that way once, remember? But the sun from the market has dried my bones. Every time I move they crack into ash and fall into my womb. But I did, I moved like him, better than him. You used to say to watch me dance, moved something carnal in you

EDWIN. It was a bargain. He builds his boat and I get to paint him

JUDITH. But maybe he is better than me. 'Cause to be with him makes you feel more than carnal

EDWIN. It's just a painting

JUDITH. I saw you touch him

EDWIN. His scars

JUDITH. You touched them all

EDWIN. He's a peasant, he's nothing

          (JUDITH *sucks her teeth.*)
You're my wife

(She presses her body against his.)

JUDITH. Then show me that I'm wrong

EDWIN. I can't be the man you fell in love with

JUDITH. You just need to remember how

EDWIN. Nor can you be the woman I fell in love with

JUDITH. I'm still her

EDWIN. That's a foolish thing to believe

JUDITH. You always want it both ways. You belittle and admire peasants. You are a man who lives and doesn't. You've always wanted a family and you've always desired the unnatural.

EDWIN. Today, I want my wife

JUDITH. When you used to want me, you'd already have me. You never said it, you never asked, you just took it. And you *knew* how to take it. And it was violent and sweet and full of life. That's all I want right now. To feel like I can live again

EDWIN. Know that I love you

JUDITH. I'm leaving

EDWIN. You have nowhere to go

JUDITH. I'm going to the rally and joining Jean-Louis. Be part of the revolution

EDWIN. It's a trap. They won't kill you, you're a woman. You will age and die in prison

JUDITH. At least I'll feel alive again for a few moments

EDWIN. Don't go

JUDITH. Then touch me

JUDITH. ——   **EDWIN.** ——

EDWIN. I can't, not like this

(A moment.)

JUDITH. Revolutions arise when our past cries out to us. To die for it is a fine thing.

(JUDITH exits. EDWIN watches her.)

Scene Nine

Same day. Late afternoon/early evening. Split scene. The studio. HENRI MARX *is finishing the boat. He's putting together the final piece. The living room.* EDWIN *is looking for radio regime. A few moments. He finds it.*

RADIO. My heart pumps the blood of this nation, of its people. The lwas and God have chosen me, François Duvalier, to lead this land of ours. Yet, there are those who question me. And by doing so they question God. Who are they to question the divine? For God is the all-knowing and if you deceive Him, He will lay down judgment. And today He has.

A group of intellectual elitists, led by the traitor Jean-Louis, conspired to kill me. But we have caught them all and they shall be punished. God loves this nation and its people too much to have allowed them to succeed.

(EDWIN *doesn't move. He remains still.* HENRI MARX *has finished building the boat.*)

Scene Ten

The following day. The beach, near sunset, the same spot as opening. HENRI MARX *looks around, anxiously awaiting his friends.* EDWIN *enters unseen. He watches him for a moment, savoring his every movement. A beat.* HENRI MARX *turns and sees him, he's startled.*

HENRI MARX. Jesus, Edwin. You almost made me piss on myself

EDWIN. Sorry

HENRI MARX. I didn't expect to see you, standing there

HENRI MARX. ——   **EDWIN.** ——

(*A beat.*)

HENRI MARX. I waited for you yesterday and this morning, I wanted to say thank you, for everything

EDWIN. Look at me, look at me good. What kind of beast am I?

(HENRI MARX *tries to look at him, do what* EDWIN *does so well, but can't. A beat.*)

HENRI MARX. Are you okay? You look pale

EDWIN. I need you to understand, that everything I've done in my life has been about my survival

HENRI MARX. You're scaring me, what's happened?

EDWIN. Did you hear about the rally yesterday?

HENRI MARX. No

EDWIN. A group of people were planning a coup. They were caught. My wife was among them

HENRI MARX. Jesus, I'm sorry

EDWIN. Don't be

HENRI MARX. Is that why you're here?

EDWIN. Yes

HENRI MARX. There is enough room for you.

EDWIN. This was not my original plan. When a man makes a commitment to his wife he must live by it

HENRI MARX. I understand your commitment, I understand you love her, but you have no choice

EDWIN. I don't.

HENRI MARX. No one will think less of you for leaving

EDWIN. I can't leave

HENRI MARX. It's not your fault

EDWIN. You have a beauty and a hope in your pain that is arousing. And I dreamt that I could feed off of it, steal it in some way

HENRI MARX. You have no need to be afraid. You'll survive in America. I'll help you.

EDWIN. Dead men have no fear

HENRI MARX. That's the thing you don't have to be anymore

EDWIN. I'm not. I'm no longer dead

HENRI MARX. Edwin, what do you want from me? My friends will be here soon

EDWIN. For you to understand

HENRI MARX. I do. Being alive is having to choose. And it's okay, being alive is okay

EDWIN. Thank you

EDWIN. ——   **HENRI MARX.** ——

      (*A moment.*)

EDWIN. Your friends aren't coming

HENRI MARX. What do you mean?

EDWIN. Yesterday, I went to see a friend of Judith's. A journalist, Michelet Cadet

HENRI MARX. The journalist of the people?

EDWIN. Yes, he's also the journalist of the regime. I heard if someone in prison knows a political figure more important than they are, especially if the person in prison is no one, then they'd let the person go.

HENRI MARX. You're taking Judith's place?

EDWIN. No, I tried. But I'm no longer of value. They still see me as a dead painter and no one cares for a dead man's art. But your friends

HENRI MARX. You told them about my friends?

EDWIN. Yes, what they can say holds much more value here and abroad. They've already got them

HENRI MARX. ——

> (*He realizes it. He sees it.*)

EDWIN. Ah, you can see it now. The true beast that I am

HENRI MARX. How do you know that they've got them?

EDWIN. I led the Macoutes here. I saw them grab your friends. I didn't want to watch you get hurt so I asked to speak to you. You're not as important and these boogeymen are kinder than the rest

HENRI MARX. Then why not let me go?

EDWIN. You know they can't

HENRI MARX. How close are they?

EDWIN. You'll never make it to the ocean on time

HENRI MARX. Fuck you

EDWIN. Don't try

HENRI MARX. I'm dead anyways.

> (*He grabs the boat, runs towards the water. We hear sounds of rustling around* EDWIN. *He watches. He watches. He watches. A rapid succession of gun shots is heard. Silence. He watches. Lights fade down.*)

Scene Eleven

Three weeks later. Evening near the time of sunset. The living room has been transformed into EDWIN'*s studio. It is filled with his canvases and materials. Visible in the corner is the unfinished painting of* HENRI MARX. EDWIN *is drinking rum and staring at a blank canvas. He can't paint.* JUDITH *is cutting up eggplant. She is dressed once again like a woman from a village. Her bald head is wrapped in a mushwa. Her bones have aged even further. The hum of the radio is heard, as before it plays daily evening news or Duvalier propaganda. It is at the same volume as it was in Scene Six, but the silence between them is so deep that it seems louder. They sit in a silence for a few moments. A beat.*

JUDITH. I found an open space at a market off of a dirt road between here and the next village. It's small and not too much traffic and I'll have to leave earlier and be back late, but it's something. It's been three weeks and we don't have much money left. Plus the other sellers don't know me and what I tried to do, so they aren't afraid to have me there.

(*A silence.*)

I saw Madame Lucner when I was imprisoned. Did I tell you that?

(*A beat.*)

I didn't recognize her at first. She was so small, a skeleton of what she was. And her face was blank. She was gone. She's been there for less than two months and already she is aged beyond recognition. If it weren't for that little hop in her walk, like a rabbit, I never would have known it was her.

(*A beat.*)

Thank you

EDWIN. Do not thank me for killing a man

(*A moment. They return to their silence. A beat. Suddenly, as if the radio is being changed, the static, the in-betweenness one hears when changing the station on an old dial, is heard. Slowly coming into focus, a beautiful Chansonnette Francaises plays. The sound fills the stage with a soft, echoing beauty. A beat. JUDITH smiles. As she speaks the lights shift. She enters a different space. EDWIN remains in the home watching intently. He can't be where they are. But he never fades from the picture.*)

JUDITH. Last night I had this dream. I was at Carnival, this beautiful Chansonnette Francaises was playing, just like this. People were all around me dancing, but the country was different. It was like being in the future and the past at the same time. I was dancing in front of the Palace when I saw him. He was wearing a mask and holding an ice cream cone. And he started running. So I started running after him or maybe the ice cream, I don't know. I follow him to the beach, to this spot I don't recognize. And he's waiting there.

(*Lights on HENRI MARX sitting on his boat. He is wearing a mask and holding an ice cream cone.*)

HENRI MARX. I brought this for you. Butter pecan, your favorite

JUDITH. Who are you?

HENRI MARX. You don't remember me?

JUDITH. I can't tell

HENRI MARX. You I remember perfectly

JUDITH. Do you know my family?

HENRI MARX. You're more beautiful than in his painting

JUDITH. ——

(*A slight beat.*)

Take off your mask

>(HENRI MARX *removes the mask.*)

HENRI MARX. You remember now?

JUDITH. Yes. You look different

HENRI MARX. Is that good?

JUDITH. Yes

HENRI MARX. Come sit with me

>(JUDITH *sits with him. He hands her the ice cream. She begins to eat it as they stare out into the ocean, the setting sun.*)

It's beautiful isn't it?

JUDITH. Yes. But where's the horizon?

HENRI MARX. No one ever told you that it didn't always exist?

JUDITH. No

HENRI MARX. Ah, a long, long time ago, when the country was still young. The ocean bled into the sky, as if the entire world was this island. The hills rolled into the mountains and the mountaintops were high enough that you could shake God's hands. And at night, around fires, entire villages would sing, dance and tell stories. There were no other possibilities. And no one needed there to be.

>(*They all stare out listening to the country sing as lights fade down.*)

End of Play

O GURU GURU GURU
or why I don't want to go
to yoga class with you
by Mallery Avidon

ABOUT *O GURU GURU GURU*

This article first ran in the January/February 2013 issue of Inside Actors, *Actors Theatre of Louisville's subscriber newsletter, and is based on conversations with the playwright before rehearsals for the Humana Festival production began.*

Lila does not want to go to yoga class with you. Not because she doesn't like stretching or has no discipline or worries she might be bad at it. Not because she doesn't like you. The reason Lila doesn't want to go to yoga class is not easy to explain, but that doesn't mean she isn't going to try. With both humor and sincere yearning, *O Guru Guru Guru* grapples with wide-ranging questions about identity, the nature of struggle, and the pursuit of something like happiness. When you discover that the system of belief in which you once found meaning no longer holds currency for you; when you find yourself a little older, but not necessarily wiser; when the question of "where do I go from here" feels impossibly high-stakes, but impossible to answer, what do you do? Lila is hoping to figure it out today—and she brought notes.

The play launches with a lecture and a series of false starts, as Lila, adrift at 30, sorts through memories of her unconventional childhood in an attempt to make sense of present confusions. As a child she spent time living in an ashram in upstate New York, where she devoted herself to a highly regimented daily yogic practice and to the teachings of the organization's iconoclastic spiritual leader. But over time her relationship to the ashram, its rituals and philosophies, became problematic. "When I was 14," Lila muses, "I could say, meditating makes me happy. Chanting makes me happy... But now I— Now it's just—." As her efforts to locate reason in the past give rise only to more puzzlement, the "why not" implied by the play's subtitle remains elusive. "And so you see," she says early in her talk, "not only is one sentence not enough, but neither are ten or twenty... All I really want. All I ever really wanted was to be normal. Whatever that is."

Lila's stilted search for clarity in the stories of her past carries personal resonance for playwright Mallery Avidon. While *O Guru Guru Guru* is not autobiographical in the purest sense, most of the experiences Lila recounts in her opening lecture are taken from the writer's own life. Avidon really did live for a time at an ashram in the Catskills. And like Lila, Avidon approached her daily spiritual practice with sincere discipline. But the vantage of adulthood— coupled with troubling new information about the organization's inner workings—complicated her memories of her years there. These days, the playwright's relationship to her own spirituality is much more ambivalent, and her new perspective is tinged with a sense of loss. "I have friends who, as adults and under their own agency—or okay, here I am thinking of one woman in particular," says Avidon with a wry laugh. "She has truly found some sort of center in her life that revolves around her practice of yoga. And I both judge that harshly and envy it intensely."

In *O Guru Guru Guru,* Avidon maps the collision of Western capitalist ideals and pop culture with Eastern spiritual practice, a mash-up that has both personal and social ramifications. "Part of why I wrote it when I did," she explains, "is because the movie *Eat Pray Love* was coming out, and it felt like suddenly there was a context in the culture that both changed my perspective on my own experience, and created a shared vocabulary that made the expression of that experience legible for an audience." Lila's attempts to identify the source of her unhappiness will resonate with anyone who's ever felt lost (and honestly: who hasn't?) or overwhelmed by the myriad decisions adulthood demands. Of Lila's struggles, the playwright reflects, "I want my life to have meaning. One way that people look for meaning is through religion. But how is it possible to make meaning when at every turn, people tell you you're doing it wrong, or else it feels disingenuous? The play is in some ways my attempt to work through those questions."

Avidon structures *O Guru Guru Guru* as a triptych, and while to hint at the particular nature of its three parts would spoil some of its most delightful revelations, perhaps it's worth saying: come prepared to be surprised. The playwright confesses to an abiding interest in the form of theatre itself— how to make the experience more immediate, dynamic and involving—and the play engages its audience in unexpected ways. "I think just the idea of *experience* is what I want," says Avidon of her (and the play's) formal aesthetics. "When it comes to making theatre, I am not excited about recreating the relationship between a viewer and a screen. Theatre is like church to me: it's the place I go to share a fundamentally personal experience with strangers in public. So with every project, I'm always asking myself, how can the event be as much about people being together in the present moment as it is about the story being told?"

As for "normal"—whatever that is—*O Guru Guru Guru* ultimately dismantles the very notion with disarming compassion. "I wish the idea of a prevailing normalcy would go away," says Avidon. "It's not true, anyway. And if everyone were more honest about the ways they don't fit into that mold... I mean, okay: Can we all just be a little braver? Because then maybe everyone would feel a little less alone."

—Sarah Lunnie

BIOGRAPHY

Mallery Avidon is a playwright interested in the intersection of fact and fiction. Her play *Mary-Kate Olsen is in Love* premiered at The Flea Theater in November 2013, and *queerSpawn* (a commission from the COLAGE Foundation) premiered in the spring of 2013, produced by A Collection of Shiny Objects at HERE Arts Center, New York City. Other plays include *Breaks & Bikes, fracture/mechanics, The Past is Not a Foreign Country* and *everyone they knew was famous.* Avidon's work has been produced by Pavement Group, Target Margin Theater, On The Boards, angry BLVD and Williams College Summer Theatre Lab, and developed by Playwrights Horizons, Playwrights Foundation, IRT Theater, Seattle Repertory Theatre and New Century Theatre Company, among others. Avidon is an alum of the Soho Rep., Writer/Director Lab, an affiliated artist with New Georges, an artistic associate of Pavement Group and Target Margin Theater, co-curator of The Bushwick Starr's monthly reading series, and a dramaturg for the company Saint Genet. She has taught playwriting to prison inmates, high-schoolers and college students. She is currently working on a series of plays based on a seven-week road trip she took with D.W. Gibson and M.J. Sieber in the summer of 2011 (www.NotWorkingProject.com), interviewing people across America who were laid off because of the recession. Avidon holds a B.F.A. in Theater from Cornish College of the Arts and an M.F.A. in Playwriting from Brown University.

ACKNOWLEDGMENTS

O Guru Guru Guru premiered at the Humana Festival of New American Plays in March 2013. It was directed by Lila Neugebauer with the following cast:

LILA	Rebecca Hart
SAVITA	Daphne Gaines
BOWBAY	Maya Lawson
INDU	Kristin Villanueva
RAMÁ	Gisela Chípe
JULIA ROBERTS	Khrystyne Haje

and the following production staff:

Scenic Designer	Andrew Lieberman
Costume Designer	Ásta Bennie Hostetter
Lighting Designer	Brian H. Scott
Sound Designer	Darron L West
Puppet Designer	Jay Tollefsen
Stage Manager	Sarah Hall
Dramaturg	Sarah Lunnie
Casting	Judy Bowman
Directing Assistant	Rachel Karp
Production Assistant	Leslie Cobb
Assistant Dramaturg	Naomi Shafer

CHARACTERS

LILA
SAVITA
BOWBAY
INDU
RAMÁ
JULIA ROBERTS

Khrystyne Haje and Rebecca Hart
in *O Guru Guru Guru,*
or why I don't want to go to yoga class with you

37th Humana Festival of New American Plays
Actors Theatre of Louisville, 2013
Photo by Alan Simons

O GURU GURU GURU
or why I don't want to go to yoga class with you

PART I
Why I Don't Want To Go To Yoga Class With You
A Lecture

LILA is 30 but she looks quite young.
She sits at a table.
There is a glass of water on the table.
There is a slide projector.
She is trying to look put-together.
She is giving a lecture.
She has notes.

LILA. I know not all of you have asked me.
But enough people have.

And I know not all of you are um "Yogis"
but enough of you—
Well actually none of you are
Yogis
Because Yogis are
Because Going To Yoga Class Does Not in Fact Make You a Yogi.
And not that I am.

Or who knows maybe some of you are.
But if you were you would probably not…
You would be in a cave somewhere with a long wispy beard levitating as you
meditate because of all the…

You wouldn't be here listening to…

You wouldn't be here.

You would be somewhere else.
But you are here. So Welcome.

The reason I don't want to go to Yoga Class with you
is not because I'm a Christian and think it's Devil Worship.
It's not that I don't like the heat,

or stretching
or exercise.
It's not that I don't like Hippies.
It's not that I have no discipline.
It's not that I can't open myself up to new experiences.
It's not that I've never done it before and I think I might be bad at it.
It's not that I don't like sitting still.
It's not that it's too far away.
It's not that it's too expensive.
It's not that I don't like you.

It's not even that I don't like Yoga.

Or to be more precise.
Hatha Yoga.
Which is what you want me to do.
Because there are other Yogas.

Karma Yoga And
Bhakti Yoga And
Mantra Yoga

None of which have to do with stretching.

The reason I don't want to go to yoga class isn't even that I failed yoga twice in college.

I think I might like yoga class more if there was no "Om-ing"
And no "Namaste-ing."
Maybe Yoga at the gym would be okay.
Because there would be no pretensions of spiritual practice.
Or at least I assume there wouldn't…although I wouldn't know.
Since I haven't gone to yoga at the gym.
I think that if I could in one sentence explain to you why I don't want to go to yoga class my life over the course of the last ten years would have been much easier.

But I haven't figured out what that one sentence is.

Lately I've been trying
"I grew up in an Ashram."

But that doesn't necessarily mean anything to most people.

An Ashram is an isolated Hindu site designed for spiritual instruction and meditation.
There was a *New York Times* "Sunday Styles" article about occupancy in Ashrams increasing because of the recession and if something is in the

"Sunday Styles" section of the *New York Times*
it has entered the national conversation on at least some level.

And now there's *Eat Pray Love*.

There was a posting on Craigslist looking for extras who knew the customs
of the Ashram featured in *Eat Pray Love*.
I could be an extra in a Julia Roberts movie.

When I was eight I met Gurukalika for the first time. She came to Seattle on
one of her world tours.

Gurukalika is a trademarked word so I'm probably not allowed to actually
say her name.
But I'm going to take a chance.

A chance that Elizabeth Gilbert, the author of *Eat Pray Love*, does not take,
or so I've heard.

I didn't read the book.

This would be a picture of Gurukalika from the year that I met her. 1988.
The copyright to the picture is owned by the Ashram so I can't actually show
it to you.
And you aren't allowed to take pictures of Gurukalika if you aren't an
Ashram photographer.
So the copyright to every picture of Gurukalika is owned by the Ashram.
            (*There is a blank slide.*)
In the picture Gurukalika is sitting in her Chair.
She is wearing round glasses.
The picture is black and white but I think the glasses are probably red.
As is everything else she is wearing.
Gurukalika always wore red or orange or pink. Something in the fire color
family.
She is also wearing a hat. She usually wore a hat. She had the most Amazing
Hats. And Scarves.
She's wearing this cape sort of thing which was her usual attire. I can't
exactly explain the outfit because it isn't made up of normal clothing that
I can name. But the effect is something that looks luxurious and beautiful
while still being incredibly shapeless and modest.
Her hair is short and wavy.
Her eyes are closed.
She looks incredibly peaceful and at ease.

We went to meet Gurukalika because…
And this is why one sentence is never enough…

When I was six months old my parents bought a house with two other families.
The house was called 123 House
and we lived there commune-style until I was four, when my parents split up.
My best friend Holly's family was one of the other two families.
Holly's dad is the reason we went to meet Gurukalika.

He had been
involved in Laya Yoga (that's another Trademark) for many years.
When Swami Ji (another)
was still the Guru.
Which is to say the leader of the—

And so you see not only is one sentence not enough but neither are ten or twenty
because everything requires an explanation.
And then I get self-conscious because…

All I really want.
All I ever really wanted was to be normal.
Whatever that is.

And I know of course that it isn't one thing
and even if it were I probably wouldn't want to be it
but at every juncture in any story I tell about my life I see that the path that I went down,
or that my parents went down really,
and that again is what's complicated,
because these aren't really decisions that I made
because they are things that happened before I really had agency in my life
and so then when I wish that I were normal now
I wonder at what point in all of those twisting roads that we went down
my parents would have had to make a different choice
and how many different choices they would have had to make
for me to be married to some guy who's finally getting that promotion expecting our first child and talking to a mortgage broker to see how much of a house in the suburbs we can actually afford because raising a kid in the city is ridiculous and I want to drive my Prius to yoga class at the gym.

But that isn't the point of this.

The point of this is to try to explain to you Why I don't want to go to Yoga Class.

And the reason I don't want to go to Yoga Class stems from the moment that I met Gurukalika with my mother when I was eight.

Gurukalika is the Guru of an organization called Laya Yoga
which operates in the U.S. as a non-profit called the L-A-Y-A Foundation.
Laya Yoga's definition of a Guru per its own marketing materials circa 1988:

Actually hold on...

I'm really unclear on copyright issues.
Can you copyright a definition?

Also
actually

If there is someone here who is currently in Laya Yoga it would probably be
better for both of us if you left. I think you'll be bored. And it will just make
me really uncomfortable.

Anyone?
> (*If anyone leaves say thank you. And apologize.*)

I totally understand if your answer is yes and you still didn't leave I probably
wouldn't have either.

I hate audience participation.

And one last thing.
And I'm sorry for the um insistence.
But if there is someone here who is currently in Laya Yoga and you didn't
just leave.
Please don't call the Ashram Managers.

Okay.
Sorry.

But the thing is
and again this is what makes it difficult to talk about these things
is that there's a real fear of getting Sued.

Am I allowed to talk to you about this thing that was a huge part of my life
for twelve years?
Or does the fact that it's trademarked and copyrighted mean it isn't mine
even though I lived through it?

After that initial meeting with Gurukalika my mother became deeply involved
in Laya Yoga.
She started meditating and chanting and doing Seva, or selfless service.
She started going to the Laya Yoga Center in Seattle all the time.
She put pictures of Gurukalika up all over our house.

And a few months later we went to the main Ashram in the U.S. for a short visit.

Which is when I got my spiritual name: Lila.

Spelled L-I-L-A
But pronounced Leela.
Which means "God's play."
Which my mom was so thrilled about because I wanted to be an actress and so that seemed like the perfect name and what Grace it was that I would get such a perfect name from the Guru.
So from then on when I was at the Ashram my name was Lila.

No one ever calls me Lila anymore.
But for many years that was all anyone called me.

After that first visit to the main Ashram in the U.S.
we went to the Ashram in India for part of my sixth-grade year.

This is the place Elizabeth Gilbert goes in *Eat Pray Love*.
It is an Eden for westerners in a sea of poverty and want.
Or at least it was in 1991.
When India was in the depths of an economic crisis which I, of course, knew nothing about.
Which I still know nothing about.
Because despite actual attempts on my part I cannot seem to understand world economics.

This would be a picture of me standing in Front of the Ganesh Statue at the Ashram in India.
        (*Another blank slide.*)
The statue is brightly painted and about two feet taller than I am.
There are statues all over the Ashram in India.
But this one was my favorite.
We weren't supposed to take pictures while we were there.
I think this is from one of our last days.
You could get a pass to take pictures for one day at the end of your stay.
As long as you didn't then show them to anyone.
And you couldn't take pictures of Gurukalika.

In the picture, I am wearing a blue sari that belonged to my mom.
And I'm wearing big round red glasses and if it weren't for the sari you'd think I was a boy.
I was a gawky awkward eleven-year-old with no boobs.
I loved wearing saris. The whole cultural appropriation thing was a little over my head.

After we left India I had to go back and finish sixth grade at my school in Seattle.

I went to a fancy prep school and I already didn't fit in.

The reason I had started there in fifth grade was because my dad was working in the kitchen.

So I was already one of the few poor kids at the rich kid school.

Also my mom is a lesbian and in fifth grade I was still willing to tell people that so in sixth grade although I no longer talked about it everyone knew.

Plus I left school for two months to go meditate in India.

I don't remember the rest of sixth grade, but I'm sure it was awesome.

When I finished sixth grade my mom got permission from Gurukalika for us to go live at the main Ashram in the U.S. which is in Upstate New York.

It is comprised of three former resorts.

These were the hotels where all the New York City Jews spent their summers.

But then they stopped.

Although I guess my mother used to be a New York City Jew and here we were summering in The Catskills.

More than summering we stayed for 15 months.

There are all these pictures of me in the Ashram Magazines.

Doing things.

Me and the other Ashram kids constantly surrounding Gurukalika.

Making popcorn and cranberry strands for the Christmas tree.

Putting candles on little paper boats into a lake for her birthday.

In all white dresses for Easter.

Dressed as elves singing Christmas carols on a big stage for some program.

In saris singing backup for John Denver.

I don't remember what it felt like to do these things.

Or what it felt like to be so close to Gurukalika.

But there I am in the pictures.

I do remember the Ashram kids:

Ambika: Gurukalika's favorite and therefore the leader.

Ambika was a bitch.

There was also

Dhruva and Ravi and Ramá and Savita and Bhavani and Jayshree and Malika and Arun and Arjun and Heather and Caitlin. And others. Lots of others.

Who came and went just like I did.

I sing terribly. Really. But when I lived at the Ashram I loved chanting. And in the mass of all of those voices I actually felt like I could sing.

This would be a picture of me chanting.
  (*Another blank slide.*)
There's a bunch of us in the picture.
We are all standing up and have our arms thrown in the air.
And we all have a slightly druggy blissed-out look on our faces.
Ambika's in front of me in a Poofy white dress, her hair pulled back in a French braid with a headband worthy of Blair Waldorf on her head. And there is Heather. And Ramá. And Savita.
With headbands and French braids.

I am wearing a flowered dress and a cardigan.

The dress was a gift from Gurukalika as is the bracelet on my wrist.

It's a string of silver hearts.

I'm certain you can't copyright a gift.
  (*She pulls out the bracelet.*)
The clasp is broken now. I never wear it. And I don't remember the occasion on which I received it.

Gifts from Gurukalika were a big deal.
And over the years I received many.
But aside from this broken bracelet I've lost them all.

I'm not very good at holding onto things.

After that first year in the Ashram with my mom
we went back to Seattle and I had to go back to that same prep school for eighth grade.
And while I had been busy at the Ashram meditating and chanting and doing Hatha Yoga
all the kids I went to school with had started smoking pot and cigarettes and drinking their parents' liquor and having sex.

I don't really remember eighth grade.
But again.
I'm sure it was awesome.
So Awesome that I convinced my parents to let me go back to the Ashram by myself the next summer.

It was somewhere that felt like home.
I was old enough to have real responsibilities as a Darshan Girl.
Helping get everything ready before programs and then sitting right up next to Gurukalika during Darshan.

I would get to sit right next to Gurukalika for hours.

As the thousands of people at the program came up and pranamed, leaving gifts for Gurukalika as she tapped them on the head with her wand of peacock feathers.

Sometimes people would come to the side and ask Gurukalika questions about their job or their relationship or their meditation practice or their family and Gurukalika would tell them what they should do.

Or it would be someone's birthday and she would point to one of the pieces of Jewelry on the tray I held up and suddenly some devotee was ecstatic over the new Japa mala that I was handing them, their birthday gift from the Guru.

I felt important. And included.

I went to all of the chants and programs I could.

I even meditated in the cave on a regular basis.

I made new friends.

There was gossip and scandal because we were all teenagers now.

But it was the most vanilla gossip and scandal possible.

None of us did drugs or drank or had sex or smoked cigarettes.

No one even made out.

There was a boy from Australia named Ananta who I was friends with.

He was a couple years older than me.

I'm pretty sure I had a crush on him.

After he left to go back to Australia and I left to go back to Seattle we wrote letters.

I found the letters he sent me recently.

The final one is dated

> (*She reads from the letter.*)

April 5, 1994

The letter ends

I just wanted to see if you knew that many people thought we were spending a lot of time with each other, even my Mum thought we were. It is not easy for me to say this but I certainly felt an attraction towards you, even though we were in the Ashram, I did, yet didn't act on it. Maybe it was just me but this is the truth.

It's signed

Love Always

And it begins

Regarding your stepmother having cancer, well you may remember that I had cancer and that was the reason for me going to the Ashram. When I was going through my treatment for cancer I found out it was more than a physical ailment. It was more. I got cancer for more reasons than just that I didn't look after my health, or that I had a cancer gene. It was more than that. When I wrote to Gurukalika telling her that I had cancer in her reply she said that I was gaining a lot from an old karmic ailment, and that is what it is. One just can't have chemo or any other treatment and hope it turns out. One needs to take responsibility for it and their life must change. You may want to pass this on to her or even your father and he could tell her if she is not already doing so.

I wonder if I said anything to my dad or stepmom about Karma?

I wonder how I felt reading this letter.

I'm pretty sure I never wrote back.

My stepmother died three months later.

She was 38 I think.

There is something incredibly comforting about the thought that cancer is your fault.
And if you just change your ways you will get better.

Ananta wanted to be a chiropractor and when I found the letters I looked for him online.
I found a chiropractor on LinkedIn who lived in the right part of Australia and had the right name.
I didn't contact him.

Some people's lives are a straight line. From here to where they are going.

If you grew up going to church you either keep going to church yourself as an adult or you don't.

I didn't grow up going to church.
I'm Jewish.
Or ostensibly Jewish.
Really I'm nothing.
I didn't even really grow up going to the Ashram.

There was no religion in my life until I was eight and then all of a sudden this thing—
which is not a religion it's a spiritual path which means a way of life
was in every part of me.
And it stayed that way until I was 20.

I was a person who got up at five-thirty in the morning to chant and meditate.
I did Hatha Yoga not as a form of exercise but as a real and profound expression of some deeper spiritual practice.

When I'm walking with my friends now sometimes we play Slug Bug.
You know that game where you punch each other every time you see a VW Bug Drive by?

Well we play that
only we play it with
Yoga Studios.
And girls with their yoga mats that match their tote bags and their sneakers.

The bar where I had my 21st birthday is now a yoga studio.
You probably own something from Lululemon.

So maybe I've gotten my wish.
Maybe I am normal now.
Maybe when there are as many yoga studios as hair salons on the streets of most American cities
and Julia Roberts is chanting and meditating
at the Ashram I grew up in then it is no longer an oddity.

But somehow that doesn't feel like the case.

And that isn't even really what I want.

And I have spent so much time trying to…
Or maybe…
maybe I'm not trying.
maybe forgetting is the—

People talk about regret a lot.

And the most pat answer I think to whether or not you regret something is saying something along the lines of…

"I wouldn't be who I am today if it weren't for all the things I've done."

And that is certainly true.

But the question is really
Do I want to be who I am today?

You either rebel against your parents or you turn into them right?
Or you try to rebel but then you turn into them.

When your parents take you to live in Ashrams and tell you stories about being at Woodstock and Altamont and how they got married eight months

pregnant in neutral masks and handmade clothes. How they studied with
Spalding Gray in Santa Cruz before Spalding Gray was "Spalding Gray."
Stories about how you first rolled over as a baby surrounded by people
smoking pot. When they buy a house with Four other Adults just so raising
kids doesn't have to mean growing up. When they won't get out of bed for
days and don't smile for weeks. When they move through identities and jobs
and beliefs and relationships the way other people change their shoes how
do you know if you're rebelling or turning into them?

Clearly I've been thinking about this a lot.
Because really.
I was more sure of who I was at 14 when I lived at the Ashram.
Than I am now.
At 30.

Maybe I should just go back.

But even if I did I still wouldn't go to Yoga Class with You.

>*(She leaves.*
>*We hear people faintly chanting.)*

PART II
O GURU GURU GURU

1. The Darshan Girls

The Darshan Girls come into the lecture hall.

The Darshan Girls' names are INDU, SAVITA, RAMÁ *and* BOWBAY.
The girls all wear solid-colored jewel-toned saris with matching gold embroidery.
They are all of indeterminate age they could be fifteen or they could be forty.
SAVITA *is a bit older than the other women.*
They are all very beautiful and very well-groomed.
They all wear pretty earrings and have French braids.
None of them are from India, though they have all been there.
They might be from Indiana or Australia or France or Spain or Montana or Mexico.
But they have not been to those places in a long time.
There might be more Darshan Girls required to accomplish the transformation of the space.
If more people are needed they should all be women and they should all wear saris.

The Darshan Girls all wear nametags.
They are nicely printed nametags in plastic holders.
Any additional Darshan Girls will also need nametags. Their names can be: Malika, Maitri, Jayshree, Karuna, Bhavani, Maya, Bhakti, Sita, Lakshmi…
When SAVITA *introduces the Darshan Girls she should introduce everyone…*

The Darshan Girls are going to help move us from the lecture hall into their world.
This might mean literally moving to another space or transforming the space that we are in or revealing a space within the space we are in.
The text for the transformation follows the actual needs of the space.
This text was written for the production in the Victor Jory Theatre at the Humana Festival of New American Plays.
If the piece were being done in a grand ballroom at a hotel, or in two different rooms in a convention center, or in a different theater, this text would need to be adjusted.

SAVITA. Om Shanti Shanti Shanti!

Hello!

And Welcome!

My Name is Savita!

I am so glad you all chose to join us for this Satsang!

In a moment we are going to ask those of you who want to

to Join Us sitting on the Floor!

(Really only if you want!!)

There are a few things we need to do to begin our program.

Indu, Ramá, Bowbay, Malika, Maitri and I will guide you through these steps
so that we can accomplish them swiftly and easily.

As we do this we ask that you maintain silence and try to stay present in this
room
in this place
in this moment
here
together.

> (BOWBAY, INDU *and* RAMÁ *each speak to a section of the audience.*
> *Below is the text for* BOWBAY's *instructions to her section.*)

BOWBAY. Welcome, my name is Bowbay and I will be guiding you through
this experience today/tonight.

In a moment we will invite you to take a seat with us on the floor
only if you want to
only if you feel comfortable.

If you choose to stay in your seat, you will still be included in our program.

Ramá's section will be going first, Indu's section will follow, and we will be
third,
so we have a few minutes here to prepare.

If you wish to join us sitting on the floor, you may take your shoes off now.

When it is time, we will form a single-file line to the shoe racks.
You will place your shoes in them.
Savita will give you a nametag and the lyrics to the chant we will be singing
as a part of our program.
I will have a pillow for you, and guide you to your seat on the floor.
As is traditional, men will be seated on the right of the aisle, and women on
the left.
This means you may not be sitting with the people you arrived with
But don't worry! They aren't going anywhere!
If you have any questions, please feel free to ask, my name is Bowbay.
Otherwise, please remain silent and enjoy the peace in the room.

At this time if you would like to sit with us on the floor you may stand now and join the line to the shoe racks.

2. Transformation

The Space is Transformed. Or we move to another space.
Everything has garlands and drapings.
This is what the Darshan Girls do when they have a program somewhere.
They transform the space.
Flowers and Silk to cover over the cheap tables.

Everyone needs a nametag. The cheap sticker kind.
There is a table with nametags and pens.
SAVITA *stands there and helps people write their names on their nametags.*

Everyone needs to take off their shoes.
There are shoe racks.
The shoe racks have signs on them that say:
"Leave Your Ego With Your Shoes."

3. The Hall

The Hall is the Lecture Hall Transformed.
Or it is another Space altogether.
Perhaps we were in a Grand Ballroom at a hotel and one end was dressed to look like a lecture hall. And now we have all taken off our shoes and moved into the rest of the Grand Ballroom.
Maybe we have transformed the theater in front of the audience's eyes.
Wherever we are the Darshan Girls have decorated.
This is what they do.
They go to Hotels and Theaters and Convention Centers and they transform them to look like the Ashram.

For their Satsangs.

There should not be too much waiting in line.
We hear chanting.

Men sit on the right, women sit on the left.
There is a wide aisle in the middle.

BOWBAY *and* RAMÁ *offer people cushions to sit on the floor*
which is recommended

but there are also chairs available in the back.

BOWBAY *and* RAMÁ *seat people in neat rows on the floor.*

At the front of the hall is a large chair on a dais.
If someone were sitting in it they would be facing everyone in the hall, but no one
will be sitting in it.
It looks as though it is made out of crystal…of course it is just plastic.
There are side tables with flowers and silver padukas.

The hall is quite large.
There are nowhere near enough people here to fill it, in the past there have been,
but not tonight.

There is a harmonium and a drum.
The Darshan Girls Have Microphones.

4. Introductions

SAVITA *is the Emcee.*

SAVITA. Om Shanti Shanti Shanti

Welcome.
We are all so thrilled to be here and so thrilled that you have taken the time
to be here with us.

I want to Introduce myself again
My name is Savita
I have been offering Seva, or selfless service,
as a speaker at learning and teaching events for many years
and I am delighted and honored to be your host for this Satsang.

For those of you who are new to all of this
Welcome.
For those of you who have been on this journey with us for days or months
or years
Welcome.
For those of you who are thrilled to be here
Welcome.
For those of you who are unsure what it is you have walked into
Welcome.
For those of you who think maybe you shouldn't have listened to your friend
or boyfriend or wife and that you would be much more comfortable at home
on the couch watching TV

Welcome.
There is a place for all of you here.
There is a place for everyone here.

Even if you leave here and immediately forget everything that happened.
Everything you heard.
Everything you saw.
It will not be a wasted evening.
Just taking this time to be here with us.
To be here with your Self is enough.

How often do you take time to sit in silence with a group of strangers?
Take a moment to look around you.
Take a moment to look at the people you are here with tonight.
Maybe you know them.
Maybe you don't.
Maybe you are sitting next to someone you've known your entire life.
Maybe you're sitting next to someone you pass every day but don't speak to.
Maybe you're sitting next to someone you haven't seen in months or even years.
Maybe you're sitting next to someone you've never seen before.
Whoever you are sitting with you have both made the decision to be here tonight
and I am so thrilled you did.
We are all so thrilled you are here to share in this evening with us.
Welcome.
            (She says welcome in seven more languages, ending with ALOHA.)
We have a great program for you this evening.
We call our programs Satsangs.
For those of you who ARE new to this
Satsang is a Sanskrit word that means
The Company of Truth.
Satsangs are a time we come together with other seekers to chant, meditate and learn about this path that we are all on.
Wherever you are on this Journey we are so happy that you are joining us.

Take a moment to locate the lyrics you received.

We will begin the Satsang by chanting and we hope that you will all chant with us!

5. Arati

RAMÁ *plays Harmonium.*
INDU *Plays the Drum.*
During the instrumental introduction BOWBAY *walks down the center aisle and faces the chair.*
She is holding a silver tray with a tea candle burning on it.
There are also rose petals, an odd number of flowers,
a pinch of saffron and uncooked Basmati rice on the tray.
As she takes her place all the Darshan Girls begin to chant.
Perhaps the audience will chant with them?
The English transliteration and translation of the words is provided for the audience.
Everyone could sing along if they wanted to.
During the Chant BOWBAY *performs Arati*
Waving the silver tray in smooth circles in front of her.
They Chant.
The Chant ends with
"Om Shanti Shanti Shanti."
When the Chant is over BOWBAY *walks back up the aisle and puts the tray on an altar to Ganesh at the back of the hall or perhaps in the lobby.*
As they do this SAVITA *stands again to speak.*

SAVITA. We always begin our programs with *Arati.*
Asking the Guru once again to share her love and light with us.
Now we will continue with a few short talks.
First, we will hear from Ramá
about her experiences Chanting.

> (*As she says this* RAMÁ *stands and* SAVITA *sits down.*
> *When the* DARSHAN GIRLS *are not speaking they should all sit cross-legged on the floor.*
> *Listening to the program.*
> *They all have incredibly good posture.*)

6. An Experience Talk

RAMÁ. Thank you Savita.

Om Shanti Shanti Shanti

The first thing I can remember is loving to chant.
I would toddle into programs during the chants and even though I couldn't

read and didn't know the words I would get lost in the music.

As I got older I grew obsessed with becoming a lead chanter.
I wanted a microphone.
I wanted everyone to know how GOOD I was.
I started keeping my eyes open as I chanted
and in my mind I would repeat Over And Over And Over
Make me a lead chanter.

One day in the middle of chanting I realized I didn't love chanting anymore.

I had grown so focused on wanting everyone to know how good I was that I had taken all the Joy out of it.

I stopped thinking about being a lead chanter right then and focused all my energy on actually chanting.

For the next few days I went to every chant and focused all my energy on just chanting.
I remembered why I loved chanting in the first place.
It wasn't because I was good at it.
It was because when I was chanting I truly felt the divine not only in myself but in everyone around me.

The night I remembered this, the head of the music department asked me if I wanted to be a lead chanter starting the next day.

I said no.

The next time I saw the Guru she nodded very softly at me and said

"That is the Joy of Chanting."

Om Shanti Shanti Shanti
SAVITA. Thank you Ramá.

7. An Experience Talk

SAVITA. Next I would like to Introduce Indu.
Indu is going to share an experience of Seva, or selfless service.
        (INDU *stands and* SAVITA *sits.*)
INDU. Thank you Savita.

Om Shanti Shanti Shanti

There was a period of time in my teens when I did my Seva in the Café
I was in charge of the pastries

I stood behind the counter and when someone wanted a magic bar or a chocolate chip cookie
I took it out with the little silver tongs and put it on a plate and handed it to them.

It was great.

I got to see everyone because eventually everyone came into the Café for a pastry!

Sometimes on the weekends I would have a helper because it was busy.

One weekend my helper was this older woman with long silver hair.
When she arrived I asked if she had ever done Seva in the Café before
and she said no.
So I proceeded to show her everything and explain to her where everything was and the names of the different areas and how to properly put the pastries on plates.

There wasn't really much to explain but somehow I managed to stretch this training out for ages.
Telling her every possible thing I could think of as though this woman had never stepped foot in a café before.

As we were returning to the pastry counter I was still explaining tiny details to her in my most know-it-all voice.

I had my back to the counter as I gestured to the woman to make sure to wash your hands.

From behind me I heard

"Indu. She knows."

I turned around and the Guru was standing there staring at me.
She did not look amused.

"Indu. Do you know who this is?"

I looked at the woman again and then back at the Guru and shook my head.
The Guru looked at the woman and smiled.
"Why didn't you tell her?"

The Woman with the Silver Hair replied, "She was having so much fun."

The guru just laughed.

"Remember Indu. You don't know everything"

The woman was a senior V.P. of Starbucks.

Ever since that moment no matter what Seva I do
or who I do Seva with
I assume the people I am working with are the Experts.
I never again walked into a room thinking I am the one with all the answers.

Om Shanti Shanti Shanti
SAVITA. Thank you Indu.

8. An Experience Talk

SAVITA. And now we will hear from Bowbay
about her experiences Meditating.
BOWBAY. Thank you Savita.
Om Shanti Shanti Shanti
Welcome.
Welcome to each and every one of you.
My name is Bowbay
and I am so happy to be here with all of you.

Because I was born in the Ashram I started doing the practices before I could even walk.
I loved chanting but I didn't much like meditating.
The other kids were always so much better at sitting still during meditation than I was.
I was constantly fidgeting.
Moving my legs from regular criss-cross applesauce to half lotus to full lotus and back again with an occasional child's pose thrown in for good measure.
I couldn't keep my eyes closed either and would look around at all of the other people actually meditating to see what it felt like.
This continued for years.

Until finally one day I meditated.

For some reason that day as the lights dimmed and the tamboura music started and the emcee began to softly give instructions I listened.
I closed my eyes and I listened.
As I breathed in and out deeply and easily I felt my whole body become still.
I could feel myself falling deeper and deeper into the pool of my mind
and I could feel that pool growing still.
All of my thoughts left me, all of my worries, and all of my fears.
I simply sat.
And breathed.
When the meditation ended I opened my eyes and knew no matter where my

life took me I could always come back to this place.
That I could always come back to the stillness of my Self.

After the program ended I went up in Darshan
and as I was kneeling down before the Guru she held out her hand and
touched the top of my head and gestured to one of the Darshan Girls who
handed me a stuffed white bear with a T-shirt that said
I heart Meditating.

To this day I keep that bear right next to my bed so that it's the first thing I
see when I wake up.
A reminder of all the peace and joy that meditating brings me.

Om Shanti Shanti Shanti

> (SAVITA *stands again.*)

SAVITA. Thank you Bowbay.

9. A Puppet Show

> *A Shadow Puppet Show.*
> SAVITA *is the Narrator. The rest of the ladies are puppeteers.*

SAVITA. And now we have a special treat for you.
We are going to share one of the stories from the great Hindu Tradition.

The Lord Shiva, The God of Destruction
and his wife
the Mother Goddess, Parvati
lived in a beautiful palace on Mount Kailas.

Shiva did not obey the conventions of palace life.
He came and went as he pleased,
meditating for weeks or months at a time in the forest.
a snake and the moon in his hair, and a tiger skin his only clothing.

Parvati loved her husband and did not mind his comings and goings
except when they interrupted her baths.
Her one moment of pure solitude.

When Shiva was off in the forest he always left an attendant to guard the
palace.
His attendants were called Ganas.

One day Parvati had an idea.
She went to the gate of the palace to speak with Nandi, the chief Gana.

PARVATI/INDU. I am going to have a bath.

Nandi, do not let ANYONE come in and disturb me while I am bathing.

NANDI/RAMÁ. Yes Madam.

SAVITA. So Nandi stood guard at the palace gate while Parvati luxuriated in the solitude of her bath.

Just then Lord Shiva returned from the forest.

NANDI/RAMÁ. My Lord I did not expect you back.

Your Wife is having a bath and has asked me to let no one enter the palace.

SHIVA/BOWBAY. Out of my way.

SAVITA. Shiva stormed into the palace and straight into his wife's bath chamber.

PARVATI/INDU. SHIVA!

SHIVA/BOWBAY. PARVATI!!

PARVATI/INDU. I told Nandi not to let Anyone into the palace.

SHIVA/BOWBAY. Well I'm not just Anyone.

PARVATI/INDU. Let me have my bath in peace.

SHIVA/BOWBAY. Oh Parvati!

> (*He leaves laughing.*)

SAVITA. Parvati was at the end of her rope.

All she wanted was a little solitude.

PARVATI/INDU. What can I do?

I have no one who answers only to me.

My lord's words outweigh mine with everyone.

I cannot do everything for myself

and yet I have no one to trust to help me.

SAVITA. Parvati contemplated her dilemma and the answer rose clearly through the storm of her thoughts.

PARVATI/INDU. I know exactly what I shall do.

I will make a son of my own and he will obey me alone!

SAVITA. So Parvati gathered the saffron paste from her body

and molded it into the shape of a perfect little boy.

She breathed life into him

decked him with ornaments

and blessed him.

PARVATI/INDU. You are my son.

My most beautiful valiant son.

BOY/RAMÁ. Command me, mother.

What shall I do?

PARVATI/INDU. This staff is endowed with great power.
Take it and stand at the gate of the palace.
Do not let anyone enter without my permission.
NO ONE.

BOY/RAMÁ. Your wish is my command Mother.

SAVITA. So the boy stood guard with the powerful staff his mother had given him.
Soon Lord Shiva returned.

SHIVA/BOWBAY. Who are you?
I've never seen you before.

BOY/RAMÁ. Halt!
No one enters without Parvati's permission.

SHIVA/BOWBAY. Foolish boy!
Do you know who I am?
Move out of my way Immediately.

BOY/RAMÁ. Parvati has given NO ONE permission to enter.

(*The Boy Strikes Shiva with his Staff.*)

SHIVA/BOWBAY. PERMISSION!!!
Fool! I am Shiva, Parvati's husband.
How dare you forbid me to enter my own home!

BOY/RAMÁ. No One Has Permission!!

(*The Boy Strikes Shiva Again.*)

SAVITA. Shiva did not want to fight the boy
so he enlisted his Ganas to reason with him.
The Ganas noisily approached to convince the boy to abandon his post
but Parvati sent word that he should hold his ground.

BOY/RAMÁ. Ganas of Shiva,
I am the son of Parvati.
She demands that I let no one.
NOT EVEN LORD SHIVA.
Enter the palace.

ATTENDANTS/BOWBAY & INDU. Wait WHAT?!
He is Parvati's SON?
What should we do?
We must go ask Lord Shiva!

SAVITA. And so the Ganas went to Lord Shiva in the Forest.
They found him meditating.

ATTENDANT/INDU. Lord.
It is Parvati's own son who refuses to let you in.

SHIVA/BOWBAY. (*Aside.*) O Parvati
What have you done.
I cannot let myself be seen as subservient to you.
I am your lord. And I cannot let my Ganas see you best me.
You have left me no choice.

> (*To the Ganas.*)

Go.
Fight and defeat him.
He is just a child.
It will be easy.

SAVITA. So the Ganas returned to the palace gate.
Weapons Drawn They Rushed the Boy
But the Boy's Staff, flowing with his mother's power,
made him much more powerful than he appeared.

> (*The boy defeats Nandi.*)

BOY/RAMÁ. I told you that NO ONE WAS ALLOWED TO ENTER!

ATTENDANTS/INDU & BOWBAY. My Chest!
He Hit my Knees!
A-A-AH!!!
MY Head!

SAVITA. Many of the Ganas fell.
The rest fled as fast as they could.
The boy once again took his post at the gate.
When the other Gods heard the uproar
they went to Lord Shiva.
Shiva explained what was happening.
The Gods agreed to take their armies and vanquish the boy.

They fell upon the boy from all directions.
Even though the boy was massively outnumbered, he faced them valiantly.

The gods were forced to retreat back to Shiva. Defeated.

SHIVA/BOWBAY. O Parvati
This boy is truly your son.
The only way to defeat him is with my own hands.

SAVITA. Shiva and the other gods formed a plan.
Their Vast Armies Approached

and as the God Vishnu distracted the boy

Shiva came up behind the boy and

Cut Off His Head.

The Gods and their Armies were Jubilant.

But as Shiva listened to their bloodlust he had a moment of Clarity.

SHIVA/BOWBAY. What have I done?
How shall I face my wife?
She created the boy
and so he was my son too.
What have I done?

SAVITA. Parvati learned of her son's death. She was enraged.
Out of her fury she created the warrior goddesses Kali and Durga
and hundreds and thousands of Shaktis.

SHAKTIS/RAMÁ & BOWBAY.
O Mother
　　What is your command?

　　O Mother
　　　　What is your command?

O Mother
　　What is your command?

PARVATI/INDU. Destroy all the Devas and Ganas.
Devour them!
Destroy everything!
Destroy ALL CREATION!
They have killed my son!
DEVOUR THEM ALL!
THEY DESERVE TO DIE!

SHAKTIS/RAMÁ & BOWBAY. We shall do your bidding
We shall avenge your son!
　　　　(*The Shaktis begin to eat all of the Ganas and Devas.*)

SAVITA. Kali, Durga and the Shaktis began destroying all creation.
Shiva could not face his wife
but all the other gods went to her to beg for her mercy.

PARVATI/INDU. I will make them stop
when you bring my son back to life and all bow before him.

SAVITA. The gods went to Shiva and put Parvati's conditions before him.

SHIVA/BOWBAY. It shall be done.
She will destroy the world.
This battle has gone too far.
For the sake of peace and happiness,
Go North.
Bring the head of the first creature that crosses your path.
Fit that head to the boy's body and he will come back to life.

SAVITA. The Gods set off to the north.
It was a single tusked elephant that met them.
They brought the head and fitted it to the body of the boy.
The boy sat up.

BOY/RAMÁ. What happened?

SHIVA/BOWBAY. Forgive me, Parvati.
This valiant youth shall truly be my son.
Even as a mere boy you showed great valor.
You shall be Ganesh, the presiding officer of all my Ganas.
You shall be worthy of worship forever by all the gods and goddesses and all of creation.
You shall also be called Vigneshwara, the remover of obstacles.

GANESHA/RAMÁ. Thank you Father.
Thank you Mother.
In my young short life I have already suffered many trials.
It will be my great joy to help ease the way for others.

SAVITA. Shiva and Parvati once again began to live happily in their abode at Mount Kailas,
delighted by the presence of their son.
To this day, before any venture is undertaken, be it a journey, or a job, or a performance
it is Ganesh who is invoked and whose blessings are sought.

ALL. Om Shanti Shanti Shanti

10. Meditation

SAVITA. Namaste

Meditation is a big word
literally

a lot of syllables
like community
and it's a word that gets thrown around a lot

Someone might tell you to Meditate on something
when really they mean contemplate

Or a store might decide to call its customers its community

Words have specific meanings

but we've started to stretch them

We are going to meditate

Here

But first we are going to stretch

I want everyone to stand up

yeah that's right
If you're on the floor or in a chair
please everyone join me standing

and I want you to take your arms and reach them straight up over your head

Reach your fingertips up towards the sky

Imagine beams of light rising out of the crown of your head and each of your
fingertips

stretching up through the ceiling of this building where we are standing up
through the clear air and all the way to the stars

let that light straighten your posture
allowing your whole body to fall into perfect alignment

And breathe

Deeply
in through your nose and out through your mouth

In and out

And then gently let your arms return to your sides

In a moment I'm going to ask you to sit again

but for now remain standing

sometimes people think that pain is part of meditation
that they are not really having an experience of meditation if they don't have

to fight their way through pain to get there

But this does not have to be true

When you sit back down I want you to find a comfortable easeful open position to sit in

This may mean half lotus
Or it may mean a zazen position
if you are in a chair you probably don't want to cross your legs
but maybe that's the only way you are comfortable
for now your comfort is the most important
A position in which you can focus on your breath and not your body

Now take your seats again
Find that comfortable position
find an easy stillness
imagine you are a stream and the water flowing in the stream
you are both solid and free at once
you are the container and you are the contents
and these two things are not in opposition

And now breathe
imagine that your body is the stream and your breath is the water
you are both water and stream

breathe in and breathe out

now gently close your eyes

imagine again that light lifting up from the crown of your head through the ceiling and up to the stars

As you breathe in feel that light radiating through your body
and as you breathe out let yourself relax into the ground below you

You are firmly rooted to the ground
but you are lifting towards the stars

You are the stream and the water in the stream

Breathe in

And out

try to let go of your thoughts

If you have a thought

notice it and return to your breath

Breathe in and out

let go of your expectations of this moment and simply be

> (*One minute of darkness and tamboura music.*
> *Then a quiet singing bowl bell three times.*)

PART III
EAT PRAY LOVE

We hear a male voice say "Ms. Roberts to the set, please."
We are on the set of Eat Pray Love
The re-creation of the Ashram for the movie.
Maybe the work lights are flipped on.
Maybe there are noises.
Maybe there are P.A.'s and A.D.'s and grips.
Some of them might be the extra Darshan Girls from Part Two
now dressed for P.A. work on a film set.
Maybe not.
There are also some Men.
JULIA ROBERTS enters. She is dressed as the chick from Eat Pray Love.
She is wearing a sari.
LILA is there, Maybe she was there in Part II also, she is the woman from the lecture.
She is an extra in the film Eat Pray Love.
She is wearing a blue sari.
The rest of the audience are extras also.
Maybe they are in this shot. Maybe they are not.
We are about to shoot the meditation scene from the movie.
LILA sits on a pillow. JULIA ROBERTS sits near her.
These are their marks for the scene that will be shot.

JULIA ROBERTS. You have really nice posture.

LILA. Thanks.
Um…
So do you.

JULIA ROBERTS. Thank you.
I've been working on it.

LILA. So…
Do you really meditate?

JULIA ROBERTS. No.

LILA. Oh.
I just thought…

JULIA ROBERTS. For the movie?

LILA. I don't know like method acting?

JULIA ROBERTS. Hahahahahaha
Oh
Hahahahaha
That's hilarious.

That's Precious.

I don't make movies like I used to.

When I was young I really dived into the research.

Following diabetes patients and abused wives and law students and hookers and accidental activists.

But you can't live like that.

This is a job.

I read the things they give me.

I show up when they tell me.

I go home and spend time with my kids.

I love my kids.

If I could I would just never work again.

But my career supports a small entourage and I feel

obligated. No not obligated.

Obliged.

To help them.

No. Not to help them.

To continue to employ them.

And with no career there are no

Agents

Managers

PR people

Stylists

Drivers and assistants.

So I'm doing this movie,

but Danny, my husband Danny, and the kids are coming for all the on-location stuff.

Not that there's that much.

And then we'll go home. And I won't make another movie for a while.

LILA. That's really admirable.

Most people are terrible parents.

JULIA ROBERTS. It's a luxury.

We have everything we'll ever need.

We can give them anything they'll ever want.

I love my husband.

He loves me.

Nothing is physically, mentally or emotionally out of place with our kids.

We can feed them the best food.

Provide them with the best education.

Every opportunity.

Their lives will be full of ease and joy.

LILA. I actually believe that's true.

I want to be cynical or…

JULIA ROBERTS. Cynicism.

It's the currency of our age.

LILA. Yeah. I'm trying not to be. Or I'm trying to be less.

But it's hard.

JULIA ROBERTS. Did you see Conan's farewell speech from his show?

LILA. No.

I don't watch—

JULIA ROBERTS. Oh me neither. I'm not up that late.

Danny showed it to me on YouTube.

It was wonderful.

He talked about Cynicism.

About how easy it is to be Cynical.

But it doesn't get you anywhere.

LILA. Yeah.

I…

Can I ask you something?

JULIA ROBERTS. Sure.

LILA. Are you happy?

JULIA ROBERTS. Yes.

LILA. Were you happy before you had kids?

JULIA ROBERTS. Yes.

LILA. Have you always been happy?

JULIA ROBERTS. No not always.

A lot of breakups.

And you know

your twenties.

I'm still unhappy now sometimes.

Things happen.

I have a bad day.

But I can't actually

Complain.

Some people's lives are hard.

My life isn't hard.

> (*They sit.*
> *Maybe a P.A. comes to tell* JULIA ROBERTS *that they're fixing the lights.*
> *Maybe* JULIA ROBERTS *moves, maybe* LILA *does too.*
> *Maybe there is a craft services table.*
> *Maybe one of the P.A.'s needs to vacuum.*

SAVITA *is an actress in her other life and has been cast as the emcee of the*
Satsang in the movie *Eat Pray Love.*
She is on set.
Maybe she is eating something from the craft services table.
Maybe she is having her mic checked.
Maybe she is irritated.)

What about you?

LILA. What about me?

JULIA ROBERTS. Are you happy?

LILA. No. Not really. No.

JULIA ROBERTS. Why not?

LILA. It's hard to say…

JULIA ROBERTS. Really?

LILA. I think I'm lonely.

JULIA ROBERTS. Hm.

LILA. I think if I believed in God I would be less lonely.

JULIA ROBERTS. Hm.

LILA. Also I'm terrible at having relationships.
I'm really selfish.
And I'm too Nostalgic.
I keep sleeping with people I used to know because I wish we were the
people we used to be.
But we never are.

JULIA ROBERTS. Do you really not believe in God?

LILA. I lived in the Ashram with my mom when I was young.
I think it ruined it for me.

JULIA ROBERTS. God?

LILA. God
Religion
Spirituality
The whole thing.
Or I don't know.
I tried going to um Tammy Faye Bakker's son's
Rock and Roll Church once a couple years ago.
I thought it…
I thought maybe…
I saw his show on cable and he had just moved to Williamsburg
And I thought
But it wasn't…

He wasn't even a good speaker and it didn't…
There was no music.
It was Rock and Roll Church
And there was no music.

JULIA ROBERTS. I go to church sometimes.
Not a lot.
But I like sitting there.
And I like lighting candles.
And I pray sometimes.
Tucking my kids into bed.
Just for the world to be okay.

LILA. It's not though.
The world.
It's not really okay.

JULIA ROBERTS. I guess that's why I pray.

A MALE VOICE FROM SOMEWHERE IN THE SPACE. Waiting on lights.

> (JULIA ROBERTS *and* LILA *sit*.
>
> *Maybe someone fixes the set.*
> *More P.A.'s maybe.*
> *Men, maybe.*
> *Moving things.*
> *Working.*)

LILA. I wanted to move back.
To the Ashram.
That's why I'm here.

JULIA ROBERTS. Is it a good re-creation?

LILA. I think so.
Maybe.

JULIA ROBERTS. Why do you want to go back?

LILA. It's nice to have someone else plan your life for you.
I don't know if I've been doing the best job of it on my own.

JULIA ROBERTS. Hmm.

LILA. I think that's why most people do it.
I think that's why you did.

JULIA ROBERTS. I didn't.

LILA. No. Not you you.
The character you.

JULIA ROBERTS. Oh right.

No.
I—
LILA. I didn't read the book.

JULIA ROBERTS. I think it's more complicated.

LILA. Well everyone lives in the same place
and eats the same food
and survives on the same meager budget.
And I don't mind meditating.
Even though my legs are starting to hurt.
I'm out of practice sitting for so long.

JULIA ROBERTS. You can stretch if you need to. They're fixing the lights.

> (LILA *does a sun salutation.*)

You did that very nicely.
I could never get the hang of Yoga.

LILA. I haven't done it in a long time.
But it felt appropriate.

JULIA ROBERTS. Are you really going to move back?

LILA. I can't.
They won't…
It's all different now.

Even since you were there.
I mean she. Even since she was there.

JULIA. ?

LILA. It's all different.

It seems like it's all withering away.

When I decided I wanted to go back I went online to see what I had to do to
get on staff at the Ashram.
But when I searched for Laya Yoga
I found all these sites about people leaving.
First-person accounts and discussion boards and ex-cult sites
Articles from newspapers and magazines.

I stayed up all night reading about all these terrible things that happened at
the Ashram.

And all I could think was

FUCK.

Because I wanted to go back.
And now that I knew all of these things I could never…

JULIA ROBERTS. ?

LILA. Oh.

Um.

Just like.

Well in the nineties

there was this article

in *The New Yorker*

Just about um

the Bad Stuff

about the Ashram.

JULIA ROBERTS. ?

LILA. Just you know.

Like all those dudes who came over in the seventies from India.

The whole "meditation revolution" crew.

Rajneesh

and the Hare Krishna guy

and Maharishi Mahesh Yogi, the TM dude.

JULIA ROBERTS. The Beatles' Guru?

LILA. It all ended up the same.

Statutory rape and tax evasion and fancy cars and environmental destruction and cutting people off from their families and taking people's money and trust and not really

living up to the ideals that you espouse.

Just like everything.

Just like the Catholic Church.

I mean I don't know.

Maybe it's not true.

But it.

It makes sense.

I guess.

Or it doesn't Not make sense.

The pieces fit with the things I remember.

Like in the *New Yorker* article there's this whole thing about this guy who was like Gurukalika's right-hand man and he was accused of statutory rape for sleeping with this Girl who went to the Ashram.

And he totally always was hanging around all the girls. He would drive us places in his Jeep all the time. And he always wore really strong cologne and would give us chocolates and stuff.

And not that I'm saying. Nothing ever happened.

To me or anyone I knew but I mean it makes sense.

And I weirdly trust *The New Yorker…*?

People started leaving.
And then Gurukalika kicked all these people out of the Ashram who had lived there forever. Who had no money and no job history other than "Ashram Sevite." And now…

JULIA ROBERTS. When was the last time you were there?

LILA. I haven't been to The Ashram in…

But I saw Gurukalika for the last time
ten years ago.
At the New Year's Retreat
in Ontario California.
Which is like Nowhere.

I was really depressed. I was… So my mom thought it would be a good idea to… Because she was going down with her Girlfriend, and she thought it would.

Because I had gotten kicked out of college, or um encouraged to take a semester off and then come back and start the year again, because I was, I was um… Ha. Actually going to school to be an actor. And I kept skipping class and I was just…

Um. I had accidentally gotten pregnant. I was in a terrible relationship. Or just out of a terrible relationship. I was 20. And I didn't tell my mom until… it was Christmas Eve and we got in a fight which ended with me yelling something about being pregnant and bursting into tears. And then saying: I don't want to talk about it.

So her solution was going to see Gurukalika. She thought it would, I don't know what she thought, maybe that Gurukalika would tell me what I should… And I didn't know what else to do.
So I went.

And it was. It was so weird. I saw everyone I knew from when I was 14, it had been six years but they were all just the same.
I was pregnant.
And they were all just the same.

And I didn't ask Gurukalika what I should do, because I was 20 and in no position to…
I knew what I had to do.

And it all seemed so…

I haven't been back since then.

JULIA ROBERTS. Did things get better?

LILA. Still here.

Ten years later.

JULIA ROBERTS. So you're an actor?

LILA. What?

No!

JULIA ROBERTS. You said you went to acting school. And you're in this movie.

LILA. I'm an extra.

I'm not an actor.

Acting terrifies me.

I loved it when I was little.

But I think I just wanted someone to give me their undivided attention.

Then when I grew up I developed terrible stage fright.

Also being an actor seems like a really awful life.

You always have to do what other people tell you to do.

JULIA ROBERTS. But that's what you want.

LILA. But I want it in my real life.

And not just someone planning for me.

But knowing that the plan would be the same a year from now or five years from now.

That I would be in the same place doing the same thing.

Forever.

JULIA ROBERTS. But you can't know that.

You never know what your life is going to be like in one minute let alone five years.

Or even what you'll want.

I didn't always want kids.

For a while I thought I would be in love with making movies forever.

That acting would be my whole life forever.

I would just go from set to set and that would be all I would ever need.

Then one day I woke up and I wasn't happy anymore.

And I met Danny.

And we moved to New Mexico and we had kids.

And someday my kids will grow up and maybe then I'll decide I want to be a poet or a painter or an architect.

But for now I'm a mom.

And I LOVE being a mom.

I'm not saying KIDS are the solution.

Or love. Or marriage.

Or New Mexico.

It's figuring out what you want.
Who you are.
What makes you happy.
And it might change.
And it might keep changing.
But every day.
Every minute it has to be
Who am I.
What do I want.
LILA. I don't know.

I keep trying different things and none of it sticks.

Or none of it…
Whenever I'm um sad or um depressed
my friends are like
Well what makes you happy.

And I
I don't
I don't know how to answer that anymore.

When I was 14 I could say
Meditating makes me happy
Chanting makes me happy
Doing Hatha Yoga makes me happy.

But now I—
Now it's just—

I can't sleep.
A lot.
I have—
When I try to fall asleep I can feel my heart race and my—

And I used to lie there and meditate in bed.
Just focus on my breath.
Inhale
Exhale
Inhale
Exhale
And it would
it would calm my
it would ease me into sleep

and then one day it

And then one day it didn't.

I think I was more grown-up when I was 14 than I am now.
Or I'm the same amount of grown-up now as I was then.
And at 14 it's precocious.
But at 30…

JULIA ROBERTS. It's fine.
It's fine.
Life is hard.

And yours isn't really that… Look.
My life isn't hard at all.
And yours isn't easy…but it's…
You spent your twenties doing what people with some education and some freedom do in their twenties.
You messed around.
You tried some stuff and it didn't work out.
You got some cuts and bruises.

You just turned 30.
You're single.
You have no kids.
You have food and water.
You know how to read and write.
You live in New York City.

You can do whatever you want.

You have to know what you want.
And then you have to keep fighting for it.

Like Ganesh.
He fights and fights and the battles keep getting bigger and bigger, but he keeps fighting.
And eventually he gets his head cut off.
If he didn't have help he would have died.
When he comes back he has an elephant head.
But he's A God.

You certainly have not been decapitated.

LILA. No. I certainly haven't.

JULIA ROBERTS. And if you don't keep fighting you'll never get your elephant head.
When was the last time someone cooked you dinner?

LILA. I don't know…

JULIA ROBERTS. It's taco night.
Danny is a pretty good cook.
And the kids are super entertaining.

> (*And we hear a bell for places.*
> *If they have moved,* JULIA ROBERTS *and* LILA *return to their marks.*
> SAVITA *returns to hers as well.*
> *We hear a man's voice again.*)

VOICE. LAST LOOKS.

> (*The wardrobe person and the P.A.'s check the ladies one last time.*)

SPEED.

> (*The voice is echoed by someone in the space but out of sight.*)

OTHER VOICE. SPEED

VOICE. EAT PRAY LOVE
SCENE 133
TAKE 1
ACTION

> (SAVITA *begins to speak as the lights fade.*)

SAVITA. Breathe in

And out

try to let go of your thoughts

If you have a thought

notice it and return to your breath

Breathe in and out

let go of your expectations of this moment and simply be

End of Play

GNIT
a fairly rough translation of
Henrik Ibsen's PEER GYNT

by Will Eno

ABOUT *GNIT*

This article first ran in the January/February 2013 issue of Inside Actors, *Actors Theatre of Louisville's subscriber newsletter, and is based on conversations with the playwright before rehearsals for the Humana Festival production began.*

"See, mainly, I'm a people person, in the executive mold, with good problem-causing skills."
　　—Peter Gnit, introducing himself

Meet Peter Gnit, the recklessly aspiring, self-deluded anti-hero of Will Eno's *Gnit*—a so-so specimen of humanity whose problem-causing skills may well be his most pronounced ability. Today he'll disappoint his ailing mother, arriving painfully late at her bedside, full of excuses as usual. Then he'll get distracted, careening out of the house to disrupt the wedding of an ex-girlfriend, absconding with the bride as an angry mob chases him out of town and into the mountains. So begins a lifetime of bad decisions, for Peter can't stay put for long: he believes he's on a mission to discover his Authentic Self. But in this "rollicking and very cautionary tale about, among other things, how the opposite of love is laziness" (in Eno's words), the winding road to self-discovery is both acutely funny and paved with the most profound existential peril.

Peter Gnit is Eno's version of one of literature's most famously entertaining ne'er-do-wells: the eponymous protagonist of Henrik Ibsen's 19th century masterpiece, *Peer Gynt*. Ibsen's dramatic poem about a man whose fantastical adventures in procrastination take him from the mountains of Norway to the North African desert provided enticing dramatic and philosophical fodder for Eno—who calls his own riff a "faithful, unfaithful, and willfully American misreading" of Ibsen's 1867 classic. "*Peer Gynt* struck me as a portrait of consciousness at a moment in between huge cultural shifts," says the playwright. "I wanted to take a crack at it with what I hoped would be something like the contemporary consciousness."

For Eno, the foolhardiness of Peter Gnit's relentless search for the self, mistaken for a noble quest, becomes a pivotal concern in his resonant reimagining of Ibsen's tale. Peter moves through life without ever loving anyone or anything for long, abandoning connection and dodging commitment along the path to self-fulfillment. "I responded to *Peer Gynt* with a kind of fascination and revulsion in the same way that I have divided feelings about 'work on the self,'" explains Eno. "I think it's important to feel good and arrive at better places within ourselves, but in the service of that goal, you can really let a lot of people down, and can fail to be present for the people in your life." While he describes his globetrotting central character as "amusing in his structural lack of self-awareness," Eno complicates that comedy with the slow tragedy of a man who thinks he's making positive choices but whose life is actually being shaped, step by step, by fear and avoidance. "It's perfectly understandable and entirely human," he says, "but you can get scared and you can get nervous, and then suddenly, that's who you are."

In *Gnit*, then, an incisive sense of humor about the absurdity of human striving exists right alongside Peter's losses and missed opportunities. For Eno, these comic and tragic impulses are inextricably linked. "If you're approaching the truth of something, as though moving toward the center of concentric circles," he suggests, "maybe the line between gloriously funny and gloriously sad gets very thin, and the world just moves back and forth between them." Also intertwined are the play's deeply thoughtful cautionary philosophy and the big theatrical energy of Peter's capricious exploits. As Eno has imagined the world of *Gnit*, all of the actors surrounding Peter play multiple roles, embodying the many colorful characters he meets along his path. "It occurred to me that if the Other People in the play are all a little bit more flexible and liquid, that emphasizes Peter's unchanging nature as he seeks to find change," Eno explains. "The idea of a swirl of people around him while he remains *himself* just seemed right."

As Peter Gnit wanders the world searching for *the* moment, for the lofty gesture that will finally define him, his inability to see the forest for the trees makes him a scoundrel we can laugh at. But as *Gnit* unfolds, his struggle becomes all too familiar, his miscalculation a warning. The cumulative effect of that recognition is an existential sucker punch of the highest order, one that lands fully on the heart, mind and gut. "What's interesting to me about the play, and about life," concludes Eno, "is that I guess you just do these tiny little things, and you do them every day, and *that's a life*. They're not grand pronouncements, but somehow the years pile by and that's what your personality is; that's how everyone knows you, and you're *that person*. It's so quiet how that happens. It's so quiet how you ended up being this kind of person, or that kind of person."

—Amy Wegener

BIOGRAPHY

Will Eno lives in Greenpoint, New York. He is a Fellow at the Signature Theatre in New York, where his play *Title and Deed* premiered in May 2012. His play *The Realistic Joneses* had its premiere at the Yale Repertory Theatre, in April 2012. Both *The Realistic Joneses* and *Title and Deed* were on the *New York Times'* "Best Plays of 2012" list. His play *Middletown* was a winner of the Horton Foote Prize and was produced at the Vineyard Theatre in New York and Steppenwolf Theatre in Chicago. His play *Thom Pain (based on nothing)* ran for a year at the DR2 Theatre, was a finalist for the 2005 Pulitzer Prize, and has been translated into over a dozen languages. Eno has taught theatre and playwriting at Princeton University and in China, through the U.S. State Department. He was recently awarded the PEN/Laura Pels International Foundation Award. His work is published by Oberon Books in London, and by TCG, Dramatists Play Service, and Playscripts, Inc. in the U.S. Other work has appeared in *Harper's*, *The Believer*, and *The Quarterly*.

ACKNOWLEDGMENTS

Gnit premiered at the Humana Festival of New American Plays in March 2013. It was directed by Les Waters with the following cast:

MOTHER	Linda Kimbrough
PETER	Dan Waller
STRANGER 1	Kris Kling
STRANGER 2	Kate Eastwood Norris
TOWN	Danny Wolohan
SOLVAY	Hannah Bos

and the following production staff:

Scenic Designer	Antje Ellermann
Costume Designer	Connie Furr-Soloman
Lighting Designer	Matt Frey
Sound Designer	Bray Poor
Stage Manager	Paul Mills Holmes
Assistant Stage Manager	Lizzy Lee
Dramaturg	Amy Wegener
Casting	Stephanie Klapper
Associate Lighting Designer	Seth Reiser
Directing Assistant	Kate Eminger
Assistant to the Scenic Designer	Jessica Mentis
Media Technologist	Philip Allgeier
Assistant Dramaturg	Kathryn Zukaitis

Gnit was developed at The Pershing Square Signature Center, with thanks to the JAW Festival, Portland Center Stage.

CHARACTERS

Double-cast roles are in parentheses. This suggested configuration will require a number of quick-changes, but these are certainly in the spirit of the play.

MOTHER (UNCLE JOE, BEGGAR)

PETER

STRANGER 1, Male (STRANGER 3, MOYNIHAN, VOICE, HUNTER, ROBBER, voice of SPHINX, SHACKLETON, PALE MAN, REPORTER)

STRANGER 2, Female (BRIDESMAID, BRIDE, GROUPIE, WOMAN IN GREEN, HELEN, CASE WORKER, ANITRA, PASTOR, BREMER, ANNA)

TOWN (THE GREEN FAMILY, INTERNATIONAL MAN, BEGRIFFIN)

SOLVAY (BARTENDER, DARK LADY, GRAVEDIGGER, AUCTIONEER)

Dan Waller and Kate Eastwood Norris
in *Gnit*

37th Humana Festival of New American Plays
Actors Theatre of Louisville, 2013
Photo by Kathy Preher Reynolds

GNIT

ACT FIRST, scene first.

The GNIT *home (pronounced "Guh-nit"). Lights up on* MOTHER, *alone, in bed, recovering from a hysterectomy. Any movements she makes, throughout the scene, are made with a little difficulty.*

MOTHER. Never have children. Or, I don't know, have children. You end up talking to yourself, either way.

(*Pause.* PETER *enters, with a small box.*)

PETER. Hi, Mom.

MOTHER. You're a liar.

PETER. That's a nice "welcome home."

MOTHER. No, it isn't.

PETER. God, Mom. I was trying to—

MOTHER. (*Interrupting.*) Yes, I'm sure you were.

(*Noticing the small box that* PETER *holds.*)

Is that for me?

PETER. What, this? Uh, yeah. You might not like it.

MOTHER. (*She opens it. It's a men's tie, yellow-green.*) You know, just because I can't have children anymore, because I don't have the organs for it anymore, doesn't mean I suddenly started goddamn wearing goddamn ties. Oh, but we're in luck. It's your color.

PETER. If you don't want it, I'll give it a try.

(*Begins putting it on.*)

MOTHER. How kind.

PETER. Hey, it fits.

MOTHER. Aren't you even going to ask how I am?

PETER. How are you?

MOTHER. You promised you'd be here. What a darling boy. You lied.

PETER. I said I was sorry.

MOTHER. No, in fact, you didn't.

PETER. Well, I am.

MOTHER. No, in fact, you aren't.

PETER. Why don't you ever believe me?

MOTHER. Probably because you're always lying.

PETER. I was trying to tell you, if you'd just let me—

MOTHER. (*Interrupting:*) And because, when you begin sentences with "I," I'm not even sure you know who you're talking about. Because maybe I didn't hold you enough when you were little.

PETER. You held me a lot.

MOTHER. I held you all the time. I never let you go. You were very holdable. I held you and told you little stories to cover up the sound of your father piddling our futures away. (*Pause.*) I needed you, Peter. I was scared.

PETER. I'm sorry, Mom.

MOTHER. I know you are, sweetheart. You always were.

PETER. I was trying to get home and then the—

MOTHER. (*Interrupting.*) Maybe if I'd let you babble more when you were a baby, you wouldn't still be babbling now.

PETER. I'm not babbling, this is the story of—

MOTHER. (*Interrupting:*) "Mrs. Gnit, will someone be coming to help you home?" "My son should be here any minute. I think he's going to surprise me. I'll just wait here." And we all stared down a long empty hallway. Surprise!

PETER. I was trying to—

MOTHER. (*Interrupting.*) Just be quiet.

PETER. So now I can't even open my mouth?

MOTHER. That's all you can do. Like a little fuzzy baby bird. Making little peeps for its dirty worm.

PETER. (*Pause.*) Peep peep. (*Brief pause.*) Is there any chance I could get that dirty worm now? (*Brief pause.*) I like your dress.

MOTHER. I'm glad you're home, you big old disappointment.

PETER. (*Wanting to tell a story.*) I almost didn't make it.

MOTHER. (*Not wanting to hear it.*) But you did. Where's the cat?

PETER. Probably outside.

MOTHER. Can you get me the blanket? I think it's under the bed.

PETER. (*He starts looking for the blanket, which isn't under the bed.*) So, yeah, no, I almost didn't make it.

MOTHER. There's supposed to be a frost tonight.

PETER. Huh. Anyway, so a few days ago, I'm looking around, and what do I see, but a—

MOTHER. (*Interrupting.*) It isn't under the bed?

PETER. No. What do I see, but this crazy dog. Wild, but familiar; brown fur, but with Dad's eyes. So I took off after it.

MOTHER. Okay.

PETER. What?

MOTHER. No, go ahead.

PETER. I will. So, I could so easily see the thing, shivering on a rusty tangled chain, while a family dined inside, in silence. There it sits, banished— hungry and getting smarter. Scrawniness is power, it seemed to say. I wanted to know its secret.

MOTHER. I don't think dogs have secrets. (*Admiring her dress.*) Do you really like this dress?

PETER. It's fine. Yeah, so this dog. I started screaming my own name, chasing after it. God. Wow.

> (*He stares off, dreamily.*)

MOTHER. (*Brief pause.*) And? I'm not interested— but, don't leave us hanging. Did you catch it?

PETER. Yes and no. We ran through backyards, boy and dog, together. My legs got all scratched up. Somebody shot at us, I think.

MOTHER. (*Concerned.*) No.

PETER. Yeah. I think. People screamed. I didn't recognize anything. The dog, now limping, now half-wearing a pretty dress from a clothesline we'd run though, and me. Man and Nature, Mom. On a journey without maps, through a new theology, bible-less. And I suddenly could see that the—

MOTHER. (*Interrupting:*) God, what is that smell? Do you smell that? Oh, God, it's terrible.   .

PETER. I don't smell anything. But, so there we were. I saw the world as if I'd just turned a corner onto it. This was my moment. I wanted to—

MOTHER. (*Still trying to find the source of the smell.*) Is it your shoes? Did you step in something?

PETER. (*He sniffs his shoes and is repulsed.*) Oh, God. Yeah, I did. Sorry. Fuck.

MOTHER. Take them off, Peter. Get them outside. And don't swear.

> (*He exits.*)

Love is in the air.

> (PETER *returns with his shoes off.*)

Light a candle or some matches. (*Brief pause.*) We don't have any candles. Maybe I hung that blanket up outside.

PETER. So, the dog and I. It had been a few days now and the hunger and blood loss were getting us somewhere special. I was seeing stars. I don't know what the dog was seeing. Sticks? Bones? Stars, just like me? I don't know, I'm not a veterinarian. We stopped to breathe and I was rubbing my leg and then the dog just bolted. Then I looked up, and, there was the house, and, here I was, Home.

MOTHER. Really?

PETER. Really, Mom. Mom, I never felt so alive.

MOTHER. No? Not even last year? When the exact same thing happened? And you couldn't get home in time to take me in for my tests? You told me the exact same story, last year.

PETER. What do you mean, last—. No, come on— I felt alive then, too. This was different. This time, at first, I was thinking—

MOTHER. (*Interrupting.*) Enough, Peter. I can't, okay. No more. (*Brief pause.*) God, I can't get warm.

PETER. Here.

>   (*He puts his jacket over her.*)

MOTHER. Can you tell me what you were born for? Honestly? Because I can't.

PETER. Well, you always told me—

MOTHER. (*Interrupting.*) I'm sure I told you something.

>   (*Finds a little bag of candies in* PETER's *jacket pocket.*)

What are these?

PETER. Oh, yeah, I forgot. I thought you used to like those.

MOTHER. Yes, I did, Pee-Wee. I did used to like these.

>   (*She tries one.*)

You're a good boy, Peter. You're like your father.

PETER. You hated Dad.

MOTHER. I disliked your father, and was deeply offended by him. I never hated him. You be careful or you'll end up just like him.

PETER. Oh, no. I've got bigger plans.

MOTHER. So did he.

PETER. I'm on a journey to discover, to uncover, the authentic self.

MOTHER. Yeah? Get some milk, while you're out. (*Brief pause.*) I'm sorry about what I said, Peter. You were born because I needed you. Let me see your legs.

PETER. (PETER *rolls up his torn pants.*) Dueling scars, from my run-in with the world.

MOTHER. Cuts on your legs from running in the woods like an idiot.

PETER. Well, potayto, potahto.

MOTHER. There's rubbing alcohol in there. (*Pointing to a cabinet.*)

>   (PETER *gets the rubbing alcohol.* MOTHER *prepares to put it on* PETER's *cuts.*)

That girl should be doing this. That girl you used to skate with.

PETER. Sarah.

MOTHER. I think she still loves you. With her brains and looks and her money, and your— all your wonderful things, your posture— what children you'd have. You could do worse than marrying her. Just think. We could get new windows.

PETER. Maybe I should. She's pretty.

(*He winces, due to the sting of the alcohol being applied.*)

Jesus. I should give that a go. I liked her. I should. Christ. She'd make me happy and calm. I could find myself. God, Fuck, that stings. She loved me. I should marry her. Auugh! Fucking Jesus Shit! I will. I'll marry her.

MOTHER. She's getting married this afternoon. I'm sorry, Peter. I don't know why I even brought it up. Probably some unconscious thing.

PETER. (*Very calmly, softly.*) Fucking Jesus Shit.

MOTHER. Don't swear, Peter.

PETER. Sarah's getting married.

MOTHER. Maybe if you'd worked harder at school or been born a different person... who knows?

PETER. Yeah, that's true, actually. (*Brief pause.*) You know what, I'm going to the wedding. I'll just show up. I'll have her, and with her idiot father's idiot consent. I always respected him. This just somehow feels right.

MOTHER. No it doesn't. This feels stupid and wrong. Just forget it, please. I just got out of the hospital. I need you here.

PETER. (*He wasn't listening.*) I'll need to leave, right away. And I'll need you to come with me. Talk me up, a little, with the in-laws. The Gnits will rise again!

MOTHER. No, we won't.

PETER. Yes, they will.

MOTHER. Peter, please— I just need to eat some protein.

PETER. Ah, I love you, Ma. I should put you up on the roof or something.

MOTHER. That doesn't make any sense.

PETER. Doesn't it?

MOTHER. No. Did you even hear one word I just said?

PETER. Yeah. Definitely. "Children." And, I think, "posture," a while ago. So there's two— you only asked for one. Listen, I know this seems hectic. I know I seem a little hectic, right now. But I know it's right. This is the moment. I thought it was that dog, but, no. This'll be the moment. When my whole life, everything, changed. I promise. I'm the man of the house, now. I'll take care of you. I will. I'll comfort you, Mother.

(*Motioning toward jacket.*)

Could I grab my, yeah, there we go—

(PETER *takes his jacket back, gently.*)

Wait, so who's she marrying?

MOTHER. That Moynihan. Come here, dear. Your collar is wrong.

PETER. Moynihan? I think I'd make a much better person than Moyniha—

> (PETER *has moved towards her bedside.* MOTHER *violently grabs* PETER *by the collar or tie.*)

MOTHER. (*Interrupting:*) You're killing me, Peter. I'm so tired of the cold. I'm tired of the free church food. So go ahead, you go and try to get yourself married to that girl. Because, you know what? We need help. We're poor. Did you know that? We're poor people. I have a condition. We have broken windows and medical bills. We're in trouble. And you are killing your dying mother.

> (*She lets* PETER *go.*)

PETER. I understand.

MOTHER. No, you don't.

PETER. Well, who's to say.

MOTHER. Be careful, Peter. Don't go die some ridiculous death.

PETER. I will, Mom. Thanks. I won't be long. Bye.

MOTHER. I really need you here. I need you. So come back home, soon, okay.

PETER. Definitely.

MOTHER. What did I just say?

PETER. (*He was not paying attention.*) Oh. Just, that when, or, I shouldn't, you said I shouldn't feel that I need—

MOTHER. Get out of here, Peter.

> (PETER *exits.* MOTHER *eats another piece of candy.*)

Sometimes, it's like I'm still pregnant with him. I mean, sometimes, I still get a little kick out of him.

ACT FIRST, scene second.

> PETER *enters, on his way to the wedding. Two* STRANGERS *approach.* PETER *has hidden.*

STRANGER 1. Oh, my god, yeah— half drunk half the time, just sort of stupid the rest. He's just, "Me, me, me." I mean, that's him, saying that. I heard that one time he actually—

PETER. (*He steps out of bush. Pointedly:*) Sorry to interrupt. I suppose you're talking about me?

STRANGER 1. Ah, no— sorry, buddy.

(*He turns to continue talking to* STRANGER 2.)

He's terrible with old people, unkind to animals.

(*He turns back to* PETER.)

Hey, wait a minute— you're Peter Gnit, aren't you. You're actually just like the guy I was just talking about.

(*To* STRANGER 2.)

In fact, he's probably worse.

STRANGER 2. What smells like urine?

PETER. Is this a quiz?

STRANGER 2. No. I smell urine.

PETER. Well, don't look at me.

STRANGER 1. We're both staring directly at you.

(STRANGER 1 *and* 2 *begin to walk away.*)

Anyway, as I was saying, this other guy was such a jerk, such a liar. But at least he didn't have any pride about it. That's what makes Gnit so much worse. He actually has the temerity to think he's got something to offer us all.

STRANGER 2. Is temerity like recklessness?

STRANGER 1. Sort of, yeah.

STRANGER 2. That's what I thought.

STRANGER 1. Vocabulary.

STRANGER 2. Yeah. (*Very brief pause.*) I guess in our relationship, you're the one who talks more.

STRANGER 1. (*Modestly:*) Oh, I don't know about that, but, thank you.

(*They both exit.*)

PETER. (*He tries to smell his underarm.*) I'm not a— whatever he said. I'm not. Let's see. I need a plan, here. (*Brief pause.*) That cloud looks like a cloud. That cloud looks like me, kind of. I am, in my eyes, the King of the Clouds.

STRANGER 3. (*Enters.*) Hi, I'm a person. Now, I doubt you're with the wedding, dressed like you are, smelling like you do. Are you? If so, the path to the wedding is that-a-way. If not, the path off my property is this-a-way. So, now, I've offered you a couple of different courses of action, a couple different a-ways off my land. Don't make me do something I don't want to do. Which I would very happily do.

PETER. Do you know who I am?

STRANGER 3. Yes, I do. Actually, let me be honest, here— no, I don't. I'm sure you're someone. Get off my property.

(*Brief pause. He opens his arms, in a gesture that seems to say, "I told you to leave, what are you still doing here?"* PETER *mimics the gesture.* STRANGER 3 *points off-stage.* PETER *mimics this, too.*)

Stop imitating me.

PETER. I'm not imitating you. You're just doing it sooner.

(PETER *exits*. STRANGER 3 *exits*.)

ACT FIRST, scene third.

At the wedding.

TOWN. (*Enters, a single person.*) Some nights I get so drunk I think I'm a whole fucking town. I get liquored up into such a state, into so many states, that I feel as angry and judgmental and beautiful as a whole town. Whole town. I shouldn't have smoked that cigar.

(PETER *enters, other side of the stage.*)

Hey, look— it's that Peter Gnit. What's he doing here? No, don't look, don't look. Great, he's coming over here. Hey, watch it, you almost spilled on my jacket. Yeah? I'll fucking smash this glass right into your eye. Guys, guys, guys. (*Brief pause.*) The bride seems really moody. She really loves Moynihan, though. You can tell.

(PETER *approaches.*)

Hey, the entertainment is here. Gnit, tell us a story. Here's some booze, monkey-man.

(TOWN *hands* PETER *a bottle.*)

PETER. I thank you, sir. Not a monkey, though.

(PETER *clears his throat.*)

Let's see.

(PETER *drinks.*)

A child was born one Monday or the year before, on a Tuesday. All sorts of forces assembled against him— even the shape of his head was determined by outside pressure. Nonetheless, if that's a word, feeling himself an emperor, somehow, he left to somehow found his empire.

(*A quick sip.*)

This is good. What is this?

(*He takes a quick look at the label.*)

Lingonberry— that's interesting. Anyway, he went through rain and sun and snow, unto himself, as life's many doors and trapdoors opened before him. End of story, basically. Many years later, in a private ceremony, he was crowned the Subject of Subjects and lowered into the final earth.

(*Glances at the label again.*)

You know, I bet this would go really well with another bottle of this.

TOWN. Huh. Not a bad tale. Really? That was the only bottle. So, the main guy died— did not see that coming. Sorry, where did they have cigars? You look stupid because you're poor and I'm going to punch you in the face. Hey, whoa— those are fightin' words. People, again, please, this is a wedding feast. This town is driving me crazy.

(PETER *has drifted away.*)

Hey, look, Gnit is up to something over there. Where? Right there. Oh yeah.

(PETER *approaches* BRIDESMAID. *Music playing at a low level.*)

PETER. Let me introduce the real me. Hi.

BRIDESMAID. Who invited you?

PETER. I did.

BRIDESMAID. Well then I think you should ask yourself to leave.

PETER. Do you want to fuck around? You know, weather permitting?

BRIDESMAID. That is so rude.

PETER. But is it really, though?

BRIDESMAID. Yes. (*Calling off-stage:*) Richard, this guy was just really rude to me.

(*Exits.*)

PETER. (SOLVAY *enters.*) I think she misconstrued what I said.

SOLVAY. Hello.

PETER. Hi.

SOLVAY. My name is Solvay.

PETER. What a coincidence.

SOLVAY. How is it a coincidence?

PETER. No, just, great name. "Solvay." It makes me want to ask for forgiveness. You know, "Atone, atone."

SOLVAY. I never had that reaction to it. I'm, um…

PETER. What?

SOLVAY. Nothing.

PETER. Did you want to, would you care to join—

SOLVAY. (*Interrupting:*) I'm fine. I love this song.

(*Looks at* TOWN, *who sips a drink, maybe dances a few small dance steps.*)

Look at everybody. It's quite a crowd.

(TOWN *waves a small awkward wave.*)

PETER. It's a good crowd.

SOLVAY. Are you here with the—

PETER. (*Interrupting.*) My name's Peter Gnit.

SOLVAY. "Gnit?" I've heard about you. (*Brief pause.*) I've always wondered about that name— where's it from?

PETER. It's a typo.

SOLVAY. Oh.

PETER. Yeah, some mix-up from a birth certificate but we just decided to go with it. Will you have this dance with me?

SOLVAY. I've heard about you, I said.

PETER. Come on. Dance with me. What are you afraid of?

SOLVAY. Nothing. I don't know. My father. The town. My body, and disease. Heights, small spaces, drowning, you, poverty. (*A little laugh.*) I'm not afraid of anything. Except loneliness, choking, stroke, drowning, anything socially-transmitted, the dark, weakness, guilt, this, you, I don't know, loneliness, going blind, history, this, things like this, my father, fathers.

PETER. Right, but I mean— actually, yeah, wow, that's a pretty good list. Drowning— ouch.

SOLVAY. I have to go.

PETER. No you don't. Stay.

SOLVAY. Why?

PETER. There's something here. Between us. A moment, maybe. A long moment.

SOLVAY. Did you hear all the things I'm afraid of?

PETER. Yeah.

SOLVAY. And you're not scared?

PETER. No, I'm scared.

SOLVAY. That makes me feel good.

PETER. Did you ever just want to feel— I don't even know how to say it— welcomed, in life? Just, give me a smile, world. Like I'm not in the wrong place. Just soup and a blanket, and everything's all right. Did you ever want that?

SOLVAY. Yes. (*Brief pause.*) Soup and a blanket. You're very... I don't know. I'll just say that: You're very.

PETER. Thank you.

SOLVAY. You're welcome. (*Brief pause.*) I have to go.

> (*She exits.*)

PETER. I like your worldview.

MOYNIHAN. (*Enters.*) Jesus, Jesus, Jesus— fuck.

PETER. (*To himself.*) Solvay.

MOYNIHAN. My wife-to-be won't come out of the bathroom.

PETER. Your wife-to-be or not-to-be? Do you remember your Shakespeare? Not me. See, mainly, I'm a people person, in the executive mold, with good problem-causing skills.

(TOWN *drifts nearby, stands downstage.*)

MOYNIHAN. I didn't know that. But, so, she won't come out of the bathroom. I don't know what I said. Maybe you could talk to her?

PETER. Sure.

(PETER *turns, moves a little downstage, toward* TOWN, *strikes a soliloquist's pose. Speaks to* TOWN, *and somewhat toward the audience:*)

And here the villain seeks your complicity. I do this for the benefit of my mother, for Family with a large F, and for the benefit of those who like to cry at weddings.

TOWN. Sorry, is that, are you saying that to me? Yeah, what was that? It's like he said this whole weird thing. Are we supposed to say anything back?

PETER. No, you don't have to say anything.

TOWN. Okay. Do you know... did you guys happen to know, that this whole function hall was once an old candle factory? Interesting. That wasn't interesting. Well, it wasn't uninteresting. Yes, it was. No, it wasn't.

PETER. Are you done?

TOWN. Hi.

PETER. Hi. (*To* MOYNIHAN:) Let me see what I can do, okay? That is the question.

MOYNIHAN. Thanks.

(PETER *moves upstage.*)

They used to skate together.

TOWN. (*Awkward pause. To* MOYNIHAN:) Big day, huh? Yeah, it's like: I sentence you to a sentence with life in, like, here's your ball and chain, hello?, life sentence, watch out. (*Very brief pause.*) That didn't come out right. No, it didn't. He's been drinking. We've all been drinking. But, so, yeah, congratulations. Yeah, congrats.

MOYNIHAN. Thanks. God, I'm a nervous wreck.

(MOYNIHAN *is downstage, facing audience, while* PETER *quietly jimmies open the bathroom door, disappears inside, returns with* BRIDE *over his shoulder and sneaks off.* TOWN *exits, to have a look.*)

UNCLE JOE. (*Enters.*) You should probably hear about this. Gnit just ran off with your wife over his shoulder. Or, I guess, fiancée. It happened about, I would say, ten to fifteen feet behind you.

MOYNIHAN. What? Are you serious? Where were they go—

UNCLE JOE. (*Interrupting.*) When do we eat, Paul? Hunger is all I remember from any wedding I've ever been to. Hunger and waiting. And then, finally, a cold plate of bad food. At least at funerals they get you in and out.

TOWN. (*Enters.*) Gnit made off with the unhappy bride! Wasn't her dress amazing? The unhappy bride was laughing and waving! The whole town just stood there. The pig! I'm so drunk, right now. What was that fabric? Let's kill him! Revenge! Tablecloths always make me sad— isn't that weird? I said fucking Revenge.

MOYNIHAN. I think I'm going to be sick.

UNCLE JOE. Is there any crackers or anything around here, Paul? I'm going to see if I can find some crackers.

> (*Exits.*)

MOYNIHAN. What am I going to do?

TOWN. He humiliated all of us. Me, most of all. I'm the girl's father. He is. And I swear to you all, I am going to kill him, and you will swear along with me that it was an accident. Now, let's go! Wait a minute— if she's so unhappy, why would she laugh? Shut up, Richard. Yeah, this is no time to think. Hey, your tie's all crooked, here, let me get that.

> (TOWN *straightens his collar.*)

Much better. So, Marek was just telling everyone about how this place used to be some kind of an old candle fac—. I said, let's fucking go. Factory. An old candle factory.

MOTHER. (*Enters, moving with difficulty.*) What's going on? What happened? Don't tell me. No, tell me. Is the wedding over?

TOWN. Sort of.

MOYNIHAN. That's all you have to say?

> (TOWN *shrugs.*)

The little liar ran off with her. Gnit, I'm talking about. He kidnapped her. We were going to be happy. That was the plan. I did the seating.

MOTHER. What does the girl's father think?

MOYNIHAN. He's going to shoot Gnit in the back and get one of these upstanding townspeople here to lie and say it was an accident.

MOTHER. You're not serious.

TOWN. We are. We just suddenly changed, from a little group standing around, to a bloodthirsty mob on a mission. Don't worry, Ma'am, just let me assure you he'll be dead or in serious pain by morning.

MOTHER. He's my son.

TOWN. Oh. We didn't know that. (*Very brief pause.*) I did— Hi, Mrs. Gnit. Sorry. I thought you were a caterer or something. Let's go. Time is wasting. My anger is wasting. The mob has spoken.

MOYNIHAN. Someone has to die, for all the dead things inside me.

TOWN. (*Finding the above philosophically distasteful:*) Ewww.

MOYNIHAN. What?

TOWN. No, nothing, that was great. Let's go. He's getting away.

(*Begins to exit.*)

MOTHER. Please wait. Good townspeople…

TOWN. You have one minute. Yeah, because, we really should… Yeah.

MOTHER. Please listen. People get struck by lightning, playing golf. They drown, skinny-dipping, drunk. We get skin cancer, lying in the sun at the beach. All very silly, in the end, the way of all flesh. The best of all is to die in the night, at home, quietly, just from having not died for so long. Let my son die a silly natural death. Just let him suffer the normal humiliations. Don't hurt him. I'm the boy's mother. Please. I'm asking you.

TOWN. Well, we're the boy's lynch mob and we're telling you. No, hang on, those were good points. I think I speak for all of us when I say we're a little torn. Let's go. But, wait, if we actually picture the moment of the hammer hitting the head, or the screwdriver entering the ear— I said, Let's go. You know, Richard, I don't think you should come. No, he should come. It should be everyone. We speak with one voice. Bye. Don't run. Yeah, let's pace ourselves.

(TOWN *exits.*)

MOTHER. Cartoons. You're all just thoughtless cruel cartoons. And so am I. And how do you draw a drawing of me to show what I'm feeling? How do you spell the sound of an old lady being hit in the stomach with the facts of her life? Not "pow." Or "wham." It's quieter than that. It's smaller and almost all vowels. The sound of an old woman, being hurt. Or the sound of a son, not turning out like anyone wanted. It's just a little sound. God. Ohhh.

ACT SECOND, scene first.

BRIDE *and* PETER. *In the mountains.*

BRIDE. You should've seen their faces how I saw their faces, upside-down, and so mad. Yelling, "Kill him. Kill the lucky vermin." With my former husband-to-be at the front, his new tuxedo all torn up, and tears in his eyes. Then the screams turned to wheezing and all I could hear was you breathing.

PETER. It was really something, wasn't it.

BRIDE. I was hoping you'd save me. Maybe I was just scared, but, I think I was making a big mistake.

PETER. Yeah. Listen, maybe you following me here wasn't the best idea.

BRIDE. You carried me here.

PETER. Yeah, I know. Hey, so who was Solvay? Was she with you or the groom or what?

BRIDE. Who? Should we make a fire?

PETER. I think we'll be all right. (*Brief pause.*) I'm in love.

BRIDE. I'm in love, too.

PETER. It's an amazing feeling, isn't it. (*Brief pause.*) So, yeah, are we clear?

BRIDE. What?

PETER. You should go back down, okay? You can probably still catch the end of the, you know, your wedding. I thought that other moment was the moment, the one with the dog, or running off with you, but now I have a better grasp on things. This is it. Solvay is.

BRIDE. Don't even joke, Peter.

PETER. Okay.

BRIDE. I have nowhere to go back down to. I gave up everything for you. My father's love, security, money, Moynihan. I ruined my life for you.

PETER. Thanks, I guess. But, as I said, you know— well, I already said it.

BRIDE. Are you—. Peter? I can't believe you're doing this. What about all the things you said? And all the times we—

PETER. (*Interrupting.*) I was probably drunk, okay? I can see how this could look ugly. But, what can I do— I gotta be me.

BRIDE. Do you? (*Brief pause.*) You ruined my life.

PETER. Yeah, you said. And I said I was sorry. On second thought, you were with me every step of the way.

BRIDE. You had me in a headlock, you fucking—. Do you even—

PETER. (*He interrupts.*) Sshhh. That's enough. Go away. I'm all sobered up, now. Isn't this awful. For whatever reason, I don't even want to bother coming up with something final to say. Death to your memory. That's actually pretty final.

BRIDE. Someday, if you're lucky, you'll look back and it will hurt you to think about this. You hurt someone who, admittedly, had a lot of problems, but who was still just a person who loved you.

PETER. Okay, very good.

BRIDE. (*Simply, plainly:*) Oh my God. I'm having a panic attack. Thank you so much. I'm in the woods in a wedding dress, on my wedding day, having a panic attack.

     (*She exits.*)

PETER. Panic attack. That can't feel good. It's probably just cold feet.

     (*He strolls off.*)

ACT SECOND, scene second.

In the mountains. MOTHER *and* SOLVAY.

MOTHER. I just need to sit for a bit.

SOLVAY. We'll find him. He has to be somewhere.

MOTHER. I keep seeing him, dead and broken, lying backwards in a ditch, animals gnawing on his muddy crotch. Mothers just have a sense.

SOLVAY. I have a feeling too.

MOTHER. That's nice.

SOLVAY. It really is. (*Very brief pause.*) I think he's wonderful. So full of life, and himself. He scared me. Then I liked him. He'll be okay.

MOTHER. It was good of you to come with me. People don't really help much. That's not true— people can be sweet.

SOLVAY. No, of course. I saw the whole town heading off, practically with rakes and torches. He doesn't deserve to get hurt. People don't understand him. I probably don't either, but, hurting him probably isn't going to help. Maybe I feel guilty about something, and, somehow, that explains something about me? I don't know.

MOTHER. Maybe. (*Brief pause.*) He used to come up here when he was little. I followed him once. He made a little clearing. He gathered all these little things together, some cloth and stones, an oak leaf. And he was talking to it all. He told the cloth, "You're a bad piece of cloth, because you're not a stone." And he told the stone it was disappointing it wasn't a leaf. And he had an animal bone he held up and said, "I don't even know where to start, with you." And then he said, "We're all the wrong thing. But here we are, together." And he sat there. Peter could be so quiet. I watched him till sunset. Then he put everything in a pile and said, "Bye, cloth. Goodbye, leafy. Bye, bone. I love you."

SOLVAY. Aww, that's a long story. "Goodbye, leafy." The poor thing. I used to make dolls, too.

MOTHER. We're not terrible people. I'm not a terrible mother.

SOLVAY. I know.

MOTHER. I think you'd make a wonderful person for Pee-Wee.

SOLVAY. (*She laughs.*) Ohh. "Pee-Wee." I think we'd be very happy. I don't know how I'm supposed to know this. But how do you know anything? Did you ever hear anyone say, "This is the moment. This is what I believe, now." And that was it and they made that their life, right then and there, forever and ever, and never looked back.

MOTHER. I have heard people say that. But they never followed through, or they got syphilis or something and then just disappeared. (*Very brief pause.*)

But I'm sure it happens.

SOLVAY. That's what it was like for me. And it never was like that, before. I don't know what this feeling is, or where it came from, but I feel really sure about it.

MOTHER. And why is that, dear?

SOLVAY. No, I just said, it's not something I can really articulate.

MOTHER. No, of course. Men can be very attractive.

SOLVAY. Yeah, I know that, but, this is different.

MOTHER. I understand. Peter's father was a complete idiot.

SOLVAY. Is that, that's how you're showing you understand?

MOTHER. You're very sweet, dear.

SOLVAY. Let's just keep looking.

> (MOTHER *stops.*)

Are you okay?

MOTHER. I just got out of the hospital. (*Brief pause.*) I'm amazed the world's children don't all die of guilt for the things they put the world's mothers through. (*Brief pause.*) You're very kind to care about us.

SOLVAY. Of course. I do care about you, Mrs. Gnit.

MOTHER. Oh, you don't have to call me that, dear. Wait!

> (*She freezes, turns her head slightly sideways, listening.*)

SOLVAY. (*Pause. They both listen.*) Did you hear something?

MOTHER. I thought I did. I'm a mother, you know— we have a sense. Although, sometimes, it's wrong.

> (*They exit.*)

ACT SECOND, scene third.

The mountains.

PETER. (*Enters.*) "Tall peaks in the distance. Late day, the shadows lengthen. Amid wild mountain flowers and babbling brooks, a solitary figure approaches." That's a stage direction from some play I read in school. Probably should have paid more attention. Or not, or not. (*Brief pause.*) Maybe I should go back and face the whole music and just get it over with. Start my life with Solvay. It'd be good. Good food, the indoors, love, company, the true self. I'll go back.

GROUPIE. (*Enters.*) Hi.

PETER. Hello. Beautiful evening.

GROUPIE. Isn't it. God, it's gorgeous. It's great being outside.

PETER. It can be, yup. What brings you up here?

GROUPIE. We're from the city, my two girlfriends and I. We're groupies.

PETER. I see. Groupies following some bearded guru or a promising local act?

GROUPIE. No. Just groupies.

PETER. With no… yeah, I get it. Just groupies. (*With interest.*) Really? Maybe I could join you. Or you could join me.

GROUPIE. Yeah, I don't know. We're here mainly for the air. But, do you want to have a glass of wine with us? We're kind of in the mood to be crazy and also we're a little high.

PETER. Crazy is a watchword of mine. A little high is my philosophy. Your gracious offer I gladly accept. You picked the right mountaintop of the right range on the night of the right sunset.

GROUPIE. You're funny. Not funny ha-ha, but, like, funny redundant. Come on. We're over here.

(*She motions off-stage. They exit.*)

TOWN. (*Enters, somewhat out of breath.*) Fucking. The fucking. Hey, slow down. You're not even winded. I want to see that bastard writhe, blood in his ears and eyes. Yeah, I play tennis three times a week, just try to stay active. Why don't we just go home. Moynihan did. No! I think I got poison ivy. I want to sit down. No, we're not stopping till we're dripping red.

(*Indecipherable grumbling.*)

What? I didn't say anything. Make sure you don't touch your eye. Yeah, you should wash your hands. Hey, look at this, this is Bergfrue— also known as pyramidal saxifrage. It's a nice little flower. Are we stopping or what? Death! It's almost like a little daisy.

(TOWN *exits.*)

PETER. (*Enters, with* GROUPIE, *speaking to another person off-stage.*) Please, why not, more champagne. The lamb was delicious.

GROUPIE. You're so authentic.

PETER. Yeah. I was really hungry.

(*Begins to exit.*)

GROUPIE. Where are you going?

PETER. Now? Just going to find some more kindling.

GROUPIE. Oh. Okay.

PETER. Don't sigh. Your good man shall return.

(*Aside:*)

Like hell he will. Thanks for the so-so experience.

GROUPIE. "Like hell he will"? "Thanks for the so-so experience"?

PETER. Oh. (*Very brief pause.*) Sorry about that.

GROUPIE. You know, I teach art in prison and I have several advanced degrees in molecular— why am I even wasting my breath.

PETER. I don't know.

GROUPIE. You're just like everyone else.

(GROUPIE *exits.*)

PETER. Me? No. That's probably the problem. I'm not enough like everyone else.

(*He seems a little dazed.*)

I'm wiped out. Let's see. I've got a big heart and I'm having palpitations. I could soliloquize, I could faint— lot of possibilities.

(*He faints.*)

ACT SECOND, scene fourth.

SOMEONE *walks by, looks at the unconscious* PETER *for a while, gives him a little kick, looks around, then walks away.*
WOMAN IN GREEN *enters. She puts cold water on* PETER's *forehead.*

PETER. Are you a dream? Are you an angel?

WOMAN IN GREEN. If I were a dream or an angel, wouldn't I know all about that dog you chased and how it got all caught up in a woman's dress from a clothesline?

PETER. I guess. You still look like an angel.

WOMAN IN GREEN. You look like a person.

PETER. I try to be myself. Because, really, that's just a large part of who I am.

WOMAN IN GREEN. We don't get a lot of people around here. This is really mysterious. I've dreamed about someone like you. I sit in my room and I have dreams and I'm starting to think they're about you. Do you believe in fate? Or other explanations?

(*She takes his hand and they exit.*)

TOWN. (*Enters.*) Are we— I think we're going in circles. It was good to get out of the house, but I think this is it for me. Let's stay out here, I like it out here. No, no, me too, I'm going back, too. We'll fuck up Gnit when he comes back home. The air really is n-n-nice out h-h-here. Who are you? You haven't said one word this whole time. I s-s-s-stutter. I th-th-th-thought you'd-d-d-d laugh.

(*Short laugh.*)

Hey, maybe we could fuck this guy up, instead? I mean, here he is, right here. True, we wouldn't have to go chasing him all over. Wh-wh-why would you duh-duh-do that? Let's bully this guy later— I'm famished. Y-y-you p-p-people are m-m-mean. Come on, guys. Make sure you bring your trash. Wh-wh-wh-wait for muh-muh-muh me. Okay, come on, slowpoke. S-s-slow-poke. I f-f-fucking like that.

(*Exits.*)

PETER. (*Enters, with* WOMAN IN GREEN. *His rumpled clothing is even more rumpled.*) Well, that was, you know, that was very good. (*Very brief pause.*) God, is it morning, or is daytime just starting to look sadder? You know? Jesus.

WOMAN IN GREEN. Time is funny.

PETER. Yes, it is.

WOMAN IN GREEN. Here comes my family.

PETER. Where?

WOMAN IN GREEN. It'll just be another second. (*Very long pause.*) Here they are.

THE GREEN FAMILY. (*Enters, a single person.*) Hello.

PETER. Are there more of you?

THE GREEN FAMILY. I think this is everyone.

PETER. Well then hello. Good evening. Good day.

WOMAN IN GREEN. Daddy, everyone— this is Peter.

THE GREEN FAMILY. Hello. Hi. How's it going? We'll make this quick. We're in real estate. We need a son-in-law. And a brother-in-law. For reasons you don't need to know. You and our daughter seem to be sexually simpatico. You are he. Our new son. Hey, brother. Welcome aboard. You're very rich, now. Be nice or we'll operate on you, and we aren't really doctors. Now, a toast.

PETER. This is all very flattering.

THE GREEN FAMILY. Isn't it? I know, it's so flattering.

PETER. It really is. But I'm afraid I'll need a little time.

THE GREEN FAMILY. Take all the time you want. (*Very brief pause.*) Have you decided?

PETER. Good people, good woman, I must decline. Or, at least, defer.

WOMAN IN GREEN. What about over there, before, in the willow tree? You started yelling, and I said, "Don't finish inside me," but you did, anyway. And now I might be pregnant. What about all the things you yelled? I gave myself to you. So now please just do what any fox or marmoset or the other monogamous animal would do, and stay with me.

PETER. I'm afraid I can't.

THE GREEN FAMILY. We're afraid you must. Put on this suit. Here's a briefcase.

(Puts the suit jacket on him.)

PETER. You're very insistent. You know what? Why not? Give me that.

(He grabs the briefcase. He's pleased with his new look.)

I could see this, maybe. Yeah. How's this sound? "Cancel my morning massage. Reschedule my afternoon massage. Listen, I've got a little place I'd buy myself but company policy forbids it. You really just got to see the place, owned by an old lady, never hurt a fly, used to cry herself to sleep, and she wants it to go to a decent sort, a sort like you, and like I say, I'd buy it myself, because I'm like you, but you're even more like you, so why don't we fill out some papers and put you in your new home, how do you like the sound of that, 'Your new home,' see, it's already, linguistically speaking, yours, so now all you got to do is buy it. Get me a pen, darling. Do you want a cup of coffee?" How was that?

THE GREEN FAMILY. Not bad. What did I tell you? You were born for this. If he was born for anything. That's enough, Steven. I was kidding— I'm sure he'll be fine. *(Whispering.)* Empty-headed fucking parrot.

PETER. Pardon?

THE GREEN FAMILY. Nothing. Yeah, I didn't hear anything. So, are we all right, here?

PETER. I have to say, it feels pretty good.

THE GREEN FAMILY. Does it. Our one rule around here, is, "By yourself, for yourself." Do it our way, and, things fall into place.

PETER. It's all I've ever done. This could really work out.

THE GREEN FAMILY. Here, dress it up with this pocket square.

(Puts a folded pocket square in PETER's *breast pocket.)*

Very nice. It brings out his eyes.

PETER. *(Brief pause.)* You know what? I can't. I'm sorry. Though I think that I— as a cloud-watching alcoholic— could probably do very well in a commission-driven industry, I really must say no. Good people, I am on a search, a search for the truest me. And I don't think I'll likely find him, here with you. Maybe I might, though.

THE GREEN FAMILY. Our daughter asked you nicely. So did we. So just say yes. And, just so you know, we'll gladly hear it, "Yes," as the last word you ever say, practically just a whisper, a last breath, trickling out of your bloody mouth, dirty newspaper stuck in the incisions made in your body by our unclean tools, following our failed operation. Steven, when did you get like this? Don't mind him. Hey, we're just crazy people. Or we're business people. Or just he is. Or, we're not.

PETER. I'm crazy too. I'd have to be to turn down your wonderful offer.

THE GREEN FAMILY. We asked you to be one of us. And you said no. It hurt. Now, we're going to hurt you back. Can we start, Dad? Yeah, kids— you go ahead.

> (*He nods, draws three knives out of his coat.*)

PETER. (*Pleading.*) Please, Sirs. I'm begging you—

THE GREEN FAMILY. We've seen begging before. And it hasn't made any difference. No, not true— remember the time we cut out a guy's mouth, instead of his eyes, because he wanted to see his kids grow up? Oh, yeah. Boy, we've done some awful things. But, we did them together. I always felt that, with the kids, it was important to always—

> (*They're interrupted by sirens, off-stage.* THE GREEN FAMILY *and* WOMAN IN GREEN *are frightened.*)

Run! No, let's take him hostage! Him!? Are you kidding!? Let's go, just run! No. Just walk normally.

> (*They exit.*)

WOMAN IN GREEN. I love you.

> (*She makes quote marks with her fingers around the following word, although she says it earnestly.*)

"Honestly."

> (*Exits.*)

ACT SECOND, scene fifth.

> *Stage goes dark, but for* PETER, *in a cone of light. Sirens abruptly stop. Amplified breathing.*

PETER. Who is that? Who are you?

VOICE. Me.

PETER. Who's "me"?

VOICE. I am.

PETER. That's like something I'd say.

VOICE. Interesting.

PETER. I guess. So, who are you? Or, what are you?

VOICE. I'm the middle.

PETER. This is only the middle!?

VOICE. I'm the thing in between things. The space between spaces, the little lack of sound between words. Where the air isn't going in or out. Call me peace, or, death. I'm what you can't handle.

PETER. Maybe you want some of this!

>   (*He throws a punch.*)

VOICE. I don't have a body. There's nothing to hit.

PETER. Then maybe you want some of this.

>   (*He does nothing.*)

VOICE. Now you're talking.

PETER. How can I get past you?

VOICE. I'm not really anything, so it's impossible to get past me. And I'm not actually real, so you'll never get over me. Just try to live with me.

PETER. Is this philosophy?

VOICE. I don't know. Is this philosophy?

>   (*A couple of breaths.*)

PETER. I don't know.

VOICE. Well, then I don't know either. See, I only exist in correlation to your resistance to me.

>   (VOICE *does not laugh.*)

Forgive me— I always have to laugh when I tell people that.

PETER. How come you didn't laugh?

VOICE. It didn't seem funny, that time.

PETER. Wait a minute. I think I get it. Are you telling me I should just bide my time, just go with the flow? And then whatever's going to come to me will come to me? My reward in life?

VOICE. Yes.

PETER. But, is this true? And can you be trusted?

VOICE. No.

PETER. (*He tries to get past again. He can't.*) I give up.

VOICE. Me too.

PETER. (*Brief pause.*) So now what happens?

VOICE. We wait.

PETER. Okay. Not my favorite thing. (*Brief pause.*) I wonder if Solvay is waiting for me. That must be awful. Turning and listening, at every snapped twig. She probably feels completely alone. As if nobody cares and nobody loves her. As if I don't.

>   (*He is a little choked up.*)

Sort of surprised, by that feeling. Feeling bad for someone else. (*Brief pause.*) Hello? Thing? Middle?

>   (*He looks around, something's changed and he's able to pass.*)

Hey. How 'bout that.

ACT SECOND, scene sixth.

Outside MOTHER'*s cabin.* PETER *is asleep, behind a bush.*

A HUNTER *with a gun enters and walks slowly across the stage.*

HUNTER. Bleezie! (*Looking up:*) Hey, Grandpa— you up there? My poor dog has rabies. So I'm in the middle of a kind of sad adventure. I can't even imagine what I'm about to do. (*Very brief pause.*) My wife brought it home a bunch of years ago, the dog. The kids gave it this weird name that just sort of stuck. And, all of a sudden, Bleezie was with us all the time. Morning noon and night. My best friend of my life.

(*Hears a sound from* PETER'*s hiding place. Brief pause, listens.*)

Anyway, so now here I am with a gun, trying to track her down, going to all her favorite spots, looking for a trail of foamy saliva, and wondering, if I can get a clear shot at my sick dog Bleezie-girl, will I be able to pull the trigger. (*Very brief pause.*) Plus, there's a bounty out on that Gnit guy. I could use the reward— maybe shoot him in the spine and get the kids a new sled. I think that would really be— I just thought of another place.

(*Exits.*)

PETER. (*Appearing, with pieces of grass or straw on his back.*) Jesus. I hope I never see that character again. I wonder how big the reward is. (*Brief pause.*) What a night. I made some strides, though, I think. I better go try and grab some money out of my mom's purse. Yes, sir, I've got work to do.

HELEN. (*Enters with basket of food.*) Solvay thought I might find you here. And she thought your mother might need some food.

PETER. Solvay? Where is she?

HELEN. She's waiting for me. She wanted me to drop this off.

PETER. Why didn't she come?

HELEN. This is a strange century and she's very sensitive. She didn't know where you both stood on things. But she wanted me to make you sure you didn't need anything.

PETER. Of course, right, strange century, sensitivity. Tell her thank you. I don't need anything.

HELEN. Is that the truth?

PETER. (*Looking at her intently.*) Is this the truth?

HELEN. You look really awful— are you sick?

PETER. I haven't really been sleeping.

HELEN. Weren't you just asleep a few minutes ago?

PETER. Everyone's a comedian. (*Brief pause.*) Well, okay, so maybe not everyone.

HELEN. Is there anything else?

PETER. No. (*Brief pause.*) I think about her, a lot. I have to say. All the time, kind of. I just thought about her, last night. I felt bad. It was helpful.

HELEN. She loves you.

PETER. No, she doesn't. She loves me?

HELEN. I'm a really straightforward person.

PETER. Well then I love her. I really do. Wait! Give her this souvenir pen with the little sleigh in the snow in it. See? When you go like this he goes back and forth. Give it to her, okay?

HELEN. It's not a great gift, but, okay, I'll give it to her.

PETER. Tell her not to forget me. I have to leave again but I'll come back.

HELEN. She does love you. And she's a really good person. I don't really see what she sees in you.

PETER. How could you?

HELEN. I wish you treated people better.

PETER. Yeah.

> (*He takes the basket of food, looks in it, pulls out a jar of jam.*)

Ohh, blueberry. Is there any—

> (*Rustles around through the basket.*)

Ah, good. Bread.

> (*Looks at* HELEN *for a moment.*)

See you later.

> (HELEN *exits.*)

ACT THIRD, scene first.

> PETER *is trying to start a chainsaw. A tree is nearby.*

PETER. I'm going to cut you down, Tree. Build myself a little mountain redoubt. Mr. Progress, coming through. Yee-haw.

> (*The chainsaw doesn't start.*)

Come on (*He tries it again.*), would you fucking start?! Goddamn it. (*Looking off-stage.*) And on top of all that, here comes someone, with a knife. Even my solitude isn't solitude. It's a boy, a young man. He's stopped. My God. He just cut his finger off. On purpose. There's a commitment. A lot of blood, too. Now, he's walking closer. He's holding up his bleeding hand. He's looking into my eyes, for sympathy. You got the wrong guy, fella. He's probably a draft-dodger. Probably trying to weasel his way out of fighting for my freedoms. Now he's walking away, curling his little bloody hand into his stomach. People.

> (*Brief pause. He fiddles with the chainsaw.*)

I should've tried it before I left the shop.

> (*He tries the chainsaw one more time. It doesn't start. For just a second, he almost starts crying.*)

Goddamn this thing. Probably it just needs to sit for a while.

> (*Exits.*)

ACT THIRD, scene second.

MOTHER's *bedroom.*

MOTHER. Explain this again.

CASE WORKER. (*She reads.*) "People v. Gnit. Insofar as the defendant, Peter Gnit, subtitled the Unfortunate, did knowingly and unknowingly harm and injure the plaintiff, herefollowing delightfully denominated as The People, and did pre-meditatively and without afterthought kidnap, defame, or legally interrupt the normal wedding and lives of said People, judgment is made in the amount of all furnishings now furnishing Defendant's house, and that house itself, at an appointed time, to be appointed by—"

MOTHER. (*Interrupting.*) Thank you, okay. I think I understand.

CASE WORKER. Yeah, they're taking the house. Him threatening the judge really hurt your case. You don't seem very upset.

MOTHER. Well, I'm old.

CASE WORKER. He's off somewhere, probably drunk or asleep in a pile of leaves, without a care in the world. And look at you. You don't have anything.

MOTHER. That's not true. (*Very brief pause.*) No, I guess that's true.

CASE WORKER. Peter's going to cost you everything.

MOTHER. Something was going to cost me everything. That's how it works, isn't it? (*Brief pause.*) This is his sweater. I'm going to put some patches on the elbows.

CASE WORKER. Why don't you move into a home? A retirement place.

MOTHER. Because I already live in a home. A retirement place. And I don't have any money, dear.

CASE WORKER. I'll try to get an injunction.

MOTHER. Ooh, an injunction. Yes, you try to get that. I'll stay here with this sweater. And here's a little pen from a set that I bought for Pee-Wee. See? It has a little ship in it that goes back and forth. They won't get this. They can take my house, and my security and dignity, but they can't take my son's old sweater. Or this little thingie.

ACT THIRD, scene third.

In the woods. Birdsong. In front of PETER's *new little house, which is very simple, and somewhat poorly constructed.*

PETER. A house of my own, almost a home. Just a place to hang a door, really. Which is all I really need. Didn't have to deal with any realtors, either, so that was good.

(SOLVAY *enters, with a suitcase.*)

It's you.

SOLVAY. I know.

PETER. I can't believe it.

SOLVAY. I'm sorry.

PETER. No, my God, I'm glad.

SOLVAY. Helen said you loved me. I decided to believe her. She's really straightforward.

PETER. I do love you.

SOLVAY. I hoped so. So I left everything. I probably seem silly.

PETER. You're not silly.

SOLVAY. I know I'm not. But I probably seem it. I had a feeling. A strong simple feeling.

PETER. I've had those. God, Solvay. I'm so happy. I built this for you. You and me.

SOLVAY. I know this is strange. But let's just have faith. I know it's unbelievable, but, why can't real things be unbelievable? Leaving my father was the hardest. He said I was making a mistake, but, then he said he hoped and prayed I wasn't. That was nice. It was a lonely walk, out here. But now I'm home.

PETER. You're home.

(PETER *opens the door for her, it falls off.*)

We'll just put that right back on.

(*He tries to put it back on. He can't, so he leans it against the house.*)

SOLVAY. Doors are hard— getting the hinges right and everything.

PETER. I know.

SOLVAY. This is such a perfect spot. Listen to the birds.

PETER. (*Listens for a moment.*) I hadn't even heard those.

SOLVAY. (*They sit for a while, enjoying the peace.*) It's getting chilly.

PETER. Go on inside, love. I'll get some wood. We'll make a little fire.

(SOLVAY *goes inside.* PETER *walks off, begins to pick up some wood.*)

Look at me, world. A calm man, with a little house and a nice person. Life, life, life: here I come.

SICK WOMAN. (*She is the* WOMAN IN GREEN. *Enters, incredibly aged and sick-looking, with* SWADDLED BABY.) There you are, my love.

PETER. Your "love"? Who are you? Anyway, I'm going to have to ask you and your great-grandson to excuse me.

SICK WOMAN. We were both so different, then.

PETER. When, "then"?

SICK WOMAN. When you married me.

PETER. I married you? I don't think I'd do that.

SICK WOMAN. I've been sick. I was pretty, that night. When you took me in the woods. Then I got sick.

PETER. Okay. How can I, let's see— I've done some drinking here and there, taken part in some ceremonies I probably shouldn't have, but, please, no offense, but, I'd remember you.

SICK WOMAN. We were married in a tree. You were drunk.

PETER. Good one. "We were married in a tree." See you later.

SICK WOMAN. My family's in realty. We offered you a job. You're still wearing the suit we gave you.

PETER. (PETER *remembers immediately.*) This? No, I think I got this at a… Realty, you said? I can't, um, that's not ringing any bells. (*Brief pause.*) Sorry, I have to take a stand here. You're going to just have to leave me alone.

SICK WOMAN. I'm not going to leave you alone.

    (*She tends to the* SWADDLED BABY.)

How do you like your little boy? I think he gets his sleep schedule from his father.

PETER. Father? How could that be? (*To himself.*) It was only, like, thirty-eight to forty weeks ago, and… Listen, um…

    (*He looks into the house, toward* SOLVAY, *then at* SICK WOMAN *and* SWADDLED BABY.)

Solvay? Wait for me. Please wait for me.

    (*He runs into the woods.*)

SICK WOMAN. If I were a witch, I'd make him get sick and old, like me, overnight. But I'm not. So I'll let him get sick and old like everyone else, in real time. So that it takes the rest of his life. It'll break his heart more, that way. It'll be more of a surprise.

    (*She exits.*
    SOLVAY *comes out of the little house. Lights fade.*)

ACT THIRD, scene fourth.

> MOTHER*'s room. Door and windows are missing.* MOTHER *lies in a corner, very sick, wrapped in a tattered blanket. She is alone in the room, save for a dead cat lying in the middle of the floor.* PETER*'s sweater, mended, sits neatly folded on the floor.*

MOTHER. I think I hear snow. This was always a good blanket. You were always good to me. We thought we'd lost you, bankie. Everything went so fast. Is that a bunny, over there? This air can't be good for my breathing. Good riddance, all of it. My son was a good boy. What's-his-name loved me. Was I too strict? I wasn't strict. I was lonely. I wish I could cry, silly old person. Or walk in the sun along some nice canal with a pretty granddaughter. Instead of sitting in a cold smelly room, talking to myself. Hello, bunny rabbit. Do you want a carrot?

> (*Pause.* PETER *enters quietly. He smells the cat. Holding his nose, almost gagging, he carries it outside.*)

MOTHER. Henrik? Is that you?

PETER. It's me, Mom. Pee-Wee.

MOTHER. What are you doing?

PETER. I was just taking the cat out.

MOTHER. Good boy. It was beginning to smell.

PETER. You knew it was dead?

MOTHER. Remember this blanket?

PETER. I do, yeah.

MOTHER. Where have you been?

PETER. I was out kind of perfecting my—

MOTHER. (*Interrupting, quietly:*) I don't care, sweetie. (*Brief pause.*) I'm freezing, Son. You ruined that wedding and then left that girl. That was stupid, dear. They sued me. They're supposed to take the house, but they said because they're Christians, they'd just take the windows and door, for now. I never imagined I'd go blind. (*Brief pause.*) How does my hair look?

PETER. It looks nice, Mom.

MOTHER. I haven't washed it. I must look awful.

PETER. You look pretty.

MOTHER. Liar. (*She smiles.*) I'm glad you're here. (*Brief pause.*) I'm scared.

PETER. Don't be scared.

MOTHER. Don't tell me what not to be. You don't know anything, Peter. I love you but you don't know anything. (*Very brief pause.*) I never used to think about my eyes, when I was watching you try to grow up.

PETER. I'm sorry, Mom.

MOTHER. You were searching for yourself from when you were very little. You used to ask, "Who am I?" And I would say, "You're very little." I told you crazy fairy tales. Maybe that was wrong. I tried, with you, Peter. I tried to do a good job loving you.

PETER. You were a great mother.

MOTHER. I am a great mother.

PETER. You are a great mother.

MOTHER. Not anymore. Tell me a story.

PETER. About what?

MOTHER. About this, Peter. My reality here, about which you know nothing. Make something up.

PETER. Once, in a kingdom—

MOTHER. (*Interrupting.*) No kingdoms, Peter. Don't make anything up.

PETER. Once, in a cold little room—

MOTHER. Good.

PETER. —a boy stood before his mother.

MOTHER. His dying mother.

PETER. His dying mother. Not knowing what to say or where to look. The boy was hardly a boy anymore. He was getting old too. He'd never really found his way into life. Yes, he had some history, he'd met a few women in his—

MOTHER. (*Interrupting.*) Keep it on the mother.

PETER. The mother held onto her blanket, and her hair looked nice, and she looked calm.

MOTHER. But she wasn't.

PETER. But she wasn't. She was afraid. She didn't know what was next.

MOTHER. She was afraid.

PETER. Her boy could see this. (*Brief pause.*) There is a limit to the magic powers of language.

MOTHER. A limit.

PETER. And they both knew, she more than he, what was coming next. Or, no, they didn't know.

MOTHER. Wait.

(*She suffers, without making a sound, through a momentary pain.*)

I'm sorry. (*Brief pause.*) Keep going. Go ahead, sweetie.

PETER. She knew. That there would be no kingdom. And no king. And no stories, left.

(*She winces, again.*)

There would be no gates, no calm, no bright light. The body knows what to do.

(PETER *is having trouble breathing, perhaps crying or trying not to cry.*)

The magic act of the body was over. There wouldn't be any more magic. But, there had been, before. The mother sang beautifully. She had beautiful eyes and looked out for her son. She could see. The world was magic. The boy loved his mother. The boy loved his mother.

MOTHER. He's a good boy. Keep going. Don't lie.

PETER. I won't, Mom. So. Whatever it all was, it was all about to end. And the boy who was no longer a boy looked into the eyes of the mother who could no longer see. She breathed with difficulty.

MOTHER. (*Breathing with difficulty.*) Yes. It was hard for her to breathe. And him?

PETER. He breathed with difficulty. (*Brief pause.*) And so— unknowing as ever as to how to comfort the woman who had given him nothing but comfort for every day of her life, and his life, for the whole uncomfortable time— the boy who might never be a man stared at his shoes.

MOTHER. Did he hold her hand?

(PETER *is not holding her hand, and, will not be.*)

PETER. He did. Tightly.

MOTHER. Good boy. Did she smile?

PETER. She did. She looked beautiful. She looked ready.

MOTHER. That's nice, dear. No, she didn't.

PETER. Didn't what? Just let me tell the story, Mom. Mom? (*Brief pause. Quietly:*) Mom?

(MOTHER *has died.* PETER *looks out the window. Takes a deep breath. He closes her eyes with his fingers.*)

This is what people do.

CASE WORKER. (*Enters.*) She was wondering if you'd make it. How is she?

PETER. And, just like that, someone walks in.

CASE WORKER. (*Realizing what's happened.*) Oh, no. I had a feeling, so I came right over.

PETER. This is one of those momentous things. (*Brief pause.*) There's a family plot. I don't know where it is or if it has to be paid for, or, if you just… I'm sorry, I have to go.

CASE WORKER. Now? Where are you going? You're not even going to—

PETER. (*Interrupting.*) Not even going to what? (*Brief pause.*) I'm sorry. Thank you. For looking after her. She and I… Mom and I, um… What do you say?

A person says what?

> (*To no one in particular:*)

Thank you.

> (*Walking out the door.*)

Bye, Mom.

Intermission

ACT FOURTH, scene first.

A seaside bar in Morocco. PETER, *well-dressed, much older, is holding a leather travel bag, standing at the bar, while a* BARTENDER *is cleaning glasses. A German, an Englishman, and a Russian, all played by* INTERNATIONAL MAN, *sit at a table nearby.*

BARTENDER. How you doing, buddy— what's new?

PETER. (*Fairly quickly, throughout. Perhaps occasionally chewing on a swizzle stick.*) Oh, Jesus, let's see. Went to a wedding a bunch of years ago, met this great woman Solvay, then ran off with the bride but changed my mind, and I had to leave town and these people sued my mother, and then I got lost and had a run-in with these crazy people— realtors, I guess— impregnated one, supposedly, then met up with something called "the middle," that was challenging, then built a little house, got back together with the great woman from the wedding, but the realtoress— who turned out to be a magical witch or had gotten sick or something— came around with my so-called son, and that ruined that, so then I had to leave again. These last few years, on the lookout for my true self, I got into the baby trade, sold plots of fake land, formed a little church, a strictly paper-based sort of thing, got very wealthy, met some more women, had a string of really successful relationships. Before that, Mom went blind and died, that was hard. She was an angel, in retrospect. I left before the funeral, I don't know why, it was a confusing time— I trust she got buried all right. We always do, eventually. Then I did some more shit, tried to make some people pay for my mother's death and my dad's life, ugly stuff, nothing you'd really put on the resumé. Anyway, now I'm here: Sunny Morocco! I'm hoping to get into some arms dealing, some really serious money, as I'd like to be even richer, as I've got this massive inferiority-complex, or, this tiny superiority-complex. I'm standing here right now, with my life in a bag, all my money in a bag, no reason to look back, nothing to look back at. I'm staring at you, and, I want to be the fucking Emperor. Your fucking Emperor.

BARTENDER. (*Shaking his head, smiling, agreeing, hasn't been listening.*) Women. What can I get you?

PETER. (*Brief pause.*) Did you hear one word I just said?

BARTENDER. (*Agreeing:*) Oh, man. What'll it be?

PETER. Two scotches.

INTERNATIONAL MAN. Four!

PETER. Oh, yeah— four.

INTERNATIONAL MAN. Thank you.

BARTENDER. Coming right up.

> (*He serves* PETER *the drinks.* PETER *returns to table with drinks.*)

INTERNATIONAL MAN. Jolly good.

PETER. Not at all.

INTERNATIONAL MAN. Danke.

PETER. It's nothing.

INTERNATIONAL MAN. Sposiba.

PETER. Okay.

INTERNATIONAL MAN. Ah, drinks. Wonderful drinks. Yes.

PETER. Let us talk about the nature of the self.

INTERNATIONAL MAN. Yum.

PETER. My single rule: "By yourself." Just do it all by yourself. A terrible man once told me that. He might not have even been human. Weird, I got my life lesson from him, but, I did, and it's stood me in good stead. Yes, a little money doesn't hurt.

> (*He pats his bag, which is sitting next to him.*)

Nor does a lot. But, for me, personally, selfhood was always the thing. The goal. "The Self."

INTERNATIONAL MAN. That takes discipline. Discipline! And one needs a little garden in which to sit, remark the flowers, enjoy a spot of tea. I enjoy to sit in the sauna. It's so hot, in there. I think it also requires— and this will seem like a bit of a strange word choice, but— sympathy. Ja, this is correct, mein friend. We find ourselves in other people's hearts.

> (*Russian man is perhaps imitating English man:*)

"We find ourselves in other people's hearts." Well, it's true, old man. Okay.

PETER. Well, we all have our ways. You're wonderful company, by the way. You remind me of someone. I don't care who. But I like the way you people think. Let me get another round.

> (PETER *is getting drunk. He gets up to get more drinks, only hearing the first three sentences.*)

INTERNATIONAL MAN. Three cheers for you. Ja. Get me some ice, will you?

(PETER *is out of earshot.*)

We should take this idiot's money. We should. To teach him a lesson about the value of things. And, to take his money. He is shrewd, very shrewd. We'll have to be sly as the fox, though. We must be calculating, our strategy will have to be near-perfect, to outsmart him and get his money. I have a plan. (*Whispers.*)

PETER. (*Returning with more drinks, drunker.*) So, as I was saying, I made the great refusals, suffered the lonely nights and mornings, forever in search of this (*Pointing to his chest.*), the inside, the unvarnished mess, the thing that will die, the thing that quivers at the question "What is the thing that dies?" Yeah. I played jai alai once. Worked in finance, sort of. I met this Swiss girl, she did ballet or some kind of dancing— wow.

INTERNATIONAL MAN. (*He grabs* PETER's *bag, and runs off.*)

PETER. Hey, whoa! Where's the fire? (*Brief pause. To* BARTENDER:) Anyway, I slept in my shoes many many nights. God, the smell. But, you know, there was learning there. Philosophy. The self. Plus, I got rich. Here are my real friends, here.

(*He goes to pat his bag, which is gone.*)

Damn it. Fuck.

(*He gets up.*)

Who were those guys who just left?

BARTENDER. Ah, those guys. Hey, we're closing pretty soon. You don't have to go home, but, you can't stay here. "Laimigu celu," as they say in, um— Latvia, I think. Right? Latvia. Whooo, long day. It's been a long day.

(BARTENDER *turns lights off, exits.*)

ACT FOURTH, scene second.

INTERNATIONAL MAN *enters dark stage, with* PETER's *bag.* ROBBER *appears, with a gun.*

ROBBER. Give me the bag.

INTERNATIONAL MAN. Kill these two and take the money. No, kill those two. Bloody coward. "Bloody coward." Please, there's no money in here— it's just shells, some interesting rocks and shells I found. Please. These hands are lethal weap—

ROBBER. (*Interrupting. Three gun shots.* INTERNATIONAL MAN *is dead.* ROBBER *rifles through bag.*) Look at all this. I'm rich!

(*Pulls out an old photograph.*)

And here's an old picture of a little girl sitting on a small horse. She seems sad. Looks like it's hard to hold up the smile, like she's kind of bashful about having a face. Might as well describe the whole thing. There's some Bergfrue growing in the background. And somebody's arm, holding the reins, cropped at the wrist. There's mountains. A cloud that looks like something very personal. I think it had just rained. It's a nice little picture. Someone wrote on the back, "Mom on a horse." It's funny, we're sons and daughters into the grave. I mean, not funny, but, you know, worth noting.

(*He looks again at the photograph.*)

She looks worried, even though she's smiling. I'm going to stay in a fancy hotel, tonight. I like the little soaps. No one is ever going to hear from me again.

(*Exits.*)

ACT FOURTH, scene third.

A woman, ANITRA, *is standing somewhere, with a cigarette-girl tray, filled with maps and perhaps gum, etc. She speaks with an accent.*

PETER. (*Enters. Fine clothes now ragged, exhibiting signs that this life is wearing on him. He stands to the side.*) God, I smell. I can't keep doing this. I'm making myself sick.

ANITRA. Welcome.

PETER. That's the word I was looking for. What have you here?

(*He approaches her.*)

I'll take one of your wonderful maps, please.

ANITRA. (*She hands him one.*) Two.

PETER. Here you go.

(*He gives her two bills. Sees her name tag.*)

Your name is Anitra?

ANITRA. Anitra.

PETER. That's quite a coincidence.

ANITRA. Thank you.

PETER. No, I mean, I knew someone with that name. It's quite a story. Unbelievable story, really.

ANITRA. Yes. Not believe story.

PETER. Maybe we could go somewhere and I could tell it to you.

ANITRA. Yes.

(*She doesn't move.*)

English?

PETER. What, who me? No, no. Oh, but I do speak English.

ANITRA. Hey, sailboat.

PETER. Hey. The thing is, Anitra, I've been going around and around the world. I got robbed, lost everything. Just had a little moment of doubt back there, but, I think I'm getting closer. I'm almost there. To the real world, the world inside. I'm different from the old me.

ANITRA. The old you.

PETER. Right. Then, sometimes, I wonder. I worry. I don't know how a person is supposed to make it all the way to his death.

ANITRA. He will be fine. He feels he is robbed. You are the old you. You don't know how.

PETER. You're very beautiful.

ANITRA. From your perspective, yes. But try to see these things like I see these things— with you standing there, next to me, so ugly inside you. In this picture, I become less attractive.

PETER. Well, I lost my luggage.

ANITRA. I just said something smart.

PETER. Yes, you've certainly got a philosophical bent.

ANITRA. I am a journalist. Enjoy some of my journalism. Thank you.

(*She reads from a note pad.*)

The house—

PETER. (*Interrupting.*) Your house? Do you live near here?

ANITRA. (*Brief pause.*) The house is black. The horse is breathing. The sea is water. The man is yelling. The tree is great. The life is true. This is English. Honesty is policy.

PETER. It's very good. You speak very well.

(*He puts his hand on hers.*)

If you like, I could give you—

ANITRA. (*Interrupting.*) Thank you so much for never touching me. That's really great. My family is waiting. I am off. Try to never imagine me. I am grateful. I am closed.

(*She begins leaving.*)

PETER. No, come on, don't close. Come back.

ANITRA. What part of every word I know don't you understand?

(*Exits.*)

PETER. (*Pause. He looks at the map.*) Egypt!? We're in Egypt?

ACT FOURTH, scene fourth.

> PETER's *hut.* SOLVAY, *much older, is sitting with* PASTOR. *She is working on some knitting.*

PASTOR. It's coming along.

SOLVAY. I have to undo all this, I counted wrong, so, it isn't really. But I'll get it right. This is what my life is, I've decided. Sunshine, nighttime, watching the horizon, learning to knit. Oh, and eating, cooking. Sleeping. Dreaming and thinking. I guess there's a lot.

PASTOR. And of course God.

SOLVAY. Of course? I don't know about that.

> (*A bird sings.* SOLVAY *listens.*)

Birds sing. I thought that, the other day, and I almost fell over. Birds sit on branches, and sing. It's just almost too much. That was a grackle, I think, or a starling. Either way, it doesn't care. It doesn't know what its name is, and it's doing just fine. I like my life.

PASTOR. I like my life too.

SOLVAY. I'm not trying to compete with you.

> (*She holds up some yarn.*)

Is this gray?

PASTOR. Yeah, that's gray. How come I don't ever see you in church?

SOLVAY. Because I never go. Dark gray?

PASTOR. It's fairly dark. The funniest thing happened on the way over here.

SOLVAY. (*Small laugh. Supportively:*) That's so funny. (*Brief pause.*) I'm sorry, I'm in sort of a solitary mood. But I'm glad you're here.

PASTOR. Of course. You should come. To church.

SOLVAY. Why?

PASTOR. Salvation.

SOLVAY. Oh. Maybe I already have that. But I guess it's not for me to say. Or you, either.

> (*Holding up the knitting to look at it.*)

My eyes aren't very good. I've always thought you were very nice.

PASTOR. Thank you.

SOLVAY. You're welcome. Pastor, did you know, I used to be a girl.

PASTOR. Of course. Everyone was a girl. I mean, all females.

SOLVAY. You're a very wise man.

> (*Brief pause, knitting.*)

This is my life.

>(*Birdsong, sparrow.*)

That was a sparrow.

ACT FOURTH, scene fifth.

>*In the vicinity of the* SPHINX.

PETER. Now (*He looks at his map.*), seriously, where are we, exactly?

SPHINX. (*Voice, off-stage.*) This.

PETER. Who said that? What?

SPHINX. Nothing. I just said: This.

PETER. Oh, Jesus, are you like that other thing?

SPHINX. Yes. (*Very brief pause.*) What other thing?

PETER. The middle.

SPHINX. Yes. And I have a riddle for you to solve. Solve it or Die. What goes "Tap, Tap, Pause, Pause, Tap"— you know what, actually?— forget that, forget about that. Instead, tell me, have you learned anything since last we met?

PETER. I am continuing to explore the self.

SPHINX. So that's a "no"?

PETER. I have to ask again, who are you?

SPHINX. Who are you?

>(*Voice of* BEGRIFFIN*, doing a gentle echo:*)

Wer bist du? Wer bist du? Wer bist du?

PETER. That's crazy. The echo echoes back in German. Seriously, hello? Who are you?

SPHINX. Why do you think you're so special?

PETER. I don't. I mean, I do, but, you know.

SPHINX. The truth is outside.

PETER. Interesting. But, no, just explain to me what—

SPHINX. (*Interrupting.*) And, suddenly, strangely, but logically, but oddly, and sadly, but truly, I'm gone.

>(*A German-looking* MAN *appears from behind the* SPHINX.)

PETER. Jesus. I thought I was alone.

BEGRIFFIN. Guten tag. Sorry— I mean, Good day. I was doing the German echo.

PETER. (*Little laugh.*) So that's what that was. You had me wondering.

BEGRIFFIN. Did I. Begriffin.

PETER. Sorry?

BEGRIFFIN. Is the name. Begriffin. Touring around, are you? On holiday, are we? Just having fun, is he?

PETER. Are you just one person?

BEGRIFFIN. Yes.

PETER. I thought so. Can't hurt to ask, right?

BEGRIFFIN. Oh, it can hurt. But, go on.

PETER. Well, okay, so, I'm visiting all those places in the world that remain, like myself, great mysteries. I've wanted to solve the mystery of the Sphinx all my life.

BEGRIFFIN. Und? Excuse me— and?

PETER. It's only a mystery because it's perceived by a mystery. But we are not neutral, we are not un-mysterious. So it takes on shadows. Look on it and gaze upon the strange and crumbling statue inside yourself.

BEGRIFFIN. Okay.

   (*He stares at the statue.*)

Not bad. But, this is interesting. You think the Sphinx is you.

PETER. I can only claim this as I am, first and last-most, myself. The only actual person I know.

BEGRIFFIN. Are you.

PETER. I want to be the Emperor. Bring back the Empire, and, be its Emperor.

BEGRIFFIN. Tell me, would you like to speak to some people? I'm the director of a— I don't know what the word would be— area? Let's call it an area. I think the— what would be the word? People? Let's call them people— I think the people there might appreciate your theory.

PETER. Really?

BEGRIFFIN. Ja. Sorry, again— yeah.

PETER. A think-tank, is it, you say? Well, I'm very flattered. You mean luncheons and dinners, that kind of thing? I do have some experience. So, absolutely. Of course I will be the new artist-in-residence of your research center.

BEGRIFFIN. It's really more of an area. A place where they stay.

PETER. Finally. Someone who sees me for what I am.

ACT FOURTH, scene sixth.

They walk across the stage, enter a high-security building. PETER *sees it for some sort of research institute.* SHACKLETON *is standing against a wall.* DARK LADY *is there.*

BEGRIFFIN. I'll be right back. Have a look around.

PETER. (*To* SHACKLETON:) Hello, sir. Dr. Peter Gnit. Enchanted.

SHACKLETON. Also enchanted. Totally enchanted, now that I think of it.

PETER. What's your specialty?

SHACKLETON. Oh I think they're all pretty good.

PETER. I think I would agree.

SHACKLETON. Say that again. I can't hear out of this ear. And I wasn't paying attention.

DARK LADY. (*Shaking her head.*) Women. I mean, men. No, I was right the first time. Watch out for me. Just a thought.

PETER. Yes. Interesting group. (*Very brief pause.*) Now, I'm looking around for a podium. And perhaps some bottled water. Will it be held in here? And, when do we begin?

DARK LADY. Ahem. Yes, you heard right— a female can say "ahem." So. The world is two-thirds water, one-half women, leaving men the last little rest. The world is one-sixth men. I used math to come to my conclusion. Fractions, if I have to come right out and say it.

SHACKLETON. (*Trying to free himself, revealing that he is chained to the wall in shackles.*) Agh, these things are (*He squirms, a little.*), God, it's just really hard to move around.

PETER. Oh, no. You're— is this part of an experiment?

SHACKLETON. Yeah, I guess.

DARK LADY. People seem to enjoy what I have to say. Or, they would.

PETER. So, you're all— it's my understanding— you're all investigating the Self?

(*Brief pause, as no one responds or says anything.*)

I've been invited here to speak.

DARK LADY. (*Pause.*) So why isn't he saying anything?

SHACKLETON. (*To* PETER.) But, seriously, very nice to meet you. I'm in Men's Clothing. What do you do?

PETER. As I said, I'm here to give a lecture on a subject of some mystery. Me. This, along with a theory of mine that I think some people will find very interesting.

DARK LADY. Hey, when's lunch?

SHACKLETON. I know, I'm starving.

BREMER. (*Enters, pushed in by an unseen hand.*) Hi. (*Brief pause.*) I just got here.

PETER. Yes. Hello. Me too.

BREMER. No time for niceties.

PETER. No, of course. Are you also speaking today?

BREMER. I was just speaking five seconds ago.

DARK LADY. He was. Probably closer to ten seconds, now.

PETER. No, I mean, are you, like myself, going to expound on a subject in which you're an expert?

BREMER. (*Very brief pause.*) Don't ever change. Hand me that pencil, would you.

(PETER *hands the pencil to* BREMER.)

SHACKLETON. What's your speech about, again? Me?

PETER. No. Me.

(*Trying to ignore all the disturbing signs.*)

Where did the gentleman go? Begriffin, is it? I'm not sure that this is—

BREMER. (*Interrupting. He sticks the pencil in his eye.*) Ah, fuck— my eye. I've made a terrible mistake. But, you know, I learned something. Now what's my next step here.

PETER. (*In horror.*) Oh, God.

SHACKLETON. I wanted to stop him. Part of me did. The rest of me thought: no, let's just see where this is going. (*To* PETER.) You were right next to him.

DARK LADY. It's true. Either you ignored your instincts, or your instincts were wrong, or, you don't have any instincts. And that's just three things.

BEGRIFFIN. (*Enters.*) Oh, Jeez. Medic!

(*He shuttles* BREMER *out the door.*)

There we are. Have you met everyone?

PETER. What is this place? I don't think—. I'm not sure that I should really—

BEGRIFFIN. (*Interrupting.*) Nonsense— you're just filled with fear because it's all so scary. We'll get you your washcloth. And you get a cup, in addition— make sure you put your name on it. Then you can settle in, get the feel of the place. I just did your paperwork.

PETER. My paper—

BEGRIFFIN. (*Interrupting.*) Yes. Paperwork. You're in, officially. All stamped up and stapled.

(*Sounds of medic screaming, off-stage.*)

I think we can help.

PETER. Help? Help what?

BEGRIFFIN. You.

PETER. I don't need help. These people need help. I'm just myself. My true self.

BEGRIFFIN. So are they. They're nothing but themselves. All reason, no sympathy. Hi, everyone. You can be their Emperor. Some of your ideas would make a nice little footnote in an article I want to write. This is great. You'll be fine, here. Feeding is at seven. Excuse.

> (*Exits.*)

SHACKLETON. He's serious— make sure you put your name on your cup. I never did and someone took mine. You're thinking, "Mister, you must be thirsty." I'm thinking, "Mister, I really am."

DARK LADY. Collective nouns. You know? (*Brief pause.*) I have theories. (*To* PETER.) You do look scared. Deep down. What was your name, again? No, wait, let me guess. (*Pause.*) You know what, I don't want to guess your name.

BREMER. (*Enters, pushed into the room.*) That medic needs a medic. (*To* PETER.) Could you hand me that other pencil?

PETER. I'm not supposed to be here. I'm a sane person.

BREMER. I need that pencil, yesterday. I mean, today.

PETER. I have to get out of here. How do I get out of here?

> (*A low rumble.*)

SHACKLETON. That's an earthquake. I can sense these things. Not to be negative, but, I think it's going to get worse.

> (*The rumble becomes almost deafening. A section of wall collapses. All is very quiet.*)

DARK LADY. (*Pause.*) It's so quiet. Did you see me shaking, just then?

> (PETER *runs off, through the hole in the wall.*)

Typical.

> (*She and* BREMER *drift off.* SHACKLETON *is still handcuffed to a section of wall.*)

SHACKLETON. (*Brief pause. A fire has quietly started.*) Huh. That's a pretty good fire going there. (*Very brief pause.*) I wish I were the type to write memoirs. History never really hears from people like me. (*Very brief pause.*) But anyway, here I am. It's weird. It's a big world. So many different people— high and low, weak and strong, dying presidents and little girls with eyeglasses. Where does a guy like me, chained up in a burning building, fit in? What's an important human being? You know? How do you be good, in life, on earth? At least I never really hurt anyone. That's sort of a comfort. But not for you.

> (*Lights fade as he is consumed by the flames.*)

ACT FIFTH, scene first.

Home. A sign announces "Arrivals." Another sign says "Welcome. Willkommen. Bienvenue. Bienvenuto. Maligayang pagdatang." PETER enters, older still, carrying a bag, passing under the Arrivals sign. BEGGAR, one-legged, is dressed in rags and sitting on the ground, with a paper cup before him.

PETER. Ah. And so, after all the years, all the other times and places I stood and said, "Here I am," I now stand here, now, and say—.

BEGGAR. (*Interrupting.*) Help. Please. Thank you.

PETER. Don't get up, don't get up— I prefer this arrangement. Help is on the way.

(*He is reaching into his luggage.*)

In fact, I owe a stranger a favor or two. I just had some lucky years. So, guess what, I want you to have half of what I have. Why not. I'm feeling just that grateful. Just that happy to be home.

(*He begins opening the large bag.
A* PALE MAN *in a dark suit enters, crosses upstage, lingers.*)

BEGGAR. You're too good, sir.

PETER. I know, I know.

(*Glances at* PALE MAN.)

BEGGAR. This is too kind. You're a good person.

PETER. No, no— I understand life. I understand living.

(*To* PALE MAN:)

Yes?

PALE MAN. Are you, by any chance, an organ donor?

PETER. Excuse me?

PALE MAN. Nothing.

(*He mumbles a sentence, the only audible part of which is the words "Kierkegaardian Dread."*)

PETER. What?

PALE MAN. You have nice eyes.

PETER. I'm sorry?

PALE MAN. Oh, yeah? Bye, now.

(*Exits.*)

BEGGAR. What did he say, in the middle? Kiergegaardian what? That was weird. But, I can't tell you how much this means. My family will be so happy.

PETER. (*Brief pause. Still slightly preoccupied with* PALE MAN, *but only for a moment more.*) Right. Family. Family meaning mother and father? Some brothers, a sister?

BEGGAR. Children. Two daughters, sir. And a wonderful wife who deserves more.

PETER. Ah. I see. (*Brief pause.*) Take us through the scene. When you walk through the door, with your new-found riches, which are half of my hard-fought gains.

BEGGAR. Ah, okay— happily. Probably the dog greets me, wiggling and ducking into me. The children run to my side. My wife smiles, sees what I have, she starts to cry. We stand together in our little room, crying and laughing and praising your name, with the dog, wagging, jumping up. The happiest house in the world. In the evening, after a filling meal, before the fire, we'll sit together and plan tomorrow. Maybe a boat ride. We all cuddle together, feeling sleepy and safe. There's a beautiful glow. A glow that never fully went away, even in the hardest times. And now it's blazing. Love and hope, sir. Love and hope are blazing.

PETER. What'd you have children for? Knowing you couldn't provide for them.

BEGGAR. Oh, I could provide, sir. And did.

(*Raises his stump of a leg.*)

Then I lost this, in a machine. I hear my family's stomachs growl, at night. And in the morning. So I sit out here, on the ground, looking up at everyone, asking for help. Just until I find something else.

(*He laughs, humbly.*)

Something I can still do.

PETER. I see. Tell you what, Dad— I changed my mind. This is probably going to sound harsh, but, fuck you and fuck your family's growling stomachs. Ooooh. It sounds so much worse when you say it out loud.

(PETER *looks at his watch, looks off.*)

BEGGAR. I don't think I… You're not going to help me?

PETER. Is there still a steakhouse down this way? Ah, how would you know. (*Very brief pause.*) I think we're done here. Unless you can think of anything you wanted to add? Great.

(*Exits.*)

BEGGAR. Mankind.

(*Brief pause. He is trying not to cry, mainly succeeding.*)

I can't even tell anyone about this.

ACT FIFTH, scene second.

A graveyard, a funeral in progress. Mourners gathered around.
GRAVEDIGGER waits, to the side. PETER saunters by, with a linen
napkin tucked into the opening of his shirt. He stands nearby, listening.

PASTOR. In death, the hearing is one of the first things to go. So this eulogy is mainly meant for you, the still-living, the still-hearing. We all knew the recently departed as Gimp. But there was more to him.

(PETER *saunters nearby.*)

Hey, great— hello, hello. Didn't know people still cared. Anyway, the first time I saw Gimp was while I was a member of the local Draft Board. You all remember how he cut off his finger, because he didn't want to fight. He believed in peace. On that day, as he left Town Hall, everyone threw trash at him and called him a traitor, and he ran for the hills. There, he started a small ski resort. He married his childhood sweetheart, had three beautiful boys. An avalanche destroyed the ski resort and he rebuilt it as an emu ranch, which went broke. The boys moved away and the childhood sweetheart died, as childhood sweethearts do. Gimpy came to church, from time to time. And he came with humility. Not shame, but humility. He could have made like Job, made a big stink about his terrible luck. He didn't. He took up gardening, instead. He grew beets, which were delicious. I have a weakness, some of you know, for beet salad— some bleu cheese, some balsamic vinaigrette— right, Nancy? Is Nancy here? The point is, he tried. That's a life. Trying, and, loving. That is a real life. He now stands before his God, intact, resplendent. Imagine that, standing before God, and being proud of yourself, quietly and humbly proud of yourself. I think that's what God wants. If there is a god. And I think there probably is. Anyway, please stop by the house for coffee and pie and we'll keep saying bye-bye deep into the night. Let us go in peace.

(PASTOR *and* MOURNERS *exit.*)

PETER. Let us go however we want.

(*Looks into the grave.*)

Was this him, all those years ago, the boy I saw cut his finger off? Kindred spirit. Both of us: ourselves. He at least had a family who turned against him or died. I don't even have a skull to talk to. (*Brief pause.*) I wonder if I was too hard on that beggar. Nah. Beggars are beggars for a reason. And he's got his wife and kids.

(*He looks into the grave again.*)

GRAVEDIGGER. (*Enters, with a shovel. Quietly, hoarsely:*) Show time.

PETER. Hi.

(*Watches him dig for a while.*)

You've seen some things in your day, I imagine. All the weeping and gritted teeth. It must give a man a certain perspective, looking at life like that.

GRAVEDIGGER. (*Hoarsely:*) I have laryngitis. Sorry. I shouldn't talk.

PETER. No, of course. You know, I knew him. Not well, but, I knew him. You might say that he and I were—

GRAVEDIGGER. (*Interrupting sharply, same as above, but a little louder:*) I have laryngitis.

PETER. Right, okay. Take care of that.

GRAVEDIGGER. Oh, I will. I need some more dirt.

(*Exits.*)

PALE MAN. (*Enters.*) Remember me?

PETER. Yeah, just from a few hours ago, I think I—

PALE MAN. (*Interrupting.*) We have some history. Dot dot dot dot. I'm hoping you'll give your body to science. Remember? So that some good will have come of it. But first…

PETER. (*Brief pause.*) Yes?

PALE MAN. (*Making a little gesture with his hand.*) "I'm a piece of lint!"

PETER. (*Trying to play along:*) Oh, okay. Hello, piece of lint.

PALE MAN. I'm not a piece of lint. I was testing your lack of integrity. And, good news— you passed. (*Brief pause.*) I just have to say this. (*Very quietly and plainly:*) Repent.

PETER. Excuse me?

PALE MAN. Nothing. Just, you know, an imperative. Sometimes, it's only that loud. I'll see you soon.

PETER. I don't know what this was about.

PALE MAN. I know you don't. I know. Don't worry— everything's going to be fine. (*Brief pause.*) Did I just say "everything"? And did I say "fine"? Sorry— I was thinking of something else. Well, I've to go get some milk. See you later, body.

(*Exits. PETER begins to exit, has a thought, stays. Lights cross-fade.*)

ACT FIFTH, scene third.

An outdoor auction. TOWN *is there, with others.*

AUCTIONEER. (*He pulls PETER's old sweater out of a box. He speaks calmly.*) Okay. Last item, here we go. Don't know where this stuff is from. It's a whole box, here. We have a, let's see here, a sweater. Do I hear… one dollar? Two dollars? One. For the sweater.

(TOWN *nods.* AUCTIONEER *points.*)

Okay, I've got one right here. Now, let's really get it going. Looking for two dollars. For the sweater.

PASTOR. Is it wool?

AUCTIONEER. Is it wool.

(*He looks for a label.*)

You know, I don't know, it doesn't say. Handmade, so there's no label. It's got two nice patches. Somebody really loved somebody. A good heavy sweater. Might be a blend. Couple of stains. Probably tears, right? But, seriously, here we go, for one dollar. Going once. Going twice. Sold. Right here. One dollar.

(TOWN *hands over a bill, takes sweater.*)

Now... let's see.

(*Looking into the box.*)

We have some more stuff in here, and then we're done. All junk, looks to be. A novelty pen, an old cat collar, and some other stuff. The things people save. A dollar for the box. Do I hear a dollar? I do not. Going, going, gone.

TOWN. Nobody bid anything.

AUCTIONEER. I know.

(AUCTIONEER *puts the box in a trash can.*)

TOWN. Can I have that?

AUCTIONEER. Yeah, I don't care.

(TOWN *gets the box from the trash.*)

Next week, we have some interesting stuff.

(*He refers to a piece of paper.*)

Let's see here (*Reading:*), "Blank gravestones, a tandem bicycle, paper." A lot of paper, in fact— I think it's from a stationery store that closed or moved. See you then.

(AUCTIONEER *exits.* PETER *enters.* PALE MAN *walks by, opposite direction as he last exited, carrying a bottle of milk.*)

PALE MAN. Milk. Good for the bones and teeth.

(*He exits.*)

PETER. (REPORTER, *wearing a sweater, enters, with a camera, a notepad.*) Who was that, do you know? That just walked by?

REPORTER. Him? The guy with the milk? I did a feature on him, once. He runs sort of a medical clinic, here. His son-in-law killed himself— Moynihan was the name. Then his daughter died. He had some really dark years, lot of anger about everything, but then he, you know, I don't know, he changed. He got into suicide prevention and started a hospice. He delivered both my kids. Good guy. Weird, but, good guy.

PETER. Well, the world needs doctors.

REPORTER. Yeah. Yes it does.

PETER. You were saying, you did a feature?

REPORTER. I do a column. It's called "Total Individuals."

PETER. Well, I can see why you've approached me.

REPORTER. Didn't approach, just was walking by.

PETER. I am, yes, how shall I say it, something of an individual. Total? That'll be for the reader to decide. But I suppose I am, drum roll… myself.

REPORTER. Okay. Drum roll… how so?

PETER. Well, I've traveled around the world. Seven seas, all that.

REPORTER. Yeah, that's great. I love traveling.

PETER. Ah, yes, but I was always traveling in pursuit of myself. I always marched to the beat of my own drum.

REPORTER. Yeah, nice. I guess my thing, my column, it's more devoted to people who kind of used their selves to pursue Some Other Thing, you know?

PETER. You're not getting me.

REPORTER. Mmmh, no, I think I get you. And I think it's great you weren't tied down and you did a lot of going around.

PETER. It was more than that.

REPORTER. Yeah, you said.

PETER. My name— I guess for some legal reason you need me to officially say it— my name is Peter Gnit.

REPORTER. Okay. (*He writes it down.*) "Peter Gnit. Travel buff."

PETER. No. "Peter Gnit. Self. Actual Self." (*Brief pause.*) I said it was more than traveling. I overcame things. I came from nothing. My slogan was, "By yourself."

REPORTER. Everyone has a self. It's great you have one, but, you know, so does everyone. (*Brief pause.*) It's funny, I think "By Yourself" was an old advertising slogan for a real estate agency. They were trying to encourage home-ownership.

PETER. What?

REPORTER. Yeah. They got shut down, I'm pretty sure.

PETER. (*Very brief pause.*) I went to America.

REPORTER. Beautiful country.

PETER. I saw the Sphinx.

REPORTER. Wow! You've really done all the cruises and stuff. You know, we do another little feature, kind of a fun thing, called, "They Eat What?"

It's about exotic foods from different countries. I bet you've eaten some of those.

PETER. I've suffered. I've made myself suffer, all my life. We are talking about my soul. About the achievements of my soul on Earth.

REPORTER. It comes out every other week. (*Brief pause.*) I'm sorry.

PETER. I'm sort of panicking and drawing a blank. There's more to me than what I'm saying.

REPORTER. Hey, no, come on. I would love to see the Sphinx, you know? (*Brief pause.*) What brought you back around here, anyway?

PETER. Love? A woman I loved. I still love.

REPORTER. Oh yeah?

PETER. I haven't seen her in 30 years. I don't know if she's still here, or if she's married or even still alive.

REPORTER. Now that could be something. "Lovers reunited after 30 years." That really would be interesting.

> (*Hands him a business card.*)

I mean, potentially. Keep me posted.

PETER. My life started on a Tuesday night, and, here it is, here I am, an old man, on Friday morning.

REPORTER. It kind of ruins the joke, when you explain it.

PETER. It's not a joke.

REPORTER. No, I know.

PETER. I've gone through my life like a person cutting through a train station to stay out of the rain.

REPORTER. Yeah, no, that's pretty good, quite the poet— wow. It does go pretty fast, doesn't it. (*Brief pause.*) I have to run. Let me know about your love story. And send us something for the food thing, okay? If you want. Although, nothing on weird bugs or whale blubber— we've already had that.

PETER. (*Brief pause.*) One time, I had a meal that was—

REPORTER. (*Interrupting:*) Sorry. Good meeting you, Mr...? I'm sorry, I forget your... wait, don't tell me. Gynt, right? See, that's the mind of the journalist, at work. Never forget a name. See you later.

> (PETER *stares at him, sadly.* REPORTER *exits.* TOWN *enters, carrying the box from earlier, and* PETER's *sweater.*)

PETER. Hi.

TOWN. Is it?

PETER. What?

TOWN. Oh. I thought you said, "Good day."

PETER. No.

TOWN. Hi.

PETER. What's in the box?

TOWN. Nothing. Details.

PETER. I remember you.

TOWN. Yeah?

PETER. (*Brief pause.*) Didn't you used to be more talkative?

TOWN. Yeah. People moved, people died. Now it's just me.

PETER. Ah. (*Brief pause.*) Do you remember Solvay?

TOWN. Of course. She went blind.

PETER. That was my mother who went blind.

TOWN. More than one person can go blind. She lives in the woods.

PETER. No. In our little house? She's still there?

TOWN. I think so.

PETER. Can you take me there?

TOWN. It's a free country.

ACT FIFTH, scene fourth.

> *They walk slowly around the stage.*

TOWN. Are you all right with this pace?

PETER. I've walked these mountains all my life.

> (*Sound of a seagull squawking:*)

What was that?

TOWN. Seagull.

PETER. How is Solvay? Did she ever, is she married?

TOWN. Don't know. Do you ever go like this?

> (*He puffs up his cheeks with air, and then blows it out in four quiet puffs.*)

I do. I mean, obviously. (*Brief pause.*) Oh, this is funny.

> (*He points to a house.*)

A couple used to live back up there. You remember them? Moynihan? He hung himself. She died later, of a broken heart and an auto-immune disorder. Of course you remember them. (*Brief pause.*) Funny is totally the wrong word. It was so sad.

PETER. That is sad.

TOWN. That's exactly what I just fucking said, verbatim. (*Brief pause.*) I think my blood sugar is really low.

> (PETER *picks up a wild onion.*)

PETER. Do you know why this onion is like my life?

TOWN. I don't know, because it smells and it makes you cry? Because it's no good by itself? Because if you peel it, I don't know, you just keep peeling it, and there's nothing there except layers? Because there's no, whatever, center to it? Is that what you mean? But more importantly, here's a question for you: why would you want to stop, on your way to see a woman who's been waiting for you for thirty years, to philosophize about an onion?

PETER. That's a good… You've raised a very—

TOWN. (*Interrupting:*) You don't have to say anything.

PETER. Then I won't. (*Very brief pause.*) I know I don't have to say anything.

TOWN. Hey, little advice: ssshhh.

>   (*They continue walking, and approach the little house, on the front of which is an old torn banner that says, "Welcome Home My." Woodland birdsong is heard.*)

PETER. I'd forgotten what a beautiful spot this was. It was here all along. My place on Earth.

>   (*The voice of a woman is heard, singing.*)

TOWN. You're in luck. Sounds like she's home.

PETER. (*Moved, to tears, or almost.*) Oh God. What a beautiful sound. She waited. Solvay! I'm home!

>   (*Brief pause.* ANNA *steps out of the little house, with cleaning supplies.*)

ANNA. Solvay Breeland? I'm so sorry. Are you a relative? I was just cleaning up.

PETER. No. No she didn't.

ANNA. Can I ask who you are?

PETER. Peter.

ANNA. Peter Gnit? I recognize you from the drawings she used to do. (*Brief pause.*) I thought what you did to her was horrible. But she told me, right before the end of her life, how much she loved her life. She said she learned the genius of staying in one place, thanks to you. And how much of the world you get to see when you just stay looking for one thing. She got to be quite a bird expert.

PETER. (*Close to devastated. Almost without affect:*) I don't think I can—. (*Brief pause.*) It's too late, but now I'm home. Solvay, darling, I'm still your boy inside, and I'm home.

ANNA. I don't know if you know this, but, she bought all this land.

PETER. She did? Oh my darling. She was a very smart woman.

ANNA. And she willed it to the Nature Society. As a bird sanctuary. She loved people but she said no people could live here. She loved you and said if you loved her, and you ever came back, you'd understand. People offered her a lot of money but she said no. It was just who she was.

PETER. Yes. (*Brief pause.*) I don't imagine there was any kind of a clause?

ANNA. No, it was very simple.

TOWN. When she believed a thing, she believed a thing. It's beautiful up here. They flock from all over, rare crazy birds from all over.

PETER. I don't know how to live. I never did. Not once. I don't know how to live.

ANNA. Oh. I'm sorry. (*Brief pause.*) Is it— this is going to sound awful, but— is it that hard? Other people figured it out. It's in thousands of books. It's in every religion.

TOWN. There are clubs and groups that are good, too. I think it's important to just—

PETER. (*Interrupting:*) Oh, I could have read a book, you say? Sung in a choir?

TOWN. No, no— we were just saying—

PETER. (*Interrupting:*) Could you please take pity on an old person with nothing, not one single fucking thing, and leave me alone!?

(*The birdsong stops. All quiet.*)

ANNA. (*Brief pause.*) I'm sure we were only trying—

PETER. (*Interrupting.*) I don't need you to try. I need you to go away.

ANNA. Stay as long as you need. You can't stay, though. The charter is very clear about that, that nobody...

(PETER *glares at her.* ANNA *and* TOWN *exit.*)

We'll leave you alone for a bit.

PETER. (*A long pause.* PETER *looks at the little house, touches some of the woodwork.*) Solvay? Hello, sweetie.

(*He* listens for a moment. Quietly, to SOLVAY, and the silent birds:*)

Where are your little birdies?

(PETER, *in a rage, but very slowly because he's old, partly pulls down the banner, and begins to try to tear the little house down. He can't. Quietly, again:*)

I can't even wreck anything right. God.

(*To audience, in what should feel like the first true direct address of the play:*)

You. Sympathize with me, if you're so sympathetic. Love a cruel old man who hates you, if you're so loving. I hate you. (*Very brief pause.*) I'm sorry. I'm so sorry. (*Brief pause.*) Solvay, come back. Don't leave me. (*Brief pause.*) This isn't literature. (*Brief pause.*) Mom?

TOWN. (*Pause. Enters.*) Sorry, Peter? Mr. Gnit?

(*Looks at a broken window or other small sign of damage.*)

Wow, look what you've done. (*Very brief pause.*) Hey, I know you were going to sit for a while, but, I haven't eaten. And I was thinking maybe you'd like to go down to the—

PETER. (*Interrupting.*) No. Forgive me. That's nice of you, but, I've eaten enough.

TOWN. Yeah? You already ate? Okay. Just thought I'd ask.

(*Exits.*)

PETER. (*Out, to audience:*) My little poem is over. I'm gone. Who's next? You? You? You? You? You?

(*Looking at the audience. With simple gentleness and affection:*)

Ahh. Look at everyone. All dressed up and... and with your hair nice and combed.

(*A rueful but not completely cold smile.*)

I wish this had been happier.

(*He picks up a piece of lumber, then, using it as a cane, he walks upstage into the black woods. Stops and pokes at something on the ground for a moment, then walks off and disappears. A single bird begins a sparse song. Lights fade.*)

End of Play

APPROPRIATE
by Branden Jacobs-Jenkins

ABOUT *APPROPRIATE*

This article first ran in the January/February 2013 issue of Inside Actors, *Actors Theatre of Louisville's subscriber newsletter, and is based on conversations with the playwright before rehearsals for the Humana Festival production began.*

As Branden Jacobs-Jenkins' crackling, combustive drama *Appropriate* begins, it's a hot summer night in Arkansas, the air thick with the song of cicadas. A crumbling former plantation house sits cluttered with its late patriarch's hoard of possessions, and the graves of many generations of its inhabitants lie in ghostly repose just outside. Suddenly, a figure hoists himself through the window and out of the night—setting in motion the uneasy reunion of the Lafayette siblings, who are descending upon their ancestral home to liquidate their dead father's estate. Franz, the youngest, climbs into the living room after more than a decade's estrangement; beleaguered eldest sister Toni has been shouldering all of the arrangements, while middle brother Bo swoops in just for the weekend. Arriving with partners and kids in tow—not to mention their own agendas—they've come to dispense with the past and claim their inheritance.

But as the play unfolds and the secrets of this fractious family begin to tumble out, the nature of that inheritance becomes an increasingly fraught question. And when a disturbing discovery surfaces among their father's belongings, it brings the heated gathering to an outright boil. Conflicting accounts of who Dad really was mix with accusations of blame, and Jacobs-Jenkins spins a riveting tale of a family haunted by its past—both the contested histories of their own making, and the debts passed down to them.

While *Appropriate* resulted from several converging inspirations, one of the most central for Jacobs-Jenkins was a fascination with the American family drama. "I do a lot of work with genre, taking these generally 'American' dramatic forms and trying to re-appropriate them in some way," says the playwright. "It is said that one of America's main contributions to Tragedy as a historical genre is locating it firmly in the family. The theory is that in this 'country of immigrants,' the only social unit you had was the one you immigrated with, and that—as opposed to your little Bavarian village or your *shtetl*—became the battleground for all these conflicts of the soul." So Jacobs-Jenkins immersed himself in the genre, looking at seminal plays from *Long Day's Journey into Night* to *Cat on a Hot Tin Roof* to *Buried Child*. "Why are we so compelled by family dysfunction and buried secrets—by bearing witness to the pain of not just one person, but of an entire gene pool?" he wondered.

In Jacobs-Jenkins' version of the drama, that compulsion to *look* and make meaning of dark discoveries is part of the fabric of the conflict itself, since the characters tangle over their varied interpretations of the evidence before them. "I've always been obsessed by the act of looking," notes the author, "and I'm interested in what it means to be an audience member and sit in judgment of characters, how the experience of simply watching is so charged—politically and otherwise." In the world of *Appropriate*, our judgment never rests for long, thanks to deftly-orchestrated revelations and differing accounts of history that constantly reframe the audience's perspective.

Even more stressful for Ray Lafayette's heirs than sorting out his dilapidated house, then, is dealing with each other. The three siblings have traveled divergent paths, which for Jacobs-Jenkins came from an allegorical impulse. "Franz has gone West to reinvent himself, to start over," he explains. "The West has always represented the possibility of wrestling some sort of new fortune or destiny for yourself out of the world where you had none." Franz's troubled history has led to his banishment, and he's regarded with suspicion from the moment he arrives with his young fiancée. Seeking forgiveness, he gets a cold reception from older sister Toni, who's been saddled with handling their father's affairs in the wake of her own crushing personal hardship. Jacobs-Jenkins recalls driving through "depressed little cities that have taken a real beating" on his way to visit his mother's hometown in Arkansas. "Toni is the New South," he observes, "with that sense of a lost kingdom that has been repeatedly betrayed by the rest of the country." Meanwhile, Bo flies down from New York City with his wife and two kids, smartphone in hand, eager to get things done. "He thinks of himself as having a connection to a bigger world and is obsessed with forward momentum," says Jacobs-Jenkins.

However, absolution from past wrongdoings doesn't come easily, and moving forward without taking a clear-eyed look backward comes with a price. The impulse to reinvent or sell off a loaded history means that we're left with its scars, but with no understanding of how they got there. "I'm interested in the relationship between collective memory and collective forgetting. I wanted to show how something is forgotten over three generations, or transformed to the point that it's unrecognizable," notes Jacobs-Jenkins. "Recently I read somewhere that the invention of grandparents was instrumental in human evolution. When life expectancy stretched far enough to provide access to an extra generation of knowledge, we could remember things like which plants were poisonous. But when it comes to other kinds of 'poisons,' like shame, there's also a survival impulse to move on, to let go." In depicting a family caught up in the fine art of repression, *Appropriate*'s questions live at the heart of that paradox.

—Amy Wegener

BIOGRAPHY

Branden Jacobs-Jenkins' plays include *Neighbors* (The Public Theater), *Appropriate* (Actors Theatre of Louisville, Victory Gardens Theater, Woolly Mammoth Theatre Company, and Signature Theatre in New York, Spring 2014), *An Octoroon* (Soho Rep, Spring 2014), and *War*. He is currently a Residency Five playwright at Signature Theatre and a Lila Acheson Wallace Fellow at The Juilliard School. Additionally, his work has been or will be seen at the Vineyard Theatre, The Matrix Theatre in Los Angeles, Company One in Boston, and the HighTide Festival in the United Kingdom. He has taught at New York University and Queens University of Charlotte, and his honors include a Paula Vogel Award, a Helen Merrill Award, and the inaugural Tennessee Williams Award. He holds an M.A. in Performance Studies.

ACKNOWLEDGMENTS

Appropriate premiered at the Humana Festival of New American Plays in March 2013, in association with Victory Gardens Theater. It was directed by Gary Griffin with the following cast:

FRANZ	Reese Madigan
TRISHA	Natalie Kuhn
RHYS	David Rosenblatt
TONI	Jordan Baker
RACHAEL	Amy Lynn Stewart
AINSLEY	Gabe Weible
BO	Larry Bull
CASSIDY	Lilli Stein

and the following production staff:

Scenic Designer	Antje Ellermann
Costume Designer	Connie Furr-Soloman
Lighting Designer	Matt Frey
Sound Designer	Bray Poor
Stage Manager	Michael D. Domue
Dramaturgs	Janice Paran and Amy Wegener
Casting	Stephanie Klapper
Directing Assistant	Jane B. Jones
Fight Director	Drew Fracher
Assistant Set Designer	Jung Griffin
Production Assistant	Jessica Potter
Assistant Dramaturg	Naomi Shafer

The character name "Trisha" was changed to "River" during subsequent productions.

Appropriate was developed, in part, at Vineyard Arts Project, Ashley Melone, Founder and Artistic Director; the 2012 Sundance Institute Theatre Lab at the Sundance Resort; and Victory Gardens Theater, Chicago, Illinois, Chay Yew, Artistic Director, Jan Kallish, Executive Director, as part of IGNITION 2012.

DRAMATIS PERSONAE

ANTOINETTE "TONI" LAFAYETTE, the oldest, white, late 40s/early 50s
RHYS THURSTON, her son, white, late teens

BEAUREGARDE "BO" LAFAYETTE, the middle, white, late 40s/early 50s
RACHAEL KRAMER-LAFAYETTE, his wife, white, mid-late 40s
CASSIDY "CASSIE" KRAMER-LAFAYETTE, their oldest child, white, early teens
AINSLEY KRAMER-LAFAYETTE, their youngest, white, a child

FRANÇOIS "FRANZ/FRANK" LAFAYETTE, the youngest, white, late 30s/early 40s
RIVER RAYNER, his fiancée, white, early 20s but looks younger

SETTING

The living room of a former plantation home in southeast Arkansas. Summer.

NOTE

The script published in this volume reflects changes made following the Humana Festival run, during *Appropriate*'s productions at Victory Gardens Theater and Woolly Mammoth Theatre Company—but this book predates the 2014 production at Signature Theatre in New York.

"LOPAKHIN: If only my father and grandfather could rise up out of their graves, and see all that's happened—how their little Yermolai, their abused, semi-literate Yermolai, who used to run around barefoot in winter—how that same Yermolai has bought this estate, the most beautiful spot on earth. Yes, I've bought the land on which my father and grandfather were slaves, where they weren't even allowed in the kitchen."

—Anton Chekhov, *The Cherry Orchard*

"No 'we' should be taken for granted when the subject is looking at other people's pain."

—Susan Sontag, *Regarding the Pain of Others*

"I realized that the only character I could identify with was Karl."

—Bruce Norris, on *A Raisin in the Sun*

Larry Bull and Jordan Baker
in *Appropriate*

37th Humana Festival of New American Plays
Actors Theatre of Louisville, 2013
Photo by Alan Simons

APPROPRIATE

act one: the book of revelations

prologue

Light abandons us and a darkness replaces it.

Instantly, a billion cicadas begin trilling in the dense, velvety void—loudly, insistently, without pause—before hopefully, at some point, becoming it.

The insect song fills and sweeps the theatre in pulsing pitch-black waves, over and beyond the stage—washing itself over the walls and the floors, baptizing the aisles and the seats, forcing itself into every inch of space, every nook, every pocket, hiding place and pore until this incessant chatter is touching you.

It is touching you.

This goes on and on and on and on and on until the thought occurs in each head, Is this it?

Is this the whole show?

1.

Then something happens.

Light seeps in through an upstage window and barely reveals a very large and very disorderly living room, claustrophobic and decrepit: a mixture of old and new furniture scattered beneath a dead chandelier; bookshelves packed with dusty hardcovers, paperbacks, and assorted curiosities; and all over the place there is junk—just a ton of it—a whole lifetime of clutter and crap just everywhere it can possibly be.

Somewhere, a staircase disappears into another floor; a swinging door swings onto a dining area/kitchen; through a foyer, a front door leads out and one can just barely glimpse a hallway leading to an unseen room, which is probably connected to the dining area. As the lights swell and swell, the sounds of the cicadas fade a little but never quite disappear, and just when we've gotten a good look at the place, there is a:

Sudden BLACKOUT, in which the cicadas' twittering swells before hitting a peak and dissolving back into a hum again as lights immediately come up again on the living room. It's some other time—maybe even another day—perhaps the dead of night. Beat, before, seemingly out of nowhere, a man springs up into the upstage window—FRANZ. *He jostles with the frame for a bit before he hoists it up, and a sleepy voice is heard coming from just below the ledge on the other side:*

RIVER. (*Offstage.*) Franz, what is that?

FRANZ. What?

RIVER. (*Offstage.*) That sound?

FRANZ. (*Climbs through the window.*) It's the cicadas.

(*Reaching out the window.*)

They're swarming. Every thirteen years they come out of the ground and make all this noise. I didn't even realize…

RIVER. (*Offstage.*) It's so scary…

(FRANZ *doesn't hear her. He is taking in the room. His face betrays the surfacing of ugly feelings for a beat before a weird scraping noise is heard coming from outside. Suddenly, someone else*—RIVER—*shoots up into the window, and tries to pull herself in, sort of in slow motion, but she doesn't quite make it, falling back down.* RIVER *tries to spring up into the window, again, and, again, she doesn't make it. She's too short, too weak, too…?*)

FRANZ. (*Shaken out of it, amused, confused.*) Baby, what is happening?

(RIVER *tries again, fails again.*)

RIVER. (*Offstage. An endearing whine.*) I'm sleepy! Help!

FRANZ. Jump, midget—

RIVER. (*Hoisting herself in.*) Shut up. That's offensive to little people. How long were we on the road?

(FRANZ *catches her. She's a tiny thing.*)

FRANZ. (*Dragging her in.*) Twenty hours— Watch your he—

RIVER. (*Hits her head hard.*) OW!!!

FRANZ. (*Pulling her in.*) I said, watch your head.

RIVER. (*Rubbing her head.*) Owwwww—wuh!

FRANZ. (*Holding her, rubbing her head.*) Aww, come here.

(*Kissing/kind of eating her booboo.*)

Nom-nom-nom—

(*Sudden BLACKOUT, cicadas, and lights come up again on the living room. It is later that morning. There are sounds of cooking coming from the kitchen—the hiss of grease, the scrape of a spatula*—RIVER.

Someone else is on the front porch—TONI.)

TONI. (*Shouting offstage.*) —could you grab mine, too, sweetie? Thank you!

(TONI *lets herself in, locks the door. After a moment, she hears the noises coming from the kitchen. She thinks that it's her brother,* BO. *She seems pleased. Calling into the house:*)

Bo?... Rachael...?

(*Following the noises into the kitchen.*)

What in the world are you do—?

(TONI *has disappeared through the swinging door. Beat, before she comes rushing back in, freaked out of her mind. She paces around the living room, doesn't know what to do. Panicked, she heads outside, just as* RIVER *comes peeking through the swinging door, headphones on. She takes them out.*)

RIVER. (*Did she just hear something?*) Franz?

(*Sudden BLACKOUT, cicadas, then lights come up again on the living room. It is a little later.* TONI *is there, again, but she is now joined by* RACHAEL, *who is a little alarmed, perhaps fanning herself. They both peer through the swinging door just a crack, trying to see what's happening. They semi-whisper.*)

TONI. We just got back—

RACHAEL. From where?

TONI. I had to drive back to Atlanta to pick up Rhys. We saw that car out front and I thought it was you all. I come in and she's in the kitchen—

RACHAEL. Oh my god— What did you do?

TONI. Well, first, I almost jumped out of my skin. She looks like a teenager—a runaway, probably— Didn't Juanita warn us about this—squatters?— So I was just like, "You know what? Rhys and I just need to sit our little behinds in our Volvo outside and wait for you all—because this girl could be hopped up on drugs for all we know—crystal meth!—and I knew you guys were going to be getting here soon and I thought, "Bo—Bo will handle this."

(*Peering through the door.*)

He's good at this sort of thing.

RACHAEL. Do you know how long she's been here?

TONI. There was no one here yesterday when I left so she must have come in last night?—this morning? Do you think she might have been hiding out somewhere around here—waiting for me to leave?

RACHAEL. Why didn't you just call the police?

TONI. I panicked—and you know you can't trust these small town cops—I mean, she's probably somebody's cousin, and I knew you all were going to be getting here soon...

(*Peering through the door.*)

Bo is certainly taking his time with her...

(AINSLEY *comes running through the foyer, making a toy fly. He seems to be heading for the swinging door, but* RACHAEL *cuts him off.*)

RACHAEL. Heyheyhey— Not in there— Not in there! Where is your sister?

(AINSLEY *shrugs.*)

TONI. She wandered off with Rhys. I told them to stay away until we knew what was going on.

RACHAEL. She is supposed to be babysitting—

TONI. Why don't you just send Ainsley outside?

RACHAEL. Not with those bugs everywhere— It's like a horror movie—

TONI. I forgot about the / cicadas—

RACHAEL. (*To* AINSLEY.) Stay on the porch, sweetie, okay? And no running. It's too hot.

> (AINSLEY *takes off for the porch.*)

TONI. He's shot right up since the funeral.

> (RACHAEL *sees her sister-in-law, spying at the swinging door, and takes a moment to inspect the place with some concern.*)

RACHAEL. You've really been here by yourself all week?

TONI. Yes—

RACHAEL. Uh huh… And the auction's still happening, right?

TONI. Yes, tomorrow afternoon—

RACHAEL. So then what are we planning to do with this stuff?

TONI. Oh—I got the idea that we could do a kind of tag sale in the morning beforehand—I already ran it by the lawyers. I thought it might be a good way to get rid of some of this, make a little cash—

RACHAEL. Okay and—Bo didn't really tell me the whole story—these liquidators quit?

TONI. No, no. I fired them. They were trying to rob us blind—

> (*Suddenly,* BO *enters from the kitchen, looking overextended, iPhone in hand. Beat, then:*)

BO. So. Her name is River.

TONI. Excuse me?

BO. River. As in the body of water. And she is here with Franz.

RACHAEL. There's another one?

TONI. And who the hell is Fronds?

BO. Franz is Frank.

TONI. / What?

BO. I need to sit for a second. Jesus, is there anywhere to sit down / around here?

TONI. Wait—are you telling me that Frank is in this house right now?

BO. Yes. He's upstairs, sleeping. "They've been driving all night," she said.

TONI. Are you fucking kidding me? / What?

RACHAEL. Toni—your language—

TONI. Sorry—

RACHAEL. It's okay. Ainsley's just picking up / all sorts of—

TONI. Wait— How old is this girl?

BO. Was I supposed to ask her that?!

TONI. Yes! Did she tell you what they are doing here? What are they doing here?

>   (AINSLEY *comes running through.*)

RACHAEL. (*To* AINSLEY.) / Hey! What did I say? No running!

>   (AINSLEY *exits.*)

BO. I have no idea, Toni! Can you give me a second, please?! The flight was exhausting, I pull up and you're on the lawn, raving like a lunatic—

TONI. Bo, I just had the crap scared out of me by a teenybopper banging around my dead father's kitchen and now you're telling me Frank is here, that Frank the family pedophile is here—

RACHAEL. / Toni—

TONI. —and that he is upstairs? What is he doing here?

BO. How am I supposed / to know?

TONI. Is this really happening? Where was he at Daddy's funeral? Wait— Did he know we were here!?

BO. It sounds like they were expecting us—

TONI. Where has this bastard even been for the last—how many— Oh my god, has it been ten years? Has it been a decade, Bo? Why would he— Oh my god—he's here for— Is Frank here for money? Oh my god, he's here for money! Are you— I literally cannot believe this happening— I'm going to have a panic attack— I'm going to kill him!— We have to get him out of here, Bo!

BO. Jesus, Toni, will you stop—the man is upstairs asleep, okay? Relax!

TONI. Then go wake him up! / He cannot be here!

BO. No, Toni! No!

TONI. Then I'm calling the police!

BO. And what are they going to do? What are you going to say? That he's trespassing? Will you just calm the frick down! Please!

>   (*Beat.*)

What is the use of your whipping yourself into a conniption right now? Just let the man wake up and then we'll deal with it, okay!? Okay!? Just let me sit for a second! You were the one gunning for some sort of family reunion.

>   (*Beat.*)

TONI. This is not a reunion. We have work to do. And how are we supposed to get anything done with this little girl prancing around in there?

BO. You could start by telling me what the hell is going on here? I thought you said you've been here all week?

TONI. I have.

BO. Then what have you been doing? This place is a pigsty—the front porch, the kitchen— How long has this place been looking like this? Since when was our father a hoarder?

TONI. / Our father was not—!?

BO. No wonder those estate people wanted more money! I would have given it to them if I'd known it was this bad. I can't believe you thought you could do this by yourself! I mean, what was I paying that Juanita woman for?

TONI. Juanita was a caregiver, Bo, not a housekeeper and for your information, a lot of this is stuff I brought down from upstairs—

BO. So you just spent the last week moving crap from one room to another!?

TONI. I figured that you and your kids probably wanted some place to sleep!

RACHAEL. And Toni, we are very grateful! I wasn't trying to be any sort of trouble, / on top of—

TONI. You are not being any sort of trouble, / Rachael—

RACHAEL. If I'd known that things were going to be in such a…state of flux, I would have found a hotel—

TONI. It's fine—I already cleared out the bedrooms by the / big bathroom—

BO. (*To* RACHAEL.) I told you this was a terrible idea—

RACHAEL. Well, I'm sorry!

> (*To* TONI.)

I just thought it might be nice for the kids to experience some of their father's childhood before it up and disappears—one of these big romantic / Southern mans—

BO. This is not my childhood—

RACHAEL. Childhood summers—

BO. Barely.

TONI. Rachael, it's no use. Bo's always been the biggest brat about this place—the summers we spent here— He's the reason we stopped coming.

BO. We stopped coming because Aunt Claudette died.

TONI. No. We stopped coming because you had a miserable time and Mommy and Daddy were tired of watching you sulk and complain all day. Daddy told me.

BO. I did not sulk and complain all day.

TONI. Why did you hate this place so much?

BO. I don't know. I just never liked the place. Summer was always this swampy, humid nightmare—the furniture sticking to your skin— No air conditioning. —And people's idea of fun was killing some animal or tying an old tire to a tree and swinging from it or swimming into that disgusting lake. "Go take a cool dip in the lake if ya get hot!" That lake is a health hazard—covered in algae and they treated it like Niagara frickin Falls—this cesspool— People always taking us out to stare at those gravestones, boring us with these endless stories about how Great-grand-cousin Bubba Jo hid sacks of flour from the Yankees in a well or some crap. I just didn't get it—I just didn't fucking get it— Bugs everywhere. What did you like about it?

TONI. I don't know. I've always had a fondness for old things. I always liked the stories about the gravestones. The stories about the furniture—I always liked the stories—how much this old place had seen. It was like a castle in a fairytale, like a little kingdom.

BO. I can't believe we're talking about the same place.

TONI. Well, we're not. This isn't exactly the place we spent our summers. Not anymore.

RACHAEL. Why not?

TONI. By the time Grandma died and Frank and Daddy moved in, the cousins had taken everything—the furniture, everything—picked the place clean. This is just a shell of the place... Anyway, I think it's a lovely idea. I think our father would have really appreciated it—

RACHAEL. Yes, I regret that Cassidy and Ainsley never really...got to spend a lot of time with Ray. And ever since his funeral, these two have been nothing but questions. And since we can't do a Europe trip this summer, I thought, Why not? Why don't the kids and I just do a little road trip through the South—start here, rent a van, and drive back home through Mississippi, Louisiana—all those places—experience some of Daddy's heritage for once—

BO. Rachael, I grew up in D.C.—

RACHAEL. D.C. is the South.

TONI. No it isn't.

BO. She thinks anything south of Brooklyn is a trailer park—

TONI. You can't do a "Europe trip"?

BO. We can't afford it.

RACHAEL. But now that I see how big of a job you have here, Toni, and how hard you've been working, I'm glad we've all come. I'm sorry we haven't been around more to help out, but now that we're here, we're all going to make sure we pitch in and—

(*To* AINSLEY, *who runs through.*)

HEY! WHAT DID I SAY? STOP RUNNING BEFORE YOU KNOCK SOMETHING OVER!

(RHYS *and* CASSIDY *enter tentatively through the front door.*)

RHYS. Mom?

RACHAEL. (*Seeing* CASSIDY.) Cassidy, where have you / been!?

RHYS. / Is everything okay?

CASSIDY. Rhys and I just / walked down to the lake! What's the big deal?

TONI. It's your Uncle Frank.

RHYS. What? Where is / he?

RACHAEL. You are supposed / to be watching your brother!

TONI. He's upstairs.

CASSIDY. Why?

RACHAEL. Because I said so! Now take him please?

CASSIDY. Take him where?

RACHAEL. Toni, can Cassidy and Ainsley start doing something for you?

CASSIDY. / Oh my god.

TONI. Actually, you guys wanna finish cleaning out your grandpa's study for me?

(*Hands them some supplies—boxes, bags.*)

Just put anything that looks like we can sell it in these and throw everything else away, okay?

RHYS. Okay.

RACHAEL. And take your brother—!

CASSIDY. Ugh!

TONI. And if you see your Uncle Frank, you tell him to get his butt down here, / pronto!

(RHYS, CASSIDY, *and* AINSLEY *exit upstairs.*)

BO. Where did she just come from?

RACHAEL. She was "down by the lake with Rhys," she said.

BO. We'd better put a stop to that.

TONI. Stop to what?

RACHAEL. We just think Cassidy's developing a little crush on her cousin.

(*Off* TONI's *reaction.*)

Didn't you see them at the funeral together? Afterwards, all she could talk about was Rhys, Rhys, Rhys—went around posting these photos of the two of them together on Facebook and we were like, "Honey, please—those are from a funeral." With the casket in the background and everything—

BO. So let's keep an eye on the two of them please. I know we're in Arkansas or whatever but—

RACHAEL. Bo, ew! Toni, it's innocent— She's just…discovering boys. Bo is freaking out—

TONI. Well, she is sprouting into quite a pretty young thing—

RACHAEL. Those braces finally paid off.

BO. Meanwhile, we're still paying the braces off—

RACHAEL. / Bo—

BO. And don't get me started on the dermatologist, the contact lenses— Raising a teenager in New York is a Ponzi scheme, Toni. I bet in Atlanta you get to have as ugly a kid as you want.

(*Beat.*)

RACHAEL. Rhys is looking so great. Did I already say that? So healthy—

TONI. Well…

BO. Must be that juvvie diet. What were they feeding him in there?

(*He is swatted by* RACHAEL.)

What? It was a joke! We can't joke about it?!

(*Beat.*)

RACHAEL. Have you guys figured out what you're going to do in the fall?

TONI. Not really. Technically, he has to get his GED now, so he's taking a year off. Also wants to spend some time with his father, he says…

BO. What does that mean?

TONI. I guess he's moving in with Derek for a little bit and… I don't know—

(AINSLEY *runs right back down the stairs.*)

RACHAEL. (*Re:* AINSLEY.) Oh my god— THAT'S ENOUGH! COME HERE! SIT DOWN! SIT DOWN!

(*Grabbing a photo album off the shelf.*)

/ HERE! LOOK AT SOME PICTURES OR SOMETHING. DISTRACT YOURSELF.

BO. (*Looking up from his phone.*) Hey—so please tell me you're not running the auction, too.

TONI. Of course not. There's an auctioneer.

BO. Who?

TONI. Some guy I found on Craigslist.

BO. (*After a beat.*) What? You hired "some guy" off Craigslist to handle an entire estate?

TONI. What else was I supposed to do?

BO. Daddy's moron lawyer didn't have any recommendations?!

TONI. This man's perfectly fine! I talked to him on the phone!

BO. / Oh, okay!

TONI. What is your problem?!

BO. My problem is your not consulting me before making all these dumb decisions that I am ultimately paying for! Firing the liquidators, / hiring some random—

TONI. Whoa— That you are ultimately paying / for?!

BO. Toni, who has been bankrolling our father's convalescence the past two years—

TONI. What!?

BO. Who was keeping the lights on? Who was footing the bill for this so-called "caretaker," that took / care of what exactly?

TONI. Wait, I'm sorry—so you're looking for a return on your investment? / Our father was dying!

BO. I'm saying this has been a very expensive journey Toni, and I think I deserve not to have the little that I'm entitled to jeopardized by your shortsightedness—

TONI. And what about my time, Bo? Do you think I'm going to get back every twelve-hour drive to deal with doctors, / and arrangements for the funeral—

BO. / Oh, here we go—

TONI. —and locking everything up so you and Rachael couldn't miss whatever dinner party you / needed to be at?

BO. No one told you to do all that stuff by yourself. If you needed help, you could have asked for it, which you didn't do, / which you never do, because you're a control freak!

TONI. Oh, I'm sorry! I didn't know I was supposed to be applying for your assistance!

BO. I'm sorry I thought you were competent enough to do / what you said you could do!

TONI. I'm sorry some of us's time isn't more important / than everyone else's!

BO. I'm sorry some of us don't have our fat alimony checks to fall back on!

(*Beat.*)

TONI. I wasn't aware that my divorce was such a wonderful luxury—

BO. That is not what I— Look, Toni. You and I and everyone knows that you have had—have been having—a very, very difficult year, years—but I feel that it has been irresponsible and unfair of you to hold the rest of us... hostage to your own...hardship. Our father just died. You have been going through a divorce. There was Rhys's whole...ordeal with his school. You were obviously in no position to accept the responsibility of executor of our

father's will and you should have had the foresight and self-awareness to say
something.

(*Beat.*)

TONI. Well. Fuuuuuuuuuuuuuuuuuuuuuuuuck—you!

RACHAEL. Toni, your / language!

TONI. Rachael, why don't you just take your kid in the other room, because
we're having an adult conversation in here!

(*Beat.* RACHAEL *gives* BO *a look like, "You're on your own," and crosses
to stand near* AINSLEY, *but keeps an ear on the fight.*)

You know, despite my trials, Bo, I am not suddenly some sort of idiot. I'm
sorry I'm not milking this tragedy for every penny like some kind of shylock.
I'm sorry I couldn't just line your pockets. I'm sure that, had you been named
the executor, you and your personal assistant Sonya would have done an
effortlessly more wonderful job and come tomorrow we'd all be wiping our
behinds with hundred dollars bills but I think that whatever remainder we
split tomorrow after the estate sale and the auction are over—both of which
I have organized by myself—might be just enough to cover your expenses,
alright? But if that's not enough for you, how about you just take my share—
you greedy sack of crap.

BO. What estate sale?

TONI. We're having an estate sale before we have the auction tomorrow.

BO. What!? Why!?

TONI. Because the liquidators didn't finish cataloguing everything! Don't
worry— / I already ran it by the—

BO. Toni, that was the point of your coming down here! You were supposed
to finish everything!

TONI. Well, I didn't have enough time!

BO. So we're going to give everything away!?

TONI. We're not giving anything away! It's a sale!

BO. Toni, you do not make actual money off of— We are not going to pay
off half a million dollars from a junk sale!

TONI. Bo, that is why were are auctioning off the house!?—to pay that
down!

BO. You actually think we're going to— Oh my god! This is / an actual
disaster!

TONI. Okay, you know what, Bo, how about this!? How about you take over
then, since I'm so goddamn stupid! How about that!? By the powers invested
in whatever, you, Beauregarde Moneybags Lafayette, are now the flipping
executor! Please take over!

(RIVER, *in an apron and with an oven mitt, pokes her head in through the swinging door, interrupting the conversation.*)

RIVER. Soup's on!

(*Everyone looks at her.*)

BO. Thank you.

(RIVER *exits.*)

TONI. Lord help us.

(BO *walks away from* TONI.)

BO. (*To* RACHAEL, *pleading.*) Rachael…

RACHAEL. (*To* AINSLEY.) / Hey, monster, you hungry? Let's go get your sister.

TONI. That's it, Bo. Just walk away. Walk away.

BO. Please tell me that you are aware of the cemetery sitting outside our window.

TONI. Oh what does that have to do / with anything?

BO. Well, while you were sitting around being a nightmare, I consulted an actual estate lawyer—a friend of mine—who told me the only people interested in property like this are retail developers, but unfortunately we've got a serious liability on our hands in the form of a graveyard. No one's gonna want to fork over the money it will take to dig up and move those bones outside to turn this place in a Walmart or whatever the hell—

RACHAEL. (*To* AINSLEY.) / I said, let's go. What are you—

BO. Which means it's highly unlikely we're going to make the payoff from just the property auction, since the debt is more than its value—

RACHAEL. / Oh my god.

BO. So now we're going to / lose everything tomorrow— There won't be anything to "split."

TONI. Oh, because one of your New York friends swooped in and decided / everyone else was incompetent!?

RACHAEL. (*A little louder, disgusted.*) / Oh my god!

BO. Okay, you know what? The answer is no. I don't want to be executor. I want you to know that the responsibility is yours / tomorrow when there is literally nothing left—

RACHAEL. (*Snatching the photo album away.*) Give me that! Go—go to the dining room— / Go!

(AINSLEY *runs off to the dining room.*)

BO. (*Distracted, to* RACHAEL.) Rachael? What's going on?

(RACHAEL, *not hearing* BO, *opens the photo album and stares. Her eyes scan the page for a beat, slowly, taking it all in, but repulsed.*)

TONI. Rachael, what's wrong?

BO. Honey?

> (*Standing there,* RACHAEL *flips to the next page, just as* TONI *and* BO *rush over to look at what she's looking at. Once they see, their faces register an immediate shock, but not yet disgust.*)

RACHAEL. (*Overwhelmed.*) Oh my god.

> (*BLACKOUT, cicadas.*)

2.

> *The living room, a bit later.*
>
> FRANZ *sits somewhere, the album open on his lap, his groggy face gnarled slightly with a combination of feelings.* BO *and* TONI, *standing or perched nearby, study him closely.* RACHAEL *sits some distance away, dabbing her eyes, trying to get a hold of herself.*

FRANZ. Why would you wake me up to show me this?!

BO. Toni thought they might have been yours.

FRANZ. No, these are not mine! What would I be doing with something like this?

TONI. You're the one with the track record for freaky stuff! And half this crap is yours, anyway, or did you forget?!

FRANZ. Of course, I didn't forget! I'm the one who fucking lived here!

BO. Hey! Hey! Alright! So they don't belong to Frank—!

FRANZ. No.

BO. Great. Now can we hurry up and get rid of these things? It's bad enough my kid has already been exposed to this bullshit once.

FRANZ. Your daughter found these?

BO. No, my son.

FRANZ. Whoa, whoa, whoa… You have a son?

BO. …Yes, Frank. I have a nine-year-old… His name is Ainsley.

> (*Beat.*)

TONI. (*Wryly.*) Welcome back.

> (*Beat.*)

Now who's your kid?

> (*Off his reaction.*)

That co-ed in our kitchen— / Brook—River—Seabreeze?

FRANZ. Oh my god—

TONI. And why is she calling herself that?! And why is she calling you Franz?

FRANZ. Because my name is Franz!

TONI. No, Frank! Your name is Frank! And while we're on the subject, where the hell did you just come from and what are you doing here?

FRANZ. I'm here to see you all!

TONI. See us about what?

FRANZ. Why didn't anyone tell me about Daddy's dying?

> (*Beat.*)

TONI. We had lawyers trying to find you, Frank. It is not our fault you fell off the planet! Where have / you even been!?

FRANZ. I've been in Portland, Oregon.

TONI. Oregon? What's in Oregon? Besides all-you-can-eat jailbait—

FRANZ. You're going to shut your fat mouth about River!

TONI. Ugh, don't make throw up. What kind of name is River?

FRANZ. She feels a deep connection to the natural world!

RACHAEL. Hello!?!?

> (*Beat.*)

Can we sit around being casually dysfunctional later and focus for one second?

BO. / Rach—

RACHAEL. What are we going to do with these photos? I mean, what in the world was your father even thinking having them out in the open like this?

TONI. Rachael, we are just as upset as you are, but let's not get irrational. We have no idea where these came from.

RACHAEL. Frank just said they weren't his, Toni, and he's the only other person who lived in this house—

TONI. They could have been here when he and Daddy moved in—

RACHAEL. You just said the place was empty when they got here—

TONI. Rachael, there was still stuff in the attic, there was—

RACHAEL. We didn't find these in any attic. They were sitting on the shelf right here with all of your father's things!

BO. Rach—

RACHAEL. Bo, you've got one more time to try and shush me!

TONI. There were all kinds of people in this town coming through here—

RACHAEL. Okay, so you want me to believe that some "friend" of your father came over and was just like, "Doop-de-doop, let me just leave my disturbing photographs of dead black people I carry around with me all the time on this shelf over here while I pay old Ray a visit?"

(*Beat.*)

These belonged to your father. And let me just say I resent you standing there and calling me irrational. Your child was not exposed to this...sickness. A small child!

(*Beat.*)

TONI. Well, what would you like us to do, Rachael?

RACHAEL. Excuse me?

TONI. Tell me what you would like the adults in this room to do right now to help you deal with that? I mean, you handed these things over to Ainsley yourself.

RACHAEL. Oh, okay, so whatever psychological damage that my child is going to...suffer due to his grandfather's...perversity is now my fault?

TONI. Perversity?

RACHAEL. Prejudice!

(*A breath, then.*)

Listen, Toni: I appreciated Ray just as much as anyone and, yes, he cannot be held responsible for how he may have been brought up to feel or think about other people—

TONI. What?

RACHAEL. Toni, none of us are strangers to the history of the South. We're all standing in the middle of your family's plantation for / crying out loud!

TONI. Our father spent half of his life in Washington!

RACHAEL. But he came back here, didn't he? Because he wanted to—This is the soil upon which / his worldview was fashioned—

TONI. Rachael, you didn't even know this man!

RACHAEL. Toni, he was the grandfather of my children. I am / not some stranger.

TONI. Being a daughter-in-law does not make you privy to the full understanding of a person, my dear.

RACHAEL. And neither does being a daughter. My dear. Your father was a somebody long before you came along. And certainly somebody else when you weren't in the room. Now, I'm not saying Ray took these photos. I'm not saying he was involved in any of these lynchings... I don't know and frankly I don't care. I am just saying he was a slave to his upbringing just like everyone else and, like everyone else, he had issues. Now can we just own that and figure out what we're going to do, because there are still children in this house and I'm not interested in any more surprises!

>   (*Beat.*)

TONI. No. I want to talk about my father's "issues."

BO. Okay, you two—

RACHAEL. / Bo, shut up—

TONI. Shut up, Bo!

>   (*To* RACHAEL.)

Go ahead.

>   (*Beat.*)

RACHAEL. Fine, Toni. You want to look at the way he treated me?

TONI. What about the way he treated you?

RACHAEL. Ray obviously had real problems with me because of my heritage and this…anti-Semitism was always very uncomfortable for Bo and I… So I don't think his…race issues are so far of / a leap—

TONI. Wait, wait, I'm sorry, so Rachael, let me get this straight: you think our father is a racist because you think our father is an anti-Semite because you feel like he didn't like you?

RACHAEL. First of all, I did not call him an anti-Semite. He was in possession of latent anti-Semitic traits—

TONI. Anti-Semitic traits like what?

RACHAEL. Anti-Semitic traits like wh— Like having a problem with / Jews, Toni!

TONI. No, give me a concrete example, Rachael, of our father's "latent anti-Semitism."

>   (*Beat.*)

RACHAEL. I don't have to prove anything to you.

TONI. That's right. Because you're full of it.

>   (*Beat.*)

RACHAEL. I once overheard your father referring to me as Bo's "Jew wife." We were visiting him the summer I was pregnant with Cassidy and he was on the phone and he didn't know I was standing there and I overheard him refer to me to someone as "Bo's Jew wife." "Bo and his Jew wife are here from New York." Now would someone like to explain to me why it was necessary to distinguish to whoever this person was that I was, in fact, a Jew? Why couldn't I just be Bo's wife?

TONI. Are you kidding?

RACHAEL. And that's just a small example. Your father had a very difficult time with me and the fact that I was Jewish, which is maybe why he was very distant to me and Bo and our kids. And did I feel the need to say anything to him? No. He was an old man. You can't blame people for the ways they were raised… And I don't expect you guys to totally…be able to grasp this, because you've never been discriminated against, but that's how it is.

(*Beat.*)

TONI. Bo, I think it's time to take your wife upstairs. This is now a family-only discussion.

RACHAEL. Am I next in line for the Toni Bully Treatment? That must make me family.

TONI. No, Rachael. You're a Jew. And you're being kicked out because I subconsciously hate Jews and you, my dear, are a big ole Jew.

(*Beat.*)

RACHAEL. Well, if it's how you were raised. Why don't you just call me a shylock?

TONI. Sure: shylock.

RACHAEL. How about a kike?

TONI. Sure, kike.

(*Beat.*)

RACHAEL. Excuse me—

BO. / Rach—

RACHAEL. I'm going to go check on our baby kike.

(RACHAEL *exits.*)

BO. (*Going after her.*) Rachael! Rachael!

(*Wheels around.*)

TONI! WHAT THE HELL WAS THAT!?

(BO *exits after* RACHAEL.)

TONI. (*Calling after* BO.) How long was I supposed to stand there and let her insult my Daddy?

(*Turning on* FRANZ.)

You piece of shit.

FRANZ. What?

TONI. You know our father wasn't guilty of a single thing that harpy just accused him of—and you and Bo just sat there while she spat on the man's memory—in the middle of his living room! I'd tell you to be ashamed of yourself, but I already know you have no shame!

FRANZ. Oh my god what am I doing here?

TONI. Good question! What are you doing here, besides picking a dead man's pockets!?

FRANZ. I am not here to pick anyone's pockets!?

TONI. Oh, really!? So what do you call skipping a funeral but showing up the minute everything's getting sold off!?

FRANZ. That is not why I'm here!

TONI. Then why are you here, Frank!?

FRANZ. I'm here to— / to—

TONI. To—to—to what?!

FRANZ. To apologize! Actually. I came here to apologize to you and Bo.

(*Beat.*)

TONI. "Apologize"? That's the best you could come up with?

FRANZ. I'm a different person now, Toni! I came here to show you that I've changed! I'm here to make peace!

TONI. And you've never heard of e-mail?

FRANZ. And where was I supposed to get your e-mail?

TONI. From whoever it was that told you we would be here—which was who exactly?

(*Beat.*)

Hello?!

FRANZ. The lawyers found me.

TONI. When?

FRANZ. I don't know. A couple of weeks ago. I guess it took them so long because I...I changed my name and moved around a lot.

(*Beat.*)

TONI. And how old is that little girl? Please tell me / she is legal.

FRANZ. She is twenty-three!

TONI. Oh, she's twenty-three! She's twenty-three! You have some nerve showing up here with a "twenty-three-year-old" after how you / left—

RHYS. (*Offstage.*) Mom?

(RHYS *and* CASSIDY *enter from upstairs.* TONI *and* FRANZ *freeze. The kids freeze.* CASSIDY *holds a box of something in her hands.*)

TONI. Rhys—

CASSIDY. Hey, Uncle Frank! You're here!

FRANZ. (*A little nervous.*) Hey, Cassidy—

(*Throwing focus.*)

Whoa, Rhys! You look like a dude, dude!

RHYS. (*To* TONI.) What happened?

TONI. Nothing happened. We were just talking.

RHYS. About what?

TONI. Adult stuff.

CASSIDY. (*Setting the box down somewhere.*) We're almost adults.

TONI. Not quite. Are y'all finished upstairs?

RHYS. Almost, but we found a box of weird stuff in the study we don't know what to do with?

TONI. What kind of stuff?

(CASSIDY *removes a couple of jars from the box and hands one to* TONI.)

CASSIDY. Old scraps of cloth and stuff, but also these jars of like…weird stuff.

TONI. (*Taking the jar, looking at it.*) Ew…

CASSIDY. Right?

TONI. Frank, what is this? Are these bones?

FRANZ. (*Looks at another jar.*) I don't know. Meat? This looks like some sort of jerky?

CASSIDY. (*Another jar.*) I think this one looks like an ear.

TONI. Cassidy—

CASSIDY. What should we do with it?

TONI. Well, obviously throw it away—

CASSIDY. The whole box?

TONI. Yes. This is disgusting.

RHYS. (*Having noticed the open album somewhere.*) Oh shit!

TONI. / Rhys!

FRANZ. (*Snatching the album away.*) Whoa.

RHYS. Sorry! What—

FRANZ. Don't touch / those.

CASSIDY. What / happened?

RHYS. I thought they were just some—

CASSIDY. What's going / on?

RHYS. What are those?!

CASSIDY. What's in that? Can I see?!

TONI. We'll explain later. Go finish upstairs, you two.

CASSIDY. (*To* RHYS.) What did you see?

RHYS. (*Gesturing.*) They were pictures of / like—

TONI. Rhys! What did I just say?

CASSIDY. Why can't I know?!

(BO *re-enters, ready for a fight.*)

BO. Toni!

CASSIDY. (*Running to her father.*) Daddy!

BO. What is it, sweetie?

(*Re: the jar in her hand.*)

Jesus, what is / that?

CASSIDY. What are those photos?

BO. (*Shooting his siblings a look, incensed.*) What!?

TONI. Rhys accidentally saw it. And then we took it away before Cassidy could.

CASSIDY. Is it naked pictures or something? I've seen pornography before.

(*Beat.*)

BO. Excuse me!?

CASSIDY. I mean—I don't like look at it, but I've seen it. I'm almost an adult!

BO. (*Explosive.*) Cassidy, enough! Do you want to lose your phone?

(*Beat.*)

Go find your mother. She needs help with your brother.

(*Beat, before* CASSIDY *exits grumpily through the kitchen.* RHYS *stands there.*)

RHYS. (*To* TONI.) / What's happening?

FRANZ. (*To* BO.) She didn't see anything.

TONI. (*To* RHYS.) / Throw that stuff away and finish the study, please. I'll be up in a little bit. We'll talk.

(RHYS *exits.*)

BO. (*To* FRANZ.) I don't give a shit! Get rid of those things right now before she does and—

(*Wheeling around on* TONI.)

Toni, what are you thinking? Rachael came all the way down here because she actually wanted to help!

TONI. Implying, based on nothing, that our father was some sort of bigot— She calls that / help?

BO. So you call her a kike?

TONI. You know I didn't mean it like that! It was a joke!

BO. Oh! Well, it didn't sound like a joke, Toni! She didn't take it like a joke—!

TONI. So am I now the anti-Semite? And what's the word for her? What was that "Jew wife" moment? "Bo and his Jew wife"— Our father doesn't even sound like that!

BO. Rachael's relationship to our father was her relationship! Okay?! Leave it alone!

TONI. (*Gasp, realizing.*) Oh my god— You agree with her, don't you!? You think he was a—

BO. I'm not getting into this with you— In fact, I don't care! Just go frickin' apologize!

TONI. I am / not apologizing!

BO. Fix something! You lost the house! You've screwed up the auction! Just do one thing that is actually going to help everyone! Stop being such a terrorist!

> (*Reaching for the photos.*)

Frank, give me the photos— I'll toss them out—

TONI. Name one thing—name one instance of our father's…prejudice. Either of you! Yes, he was a little aloof—kept to himself—but that was just his personality. And, okay, he didn't like Rachael. It wasn't because she was Jewish. It was because she is an annoying person—

FRANZ. Wait a minute. Back up.

> (*Beat.*)

Toni, you lost the house?

> (*Beat.*)

TONI. No, I didn't lose the house!

FRANZ. Then what is Bo talking about? I thought you guys were selling the place tomorrow?

BO. We're supposed to. To pay off the debt…?

FRANZ. What debt?

BO. Frank, we're paying back a half million dollars in loans?

FRANZ. What loans?

BO. The ones our father took out to turn this place into the Bed and Breakfast that never was—

TONI. The lawyers didn't tell you any of this?

BO. Yeah— What did you think is going on here?

FRANZ. I thought you were just getting rid of the place and splitting the money—

TONI. I thought you weren't here for money.

FRANZ. I'm not.

TONI. Then why are you suddenly so worried about it—

FRANZ. I'm not worried about the money. I'm worried about the house—

TONI. Why?

FRANZ. Because I grew up here! How did you lose it, Toni?

TONI. I did not lose it!

BO. Daddy either stopped making payments or forgot to make payments and Toni didn't catch it in time—

TONI. I didn't catch it—

BO. Toni, it was your job to keep track of his mail!

> (RIVER *has quietly come through the swinging door and stood next to* FRANZ.)

TONI. My— / What?!

RIVER. (*To* FRANZ.) What's happening?

FRANZ. Toni lost the house.

> (BO *and* TONI *stop fighting, having noticed* RIVER'*s presence.* TONI *wheels around.*)

TONI. I did not lose the house and if I hear someone say that one more time, I'll beat the piss out of all of you!

> (*To* FRANZ.)

If anyone lost the house, it's you! This debt is all yours anyway!

FRANZ. How is this my fault?

TONI. Does this place look like a Bed and frickin' Breakfast? Did any of that money go into this house? Or do you think it went into taking care of you for twenty-odd years—keeping you clothed and fed? Or did you take it, Frank? How much did you drink through? How much did you smoke through? How much did you need to run away to Oregon?

> (*Turning on* BO.)

And your job was handling the finances. Why didn't you catch this? Why couldn't you talk to the bank? Oh, right—because you pawned it off on Tanya or Sonya or whoever-the-hell.

> (*Turning on* RIVER.)

And what are you still doing here!?

FRANZ. Hey! Do not scream at her!

> (*To* RIVER.)

Why are we here?! / Why am I doing this?

TONI. Bo, he's wide-awake now. Can we get them out of here please? We've got work to do.

BO. What is going on?

RIVER. Do it now. Now is the time. You can do it.

TONI. Oh my god— Actually, Frank, she's right. Since we're all here, why don't you go ahead and tell Bo what you came here to do? See if he can use it, because I sure as hell can't—

BO. Will someone tell me what is going on?

TONI. He came here to "apologize"!

FRANZ. TONI!

TONI. You know, maybe you can give that apology to Bo to give to Rachael, since she is apparently looking for one? And then when you're done, you two can go!

> (*Beat.* FRANZ *looks to* RIVER, *who gives him an encouraging look, maybe mouths something like, "Now," and tries to disappear into the background.* FRANZ *addresses his siblings.* RIVER *mouths along for part of it.*)

FRANZ. So. Um. I know it's been a very long time since we've all seen each other—let alone been in the same room together—over ten years now— even longer since I've seen you, Bo. And I know that those last few years were extremely rough and I did a lot of things that I am not proud of but I am here to let you see that I have been working very hard for a while now to become a better person—the person that I know, need, and want myself to be—and part of that recovery is about forgiveness—asking for forgiveness and also forgiving those who you feel have wronged you in some way. So I am here to apologize, because I want you all to be a part of my life again and I would like to be a part of yours.

> (*Beat, before* TONI *raises her hand.*)

TONI. Pardon me, and what exactly are we being "forgiven" for?

FRANZ. I don't think that's important.

TONI. I kind of think it is, because maybe we want to apologize, too. What exactly did we do?

> (*Beat, in which* FRANZ *looks to* RIVER, *who nods.*)

FRANZ. You two left me here with a mentally ill man when I was just a kid. And I've had to live with the consequences of that my whole life.

> (*Beat.*)

TONI. (*Head in her hands.*) Lord, what else!? What else can we say about this man?

> (*Beat, breath, looks up.*)

Okay. Well, first of all, our father was not mentally ill—

FRANZ. Okay— Mentally unstable—

TONI. He wasn't "unstable" either—

FRANZ. Toni, you didn't live in this house with him!

TONI. And how would you describe this "instability," / Frank?

FRANZ. I think our father was bipolar—undiagnosed. He was obviously a hoarder—not to mention severely depressed after our mother died—but you and Bo never saw this, because you were never here! I was!

> (*Beat.*)

TONI. Okay and, second of all, what are these consequences you feel you've been living with as a result?

(*Beat.* FRANK *hesitates, again.* RIVER *encourages him, again.*)

FRANZ. I just believe that that experience may be why I abused certain substances, why I drank—

TONI. Okay— And is it also our father's fault that you got caught with all these little girls you found on the internet—

FRANZ. That is not what— Why would you / bring that up—!

RIVER. (*Raising her hand, beat.*) ...Franz, it's fine. It's okay. Answer her question.

(*Beat, as* TONI *is dumbfounded by* RIVER. RIVER *encourages* FRANZ *again.*)

FRANZ. (*Uncomfortable.*) I take responsibility for my actions, but I did those things in a time when I was struggling with addiction—I was not myself and I believe that this environment and growing up with that man had a lot to do with that.

TONI. Okay, Frank. And, finally, where was this lunatic, bipolar father these last ten years I was taking care of him? Or, better yet, the ten years before that when I was taking care of both of you?

FRANZ. / What are you talking about?

TONI. You are the last person to accuse me of abandonment. When I took you in every holiday—every Christmas, every Thanksgiving—when I was here every other month—cooking you meals, doing your laundry, breaking up fights. But this isn't about me. If Daddy was crazy it was because you drove him there. This man wore himself down trying to save you. We all did. Do Bo and I have a childhood home to cry over? No, because when our mother died and you started acting like a menace back in Washington, getting kicked out of every school for getting into fights, drinking at the tender age of thirteen, our father uprooted our entire life, our entire family, for you—to bring you out here—

FRANZ. To start a Bed and Breakfast—

TONI. No, this house was supposed to save you—

FRANZ. How was moving me out to Bumblefuck supposed to save me?!?

TONI. Because it was a chance to be good, Frank!— Which you were obviously incapable of, because guess what? You are a poison—as you've proven over and over again. So I don't buy this. There is nothing new about you. Don't you see? You are not different. You are the same thing you've always been—chaos—a selfish chaos! Even now—the only man we all shared is dead, we are in mourning, and we are literally left with nothing— and you thought this would be the perfect time to show up out of the blue—

making this all about you and your healing with your walking rape fantasy over here—

(RIVER *takes a step forward and maybe grabs* FRANZ's *hand defiantly.*)

RIVER. Let's keep this about his relationship with you.

TONI. Wow. Thank you.

(*To* FRANZ.)

And how exactly was this supposed to end, Frank? You apologize and we all hug it out and tomorrow, after the auction, you'd get your share? Or what? How stupid do you think we are?

(*Beat.*)

RIVER. For the record, you don't have a legal right to withhold anything from him, unless you can show us a will that states otherwise.

TONI. And what are you—a lawyer?

RIVER. My parents are. I'm just his fiancée.

(*Beat.*)

TONI. (*Flabbergasted.*) Uhhhhhhhhhhhh / hhhhhhhhhh—?

BO. Frank… I accept your apology and I apologize for any wrongs you feel I've done to you. I know how hard it must have been to come here and do this—

TONI. What are you doing?

BO. I'm talking to Frank.

TONI. You have got to be kidding—

BO. What are you suddenly? The forgiveness police?

TONI. (*To* BO.) I might be, because this here is a crime! That apology isn't yours! I lost the hours! You lost nothing! I looked after him and Daddy, exposed my kid to this shitshow and probably fucked him up as a result! I took care of our father when he ran away, while you just got to sit back, write a check and watch from the box seats! This man might as well be a stranger to you. So guess what? That apology isn't yours! That forgiveness isn't yours! It's mine! You don't get anything!

BO. You are so disgusting. Can you even see yourself right now—?

TONI. I just realized: you two are the same—

BO. Have you lost your mind?

TONI. No! It was stolen from me— You two took it— The same way you took everything—the same way you took my life, my time, and I'm wasting even more of my life sitting here and fighting with you—and for what?

BO. Good question, because, at this point, there's not a single person in this house that's on your side. Not me. Not Rachael. Not Frank. Not even your own son can stand you, Toni. So ask yourself why. Ask yourself… You're like—like—like toxic— You might be the poison.

TONI. You're right. I quit. I quit.

(TONI *grabs her purse, maybe a jacket, and starts to leave.*)

BO. (*Exasperated, annoyed.*) Please. Please be done, Toni. Sure.

TONI. Enjoy forgiving each other! I hope you forgive each other all night long. Allow me to suck the poison of my sick, toxic self from your sorry, sorry veins, you bunch of sorry, sorry people.

(TONI *holds her keys above her head, presses a button, and there is the brief electronic tooting of her car unlocking itself outside. Beat, before she quickly exits out the front door.* BO *and* FRANZ *and* RIVER *look at each other. There is the sound of* TONI *crunching across gravel, getting into her car, slamming the door, the car starting, the car driving away.*)

BO. I shouldn't have said that.

FRANZ. Said what?

(*Beat, as* BO *remembers his brother is there.*)

BO. The thing about Rhys.

FRANZ. What happened with Rhys?

BO. Oh, right… He's moving in with his father.

FRANZ. Why? Wait—Toni and Derek split?

BO. Yes—a year ago. Then Rhys was caught last fall selling pills at school. Some kid died. Rhys got convicted. Toni was fired.

FRANZ. Why was she fired?

BO. She was principal at the school… She was forced to resign. It was a whole thing… I can't tell if she's losing her mind or if she's already lost it.

FRANZ. She thinks I had something to do with it? She said I fucked him up—I—

BO. Rhys is not fucked up. His life is over, but he's not fucked up. He's a good kid—and lucky— They tried him as a minor. And I think moving out isn't such a bad idea for him. Obviously. Still, I shouldn't have said that.

RIVER. Should we be worried about her?

BO. No. What's she going to do? Kill herself? She'll be back.

(*Beat.*)

Where else does she have to go?

(*Beat.*)

Maybe now I can actually try to figure out how to salvage this mess.

RIVER. What needs to happen?

BO. A miracle. We probably won't be able to give this place away tomorrow—

FRANZ. Why not?

BO. The graveyard's depreciated the property value. This whole thing is a nightmare.

> (*Beat, as* BO *doesn't know what to do.*)

I need to find Rachael.

> (*Re: the photographs, to* FRANZ.)

Throw those things in the trash, will you?

> (BO *exits up the stairs.* FRANZ *and* RIVER *are alone. Beat.*)

RIVER. She's meaner than you'd described.

FRANZ. She's meaner than I remember.

RIVER. It sounds like she's been through a lot.

> (*Beat.*)

Well, anyway, you did it.

FRANZ. Yeah, right. You told me I'd feel different. I don't feel any different. I feel like shit.

RIVER. It's a process, Franz. That was just a step. The place is still in your bones and you need to let it go. And, tomorrow, when you see it's gone, you won't be haunted by it anymore. We'll be done and you'll be free. It'll become someone else's problem.

FRANZ. Unless they can't sell it. You heard Bo. Because of the cemetery.

RIVER. Yeah—what was he talking about?

FRANZ. The one outside?

RIVER. What?

FRANZ. (*Gesturing out a window.*) See all those stones? That little gate?

RIVER. (*Looking out the window.*) That's not a garden? I thought it was a cute little— Stop! / Stop messing with me.

FRANZ. (*Looking out the window.*) I guess it sort of looks like a— What, it's true! It's just overgrown. And the tombstones were just knocked over. See? It's the family plot. Five generations of us are out there.

> (*Beat, then* RIVER *hits him.*)

River—

RIVER. Why didn't you tell me we were sleeping next to a cemetery!

> (*Gasps, realizing.*)

I forgot my candles! I knew I should have brought sage!

FRANZ. Will you stop it—

RIVER. Stop what? Spirits are real and our bodies are just porous vessels of energy waiting to be…occupied and corrupted, okay? Don't look at me like that— We have to respect the dead. They are everywhere. No wonder I've been feeling so weird! You know I'm sensitive!

FRANZ. River, there are no ghosts here. Trust me. I would know. No one is being possessed— You and these stupid fortunetellers—

RIVER. (*Looking out.*) Spiritual advisors. And they are not stupid.

(*Beat.*)

Your father's not out there, is he?

FRANZ. No. I think they had him buried back in D.C., next to my mom.

(*Beat, then pointing out the window.*)

You see that lake there?

RIVER. Yeah...?

FRANZ. Well, through those woods alongside it is where all the slaves were buried, but you have to go looking for that. They don't have grave markers or anything... I wonder if that's the one Bo was talking about...

(*Beat—a long one.*)

BOO!

RIVER. (*Shrieks a little, then:*) STOP! YOU JERK!

(*Re: the album between them.*)

What is this?

FRANZ. (*Embarrassed.*) Something I gotta throw away.

RIVER. What? Are they baby pictures or something?

(*Wrestling it away.*)

Give it to me—

FRANZ. River No!

RIVER. (*Looks at it.*) Oh my god!

(*Drops the album, having felt something.*)

Franz, what was that?

FRANZ. (*Looks at her, confused.*) What was what?

(*BLACKOUT, cicadas.*)

act two: walpurgisnacht, or possessions

The living room, the middle of the night.

CASSIDY *and* RIVER *are huddled up together on the couch, looking through the photo album. For a substantial stretch of quiet, they page through the album, slowly, deliberately and with a certain solemnity.*

A candle is lit on the table in front of them.

There is a faint scent of order in the air. Display tables or pallets seem to be set up, fewer things seem to clutter the floor. Something has been done with the place, which is barely discernible in the dark.

CASSIDY. (*Sniffs the candle.*) This doesn't smell like anything.

RIVER. I don't think it's supposed to.

CASSIDY. Then why did you light it?

RIVER. (*Shrug.*) I just like candlelight sometimes.

CASSIDY. Why?

RIVER. It helps me feel safe.

CASSIDY. Safe from what?

RIVER. I don't know. I just feel weird around cemeteries.

CASSIDY. Why? What are you afraid of? Zombies? Ghosts? Ghosts are for children.

RIVER. I wouldn't be so sure about that.

(*Beat, in which they return to looking at the photos.*)

CASSIDY. (*Seeing something.*) Ew.

(*Beat.*)

RIVER. Wait— Are your parents okay with you seeing these?

CASSIDY. Yeah— I've already seen them— Like when we found them— How did you get them?

RIVER. I guess I'm supposed to throw them away, but... I don't know... It just seems like it would be disrespectful.

CASSIDY. To who?

RIVER. To the people in these pictures.

CASSIDY. You think they care? They're dead.

RIVER. I do.

CASSIDY. Uh, okay...

(*Pointing.*)

Ewwww— What happened to that guy's eye?— Why are his pants around his ankles?— OMG, look at that little girl in the crowd... She's smiling... What do you think they did?... Hello?

RIVER. Hm?

CASSIDY. These guys are being punished, right? Isn't that why they hung people back then? What do you think they're being punished for? Or do you think it's just random—what's happening to them?

RIVER. I don't know…

CASSIDY. Why do you think Grandpa had all these?

RIVER. I didn't know your grandfather but people collect all sorts of things…

CASSIDY. But isn't this sort of like…racist?

RIVER. Your parents didn't tell you anything about these?

CASSIDY. No… I never really knew Grandpa, either. We used to, like, call him on his birthday when I was little, but that stopped. And I have this memory of going to Thanksgiving at Aunt Toni's house once and he was there, but…that's it. This whole family's like that though—I barely even knew Uncle Franz like even existed…

> (*Beat.*)

It's probably good you're keeping these. They might be worth something.

RIVER. Really?

CASSIDY. Yeah—you can sell anything on the internet.

> (*Pulling out her phone to Google.*)

Let's find out. "Money…for…photos…of…dead…people—question mark?"

RIVER. Do not Google that! Use, um…"antique photos—"

CASSIDY. "of dead people?"

RIVER. (*Back to the photos.*) Yes…

CASSIDY. (*Types then the page loads.*) There's definitely stuff… "19ᵗʰ century war photos"… "Post-mortem photos"… Yeah, there's a lot.

> (*Typing.*)

"… dead black people…"

RIVER. Cassidy…

CASSIDY. What? I mean, they are black…

> (*Something loads.*)

Same stuff— Oh, they think I mean "Black and white photos"—

> (*Typing again.*)

"African… American…"

RIVER. (*Closing the book.*) Okay, you know what? That's enough. We should stop.

CASSIDY. Why? I wasn't done looking.

RIVER. Aren't these upsetting?

CASSIDY. Am I supposed to be upset?

RIVER. I don't know…

    (*Beat.*)

CASSIDY. Do you have Daddy issues?

RIVER. Excuse me?

CASSIDY. Whenever we see a younger woman with an older man, my mom is always saying she has "Daddy issues."

RIVER. Has she said that about me?

CASSIDY. No. But I bet she's thinking it.

RIVER. Well, I don't have any "Daddy issues."

    (*Beat.*)

CASSIDY. What are "Daddy issues"?

RIVER. Why don't you Google it?

CASSIDY. I already have. I don't understand it.

RIVER. You'll understand when you're older.

CASSIDY. (*A little explosion.*) Why do people always say that?! Don't you know that every day my brain has less and less gray matter? Pretty soon, it'll be too late for me to learn anything new. Every time you keep a secret, you're retarding me!

RIVER. Sorry. It's not a secret. It's just nonsense that's a waste of your time.

CASSIDY. I'm assuming you know why Uncle Franz ran away?

RIVER. I do.

CASSIDY. OMG tell me— Did he kill someone?

RIVER. What? No? Your parents never told you?

CASSIDY. No. They don't tell me anything. And I asked Rhys and he doesn't know either.

RIVER. Well… Your Uncle Franz had to leave because this wasn't a good environment for him. It made him do things that weren't good for him. Like drink a lot. He got into a lot of trouble.

CASSIDY. That is so vague. What kind of trouble?

RIVER. Well, like, he did some kind of not so great things to some friends, who were girls.

CASSIDY. What kind of things?

RIVER. He just…didn't respect their boundaries. He touched them… inappropriately.

    (*Off* CASSIDY's *reaction.*)

But, like I said, he was drinking a lot and that impairs your judgment. That's why you shouldn't drink. You're not your real self when you drink.

CASSIDY. Okay…

> (*Beat.*)

Hey… Am I sexy?

RIVER. Uh— I don't— You should ask your mom—

CASSIDY. Ew. No. Never. Why can't you tell me?

RIVER. I don't know if I should be talking about this with you.

CASSIDY. Why not? Aren't you, like, family?

> (*Beat.*)

RIVER. You're just too young to worry about being sexy.

CASSIDY. When will I be old enough?

RIVER. Um—when you're eighteen?

CASSIDY. Hm… Do you think Rhys is sexy?

RIVER. Uh—no—do you?

CASSIDY. I don't know. Do you think he's gay?

RIVER. I don't know— Do you?

CASSIDY. My mom is always saying Aunt Toni's turning him gay.

RIVER. I don't think that's how it works…

CASSIDY. We'll see…

> (*Beat. Quietly,* TONI *has entered through the front door. She sees the two girls and silently creeps up behind them on the couch. She sways a little, tipsily.*)

RIVER. Oh my god, do you have a crush on your cousin?

CASSIDY. No!

RIVER. You totally do!

CASSIDY. No I don't!

RIVER. It's okay. Aw, I used to have a crush on my cousin when I was your age. It's very common actually. You'll grow out of it. I grew out of mine.

CASSIDY. Rhys is sort of cute, but I don't have a crush on him!

RIVER. Mhm…

CASSIDY. Stop! I'm just obsessed with this family. My mom's family is so boring and judgmental. At least these people are interesting, but my parents won't tell me anything. The whole point of this trip was to learn about Daddy's family and, instead, all I've done is babysit all day and I could have done that in New York and taken an extra bio class and been with my friends. I'm so bored. Wait—can we take a picture together?

RIVER. Sure.

CASSIDY. You're so West Coast. My friends are gonna flip.

> (*They huddle together and pose for a picture in front of* CASSIDY's *camera before they notice, in the phone's camera, that* TONI *has been standing behind*

them. They startle, perhaps scream. TONI *looks around at the space, takes in the order, bristles and breathes.)*

Aunt Toni!

RIVER. Oh my god, Toni! You scared me!

TONI. Good.

RIVER. How long have you been standing there?

TONI. Wouldn't you like to know.

(Re: *the order.)*

What is going on here?

RIVER. Oh, uh— We've almost set everything up for the sale tomorrow! All the soft goods and small appliances are in here; the big electronics are in the dining room; kitchen stuff's in the kitchen. The only room we still have to do in the morning is your father's bedroom. Rhys said he wasn't feeling well so we left him alone in there to rest.

(TONI *has noticed the photograph album near* CASSIDY, *snatches it away.)*

TONI. Cassidy, what are you doing with this?!

CASSIDY. Please don't tell!

RIVER. Uh— I'm sorry I was down here looking at them and she walked in and—

TONI. And what are you doing with them?

RIVER. I was supposed to throw them away but I thought I would hang onto them—

TONI. These are not yours to hang on to—!

CASSIDY. Don't be mad at Aunt River! It's my fault—I just wanted to know and it's not fair that Rhys got to see them and I didn't! I'm almost an adult.

TONI. No you are not—

CASSIDY. Please don't tell! I'm not, like, traumatized by them, see?! And you know how Mom and Dad will just overreact like they do about everything and then they'll take away my phone and then I'll have nothing else to do around here but kill myself and they were just going to throw them away anyway. And I probably already know more about them than they think I do—probably more than they do!

RIVER. She was very mature about them. She was asking all the right questions. She was using the internet. We even figured out that they might be worth something.

(Beat.)

TONI. (*Not taking her eyes off* RIVER.) Cassidy, go put these in my car.

CASSIDY. Why me?

TONI. Your "Aunties" need to talk. You're lucky I think you're smarter than your parents, too, but if I catch you with these again, you're in big trouble.

(CASSIDY *exits through the front door with the photos.* TONI—*sizing up* RIVER—*raises her keys over her head and presses the button on the door unlocker thing. There is a brief electronic tooting outside.*)

RIVER. She told me she had already seen them but I was here with her the whole time—

TONI. So what's your real name, River?... You're not going to tell me your parents actually named you that?

(*Beat.*)

RIVER. (*A concession.*) My name used to be Trisha, but I changed it. Like Franz. Because we both needed—

TONI. Uh huh and how old are you really? Eighteen? Nineteen? Eighteen?

RIVER. I'm twenty-three, but thank you.

(*Beat.*)

I may look young, but I know a few things, okay?

TONI. Well, do you know what's happening here? That tomorrow, the bank is taking everything? So there's no money to be made—

RIVER. Toni, we have our own money. Do you really think we got in our car and drove twenty hours across the country to come make a fuss over some old junk? If we wanted to, we could have taken what his father left him with a phone call—but we didn't. This is mostly my fault—his being here—When Franz heard the news, he was...a mess. Not eating, wouldn't get out of bed. Wouldn't talk. Dark... Just darkness—and Franz has worked too hard on himself to go...back. So I told him, "Get up. We have to go." Because Franz is haunted, Toni— And I know—the timing may not have been the best for you—but grief is an old, powerful thing—so is mourning. So is family. That's why we need things like forgiveness and rituals—funerals—to heal—to move forward. And Franz was denied his, so we're having our own. He's entitled to closure.

TONI. And how's your mother, River?

RIVER. She's fine.

TONI. Oh, okay, because when I was your age, mine was dead and it was a very ugly and slow and painful death. So I don't need you to come in here with your "old soul" giving me the notes from your hippy community college Anthro seminar on grief and mourning because I've been through the real thing. Twice—

RIVER. Toni, I know you're hurt. I hated watching the way you and your brothers were speaking to each other earlier. I hope that isn't how it's always been.

(*Going in for a hug or just touching her.*)

You know what you need? You need a sister. I have three of them and you wouldn't imagine the difference it makes. Women need other women. We need other women to talk to, to share secrets with. Otherwise, I think we become monsters—to each other—to ourselves.

TONI. I'll tell you what I need—I need you to get away from me.

(*An a-ha moment.*)

Oh no. I've had you all wrong. I just figured you out. You're one of those sweet girls, aren't you? Aren't people always calling you that? "Sweet." You think I was never twenty-three, running around being "sweet," thinking I knew everything, that I was gonna save somebody with my love. And do you know what happens to sweet girls? Life gobbles us up. And do you know why? Because we run around making ourselves so tasty, thinking we've got some unlimited supply of sugar to run around sprinkling all over everyone's shit—but here's something no one ever told me: it runs out. And there are people out there with a sweet tooth, like Frank, and if you're not careful they'll take it all—so you better be careful. Save some of that sweetness for you. You'll need it.

RIVER. Franz has got sweetness in him, too, Toni. Why can't you see it?

TONI. You're not going to save a grown man! Especially not Frank. Can't you see I already tried? This whole family's tried. Look around you. This whole house was one big try.

(CASSIDY *has snuck back into the house, the photos in her arms, but she holds back—eavesdropping.*)

RIVER. Well, no offense, Toni, but we're not the same person. And Franz and I are in love. And love is not something that runs out. Real love is infinite. Real love changes.

TONI. And how do you do that?

RIVER. Do what?

TONI. Love a pervert.

(*Beat.*)

RIVER. The secret, Toni, is that I don't care. I forgive him. It's that easy. People can't live their whole life under all that guilt—especially guilt for things you did when you were under the influence. God knows I know something about that. And that's something hard for people to understand—especially people who I guess have never done a thing in their lives they regret—but me and Franz—get that about each other. That's a place where we connect—where our love begins—because love changes. Love is changing us. It's giving us a second chance.

TONI. Well good luck.

RIVER. We're already having it because we're having a baby!

TONI. What?

RIVER. (*Giddy.*) Oh gosh! I haven't told anyone yet! Not even Franz.

TONI. What?

RIVER. I was planning to—tomorrow—as a part of our ritual. After the house gets sold, we're going to camp in the woods out back. We are going to reconnect with the Earth—this old Earth—and with the land this old house is built on—build a fire, tell stories, make s'mores—once we were climbing into our sleeping bags under the stars—that was when I was going to tell him—let his final memories of this place be filled with joy, let him know his life was really, truly, finally about to change!

> (*Beat.*)

See? Now we're going to be sisters and we have a secret.

> (BO *comes down the stairs, heavily. He sees* TONI *and freezes.*)

BO. Toni? Where the heck have you been?

> (CASSIDY, *hearing her father's voice and afraid of being caught with the photos, sneaks back out!*)

TONI. Out.

BO. Hey River, where is Frank?

RIVER. He should be upstairs sleeping— Do you want me to get him?

BO. No, it's okay—but do you know where he threw away the photos?

TONI. He didn't throw them away. She's got 'em.

RIVER. I just couldn't throw them out— I'm sorry—

BO. No— That's good! Where are they now?

> (RIVER *and* TONI *exchange glances.*)

RIVER. Uh—

TONI. I put them in my car. Why? You suddenly want them?

BO. Rachael does.

TONI. Oh really?

BO. Yes, because tomorrow we have to have an Emergency Family Meeting about the entire history of our country's…bullshit and she apparently needs visual aids.

RIVER. I'll leave you two alone…

> (*To* TONI.)

Between us girls, okay?

> (RIVER *exits.* BO *seems puzzled.*)

TONI. She's pregnant.

BO. What?

TONI. She and Frank are going to have a baby—

BO. What am I supposed to do with this information?

TONI. You could mourn that poor little girl's life. She doesn't know what she's done.

BO. Toni— Have you been drinking?

TONI. Yup.

BO. Alone?

TONI. Nope. I found a friend. Since I don't have any in this house.

BO. Who?

TONI. Juanita.

BO. You got drunk with our father's nurse?

TONI. Yes. I needed to find somebody who actually knew Daddy—who actually might have liked the man, maybe even missed him. Just to make sure I wasn't going nuts. Because I was beginning to think I'd hallucinated a father. She said he was the nicest man she'd ever worked for. Also! She didn't think he was a racist, and she's black.

BO. You actually asked her that? She was our employee, Toni. What else was she going to say?

(*Beat.*)

TONI. How long have I been a villain?

BO. What?

TONI. The family crazy? How long have I disgusted you? Or is this a new thing?

BO. Toni, you're drunk—

TONI. You see there's something wrong with me. What is it, Bo? I can't see it? I go back over my entire life and— Wasn't I doing the right thing? Wasn't I taking care of people, taking care of Daddy? Wasn't I loving?

BO. I guess…

TONI. Then why am I so unhappy now? What's wrong with me? Help me— Tell me!

BO. Toni, I don't know! I don't know, okay? I don't know why we are the way we are, Toni.

TONI. Is this the way I am? Have I always been this way? How can I change?

BO. You're drunk. You need to just go to bed.

TONI. Why doesn't Rhys want to be with me? Am I a bad mother?

(*Beat.*)

BO. There's no rulebook, Toni. Besides, how were you supposed to know what a mother was?

TONI. I had a mother. We had a mother.

BO. Not long enough.

TONI. How long do you need one?

> (*Beat.* CASSIDY *is seen, poking her head in, annoyed that her father is still here.*)

BO. Well. Look at Frank.

> (*Beat.*)

How did we ever think that this Bed and Breakfast nonsense would be a good idea for the two of them?

TONI. We thought it would give them something to do.

BO. And what did they do with it? I mean, look at this place. What's the point of owning anything? Possessions—they just become a burden, an embarrassment. Do you think Daddy even had any idea what half of this stuff was?

TONI. Who knows? It's just life. Being alive, you just accrue things.

BO. How in the world do you accrue this much crap in twenty years?

TONI. You think you've got time to use it.

BO. Well, let it go! I think that's our lesson today. Let it all go! It's not like any of us wanted this godforsaken place anyway—or any of this crap.

> (RACHAEL *comes downstairs.*)

RACHAEL. Bo—!

> (RACHAEL *sees* BO *and* TONI. *She freezes. There is a seething between the two women.*)

Did you find them?

BO. No, but they're in Toni's car.

RACHAEL. Fine. Well hurry up so we can finish up our plan. I'm getting sleepy.

> (RACHAEL *exits into the kitchen.*)

BO. Why don't you just apologize?

TONI. Why doesn't she?

BO. All she tried to say was that these things were his.

TONI. We don't even know if they're his.

BO. We don't know they weren't. And now we'll never know. You think you'd be sure to burn something like this before you die—

TONI. Well your pal River didn't seem to think so. She told me she thinks they're valuable.

> (RHYS *is seen at the top of the stairs, carrying his pillow, the quilt.*)

BO. Really? The thought actually crossed my mind that these things might be worth something. It looks like these are some sort of weird...historical thing. And there's a lot of them. So maybe they are some sort of sick-o collectors' item. I'm half-tempted to try selling them off tomorrow to one of these local yokels with everything else— Though they are pretty old— I wonder if we should try to get a proper appraisal. I should talk to someone.

TONI. What happened to "let it go"?

BO. Toni, shut up.

>   (*Beat.*)

How did you deal with this, by the way?

TONI. What do you mean?

BO. With Rhys— What did you tell him?

TONI. I haven't told him anything. I mean, what is there to explain that he hasn't had in a history class?

BO. I don't remember hearing about these in any class…

TONI. Am I a bad mother—yes or no?

>   (RACHAEL *re-enters from the kitchen with a class of water.* BO *and* TONI *notice. Beat.*)

RACHAEL. Bo…

>   (BO *gets up to exit.*)

BO. Go to bed, Toni.

>   (*Seeing* RHYS.)

Hi Rhys.

RACHAEL. Feeling better?

>   (RHYS *nods.* RACHAEL *and* BO *exit upstairs.*)

TONI. Are you sick?

RHYS. No. But I had to tell them something so they would leave me alone. Where have you been? I've been calling you.

TONI. My phone died— I'm sorry— I went to Juanita's—

RHYS. For eight hours? Why did you leave me here with them? I fucking hate these people!

TONI. Don't say that.

RHYS. I do. They're so condescending to me—and to you. I don't like seeing people act like that to you. Why is Uncle Bo such a dick?

TONI. He isn't.

RHYS. Yes he is. He and Rachael both, bossing everyone around like a couple of Jews—

TONI. (*Scolding.*) Rhys—don't say that!

RHYS. All they talked about was money and how much they thought everything was worth. It was disgusting.

(*Beat.*)

TONI. Well… Don't worry about that anymore. I fixed it.

RHYS. You did?

TONI. Yup. You'll see. Tomorrow, we take back what they stole from us.

RHYS. Take back what?

TONI. Our time. We're even.

RHYS. Are you drunk?

TONI. No, I'm not drunk.

> (CASSIDY, *seeing her father gone, finally comes back inside—but stops short and hangs back, noticing* TONI *and* RHYS *having an intimate something or other.*)

RHYS. I've never seen you drunk before.

TONI. I'm not drunk, Rhys.

> (*Beat.*)

Do we need to talk about those photos you saw earlier?

RHYS. I don't know. Do we?

TONI. Did you learn about them in school?

RHYS. No, but, I mean, I can guess.

TONI. Okay. Do you have any questions?

> (*Beat.*)

RHYS. Did they belong to Grandpa?

> (*Beat.*)

TONI. We don't know. We'll never know.

> (*Beat.*)

Are you sleeping down here?

RHYS. Yeah. Uncle Frank took the extra bedroom.

TONI. Oh, crap—that's right. Well, do you want to come up and sleep in Grandpa's bed with me?

> (*Beat.*)

RHYS. No.

TONI. Okay…

> (*Beat.*)

Well, can I have a hug?

RHYS. Uh, sure.

> (TONI *embraces* RHYS *with intensity.*)

TONI. You are such a good son.

RHYS. You're drunk.

TONI. Fine. I'm drunk, but I still wake up every morning and I thank God you're mine. Sweet dreams.

(TONI *exits.* RHYS *takes a minute to recover from that before he starts to set up his pallet on the couch, during which* CASSIDY *emerges from the shadows. She's relieved to see* RHYS *alone.*)

CASSIDY. Rhys!

RHYS. (*Startled.*) Cassie! WTF!

CASSIDY. Hey, sorry—

RHYS. What are you doing up?

CASSIDY. I was supposed to put these in your mom's car—

RHYS. Are those the—

CASSIDY. Yeah, long story—but she didn't unlock it right, because I think she was drunk, and now I don't know what to do. So can I just leave them with you? And in the morning, maybe you can put them in your mom's car?

RHYS. Uh…sure?

CASSIDY. You're the best.

(*Beat.*)

Are you feeling better?

RHYS. Yeah. A little. I just had to sleep.

CASSIDY. Okay…

(*Beat.*)

RHYS. Are you okay?

CASSIDY. Uh, yeah, sorry—uh—do you know anything about cicadas?

RHYS. Not really.

CASSIDY. Did you know that they're the oldest bugs on earth? They only appear every thirteen years and these bugs outside—they're thirteen years old. I just realized…they're about as old as I am. But this is, like, the end of their life. They're about to die. Can you imagine if I just like died last year? And do you know why they're singing?

RHYS. Not…really…

CASSIDY. It's because they're trying to find each other—to mate… But isn't it weird that they spend like all this time underground becoming teenagers, waiting to hatch, and then they just sing and sing for a few weeks in the summer and then they die? This is like—this song is like the peak of their existence. Like the whole point of their lives is to be able to sing so that they can get with another cicada and then they die before the kids are even born? And, also, how do the baby cicadas learn the song? Is it just something that's programmed in them? Or maybe they just pick it up somewhere, listening when they're eggs. Maybe they're hearing it in their sleep, and that's how they learn? And their parents are dead, but they have this memory of a song that they think is just a part of them?

RHYS. Cassidy, I don't know... Did something happen?

CASSIDY. I...don't know. I think I'm upset... See you in the morning.

RHYS. Good night.

(CASSIDY *exits upstairs.* RHYS *is left with the album of photos. He goes over to the couch, and sits down with them. He starts looking through them. There is a long while of* RHYS *looking at the photos, sort of distractedly. After a while, he puts the open photograph album to the side and stares into space, thinking. At some point, he tries to get to sleep. He can't. He takes out his smartphone. He clicks around on it. Something comes up and he starts playing it. There are the sounds of two men having sex. He puts his phone on mute quickly. Keeping his eyes on the screen, he puts his hand down his pants and starts masturbating. The photograph album stays open near him. This goes on for a little bit before we see* FRANZ *come down the stairs. He stops on the landing and watches* RHYS. *He doesn't exactly see what's going on, but he knows something is.*)

FRANZ. Hey, Rhys?

(*Panicked, frantic,* RHYS *quickly turns off the phone and hides it under the blanket and stops what he's doing.*)

RHYS. Hey— Yeah?

(FRANZ *comes downstairs over the following and stands next to* RHYS, *examining the scene.*)

FRANZ. What's going on dude?

RHYS. Nothing.

(*Beat.*)

FRANZ. Are you feeling better?

RHYS. Yeah, just...just trying to get some sleep now.

FRANZ. Okay.

(*Beat.*)

Do you remember me from when we used to hang out? You were just a kid, but do you remember—

RHYS. Yeah—at Christmas you would come...

FRANZ. Yeah. Well, I want to apologize if I was... You know, not a good Uncle or something— If I like, fucked you up, or something— I was like... another person then—

RHYS. (*Shrugging.*) You were a fine Uncle...?

FRANZ. Really?

(*Beat.*)

Do I seem different to you?

RHYS. Not really. A little older.

FRANZ. Cool. Well, good—

(*Noticing the photographs, beat.*)

Are those the—?

RHYS. (*Covering.*) Yeah… I was just, um, looking at them…

(*Beat, in which* FRANZ *doesn't know what to do and then suddenly decides to just go for it.*)

FRANZ. Okay dude—you know what?… I saw what you were doing— And, you know—I totally get it.

RHYS. (*Confused.*) You…do?

FRANZ. (*Struggling.*) Yeah, you know, it's like… You know, who are we? We're just things—these kind of bundles of nerves and feelings and confusion and we have so little that allows us to deal with ourselves or any of these things and like, you know. And, like, don't be ashamed or whatever— shame is deadly—but also know, you know, there are other ways to, you know, feel… There are other ways to deal with…urges—any urges—you know? Like you can always sort of…rewire…yourself, you know? If you need to.

RHYS. (*Not really sure what's going on.*) Uh huh…

FRANZ. I really struggled for a long time with something similar, you know, and I thought this thing was me, but it's not…you know. You…you… are bigger than that—than that thing. There's nothing wrong with being… with having these things, but…if, you want, you can be "normal," you know. I mean, what is normal, but you know? Like…I met River and I mean she's like…yeah…and I know what people think, or whatever…but it's like we're—it's like the thing in me that made me want that—or whatever—is kind of like…silenced. Or whatever? Because sometimes you need someone to step in and help you—give you strength to…deal with yourself.

(*Off* RHYS's *blank stare.*)

And, you know what? I'm gonna take these. If that's okay with you.

RHYS. Yeah, sure. I mean… I'm supposed to put them in Mom's car…

FRANZ. (*Taking the photos.*) Okay… I'll take care of them…

(FRANZ *exits.* RHYS *is alone—he is confused, humiliated, any number of things. You would be, too. He lies down on the couch and pulls the quilt over his head.*

BLACKOUT, cicadas.)

act three: the book of genesis

1.

The living room, the next morning.

Light reveals the extent to which the place has been completely organized. Neatness abounds. The objects which populated Ray's existence here are displayed and arranged about like the organs of some dissected animal. The order is almost oppressive. It's like a museum. Or a mausoleum. Not like a home at all.

RHYS *is still a blanketed figure on the couch.* RACHAEL *sits on the sofa's arm near his head.* RIVER *stands near the swinging door with two cups of coffee, observing. Occasionally, we hear the sounds of* CASSIDY *and* AINSLEY *in the next room, playing around, making animal noises, etc.*

RACHAEL. (*Gently trying to wake him up.*) Rhys… Rhys, sweetie…?

RHYS. Hm—huh?

RACHAEL. Hey, Rhys, I'm sorry to wake you up, but I think it's going to get a little busy down here in a bit. Do you want to go sleep in our bedroom?

RHYS. No… I should get up…

RACHAEL. Okay… And do you know when the sale's supposed to start? I don't know if your mother gave these people a specific time or not…

RHYS. Hm. No…

RACHAEL. Okay…

(*Beat.*)

And do you have a number for the guy who's running the auction?

RHYS. No…

RACHAEL. Okay…

(*Beat.*)

Would you do me a favor and get the number from your mother? I have some things I need to go over with him.

RHYS. Okay…

(*Beat.*)

RACHAEL. Could you do that now, honey?

RHYS. Yeah—sorry…

(RHYS *gets up and exits slowly up the stairs, uncomfortable. There is noise in the other room.*)

RACHAEL. (*To* RIVER.) See? You just gotta give these men a little push.

(*Poking her head into the den.*)

HEY! KEEP IT DOWN! YOUR AUNT TONI'S TRYING TO SLEEP!

(RACHAEL shares a little smile with RIVER before BO wanders in from somewhere, hanging up his phone and dialing a new number.)

Any luck?

BO. He just gave me some other guy's number to call. We might have something. Hold on.

(BO wanders out onto the porch.)

RACHAEL. *(Re: the couch, to RIVER.)* Can you help me push this against the wall? I wanna set up another—

RIVER. Oh, sure—

(Putting her coffee down.)

Rhys looked better—

(They push the couch against the wall, to clear out the floor, then they set up another table where the couch was—or maybe they move an already set-up table.)

RACHAEL. If he was ever sick to begin with. Though I don't blame him. What else do you do but lock yourself in a bedroom when your lunatic mother alienates your entire family? I just feel bad for the poor boy. No wonder he was slinging Oxycontin.

RIVER. Does Toni get this from Ray?

RACHAEL. Well, if you listen to Bo, she certainly didn't get it from Eleanor—

RIVER. Eleanor—

RACHAEL. Their mother?

(There is noise coming from the den.)

RIVER. I've never heard her name before.

RACHAEL. Hold on—

(Poking her head in the den.)

HEY! WHAT DID I SAY?

(The noise quiets down—for a little while. RACHAEL starts arranging things on the new table.)

RIVER. What was Ray like? I get a sense that he was…cruel.

RACHAEL. Cruel? Oh god no—I mean, the last time I spoke to the man was years ago—years and years ago—the man was definitely unpleasant— but he was certainly nothing to be afraid of. Ray was just…warped. That's the best way to put it. As is the case with all the men in this family…warped.

RIVER. Ha.

RACHAEL. Yeah, I bet you've figured it out already. Just remember: you are the sane one.

(BO wanders through.)

BO. Uh huh… Well, I haven't gotten a good look, but I'd say at least forty, fifty, sixty… / Uh huh…

(BO *wanders out just as* TONI *comes stalking downstairs, shutting everyone up. She is clearly hung over. There is some silence before:*)

RIVER. Good morning!

(TONI *can barely look at this girl. She heads straight into the kitchen.*)

I bet she's hung over.

RACHAEL. (*Goes over to the den.*) Cassidy?

CASSIDY. (*Entering from the den.*) What?!

RACHAEL. Your Aunt Toni is finally up. Take your brother upstairs and the two of you clean out that closet in his bedroom before we start.

CASSIDY. Ugh—!

RACHAEL. Just do it! And quickly!

CASSIDY. FINE!

(CASSIDY *stomps upstairs,* AINSLEY *in tow.*)

RACHAEL. FOLD EVERYTHING UP NICE AND NEAT AND THEN BRING IT / ALL DOWN!

CASSIDY. (*Offstage.*) OKAY! JESUS!

(BO *pokes his head in from the porch and motions to everyone to keep it down.*)

BO. Uh huh…well some of them looked like postcards, / but some were like, photo-photos. I'd have to look again…

(BO *wanders back out onto the porch.* TONI *re-enters. There is a charged beat, as the women all look at each other.*)

RACHAEL. Toni— I need the auctioneer's number so I can go over the inventory.

(TONI *ignores her, goes straight to the coffee maker, snatches it off the table, and goes straight back into the kitchen.*)

I am the only adult in a house full of children.

(*Beat.*)

RIVER. Just so you know, I don't have any Daddy issues…

RACHAEL. …That's wonderful…?

RIVER. I mean, in case you thought— Franz is actually the oldest guy I've ever—

RACHAEL. (*Putting up a hand.*) Uhp! River, no offense, but I don't care. You're not my daughter. Besides, it sounds like you know what you're getting yourself into. One day you'll have to tell me how you did it, but until then: enjoy the ride.

(*Shouting up the stairs.*)

CASSIDY, WHAT ARE YOU TWO DOING UP THERE? STOP RUNNING!

CASSIDY. (*Offstage.*) WE'RE PLAYING GHOST!

RACHAEL. WELL DON'T DO THAT! FINISH CLEANING OUT THAT CLOSET!

> (*Beat, realizes she's finished.*)

We're done.

RIVER. This place looks completely different. I don't think I could have done all this after someone called me a racial slur.

RACHAEL. It was mostly for my own sanity. After we found the photos, I needed to make sure nothing else traumatic was hiding in this trash heap. The last thing I needed was for us to find a…jar of…testicles or something.

RIVER. What?

RACHAEL. You know, Bo and I spent all night reading about these awful lynchings and we found that, apparently, after these things, it was customary for people to take souvenirs—ears, fingers, toes.

RIVER. Oh no.

RACHAEL. Right? Anyway, thank you by the way for having some sense. When Bo told me he tried to throw these things away, I almost killed him— especially after Rhys had seen them, because, you know, kids talk. Ainsley's one thing— If we're lucky he'll forget all about— But Cassidy is the one to worry about. If she wants something, she'll find it. And she's at such an impressionable age. She thinks she knows everything, but she just doesn't. You have to get in the way of stuff like this—give her the context before she gives it her own—and who knows what that might be—

> (TONI *re-enters with her own cup of coffee, taking her time. Beat.*)

Let me know when you're done acting like a child, so we can all finish cleaning up the mess you made.

> (TONI *takes her time sitting down on the couch. She takes her time taking a sip of coffee. She clears her throat.*)

BO. (*Offstage, from the porch.*) You're kidding!! Oh my god this is great news… / No, seriously. Let me— I'll call you in a bit, once we— Yes, no, no. Thank you… I appreciate it… Okay, bye.

TONI. (*To* RIVER.) Good morning.

> (*Beat.*)

To answer your question, Rachael: there is no need to worry about the auctioneer because there's no more auction.

RACHAEL. What?

TONI. I pulled the notices yesterday and called and cancelled everything.

RACHAEL. EXCUSE ME!?

TONI. There is no more auction, there is no more sale. Thanks for nothing.

(BO *re-enters, hanging up the phone, a smile on his face.*)

BO. Hey— When are we starting? I think some people are just pulling up.

RACHAEL. Well, Bo, you can tell them to go on home because nothing's happening here!

BO. What? Why not?

RACHAEL. Because your sociopath of a sister cancelled it! She went behind our backs and sabotaged everything while the rest of us were here working our asses off trying to be helpful—

TONI. Well, Rachael— Did someone ask for your help?

BO. Hey! Okay. Okay. Rachael, relax—

RACHAEL. What do you mean relax?! Your sister is…a—a—a—cunt!!!

TONI. Rachael, your language!

RACHAEL. I don't care if Ainsley hears it! In fact, let's make this a teaching moment! Bring him down here so he can see you and know what the definition of a cunt is, which is you—you sabotaging cunt!

(*Quietly,* RHYS *has entered from upstairs and stands on the steps, maybe freshly showered.*)

BO. Rachael, Rachael, Rachael—it doesn't matter.

RACHAEL. What are you talking about?

BO. Let the bank have it all.

(*Beat.*)

Toni, after our conversation last night, I thought it might be worth trying to get a real appraisal of these things, and I just got off the phone with a friend of a friend, who explained to me that these photos are like…highly specialized collectors' items—like antiques. He said, if we did this right, through an actual auction house or a private dealer, we might fetch six, seven times what they would have sold for today at this junk sale—depending on the condition and how many they are maybe several hundred thousand dollars—

TONI. What?

BO. I mean, before the fees obviously. He's waiting for me to call him back with a number, so he can start reaching out to a few people he thinks might be interested in this stuff—

RACHAEL. What kind of people?

BO. Who knows? In the meantime, since I'm flying back tonight, I was thinking it might make the most sense for me to take them back with me. The best appraisers for this are obviously in the city, so can you go get them out of your car and bring them here? I need to take a look at them.

RIVER. What about Franz?

> (*Beat, in which* BO *and* TONI *look at* RIVER.)

BO. What about Franz?

RIVER. Technically, he's entitled to a third of those photos. Don't you think he deserves to be / a part of this conversation?

BO. Well, first we're going to get through today, then we'll talk about who gets what—

RIVER. That's fine but if you're taking those photos back with you, it sounds like you're not declaring those as a part of your father's estate, which is a little shady, since that gets liquidated today.

TONI. Rhys, sweetie, will you go get the photos out of my car?

> (*Beat, in which* RHYS *hesitates.*)

Go ahead.

> (RHYS *exits.*)

(*To* RIVER.) I thought y'all had your own money.

RIVER. Just because we're not here for money doesn't mean Franz doesn't get to have a say in what his father has left him. That doesn't mean he doesn't care.

TONI. It seems to me if Frank actually cared about anything, he'd be here right now.

RIVER. He's been out since early this morning. I'll call him.

TONI. Why don't you do that?

> (RIVER *takes out her cell, walking into the corner the way people do when they're on the phone. Beat, while it rings.* FRANZ *picks up.*)

RIVER. Hey, baby. Where are you?... / Why are you out of breath?... Oh, that sounds nice... Yeah? Okay, well, you should come back home... Not yet, but there's a problem. You should come back. Now... Okay. Okay. I'll tell them. Alright. Love you. See you soon.

TONI. (*To* BO.) Bo, see! They're here for money! With her pregnancy and her lawyer parents and there is no way! Frank does not get to profit off of this! If Frank makes a dime off of this, I will kill myself. / I will just die!

BO. We're talking about a substantial amount of money here! There's more than enough for everyone. There's no reason to toss this away out of spite.

TONI. It's not spite, Bo. And I mean, given we aren't 100% sure that these photos are even his—we haven't even proven this, we—

RACHAEL. (*Under her breath.*) Jesus / Christ.

TONI. Or let's donate them, or— You said it yourself—let it go! Why can't we just let it all go? Let it be someone else's problem—

(*They both realize* RIVER *is off the phone and that she has been standing there watching them.*)

RIVER. He's on his way.

TONI. Great, well, we're going to donate them to a museum or something—a university—

BO. Toni, you are going to have nothing to do with these—!

TONI. I'm the executor, Bo.

BO. If you think you are about to hold those things hostage, you have got another thing coming. Don't think I will think twice about suing you! I will sue you!

(RHYS *re-enters empty-handed.*)

RHYS. Um.

BO. Where are they?

RHYS. I couldn't find them.

BO. What do you mean you couldn't find them? I thought you said you put them in your car!

TONI. (*Looks at* RIVER.) We did.

BO. (*To* RIVER.) Alright, where are they!?

RIVER. I— How should I know?

BO. Okay, clearly you and Toni were the last people to see these things— correct?

RIVER. Okay?

BO. And weren't you the one who told Toni they were worth something?

RIVER. I'm sorry, are you implying that I stole them?

BO. I'm not implying anything, but I think it might be a good idea if you brought down your luggage so we can just be sure. Look, I get it—you've got a baby coming and you probably need the money—

RACHAEL. / Bo, calm down, come on—

RIVER. Whoa! Whoa! Whoa! First of all— Your daughter was the last person with the photos!

RACHAEL. / What?

BO. What!?

RIVER. Last night. Toni caught Cassidy and I looking at the photos and told her to take them outside.

(*Beat.*)

RACHAEL. (*To* RIVER.) What!? You and my daughter were looking at the—and you didn't tell me!?

BO. Rachael, please—!

(Beat.)

CASSIDY GET DOWN HERE RIGHT NOW!

(CASSIDY *comes down here.*)

CASSIDY. What's going on!? Are we still fighting about those pictures? I've already seen them.

RACHAEL. AGH!

CASSIDY. Mom! Frankly, I don't understand what the big deal is. I've seen worse things on the internet. I am almost an adult!

BO. You are not an adult!

CASSIDY. Yes I am!

BO. No you're not!

TONI. Can we all just calm down! Cassidy, honey, where did you put the photos? They're not in the car.

CASSIDY. They're not?

TONI. They're not there anymore.

CASSIDY. Well, Rhys had them last—

(Beat. All eyes on RHYS.)

TONI. What?

(Beat.)

Okay, somebody had better start explaining something right now.

(Beat.)

RACHAEL. RIGHT! NOW!

BO. / Rachael—

CASSIDY. The car was locked and I gave them to Rhys to put in the car!

TONI. And what did you do with them Rhys?

RHYS. Uh, I—

(The front door opens and FRANZ enters. He is shirtless and dripping wet.)

BO. Frank?

FRANZ. Good morning, everybody!

TONI. Where have you— Ew, Frank, you're soaking wet!

FRANZ. I've been swimming.

TONI. Swimming?

FRANZ. In the lake! Can you believe in all the years I lived here, I never once went swimming in that lake? It's amazing! I think— I think I baptized myself! I mean, I don't know how people do it, but I just went to the edge of the water and said, "Water. Take it away. Take everything away." And I think it did. I got out of that water and felt…different. I'm literally shaking right now. I think I did it. I think I'm a new me, finally!

(*Beat.*)

RIVER. Honey, have / you slept?

BO. Frank, we don't have time for this. We're in the middle of a crisis— The photos are missing.

FRANZ. Missing? No they're not.

BO. Well then where are they?

FRANZ. Well, I couldn't sleep last night— I had this terrible feeling, suddenly, I couldn't get rid of. Like a bad energy in the air just pressing down into me—on all of us—everyone's been so angry, doing crazy things—and so I just had to get out of bed, because I couldn't take it anymore. I couldn't sleep. I came downstairs and I went outside, because I needed to get out, but there was nothing for me to do and I remembered the photographs and, without thinking too much about it, I decided to go looking. I guess I had this idea that I was going to figure out if Daddy or anyone in this family had anything to do with these photos. I would see if I could find the trees. I know the property well enough. If any of these trees were on our property, I would know. But while I'm wandering around, all these memories start coming back to me—every memory from this place that I've buried—memories of memories, the things that went through my head when I used to pace through these orchards, trying to hatch my escape plan and I'm just chasing these trees, not finding anything, and I'm like, François, What are you doing? These pictures are so old. The trees in them are probably completely different-looking by now, and by the time I realized this, I was standing by the slave cemetery—that little clearing in the woods where all the slaves are buried. You hardly realize you're there until you're right up on it and I'm sitting in the middle of this graveyard and I'm thinking about old trees and memory and family and Daddy and I was remembering all this cuckoo stuff River's been saying about ghosts and spirits and that we're not what we think we are—and I turned around and there was the lake—the water and the sun coming up over it and it's glittering and it's calling to me and then I realized there was a whole purpose to this journey! That sometimes there feels like there's this thing inside of us that's leading us and we just have to follow it and so you sometimes just have to trust it and it took me to the edge of the water and it seemed to be telling me, Go on in. Go in and cleanse yourself. Wipe it all away. Take it all in with you and leave it there. So I did. I took everything—all my pain, all Daddy's pain, this family's pain, the pictures— and I left it there. I washed it away.

(*Beat.*)

TONI. Frank. Those photos were worth a lot of money.

FRANZ. What? They were!? How much?

TONI. Hundreds of thousands of dollars! Maybe more!

(*Beat.*)

BO. YOU FUCKING IDIOT!

RACHAEL. / BO!

FRANZ. I didn't know they were worth so much money! You told me to throw them away!

BO. (*About to have an aneurysm, basically.*) OH MY GOD!

FRANZ. / I didn't know.

TONI. Oh Jesus Lord in Heaven. / I can't believe you could be so stupid.

BO. OH MY GOD FRANK WHAT THE FUCK IS WRONG WITH YOU!?

TONI. See, Bo. I told you. I bet you're actually sorry now!

RIVER. You leave him alone! If you have anyone to blame, it's yourself, it's your own selfishness! If anything, this is your comeuppance, you cruel, rotten people! Look at this place! Look at the evil and rot you're descended from— It's in your blood!—and all Franz tried to do is change it—to—to—to purify you people—and lift whatever curse it is that hangs over you—you—

BO. Let me just say something real quick. This is the exact kind of thing I can't stand. If anyone is being given the short end of the stick, it's me, alright, because I have to walk through the world, trying to mind my own business, but getting accosted every fourteen minutes by some prick like you for being white. Tell me what you want me to do. You want me to go back in time and spank my great-great grandparents? Or should I lynch myself? You people just need to say what it is you want me to do! I didn't enslave anybody! I didn't lynch anybody! I didn't burn down your fucking village! I didn't give your people any fucking blankets! You don't know my life! Nobody asked to be born and certainly nobody asked to be born into the life they're given, into this fucked up time, into this—this—this history—so how about you show some respect, sister, when you're in someone else's house—!

RIVER. What are you talking about? You people? Blankets!?

BO. Aren't you part-Indian or something!?

RIVER. WHAT?! No I'm not!

BO. Then why do you dress like that? Why is your name River?!

RIVER. Uh— I'm white! I— You think this has to do with— This has nothing to do with your…race! This has to do with you being a bunch of assholes! All of you! Except for you Cassidy! I mean, thank god he has a semi-healthy relationship with her.

RACHAEL. Excuse me?

RIVER. If it weren't for her, this man might have never found out who you people really were or that his own father was dead!

(*Beat.*)

RACHAEL. What relationship?

(*Beat.*)

BO. Cassidy, you better explain what this woman is talking about—

CASSIDY. There's nothing to explain— We're just friends on Facebook? / What is the big deal?

BO. (*Wheeling on* FRANZ.) WHAT DO YOU MEAN YOU'RE FRIENDS ON FACEBOOK!

RACHAEL. HOW LONG HAS THIS BEEN HAPPENING!?

CASSIDY. Just since Grandpa's funeral— Why are you screaming / at me?!

RACHAEL. Because it is inappropriate for a fourteen-year-old to have a secret online relationship with her Uncle!

RIVER. Really, / Rachael, is that necessary?

FRANZ. Hey, come on, you guys! It's not a / relationship

BO. / Frank, you shut up! I'm going to deal with you in a second!

RACHAEL. Well, yes, River, sorry some of us can't be so hip and relaxed around child sex offenders!

RIVER. / What?

RACHAEL. YOU ARE SO / GROUNDED!

RIVER. Child— What?

(*To* FRANZ.)

Child what?

(*Beat.*)

FRANZ. Wait—

TONI. Oh, is there some sort of confusion?

FRANZ. Toni, shut up! Shut up!

RIVER. What is she talking about?

FRANZ. Toni, that is not what happened! You know it's not true! I didn't—

TONI. / Okay, Frank.

RIVER. Who are you talking about?

TONI. Who do you think we're talking about?

RIVER. The girls he...

TONI. The girls he...what?

BO. / Toni—

FRANZ. I didn't do anything!

RIVER. Assaulted...

TONI. The word is raped, yes—

BO. Toni!

TONI. Statutory rape is still rape!

> (*To* RIVER.)

What did he tell you, sweetie?

FRANZ. / Toni, stop.

RIVER. (*Small.*) He—

FRANZ. Toni, please stop. It was not— It was consensual!

TONI. They were children! One of them was thirteen—for crying out loud!

> (RIVER *gasps.*)

Oh, you didn't know anything, did you?

FRANZ. She told me she was older, River! I thought she was older! She told me so! And we never had sex! I didn't know she was that young until—

> (*Suddenly,* RIVER *exits into the dining room.* FRANZ *starts to go after her, but stops himself. He wheels around on* TONI.)

Why did you do that!

TONI. Why didn't you?

FRANZ. That girl lied to me! You know that! I don't know how much I'm supposed to suffer, Toni! I don't know how much I'm supposed to suffer for things people think I did when the things I did were—I wasn't the real me! I wasn't me yet! I didn't feel like an adult! I didn't even understand who I was or— I'm a different person now! I'm a different person! Let me be different!

TONI. This isn't about you, Frank. It's about the truth. I didn't do anything but tell the truth.

RACHAEL. (*To* FRANZ.) AND YOU HAD NO BUSINESS CARRYING ON SOMETHING LIKE THIS WITH OUR CHILD BEHIND OUR BACKS!

TONI. Rachael, give it a rest!

RACHAEL. No, Toni! You don't get to tell me anything! I am sick of you undermining me! I'm sorry you neglected your child and now he wants nothing to do with you and I'm sorry you're suddenly realizing you might have missed a lesson or two in parenting and never figured out how to not raise a monster—Frank and Rhys both—and I'm sorry that for whatever reason you seem to be resentful or jealous of me because I'm someone who does not raise losers—I raise winners! So, here's your proof, Toni! The answer is yes—you are a crap mother—so why don't you give it a rest!

BO. Rachael?

RACHAEL. What, Bo? I'm not in this family anymore! I can say whatever I want!

> (*A silence, in which* TONI *just glowers at* RACHAEL—*like a long, deep,*

ocean of a silence that pours through the walls and fills up the entire space and takes forever to drain away, before—)

TONI. Alright, Rachael… I'm sorry.

(*—suddenly, viciously,* TONI *grabs* RACHAEL *by the hair, which sends everyone into calamity only after a moment of being like, "Wait, is what I am watching really happening?!" By the point folks are mobilized,* TONI *is halfway to the front door.* RACHAEL *shouts, twists, screams, squeals, terrified, trips, and stumbles the entire time she is being dragged. Meanwhile,* BO *is on the way to save his wife—)*

BO. NO!

(*—and, without thinking, he grabs his sister by the arm and basically throws her across the room.* RHYS *sees this and immediately throws himself into the scuffle—)*

RHYS. What are you doing?!

(*—grappling with* BO. TONI *recovers, pulls herself up, starts shouting at* BO *and trying to half-pull* BO *and* RHYS *apart, but also fighting off* RACHAEL, *who, by now, is getting her own licks in.* FRANZ *jumps in trying to pull people apart—)*

FRANZ. Hey! HEY! HEY! HEY!

(*—but he gets sort of dragged into the fight and starts sort of defending himself. There is the commotion of people screaming and fighting with each other.* RIVER, *hearing all this, comes back into the room, joins in, trying to defend* FRANZ, *but also pulling people apart—)*

RIVER. Stop! Stop! Stop hitting him!

(*It is pretty vicious and goes on for a substantial amount of time, everyone blurring the line between offense and defense, working their issues out on everyone else, tapping into whatever crazy lizard thing exists inside of us that comes on only when there's a brawl but then a child's cry—confused and scared— pierces through the air from upstairs. Everyone sort of stops and looks up at the top of the stairs, remembering* AINSLEY, *who comes slowly down the stairs, wailing—except over his head is a pointed white hood—an old pillowcase with two eyeholes. Everyone watches him cry and cry, dead silent, mortified, confused. What the—*

BLACKOUT, cicadas.)

2.

The living room, a little while later. Empty.

A bickering is heard coming from upstairs, before RACHAEL *appears, suitcases in hand, trailed by* BO, *who is trying so hard to calm her down. He may or may not have a black eye.*

RACHAEL. Then we'll fly standby, Bo! I don't care! I will wait all night in that goddamn airport!

BO. Rachael, we've already rented the van!

RACHAEL. No, Bo, we're going home! We've had enough of your family heritage for a lifetime!

BO. We can't afford four last-minute plane tickets.

RACHAEL. Bo, let me tell you what I can't afford: being physically attacked in front of my children! Do you know how humiliating that is? For them and for me? And why? Tell me why was I attacked, Bo?

BO. Everyone knows Toni is crazy—

RACHAEL. Your entire family is crazy! I mean, your brother threw himself into a goddamned lake, he was so crazy! And, in fact, it's infectious! Your family makes me crazy! I have never fought anyway in my whole life! And I hate myself! I always hate myself around these people! I can hear myself becoming this…annoying, shrill, catty, chatty…thing around these people and that is not me, Bo! That is not who I am and I know this! Why do these people have this effect on me? I ask myself this every time. How is it that they have the power to turn me into this thing? And now I know: it's this… this violence! This need for violence—some taste for it—a thirst—makes people this way and I don't have that! I don't like violence! I mean, your youngest child just walked down those stairs in your father's hood—as if we needed proof—I mean— What are we supposed to do with that?

BO. Rachael, you don't have to do anything! You heard Cassidy: they didn't even know what that was!

RACHAEL. Yes and that is not okay, Bo! Because what they do know is how we responded, which was with horror! And how are we supposed to explain that? They look to us to tell them how to deal with things— How are they supposed to deal with the fact that their Grandfather was a—a— terrorist—if we can't!

BO. Rachael—stop—

RACHAEL. What?

BO. I don't know if— I think we just don't know.

RACHAEL. Just don't know what?

BO. I think Toni might have been a little right—

RACHAEL. Right about what?!

BO. I mean, Dad was…a lot, yes, and maybe was a bit unevolved in his thinking sometimes—but I don't think— He wasn't social enough for this sort of thing… He was, like, a shut-in. You saw that funeral. There was no one there— I mean— Honestly, after all this, I'm thinking maybe this stuff was just—just—

RACHAEL. Just what, Bo!?

BO. An investment? Maybe he knew how much they were worth? Maybe it was—for the Bed and Breakfast?

RACHAEL. Oh, really? For the special Klan suite?!

BO. For a museum or something—or—or maybe it was just accrual! Just stuff he'd wound up with—stuff he didn't know what to do with.

RACHAEL. Well, Bo, I think that answer is a bunch of crap, but, whatever the case, he didn't deal with it and now he's dead, so now we have to deal with it—

(RHYS *enters from the kitchen; they fall silent, guiltily. Beat, before:*)

RHYS. Mom sent me to ask when Rachael will be gone so that you and Uncle Frank and her can talk.

RACHAEL. You can tell her I'm leaving right now.

(*To* BO.)

You've got ten minutes and then we're going to the airport.

BO. Rachael, we're not—

(RACHAEL *exits, huffily, with her suitcases.* BO *look at* RHYS, RHYS *looks at* BO, *it's intense.*)

Tell your mother five minutes.

RHYS. Okay.

BO. (*Shouting up the stairs.*) CASSIDY, LET'S GO!

(BO *exits out the door, just as* CASSIDY *rushes down the stairs.* RHYS *tries to go.*)

CASSIDY. Hey, wait, Rhys! I was…just looking for you.

RHYS. You were?

CASSIDY. Yeah. Uh, I want to give you something. But you have to keep it a secret. I don't want to get in trouble.

(CASSIDY *looks around furtively, to be sure no one is watching, and hands him a couple of photographs that she's dug out of her pocket.*)

RHYS. Where did you—

CASSIDY. I'm kind of a klepto! And I thought they were going to throw them away and I thought that was a little weird and so I took some for myself and I didn't tell anyone. Anyway, I think you should keep those. I already saved a couple for myself.

RHYS. What am I supposed to do with these?

CASSIDY. I don't know. Whatever you want, I guess.

RHYS. What are you going to do?

CASSIDY. I don't know. Use them as a bookmark?

    (*Off* RHYS's *reaction.*)

I don't know! That's what I do with old photos.

BO. (*Offstage.*) Cassidy!

CASSIDY. I'm coming!

RHYS. I'm sorry.

CASSIDY. For what?

RHYS. For hitting your dad.

CASSIDY. I don't care.

    (*Beat.*)

What if we never see each other again?

RHYS. We'll see each other again. In a few years, we'll be adults and we can, you know, we can be friends. We can see each other whenever we want.

CASSIDY. Can I have a hug?

RHYS. Sure.

    (*After a second,* CASSIDY *and* RHYS *embrace. It's awkward at first, but melts into something real.* TONI *enters at the top of the stairs, tries to conceal herself.* CASSIDY *grabs her bag, waves, and goes.*)

CASSIDY. Bye, cousin.

RHYS. Bye, cousin.

CASSIDY. Bye, Aunt Toni.

    (RHYS *tries to leave.*)

TONI. I'm sorry. You shouldn't have seen that. I'm sorry this all happened—

RHYS. Mom, just please get out of my way.

    (BO *enters.* RHYS *exits up the stairs. Beat.*)

BO. Well, are you coming downstairs?

TONI. I don't know yet.

BO. What do you mean you don't know yet?

TONI. I don't know if I want to come downstairs yet. I like standing here.

    (*Beat.*)

What happened to those people outside?

BO. I sent them away. I told him we had to reschedule.

TONI. Where is Frank?

BO. I don't care. Listen, when I get back to New York, my lawyers are going to take over. Though who knows if it will even be worth the expense. We're losing everything anyway.

TONI. Don't worry. It was lost before we got here.

(The door opens. It's FRANZ—*soaking wet, again. In his hands, he carries a pile of wet paper pulp—the remains of the photo album—a mess. He comes to the center of the room and plops it down. Beat.)*

FRANZ. That's all of them.

BO. Frank, why did you even bother?

FRANZ. I didn't know what else to do.

(Beat.)

TONI. You know what I just realized? I've known both you idiots your whole entire lives, isn't that crazy?

BO. Toni—

TONI. Let me finish, Bo. Please.

(Beat.)

I remember holding both of you, staring at you Bo, just looking down on this...helpless little thing trying to figure out the world. You, too, Frank. But there's no one alive who's held me. There's no one left in this family who might have told me about the whole me. You know, I used to think that family was an obligation, because the people who shared your blood—they knew you before you knew you and family could be the place you could come back to find yourself when you were lost. Though what does it matter? No one in this family is interested in finding themselves. They just want to be lost, lost, lost, lost, lost— Family is just a story you tell yourself when it's convenient isn't it—when you need an excuse to explain how trapped you feel or broken or unable or cheated. What story are you going to tell about this weekend, Bo? What is Rachael going to say? That I kicked her ass? No. She's going to say I was crazy. And, Frank, what are you going to go back and tell whoever it is you know about the time you asked for forgiveness? That I refused you? That you took it? I'll tell you the story I'm going to tell. This is the weekend I died. Maybe you could tell this story, too. If anyone asks, I want you to tell them that this is the weekend your sister died.

BO. Toni, what are you talking about?

TONI. Because I think— I think you're dead to me. I have to resign from holding on to you people. I never want to see you two again. Don't expect me at your wedding Frank. Don't be bothered inviting me to your children's graduations, Bo. You can invite Rhys, if you want, but I'll never ask him about it. And if anything ever happens where you wonder where a certain memory or feeling or emotion is coming from, don't call and ask me about it. Make something up—for yourself—because that's what I'm going to do. Lie to myself.

(Beat.)

That's all I have to say. I'm going to say goodbye now, go finish packing with my son, get in my car, and drive away. By the time I come back down, I really hope that, out of respect, you will not still be here.

BO. Toni—

TONI. Goodbye.

> (*No one says anything, as* TONI *goes upstairs, leaving* FRANZ *and* BO, *alone. There is a very long pause, as the cicadas chir, and they look at each other. Beat. A horn honks.*)

BO. Rachael.

FRANZ. Bo—for the record—Cassidy added me as a friend.

> (*Beat.*)

I thought you had told her about me.

BO. We did. You weren't at the funeral. She saw the obituary. She had questions.

> (*Beat.*)

FRANZ. She put up some photos from it. It looked like a nice service.

> (*Beat, re: the house.*)

What's going to happen with this?

BO. I'm…going to handle it.

> (*Beat.*)

Is everything alright between you and River?

FRANZ. Yeah. We're, uh, we're working it out.

BO. Okay. You're really camping out back? Are you sure you don't want to stay at the hotel? Let me pay for a room. Please—

FRANZ. No, no. We're going to be fine. This was part of our plan all along.

BO. Okay.

> (*Horn honks, again.*)

Well, keep in touch.

FRANZ. I'll try.

> (*After a moment, they shake hands.* FRANZ *heads out through the kitchen, leaving* BO *alone, who looks at the pile of paper pulp on the floor. He kneels down, tries to pick through it. It's useless. He gets up and crosses to the door and he starts sobbing. He sobs and sobs and sobs with his hand on the door, unable to open it. He is trying to pull himself together but the harder he tries the more he sobs. It's a flood. Suddenly the door flies open and it's* RACHAEL, *mid-shout.*)

RACHAEL. Bo!

> (*She sees him there. She is startled. She immediately closes the door behind her and reaches for him, takes him into her arms.*)

Oh, Bo! Bo! What happened? Honey, what happened?!

BO. Something's wrong. Something went wrong.

RACHAEL. What, Bo? What was it? Tell me.

BO. I don't know. I don't know. I couldn't fix it.

RACHAEL. Oh, Bo, shh… Shh… Bo…

BO. (*Sobbing into her shoulder.*) I don't know. Why don't I know?

RACHAEL. Bo, shh…

    (*Holds him for a substantial while, then:*)

Come on, we have to go— Let's go—

BO. I don't want…the kids…to see me crying…

RACHAEL. Oh, Bo, shhh… It's okay…

    (*Carefully,* RACHAEL *is leading* BO *outside, just as:*
    BLACKOUT.*)

3.

The darkness that covers everything? It comes back. It comes back and it swallows up the whole world—you, me, them, this living room, these walls—and, meanwhile, the cicadas, they just go on singing, singing loudly, incessantly, an enormously complicated, deeply layered, long and entirely improvised song, which is mostly about the morning, but also about the evening and the day but also the night and the sun but also the moon and about waking up and flying around and what it is like to fly around and about loving each other and hating each other and fucking each other and hurting each other but also about trying to find each other in order to hurt and/or fuck each other but also about falling asleep and then waking up again and the quiet and the noise that accompany each day and the sounds of each other's voices and the occasional music but most about the noise and the grass and the sky and the air and the water but also the water in the air and the heat in the air and the dry in the air and the birds in the sky and the birds on the grass and the birds on the branches and always birds—birds always—but also the sap in the branches and the sweetness of the sap in the branches of the trees but also the trees themselves on the grass and the grass on the dirt but also the dirt itself and how they miss the dirt and how they miss their homes in the dirt, the places where they came from, and the feeling of missing the thing you can never go back to and the mystery of the way one moves away from it and through the present and the mystery of the present and the mystery of the movement itself and the leaves on the branches and the birds on the branches and the birds in the leaves on the branches and the branches on the trees and the trees on the grass and the grass on the dirt and dying. All of it incomprehensible to you, though under it we see the following:

Lights immediately come up on the living room. It's some day—any day. A knocking is heard on the door. Someone says, "Hello?" Beat. Then more knocking. But no one answers. Cicadas chir.

Sudden BLACKOUT and lights come up on the living room just as a part of the floor collapses underneath one of the display tables. Everything on the tables slides off. There is a waterfall of breakage. It's some day—any day.

Sudden BLACKOUT and lights immediately come up on the living room. It's some day—any day. Giggles are heard outside—teenagers. Someone is egging someone on. A rock comes flying through the window and shatters it.

Sudden BLACKOUT and lights immediately come up on the living room. It's some day—any day. Some local scavengers—meth heads, hipsters?—are seen just exiting with a couple of pieces of furniture.

Sudden BLACKOUT and lights immediately come up on the living room. It's some day—any day. Someone's using the basement for a party.

Sudden BLACKOUT and lights immediately come up on the living room. It's some day—any day. A rodent of some sort darts across the space quickly. Or maybe animals are heard fighting upstairs.

Sudden BLACKOUT and lights immediately come up on the living room. It's some day—any day. Sudden BLACKOUT and lights immediately come up on the living room over and over again as the house ages and ages. Time moves faster. Pieces of the place have started to disappear, chunks of wood, parts of the flooring, banister beams. Cobwebs. Every time, it is some day—any day—tomorrow— thirteen years from now—twenty-six years from now. It is the future. It is the present. It is any present. It is the past—any past—now—until:

One of these days, someone, probably neither black nor white, tries to open the front door. It's locked. He tries again. He walks around the porch, peering in through various windows, trying them, before disappearing again. At some point, he springs up into the upstage window, seemingly out of nowhere. He cups his hands around his eyes and presses his face against the glass, peering in, a STRANGER. *He tries the window and opens it. He inspects the room. He takes notes on a clipboard. He tries to take a picture.*

Look at this place.

BLACKOUT, no cicadas.

End of Play

27 WAYS I DIDN'T SAY "HI"
TO LAURENCE FISHBURNE
by Jonathan Josephson

BIOGRAPHY

Jonathan Josephson's plays have been produced at theatres across the country, including *27 Ways I Didn't Say "Hi" to Laurence Fishburne* at the Tony-winning Actors Theatre of Louisville (2013 Humana Festival of New American Plays), *The Giant and the Pixie* at the Chance Theater, and *Disconnect, or, 30K Arabian Nights* at San Jose Repertory Theatre (SJREAL late-night series). Josephson's plays have also received staged readings at Seattle Repertory Theatre (via Northwest Playwrights Alliance), Remy Bumppo Theatre Company, and many others. Josephson also has the rare distinction of being a four-time finalist for Actors Theatre of Louisville's Heideman Award. In addition to playwriting, Josephson is one of the Co-Artistic Directors of Unbound Productions and one of the founders of Wicked Lit and History Lit (unboundproductions.org). For Unbound, Josephson has adapted Washington Irving's *The Legend of Sleepy Hollow*, Sir Arthur Conan Doyle's *The New Catacomb*, H.P. Lovecraft's *The Lurking Fear* (with Jeff G. Rack), Mark Twain's *A Ghost Story*, Charles Dickens' *The Chimes*, M.R. James' *Count Magnus*, and Katherine Mansfield's *The Garden Party*. These short plays have been produced at schools, theatres, museums, historic mansions, hotels, mausoleums, and cemeteries throughout Southern California as well as in Nebraska, Maryland, Cameroon and Scotland. Josephson holds a B.A. in Theatre: Playwriting from the University of California, San Diego. He is a proud member of the Dramatists Guild and a Lifetime Member of the Alliance of Los Angeles Playwrights.

ACKNOWLEDGMENTS

27 Ways I Didn't Say "Hi" to Laurence Fishburne premiered at the Humana Festival of New American Plays in April 2013. It was directed by Meredith McDonough with the following cast:

LAURENCE FISHBURNE ....Andy Lucien
JONATHAN JOSEPHSON ....Ethan Dubin, Danny Wolohan, Bruce McKenzie, Reese Madigan, Jim Frangione, Jeff White, Ian Whitt, Larry Bull, Conor Eifler, Derek Nelson, Bobby Johnson, Joseph Metcalfe, Kris Kling, Kim Fischer, David Rosenblatt, Dan Waller, Jonathan Majors, Gabe Weible, Andy Reinhardt, and Ben Vigus

and the following production staff:

Scenic Designer..Antje Ellermann
Costume Designer ....Kristopher Castle
Lighting Designer..Seth Reiser

CHARACTERS

LAURENCE FISHBURNE, late 40s, should at least vaguely resemble the actual Laurence Fishburne.

JONATHAN JOSEPHSON (a.k.a. "I" and "Me"), early 20s, should at least vaguely resemble the actual Jonathan Josephson. Or not.

SETTING

A mostly empty rehearsal hall on the campus of a major regional theatre.

NOTE

The play calls for a clock or other time-keeping instrument to be in plain view of the audience. The clock can either be a part of the set or above the set as part of the proscenium.

Also, it may help to have the character of JONATHAN JOSEPHSON (a.k.a. "Me" and "I") played by two (or more) similar-looking actors dressed in identical costumes. This will assist with the overall timing and pace of the piece as well as add to the requisite zaniness.

Andy Lucien and Danny Wolohan
in *27 Ways I Didn't Say "Hi" to Laurence Fishburne*

37th Humana Festival of New American Plays
Actors Theatre of Louisville, 2013
Photo by Bill Brymer

27 Ways I Didn't Say "Hi" to Laurence Fishburne

In the darkness, a bell rings.

Lights rise on LAURENCE FISHBURNE *sitting at a table, eating a sandwich. An unwrapped salad sits beside him.*

The clock reads 5:01.

Unseen to LAURENCE FISHBURNE, *I enter. I take a short breath, glance over at* LAURENCE FISHBURNE…*and exit out the door I came in.*

A bell rings. The clock now reads 5:02.

Unseen to LAURENCE FISHBURNE, *I enter from the opposite side of the stage. I stop and stare over at* LAURENCE FISHBURNE *with extreme intensity.* LAURENCE FISHBURNE *continues to eat his sandwich. I stare, he eats. Finally, he looks up.*

LAURENCE FISHBURNE. Can I help you?

> (*I immediately exit out the far door—walking quickly.*
>
> *A bell rings. The clock now reads 5:03.*
>
> *I enter, unseen to* LAURENCE FISHBURNE. *I clear my throat loudly. He looks up.*)

JONATHAN JOSEPHSON. I—uh, Mr. Fishburne—you've seen me, before, I work here at the theatre. It's just so great to have you here working—uh—acting with us on *Fences*—it's one of my favoritest…most favorite plays ever. (*Pause.*) Sorry.

> (*I exit.*
>
> *A bell rings. The clock now reads 5:04.*
>
> *I enter, unseen to* LAURENCE FISHBURNE. *I am about to say something when the song "All Day I Dream About Sex" starts to blare loudly from my pocket.* LAURENCE FISHBURNE *looks up at me in annoyance. I fumble with my pocket, trying to get my cell phone out so I can turn off the noise, but I suck and it just keeps playing and playing. I finally get my phone out and throw it out the door I came in. The music stops.*)

Sorry.

> (*I exit.*
>
> *A bell rings. The clock now reads 5:05. I enter.*)

Mr. Fishburne, we wanted to—

> (LAURENCE FISHBURNE *sees me immediately but he's just taken a big*

bite of sandwich so he can't say anything without being rude and talking with his mouth full. I gesture for him to take his time. He nods, then his cell phone rings—but with a normal ring tone. After a moment, he swallows.)

LAURENCE FISHBURNE. Hello? Hey, man, what's going on? (*He laughs.*) Yeah, just eating some dinner. (*Pause.*) A few minutes? Not for that I don't. (*He laughs again.*) You are a crazy son-of-a-bitch, you know that?

(*Dejected, I exit.*

A bell rings. The clock now reads 5:06.

I enter.)

JONATHAN JOSEPHSON. Mr. Fish—

(LAURENCE FISHBURNE *is still on the phone.*)

LAURENCE FISHBURNE. I know it! I know it! That's what I told him too! (*He laughs.*)

(*I exit out the opposite door.*

A bell rings. The clock now reads 5:07.

LAURENCE FISHBURNE *is no longer on the phone. He is now eating his salad.*

I enter.)

JONATHAN JOSEPHSON. ...so just wanted to update you on...yeah. The photography—photographer, is setting up he'll be ready for you at 5:27, but we may need to start a minute or two before... So, you know. Just so you know. But I'll come and get you—if needs. Be. If it's earlier than that.

(LAURENCE FISHBURNE *continues to eat his salad, nodding. I exit.*

A bell rings. The clock now reads 5:08.

I enter.)

So, there was a question—

(LAURENCE FISHBURNE *is singing* "Go Down Moses.")

LAURENCE FISHBURNE. (*Big, deep, bass, soul voice.*)
GO DOWN, MOSES
WAY DOWN TO EGYPT LA-AND
TELL OLE... PHARAOH...
GO LET ME PEOPLE GO

(LAURENCE FISHBURNE *looks at me, I look at him. He lets out a raspberry, then continues to eat his salad. I exit.*

A bell rings. The clock now reads 5:09.

I enter.)

JONATHAN JOSEPHSON. Okay. So earlier, yesterday, you made this joke that I totally got—I totally got it, but I didn't say anything at the time because... I don't know why, I guess I'm just a schmuck. I just have so much respect for you, I mean not for your movies, but for you as an actor. I mean your movies are fine, they're okay...they do great, right? Millions of dollars, you must have...done...very...

(I exit. LAURENCE FISHBURNE continues to eat his salad.

A bell rings. The clock now reads 5:10.

I enter with a bottle of water. I take the bottle of water to LAURENCE FISHBURNE *who is now reading a magazine. He nods when I set the water down, but he's reading. I wait for just a moment, then exit.*

A bell rings. The clock now reads 5:11.

LAURENCE FISHBURNE *is now reading his magazine and drinking his bottled water.*

I enter. I am naked. I walk right up to LAURENCE FISHBURNE*, but right as I open my mouth, I realize that I am naked and run out of the room.*

LAURENCE FISHBURNE *looks up, barely.*

A bell rings. The clock now reads 5:12.

I walk in, very confidently. I walk past LAURENCE FISHBURNE *but slow down just as I cross in front of him. I turn to him, trying to catch his eye, but he is reading the magazine. I move myself into awkward, invasive positions, trying to get into his line of sight. I stoop, lean, crouch, and hover. Finally...)*

LAURENCE FISHBURNE. Son—do you have something on your mind?

JONATHAN JOSEPHSON. Not really.

(And, nonchalantly, I exit.

A bell rings. The clock now reads 5:13.

I enter.)

That joke—it was, hilarious! Hilarious! Before, when, when you said... When I came in before, yesterday, when Angela wanted her picture touched up... and you said "use all of your talents and all of your skills..." and you sort of left it open? You just said that and then you looked around and Angela and even my boss were like "what was he talking about"... I got it, man. Laurence. Sir. It was *(Clears throat.)* really, clever. I wanted you to know, that I know, you're... I'm...

(I exit.

A bell rings. The clock now reads 5:14.

I enter.)

LAURENCE FISHBURNE. WHAT THE FUCK YOU DOIN' HERE?

(I exit, crying.

A bell rings. The clock now reads 5:15.

I enter, singing. The theme to "The Fresh Prince of Bel Air."

LAURENCE FISHBURNE *just shakes his head.*

I exit.

A bell rings. The clock now reads 5:16.

I enter on roller skates. I can't control myself very well and just roll all the way across the room, and then out.

LAURENCE FISHBURNE *doesn't budge.*

A bell rings. The clock now reads 5:17.

I enter. LAURENCE FISHBURNE *has finished his salad and is looking for somewhere to throw away his trash.*

For some inexplicable reason, I dodge his glances and hide from his gaze. Finally, he sees me. He offers me his trash which I gladly accept.)

Thank you. Thank you so much. Thank you.

(*He looks at me quizzically, I exit.*

A bell rings. The clock now reads 5:18.

I enter.)

Fled! Fled was a shitty movie man, that shit was shit! I can't even tell you how shitty that shit was man, that was some shitty shit.

LAURENCE FISHBURNE. I'm sorry you feel that way.

JONATHAN JOSEPHSON. Well that's how it is.

(*I exit.*

A bell rings. The clock now reads 5:19.

I enter.)

So it'll be just a few more…few more minutes.

(LAURENCE FISHBURNE *waves me away as if to say "I know, thank you" and not "Leave me alone!" He's actually a really gracious guy.*

I exit.

A bell rings. The clock now reads 5:20.

I enter.)

So, I'm a playwright, and I read *Fences* a few years ago, it really meant a lot to me.

LAURENCE FISHBURNE. Fuck you know about this play? Fuck you know about anything? You wanna be a playwright, why don't you go write a play? You wanna be a playwright, why are you working this day job? You are a bullshit nothing my friend and you better accept that and go and get me some coffee.

(*I exit, crying hysterically.*)

No cream, lots of sugar.

(*I commit hari-kari offstage.*

A bell rings. The clock now reads 5:21.

I enter with a cup of coffee. I hand it to LAURENCE FISHBURNE. *I exit.*
A bell rings. The clock now reads 5:22.

LAURENCE FISHBURNE *drinks his coffee and is now reading the magazine.*

I enter.)

JONATHAN JOSEPHSON. *The Godfather*! I got it, I got the joke, it was from *The Godfather*. The scene with the funeral director. He's the one that was supposed to "use all of his talents and all of his skills."

LAURENCE FISHBURNE. I'm sorry—what?

JONATHAN JOSEPHSON. Never mind—

LAURENCE FISHBURNE. No, I just didn't hear you—

JONATHAN JOSEPHSON. It's nothing—

LAURENCE FISHBURNE. No, tell me, I was just reading so I didn't—

JONATHAN JOSEPHSON. It's fine, thank you—it's fine. Really. Sorry.

(*I exit.*
A bell rings. The clock now reads 5:23.
I enter.)

I loooooved *The Matrix* so much. Especially your scenes. You are just... You are just... I have to pee.

(*I run offstage.*
A bell rings. The clock now reads 5:24.
I enter.)

LAURENCE FISHBURNE. You know what's great about white people?

JONATHAN JOSEPHSON. What?

(LAURENCE FISHBURNE *stands up and roars like a lion.*
I run off stage, crying.)

LAURENCE FISHBURNE. Every time.

(*A bell rings. The clock now reads 5:25.*
I enter with a fishing pole, a stuffed mastodon, a small television set, a river raft, a kilo of blow, volume "V" of an encyclopedia, some toothpicks, a cockroach trap, a metal detector, and a machete.)

That's a lot of shit.

JONATHAN JOSEPHSON. You're telling me.

(*I exit.*
A bell rings. The clock now reads 5:26.
I enter. I walk up to LAURENCE FISHBURNE.)

Excuse me, Mr. Fishburne?

LAURENCE FISHBURNE. Laurence, please.

JONATHAN JOSEPHSON. Okay—Laurence. Hi. I'm Jonathan Josephson, I'm the Marketing and Promotions Manager for the theatre.

LAURENCE FISHBURNE. (*Nodding.*) I met you yesterday, when we were looking at the photos.

JONATHAN JOSEPHSON. Yep. And that was…that was a great *Godfather* reference. "I want you to use all of your talents and all of your skills…"

LAURENCE FISHBURNE. You caught that?

JONATHAN JOSEPHSON. Right away.

LAURENCE FISHBURNE. (*After a pause.*) So, do you like it here—at this theatre?

JONATHAN JOSEPHSON. It's great. I love the people, I love being around the plays. I'm, actually, a playwright.

LAURENCE FISHBURNE. Is that right?

JONATHAN JOSEPHSON. Yep.

LAURENCE FISHBURNE. You written anything?

> (*The clock now reads 5:27.*)

JONATHAN JOSEPHSON. A few things.

LAURENCE FISHBURNE. You have anything with a role for me?

JONATHAN JOSEPHSON. Actually—yeah, I might.

LAURENCE FISHBURNE. You might?

JONATHAN JOSEPHSON. I do! I do—actually, the play I just finished yesterday, is, I wrote it with you in mind.

LAURENCE FISHBURNE. Really?

JONATHAN JOSEPHSON. Absolutely. It's sort of a Neil Simon meets Amiri Baraka thing. I'm, really, and this will sound stupid, but I'm a fan of yours.

LAURENCE FISHBURNE. That's not stupid.

JONATHAN JOSEPHSON. (*Looking at my watch.*) Really? Because—oh—it's almost time. You need to—

LAURENCE FISHBURNE. Please. I'm Laurence Fishburne, they'll wait.

JONATHAN JOSEPHSON. Okay.

> (*The clock now reads 5:28.*)

LAURENCE FISHBURNE. You really wrote a play with me in mind?

JONATHAN JOSEPHSON. Yes. *Othello* and *The Matrix*—not to mention the clips I've seen from *Two Trains Running* on Broadway—

LAURENCE FISHBURNE. You've seen that?

JONATHAN JOSEPHSON. I think you'd be perfect.

LAURENCE FISHBURNE. Really. Well, get me a copy.

JONATHAN JOSEPHSON. I'm sorry?

LAURENCE FISHBURNE. I want to read it. Get me a copy.

JONATHAN JOSEPHSON. I have a copy right here!

(*I hand* LAURENCE FISHBURNE *a copy of my script.*)

LAURENCE FISHBURNE. That's great, thank you.

JONATHAN JOSEPHSON. Thank you!

LAURENCE FISHBURNE. (*Skimming the pages.*) This looks great. If I like it, I'll even finance it.

JONATHAN JOSEPHSON. Really?

LAURENCE FISHBURNE. And get the best director in town.

JONATHAN JOSEPHSON. Really?

LAURENCE FISHBURNE. And get a supporting cast that will make your jaw drop.

JONATHAN JOSEPHSON. Really??

(*The clock reads 5:29.*)

LAURENCE FISHBURNE. Yep. Because I like you, Jonathan. And I can just tell that you are a great person and a truly gifted playwright.

JONATHAN JOSEPHSON. Thank you. That means so…so much to me.

LAURENCE FISHBURNE. Well I mean it.

JONATHAN JOSEPHSON. It's just shitty—that this is a dream.

LAURENCE FISHBURNE. Pretty shitty.

(*I exit.*

A bell rings. The clock goes back to 5:27.

I enter. LAURENCE FISHBURNE *looks up.*)

Is it time?

(*I nod.*

LAURENCE FISHBURNE *collects his things and walks towards the door. When he gets close to me, he stops, looks at me.*

He waits for me to say something.)

Something on your mind?

(*I can't think of anything to say, even though I have a million things to say.*)

Alright then.

(*He exits. I look after him—a failure.*

Lights fade.)

End of Play

THE DELLING SHORE
by Sam Marks

ABOUT *THE DELLING SHORE*

This article first ran in the January/February 2013 issue of Inside Actors, *Actors Theatre of Louisville's subscriber newsletter, and is based on conversations with the playwright before rehearsals for the Humana Festival production began.*

Imagine escaping the hustle and bustle of Brooklyn to visit an old friend at his lakeside summer house, tucked away in the scenic seclusion of New England woods. The two of you and your respective twentysomething daughters will stay up late into the night, feasting on wine and cheese and fresh-picked blueberries, indulging in intellectual discussion and banter about favorite novelists. Your old friend, a literary household name, will have read the draft of your latest novel, and his endorsement could be the ticket to its success.

Or, imagine being a college girl escaping campus for a couple days to hang out with your writer dad and his dashing friend—who's a famous fiction author! An aspiring author yourself, you can't wait to talk tricks of the trade with a master. The best part: your father has assured you that you'll be handpicked for an apprenticeship assisting his friend in translating stories by Roberto Bolaño, the current posthumous darling of the publishing world.

For both father and daughter, doesn't this sound idyllic? But in Sam Marks' drama *The Delling Shore,* the pastoral perfection of a summer home isn't enough to diffuse hostilities between its very *im*perfect inhabitants. Eminent novelist Thomas Wright has invited fellow writer Frank Bay and his daughter Adrianne to stay the weekend at his country house. From the moment the Bays arrive, though, Thomas and his daughter Ellen are out to get them. The shared love of books that should unite these characters instead becomes a battleground, where words become weapons.

Although Frank and Thomas have known one another since graduate school, deep-seated jealousies permeate their friendship. After all, Thomas' novels are critically-acclaimed bestsellers, enabling him to throw lavish book parties and go antiquing with high-profile writers like Jonathan Franzen. Frank, however, can't support himself on his writing alone. Comparatively unknown in the fiction world, he scrapes by as the editor of an educational journal. Over the course of their first evening together in years, each man's ill-concealed resentment toward the other seethes to the surface. What ensues is a verbal boxing match as wryly hilarious and syntactically clever as it is brutal. Digs, quips, and literary references are hurled through the "Delling Summer Home" like slings and arrows, tearing gaping wounds in the façade of wealth and success.

For as Sam Marks' conflicted characters ultimately see, there are many different forms of failure. Thomas and Frank focus on professional disappointments, but what about the failure to be a good friend? Or the failure to be a good father? Marks comments, "I was initially drawn to the literariness of the play and that world—and I still am, obviously—but the more I wrote, the more I figured it was about being a parent. And how the legacy of success or non-success affects a kid." For Marks, that's the real reversal in the plot: the revelation that at its core, this play isn't just about literary ambition, but about contending with the pernicious influence of our parents' mistakes.

Daughters Adrianne and Ellen are undeniably affected by their fathers' success, or lack thereof. Adrianne, desperate to achieve in a field where Frank has failed to distinguish himself, must look outside her family for someone to admire and emulate. At 25, Ellen already earns six figures, but she feels she's a disappointment to her dad; instead of following in Thomas' creative footsteps, she works at a bank. "I've always felt there was a burden for people whose parents weren't as successful as they wanted to be, but there's also a burden for people whose parents were wildly successful," Marks reflects. "I found that dynamic really interesting."

When he wrote *The Delling Shore*, Marks was well-acquainted with that dynamic. At the time, he was teaching at Brown University, where he encountered many students struggling with how to define themselves in relation to rich and famous parents. In addition, Marks had recently become a father himself. "I thought a lot about what it is to be a dad," he recalls. Therefore, his incisive look at career rivals behaving badly doubles as a coming-of-age story for Ellen and especially Adrianne. Their fathers' actions push them onto a painful path toward adulthood that many of us can relate to: Ellen and Adrianne each are forced to look at Thomas and Frank, as Marks puts it, "not just as writers, but as flawed dads." He elaborates, "Each of them must work on not just being this man's daughter, but being her own person."

You don't have to be an avid reader, or someone pursuing a literary career, to identify with the world of *The Delling Shore*. (Though if you are either, you will delight in its characters' familiarity with contemporary fiction.) In *The Delling Shore*, as some of its characters realize too late, there are more important things to focus on in life than picking apart the plot or style of this or that novel. Because, as Marks sums it up: "Ultimately this story is really about a father and a daughter."

—Hannah Rae Montgomery

BIOGRAPHY

Sam Marks' play, *The Delling Shore*, had its world premiere at the 2013 Humana Festival, directed by Meredith McDonough. Other productions include: *The Old Masters* at Steppenwolf's First Look Repertory directed by Daniel Aukin, *The Joke* at Studio Dante (Off-Broadway debut) directed by Sam Gold, *Brack's Last Bachelor Party* at 59E59, directed by Geordie Broadwater, *Nelson* with Partial Comfort Productions, directed by Kip Fagan, *The Bigger Man* with Partial Comfort Productions, directed by Louis Moreno, and *Craft* at The Bat Theater Company, directed by Robert O'Hara.

Marks is currently developing a project at HBO with Steve Buscemi and Stanley Tucci producing. He has developed several TV series, including *Sarah K.* for CBS Studios, produced by Philip Seymour Hoffman and Cooper's Town Productions.

Additionally, Marks' plays have been workshopped and read at Arena Stage, Atlantic Theater, Manhattan Theatre Club, New York Theatre Workshop, Portland Center Stage, The Public Theater, Rattlestick Playwrights Theater, Sundance Theatre Institute, Vineyard Theatre, and many others. Marks was selected as one of the "50 Playwrights to Watch" by *The Dramatist* Magazine.

He currently teaches playwriting at Harvard University. He lives with his wife Greer, his son Ozzy, and his daughter Jupiter.

ACKNOWLEDGMENTS

The Delling Shore premiered at the Humana Festival of New American Plays in February 2013. It was directed by Meredith McDonough with the following cast:

THOMAS WRIGHT	Jim Frangione
ELLEN WRIGHT	Meredith Forlenza
FRANK BAY	Bruce McKenzie
ADRIANNE BAY	Catherine Combs

and the following production staff:

Scenic Designer	Daniel Zimmerman
Costume Designer	Lorraine Venberg
Co-Lighting Designers	Russell H. Champa, Dani Clifford
Sound Designer	Benjamin Marcum
Media Designer	Philip Allgeier
Stage Manager	Zachary Krohn
Dramaturg	Hannah Rae Montgomery
Casting	Henry Russell

Directing Assistant .... Rachel Karp
Production Assistant ....Mary Elizabeth Penrose
Assistant Dramaturg..Kathryn Zukaitis

The Delling Shore was developed, in part, with the assistance of the Sundance Institute Theatre Program.

CHARACTERS

THOMAS WRIGHT, 49, a novelist

ELLEN WRIGHT, 25, Thomas' daughter, an investment banker

FRANK BAY, 48, the editor of an educational journal

ADRIANNE BAY, 19, Frank's daughter, a college student

TIME

The action of the play takes place during the summer from around 9 p.m. on a Friday night to 9 a.m. the next morning.

SPECIAL THANKS

Special thanks to Nico Baumbach and Mac Wellman for sharing their games.

"Many years later, as he faced the firing squad, Colonel Aureliano Buendía was to remember that distant afternoon when his father took him to discover ice."

—Gabriel García Márquez, *One Hundred Years of Solitude*

Catherine Combs, Bruce McKenzie, Meredith Forlenza and Jim Frangione
in *The Delling Shore*

37th Humana Festival of New American Plays
Actors Theatre of Louisville, 2013
Photo by Alan Simons

THE DELLING SHORE

AT RISE:

The deep woods.

A Country House on a lake.

The Inside of The Delling Summer Home.

The Den. It's Plush, Elegant, Tasteful. Freshly painted walls, refurbished room, new shelves.

Center, a large, sturdy, immaculate wooden table.

Left, a glass sliding door that looks out onto a hill and a lake.

Right, a doorway to the kitchen and a staircase leading to the second floor.

Downstage, a sofa and a large bookcase filled with many titles. Along the bookcase are silver framed photos of children and vacations.

Finally, upstage, an old metal wooden stove. Newspaper, chopped wood, and chrome metal pokers.

Sitting at the Table is THOMAS WRIGHT, *49, dashing, a few days' stubble, nice shirt, nice pants, and his daughter,* ELLEN WRIGHT, *25; she's dressed well, strong, forceful.*

On the table, some meats, cheeses, fruit, and sliced baguette.

Standing in front of the big glass door are FRANK BAY, *48, shorter, sweaty, coiled, and his daughter,* ADRIANNE BAY, *19, anxious, eager, dressed down.*

The Bays hold their bags. (They've arrived.)

The Wrights stare at them for a moment. (They're out to get them.)

Then:

FRANK. I did try calling.

THOMAS. (*Warm.*) My phone is useless here. Jesus, I hope it wasn't *too* hard to find.

FRANK. (*Jovial.*) *Here* we are. That's what counts.

ADRIANNE. It was actually a wonderful drive. The lilacs, the grass all of it. Really wonderful.

FRANK. Before the sun went down *it was* stunning.

THOMAS. I thought they were good directions. They usually work.

ELLEN. That's not true Dad. No one can *ever* find this place.

FRANK. Well that's the point of this place, right? *Seclusion.*

THOMAS. Trust me, Frank, *some* people have found us.

ELLEN. Stalkers.

FRANK. And us.

THOMAS. What did Ellen just say about Stalkers?

FRANK. Right, yes, right.

ADRIANNE. (*Amused.*) That's Funny.

THOMAS. Adrianne. My goodness, it's been so long. How are you?

ADRIANNE. I'm good, Thomas. You?

THOMAS. Very glad you both made it.

FRANK. (*Reassuring.*) See, Ade. It's fine.

ADRIANNE. Yes.

FRANK. She was a little worried about all of this. But Thomas used to always say how smart he thought you were. Way Back.

ADRIANNE. Okay, awkward.

FRANK. Her classmates were jealous of this trip.

ADRIANNE. Not true. I didn't tell them I was coming up.

FRANK. Did you tell them about the internship?

THOMAS. Let's wait a bit to get into all of that. Come in, already, come in.

ADRIANNE. I am very excited to talk about it.

FRANK. (*Referring to house.*) Look at this.

(*They come in and set their bags down.*)

THOMAS. (*To* ADRIANNE.) You're much taller than the last time I saw you.

ADRIANNE. Well—

FRANK. We've grown too. But in the wrong direction. Am I right? Tom?

THOMAS. You both must be fucking exhausted from that drive.

ADRIANNE. I slept in the car. Plus I don't really sleep much at school.

FRANK. We've both really been looking forward to finally seeing your new house.

THOMAS. Yes, we've been looking forward to finally having you, haven't we?

(THOMAS *looks to* ELLEN, *who is now texting.*)

Ellen?

ELLEN. (*Picking her head up.*) Oh yeah. Sorry. Yes. Totally. *Welcome.* Yes.

ADRIANNE. I thought there was no reception.

ELLEN. (*A fact.*) This phone is special. I got it from some people I know at Verizon.

FRANK. We should talk. I have a bill issue.

ELLEN. My friends are in corporate, not billing.

FRANK. Kidding. Your father tells me you're making lots these days.

ELLEN. He did? That was nice.

THOMAS. It's true.

(*Pause.*)

ADRIANNE. Is it also true that Charles Van Doren lives down the road?

FRANK. Ade—

THOMAS. That's the rumor.

ADRIANNE. I just saw *Quiz Show* at school. So incredible—

ELLEN. They're not nearly as good-looking in real life.

ADRIANNE. I had no idea of that entire story: that these people, and NBC, that they actually—

THOMAS. They keep to themselves. They smile from the car. They have a compound.

FRANK. They're cheaters.

THOMAS. They're neighbors.

ADRIANNE. I looked for them.

ELLEN. It's way too dark.

FRANK. Sure is.

ADRIANNE. You never know.

THOMAS. I've seen them take walks.

ADRIANNE. I'd love to take a walk tomorrow.

FRANK. There is a lot to do while we're here.

THOMAS. Tonight, maybe, sleep.

FRANK. (*Confused.*) Now?

ELLEN. We thought you guys might not make it.

FRANK. Why wouldn't we make it?

THOMAS. You said five. It's *nine.*

FRANK. I told you I called. The place is pretty secluded and I haven't driven for quite a while.

THOMAS. (*Nodding.*) Well, sure, of course, yes, come on, who wants a car in the city?

FRANK. Where we are a car is pretty convenient actually.

THOMAS. Is that right?

ELLEN. Brooklyn, Dad, Brooklyn.

THOMAS. Of course yes. *Brooklyn.*

(*To* FRANK.)

But I thought you had a Car. That time I stayed with you, you were worried it wouldn't make it through the night.

FRANK. Well I was

Brooklyn was

Things were different then.

THOMAS. (*Enjoying it.*) I *know:* I was 40 years old and sleeping on my friend's couch. How about that?

FRANK. (*Also enjoying.*) One of my favorite stories: How "*The*" Thomas Wright crashed on my couch for a week.

ELLEN. (*Sharp.*) When you tell the story do you say it was 'cause he got thrown out?

FRANK. (*Proud.*) I just say I was helping out my grad school bud.

ELLEN. 'Cause he was thrown out by his wife.

THOMAS. (*Keeping it light.*) I'm still in your debt, Frank.

FRANK. Well it *was* a Very Long Week. And you snore *Very Loudly.*

THOMAS. I can't imagine. With your family there too. It's not a big apartment. What was I thinking?

FRANK. Ten years ago.

THOMAS. Did we wake them?

ADRIANNE. I thought it was funny.

ELLEN. To have my dad sleeping on your couch?

THOMAS. You remember that?

ADRIANNE. Sure I was 9, it was

THOMAS. Awful?

ADRIANNE. NO.

THOMAS. Be honest. Tell me. Come on, I can take it.

FRANK. (*Encouraging her.*) Go head Adrianne, give it to him.

ADRIANNE. Oh.

I don't know.

It was.

Well.

I feel like there's all this pressure on me to say something really sharp.

FRANK. Not at all. Let's forget it.

ADRIANNE. Yeah?

FRANK. (*Reassuring.*) Long weekend, relax. You're fine.

ADRIANNE. Okay.

     (*Pause.*)

(*Trying anyway.*) Well. So. The thing is:

Thomas was on our couch and and

And

It was *funny.*

THOMAS. Funny.

ELLEN. Me and Mom didn't think it was funny.

FRANK. How is your mother?

>   (*Pause.*)

ELLEN. She's in New Mexico.

THOMAS. Living with someone now.

FRANK. Still Writing?

ELLEN. Teaching High School.

FRANK. We were both jealous of her in grad school.

THOMAS. She was very talented.

ELLEN. She still writes. I guess.

FRANK. So do we all, I guess.

ELLEN. Do you?

ADRIANNE. I do.

THOMAS. (*To* ADRIANNE.) Yes, your father sent me your Panda Story.

ADRIANNE. *What?*

THOMAS. I had asked him for a writing sample.

ADRIANNE. I have *way better* stories.

FRANK. You like the Panda Story.

ADRIANNE. I wrote it in HIGH SCHOOL.

FRANK. Well you haven't shown me your newer stuff.

THOMAS. Well, the other candidates also mentioned they weren't terribly proud of their work.

>   (ADRIANNE *looks at* FRANK.
>   *Pause.*)

ADRIANNE. Sure, the other candidates…

FRANK. (*Clarifying.*) I told Adrianne that it was sort of a formality. Getting it. That spending the weekend here was the interview.

THOMAS. Oh. Well, actually, there are other writers, graduate students, who are also being considered. And interviewed.

FRANK. But you said she'd be great for it, that we'd talk about it up here.

THOMAS. And we *will* discuss it, of course.

>   (*Pause.*)

I thought I was clear.

ADRIANNE. I had seen the posting.

FRANK. It's why I called you.

ADRIANNE. It's okay, Dad.

THOMAS. We covered a lot of ground, Frank.

ADRIANNE. I'd still like to interview.

THOMAS. (*To* ADRIANNE.) I do think your work is strong.

ELLEN. (*To* ADRIANNE.) You really think he's going to have you to the house and then not give you the internship?

THOMAS. (*To* ELLEN.) I have to talk to other people.

ELLEN. (*To* THOMAS.) You also like to keep people on the hook.

THOMAS. (*To* ADRIANNE.) You understand what it is? It's an apprenticeship. I need an assistant on a translation that I'm doing of some new Bolaño stories.

Research on certain passages. It's not unlike what I did with Kosinski when I was at Columbia.

ADRIANNE. Yes, I get it.

THOMAS. Bolaño is very scrutinized. It's to be taken very seriously.

ADRIANNE. Of course.

FRANK. I didn't realize it was that competitive.

THOMAS. Can we discuss it more later?

     (*Pause.*)

ADRIANNE. I really like the way you've decorated this house. It looks very high-modern.

THOMAS. Kristin took the new design very seriously.

FRANK. You remember Thomas' *old* summer place?

THOMAS. *That* was a very long time ago. Before the couch.

FRANK. I loved it there.

THOMAS. (*Slightly testy.*) That place didn't have more than 5 minutes of hot water.

FRANK. Something tells me that's not a problem here.

THOMAS. I can't say we're going to be having dinner tonight, so you both should definitely, please have some of this.

     (*He offers the meats.*)

FRANK. No dinner? I thought we might *sit down.*

THOMAS. You wanted to have a "meal and stay up"? "Whiskey"? "Talk"? Like that?

ADRIANNE. I could do that too.

FRANK. No no. That'd be me and Thomas.

ADRIANNE. But aren't we here so we can all talk?

ELLEN. This is what happens at the summer house. The "grown-ups" stay up till like 2 in the morning and talk about books and writers and movements from like the 1890's while the "kids" go outside, and enjoy the weather.

ADRIANNE. I just read *The Savage Detectives.* We could talk about that.

THOMAS. The Bolaño? You do want the gig.

> (ELLEN *texts.*
> *She looks up.*)

ELLEN. I'm going out soon. So if you want me to take you to your rooms—

THOMAS. You are? Where?

ELLEN. We talked about this.

THOMAS. I didn't think it would be *tonight.*

FRANK. (*Explaining.*) Adrianne, *we're* going to talk. Me and Thomas. Okay? That's what we do.

THOMAS. We're not doing anything *tonight* anyway because it's *very late.* I'm going to bed, and apparently Ellen is going out.

FRANK. If we're not talking and we're not eating, what are we going to do?

THOMAS. Jesus Frank, you *really* want a proper dinner? It's almost 10.

FRANK. (*Defensive.*) It was a long drive Tom.

THOMAS. I know, we've been waiting here.

FRANK. We came a long way to see you.

THOMAS. (*Reconciliation.*) Of course, yes. And you're a good man for doing so. Why is it that driving is so fucking exhausting? Is it the sitting? No of course, not. It's the Constant Focus. The constant use of the Survival Instinct. That, by the way, is why *writing* is *so* impossible.

FRANK. It is?

THOMAS. Don't you find?

FRANK. Of course *I* do. *You* do?

THOMAS. Of course I do.

ADRIANNE. Me too.

THOMAS. Ah-ha, you are a writer. You're fucked.

ADRIANNE. Why do people always say that?

FRANK. Tom, to be honest, I was just maybe hoping that you and I could discuss...

> (*A moment.*)

THOMAS. Your book? Yes. Yes. Of course, yes. Can we do it tomorrow?

FRANK. I guess.

THOMAS. (*Sympathetic.*) I know how it is when you finish something. You've got to know.

ELLEN. You just finished a new book?

ADRIANNE. You sent it to Thomas?

FRANK. Doesn't happen to me that often. So yes, I do want—

ADRIANNE. Dad.

FRANK. What? I'm not that prolific because I'm
Well there's editing the journal which is full-time
And there's a publisher who's maybe interested
and maybe if Thomas could write a blurb—

THOMAS. How is the journal?

FRANK. Exhausting. I was on the short list for a job at *Esquire*, thought that'd be my way out.

THOMAS. Quite an honor being on the short list.

FRANK. Didn't get it.

THOMAS. I'm looking forward to talking about your book. And catching up. It has been what?

FRANK. Two years.

THOMAS. Can we just please do it tomorrow?

FRANK. Fine. FINE.

THOMAS. Now, can I show you your rooms?

> (FRANK *picks up his own bag.*
> ADRIANNE *picks up her bag.*
> ELLEN *stops them.*)

ELLEN. (*To* ADRIANNE.) Before you go up, have some of this.

ADRIANNE. I'm not really that into cured meats.

ELLEN. You're not like *vegan* are you?

> (ADRIANNE *takes a slice of capicola.*
> *She tries to eat it.*)

Super-Gamey, right?

ADRIANNE. Yeah. Very.

ELLEN. It's capicola. My boss gets it for us because he thinks he's Tony Soprano even though he lives in Tribeca and works in a bank.

FRANK. Wait a second. We're only here two nights. If we talk about my book tomorrow night, and you still have to talk to Adrianne, when will we play "the book game"?

THOMAS. Did you want to? It's been a long time.

FRANK. It's a *tradition*.

ADRIANNE. What is it?

THOMAS. You would like it.

ELLEN. I can't play tonight. I'm going out.

FRANK. (*To* ELLEN.) The game is hard with just three.

ELLEN. My friend Ivan is spending the weekend in town.

THOMAS. (*To* ELLEN.) What about Adrianne? I don't think she wants to just spend time with me and Frank.

ADRIANNE. (*To* ELLEN.) I don't know if I'm up for going out.

ELLEN. (*To* ADRIANNE.) Ivan's friends are kinda boring anyway.

THOMAS. (*To* ELLEN.) So then why rush out and see him?

ELLEN. (*To* THOMAS.) 'Cause I never get to see him.

      (*Pause.*)

I have *plans*. We're going to go to this restaurant that apparently has an amazing wine list.

THOMAS. How could you possibly turn that down?

ELLEN. You spend a lot of money on wine.

THOMAS. Ellen's a real expert.

ELLEN. Everyone at work has been buying shares in vineyards.

FRANK. You've got us. Stay here with us.

ELLEN. Take it easy there Frank.

ADRIANNE. I think that if I had this house, I'd never leave.

ELLEN. Well, my father's always here.

THOMAS. Writing.

ADRIANNE. (*Impressed.*) You write here?

THOMAS. A little cabin out there, yes. I can show you later in the morning.

ELLEN (*Hold on.*) You're going to show her your cabin?

FRANK. I'd like to see your cabin. I've never seen it.

THOMAS. Well tomorrow we can all go and look at it. A party. It's not that thrilling. No internet.

ELLEN. That's another thing about this place. The reception is terrible.

ADRIANNE. But good for reading, writing, right?

ELLEN. You *really* are in undergrad huh?

THOMAS. Those things don't matter to Ellen.

ELLEN. (*Defensive.*) That's right. I don't "care about books," about my father's cabin, about what *The Paris Review* is going on about. I don't listen to NPR.

THOMAS. I didn't mean—

ELLEN. Frank you're in the guest room down here.

      (ELLEN *points.*)

THOMAS. Ellen come on. Don't do this.

ELLEN. And Adrianne is up there with us.

>(ELLEN *points upstairs.*
>ADRIANNE *takes a few steps toward the stairs and then STOPS.*
>*She sees something.*
>*It's a baseball in a glass case.*)

ADRIANNE. What is that?

THOMAS. You noticed My New Purchase.

ELLEN. It's *really hard* to miss.

THOMAS. (*To* ADRIANNE.) You still a baseball fan?

ADRIANNE. Yankee.

>(THOMAS *steps towards her.*)

THOMAS. So then that must mean nothing to you.

>(FRANK *joins them.*
>*He examines the ball in the case.*)

FRANK. Mookie Wilson. Is that from '86? Jesus, Tom.

THOMAS. It makes me very happy that I can still impress Frank Bay and his daughter.

FRANK. Why would someone who's won the National Book Award want to impress me?

THOMAS. We're both baseball fans, right?

ADRIANNE. That's the wild pitch?

THOMAS. No, it's the ball that went through Buckner's legs. You've seen game 6?

ADRIANNE. I wasn't born yet but I've seen it on TV.

THOMAS. (*To* FRANK.) Can you believe I actually turned the game off? Missed the play.

FRANK. No one thought they would come back. Just die-hards.

THOMAS. What a night in the city.

>(ADRIANNE *and* ELLEN *watch* THOMAS *and* FRANK.)

ADRIANNE. It's funny how Mets fans get emotional when they think of that play.

ELLEN. Looks like Adrianne's *not* impressed.

THOMAS. Well I'm not as impressive as I used to be, am I?

FRANK. Well you should know that at Ade's school they study you. Quite a bit.

THOMAS. I'm not sure anyone can teach someone to be a writer.

FRANK. Of course you can't.

ADRIANNE. (*Disagreeing.*) How would you know if you were a writer unless you took a class?

THOMAS. Well I
We
just wrote.
Right? Frank?

FRANK. Yup.

ELLEN. Until you both went to grad school for *writing*.

ADRIANNE. Our teacher had us read *The Train in South Chicago*.

THOMAS. That story is a relic. It seems that the writer should strive *not to be taught*.

ELLEN. Oh Jesus.

THOMAS. Ellen, no one wants to be a textbook. I'm still working, in the field.

ADRIANNE. I read they're about to do a movie of *Alvin's Wish*.

FRANK. Wow, really? Congrats.

THOMAS. How do you think I paid for that ball?

ELLEN. (*To* ADRIANNE.) Did people think it was annoying that you knew My Dad?

ADRIANNE. I didn't tell them.

ELLEN. Did you not want to get a better grade?

ADRIANNE. We don't have grades at my school.

THOMAS. I stayed on your couch!

ADRIANNE. I don't want anyone to be biased about my work.

THOMAS. Oh you'll get over that.

ADRIANNE. It was cool, actually, because the class was into your story without me saying anything to make them fans.

FRANK. That's a surprise?

ADRIANNE. I just think that the work should stand on its own. I know that there are favors and things and all the rest but at the end of the day—really—it's sort of about the story. I know that sounds incredibly undergraduate and pretentious, I do, I know that, but I sort of think it's true.

THOMAS. Well Adrianne, tell you what:
If you're still a fan by the end of the weekend, I think we can work out the apprenticeship.

ADRIANNE. Seriously?

THOMAS. It's looking good.

FRANK. That is something.

THOMAS. Well you practically told her she'd have it, so why not.

ADRIANNE. Well if you don't think I'm qualified.

FRANK. Hey, Ade—

THOMAS. Nothing promised. Okay?

ADRIANNE. I don't want to be just be given
My whole point was that just because I know you

THOMAS. Maybe you just don't like Mets fans.

ADRIANNE. No, no. That's not—

THOMAS. Kidding.

> (ELLEN *looks up from her phone.*)

ELLEN. (*To* ADRIANNE.) Hey, Bolaño. You going out with me? I just found out they're getting there really soon.

ADRIANNE. What about the book game?

THOMAS. (*To* ADRIANNE.) Go and see "town" with Ellen and Tomorrow, I'll cook steaks and we'll play.

FRANK. Aren't we talking about my book tomorrow night?

THOMAS. (*To* FRANK.) We can't play with three.

FRANK. (*To* ELLEN.) You really have to go out?

ELLEN. Yes, yes I do.

ADRIANNE. (*To* ELLEN.) Can I unpack really quickly?

ELLEN. Just go up and drop off your bags.
Here.

> (ELLEN *walks with* ADRIANNE *upstairs.*
> *They are offstage.*
> THOMAS *and* FRANK *alone.*)

THOMAS. (*Quick.*) I can't tell you how glad I am you made it out here.

FRANK. I'm glad to be here.

THOMAS. It's not the *actual* distance.
For a lot of people the real obstacle to coming out here is *psychological distance.* It's how far it *feels* to get here from The City.

FRANK. Light years.

THOMAS. Ha.
Yes.
Did you try these blueberries?

> (*He offers them.*)

See how *generous* I am?

FRANK. That's not fair.

THOMAS. *Generosity.* Big Thing with you.

FRANK. No.

THOMAS. I actually want to thank you. You put me in my place, last week on the phone. You reminded me—

FRANK. We don't have to talk about—

THOMAS. No, no, no. You were right. It's been too long. Kristin and I have had this place four years. You used to come to the old house a lot.

FRANK. You've been busy.

THOMAS. I haven't been a "good friend."

FRANK. Hence the "generosity" dig.

THOMAS. Just trying to make a quip.

FRANK. Authors like you make quips. Authors like me make digs.

THOMAS. Well you *used* to make quips.

FRANK. (*Referring to house.*) This here, these are some nice *digs*. Huh? Yeah?

THOMAS. Well you know all about why that is. According to your journal my wife is an heiress.

    (*A moment.*)

FRANK. That article was years ago.

THOMAS. And it wasn't exactly correct but what do you care.

FRANK. It was a puff piece: New book, new marriage—

THOMAS. And I just *graze* here.

FRANK. Most of our subscribers are poetry professors. So for you to be angry with me...

THOMAS. It wasn't *accurate*.

    (*A Beat.*)

FRANK. You don't think I'm good at what I do.

THOMAS. You're a great writer.

FRANK. But not a top-notch editor, right?

THOMAS. I told *Esquire* that no one knows more about fiction than you.

FRANK. I knew it. They *did* ask you about me.

THOMAS. Just because I know them, doesn't mean they aren't bastards.

FRANK. I could have done the job, Tom. The Article Was Accurate. *This is* The Delling Summer Home.

THOMAS. Don't say it like that. You've been to *our* apartment in the city.

FRANK. Not the parties, my friend.

THOMAS. You can't take that personally.

FRANK. Why would I take it personally? Not like we've known each other for ages? Or went to grad school together. Or in the same field. Or like I've been trying to find a book agent. Or a better job? Why on earth would you invite me to one of those parties?

THOMAS. Look, Frank, I'm sorry. You're right… I'm not perfect.

FRANK. You very much are not.

THOMAS. (*Pointed.*) You weren't supposed to say that. Okay?

I did ask you up. I did offer your daughter a job.

FRANK. If you don't want her, don't do it.

THOMAS. Frank, you told her.

FRANK. You told me.

THOMAS. I said it was a *possibility*. But you ran with that. So, here we are.

(*A moment.*)

FRANK. Look I need to talk to you.

Can I have a blueberry?

(THOMAS *hands him a blueberry.*)

Where's Kristin?

THOMAS. She's in the city with Chester and Eugene.

FRANK. The *dogs?*

THOMAS. Are you mad at me? I am sorry it's taken me a while to get to the book.

FRANK. I had this odd adventure two nights ago. I met this pretty girl at a bar. Young.

THOMAS. Ah ha. This is good for you. Very Bukowski.

FRANK. She was younger than your daughter.

THOMAS. You shouldn't think about that.

FRANK. Why not?

THOMAS. Because it's desire it's human fucking desire and you had it. How long has it been?

FRANK. She made a really clear point of telling me how she had slept with several prominent writers—

THOMAS. How was it?

FRANK. She didn't want to fuck *me* Tom.

THOMAS. Sorry to hear that.

FRANK. There *was one* she was really proud of. A Big One. That she—

THOMAS. People say things all the time. Come on—

FRANK. I know it's some girl at a bar. I know but I have to ask.

THOMAS. Wait a moment. *What* do you have to ask?

FRANK. If my daughter is going to be *working* with you—

THOMAS. Hold on. *Hold on.*

You're not suggesting that I'm

Because someone told you *a story* about me at a bar...

FRANK. You understand.

THOMAS. I don't think I do.

> (*A beat.*)

FRANK. Just be careful.

THOMAS. Are you being serious right now?

FRANK. Hey, it's my job.

THOMAS. I've known Adrianne since she was *born*.

FRANK. The offer you made her was very generous.

THOMAS. I can *withdraw* it.

FRANK. How's your marriage?

THOMAS. What is this?

FRANK. You have a a a Reputation. It's why your first wife kicked you out. And I don't judge you, at all, if anything, I think hey, this guy, he's living life. But you need to promise me that—

THOMAS. Excuse me? Promise what?

FRANK. Stop it.

THOMAS. (*Ending it.*) Do you want something to eat or not?

> (ELLEN *and* ADRIANNE *continue to come down the stairs. They have changed their clothes.*)

FRANK. I'd love some food, thanks.

> (THOMAS *goes into the kitchen.*)

So you are going out?

> (THOMAS *comes out of the kitchen. He's got hummus and one carrot. He places them in front of* FRANK.)

This is great Thomas, thanks. Thank you.

THOMAS. No problem Frank. Let me see what else I can get for you.

> (ADRIANNE *and* ELLEN *watch as* THOMAS *goes back to the kitchen.*)

FRANK. So Ellen how's the city?

ELLEN. Hold on.

> (*She's texting.*)

ADRIANNE. I didn't know you sent Thomas your book.

FRANK. We haven't talked about it yet.

ADRIANNE. What were you talking about?

> (ELLEN *looks up.*)

FRANK. I was asking how the city was.

ELLEN. I feel like I'm never home. I'm always working and if I do get to see Ivan it's always to go with him to openings of museums and shows cause of the Foundation his father set up.

ADRIANNE. Seems like fun.

ELLEN. You'll see.

> (THOMAS *comes back with some more cheese.*
> *He puts it down.*)

THOMAS. How's this? I wouldn't want to be a derelict host.

> (THOMAS *goes back into the kitchen.*)

ELLEN. (*To* FRANK.) So you're still writing?

ADRIANNE. (*To* ELLEN.) He's got a New Book.

FRANK. (*To* ADRIANNE.) You haven't even read this one.

ELLEN. She just loves her Dad.

> (THOMAS *comes out with a bottle of wine.*
> *He sets it down on the table.*
> *He places the wine glasses down.*)

THOMAS. Frank, this okay?

ELLEN. What's going on?

FRANK. Nothing.

THOMAS. Girls? Wine?

> (ELLEN *and* ADRIANNE *both raise their glasses.*)

FRANK. Now Tom, I don't know.

ELLEN. I'm 25. I can have a glass of wine.

ADRIANNE. I'd like some too.

FRANK. (*To* ADRIANNE.) Just don't go crazy okay?

ADRIANNE. Okay. I *won't.*

ELLEN. (*To* ADRIANNE.) Are you crazy?

ADRIANNE. (*Taking the wine.*) No. I'm not like crazy, crazy.

FRANK. No one said you were.

ADRIANNE. Well you actually just did say I was.

ELLEN. Most of my friends do Zoloft.

> (*A moment.*)

ADRIANNE. I spent some time in medical services around midterms.

ELLEN. My sophomore year I almost killed someone. Really.

THOMAS. She did.

ADRIANNE. Oh, cool.

(*Silence, drinking.*

Finally, ELLEN *checks her phone.*)

ELLEN. Okay, we should go soon. There's going to be a lot of people and apparently they don't have a lot of room in the back.

ADRIANNE. (*Empty already.*) Can I have another glass of wine first?

FRANK. Maybe you should take it easy.

ADRIANNE. It's two glasses.

THOMAS. It's Frank's choice.

FRANK. Far be it for me to stand in the way of Adrianne.

(THOMAS *pours her another glass of wine.*)

THOMAS. We used to give Ellen wine at dinner.

ELLEN. And now I'm about to drive 45 minutes in the dark for more wine. Nothing wrong with me at all.

(THOMAS *produces small brown cigarillos.*)

FRANK. Jesus, you still smoke cigarettes?

THOMAS. Cigarillos.

ADRIANNE. (*Bolder.*) There's definitely something about smoking and writing that go hand in hand. I think Ginsberg said that.

THOMAS. Ginsberg? Isn't that terribly old fashioned?

ADRIANNE. I read a lot of the Beats in High School actually.

THOMAS. The most overrated group ever in American Letters.

ADRIANNE. No way.

THOMAS. Do you know how Burroughs wrote?

ADRIANNE. On drugs?

FRANK. With the reams?

THOMAS. Kerouac would use the reams.
Burroughs would write and write and write.
Put his work on note cards and then arrange it randomly.
And publish.
How's that?
Is that *Genius*?

ADRIANNE. I love the first section of *Naked Lunch.*

THOMAS. Did you finish the entire book?

ADRIANNE. I'm not saying I read them now. But when I was first getting into fiction

THOMAS. (*Not letting it go.*) So did you finish *Naked Lunch* or not?

ADRIANNE. They're not the only writers I like.

THOMAS. Who else?

ADRIANNE. Miranda July, Joshua Ferris, David Foster Wallace, Nicole Krauss.

THOMAS. (*Derisive.*) Well now you're really impressing me, now you're really going out on a limb there.

ELLEN. She *is* in undergrad Dad.

ADRIANNE. So who should I be reading? Other than you, of course.

ELLEN. Don't listen to him, he's going to say Kierkegaard or something.

FRANK. He didn't write fiction.

THOMAS. Have you read Kafka?

ADRIANNE. Of course.

THOMAS. Barthelme?

ADRIANNE. Yes.

THOMAS. Something tells me you like Paul Auster.

ELLEN. Why are you talking to her like this?

THOMAS. This is how I talk to all writers.

ADRIANNE. What's wrong with Paul Auster?

THOMAS. He's a little pop, Adrianne.

ADRIANNE. You're the one with a *movie*, aren't you?

THOMAS. Auster has had *several* movies.

FRANK. How about we play the book game?
Can we do that?
Settle it on the field?

THOMAS. I'm game.

ADRIANNE. Me too.

ELLEN. Ivan's going to text really soon to tell me exactly where we're going.

ADRIANNE. One round?

THOMAS. I used to beat Frank all the time at the old house.

FRANK. That's not *all* you did at the old house, Tom.

THOMAS. That's true. I did lot of other things.
Chopped wood and burnt it. For heat. Yes. I even kept the old stove.

    (*He points to the Old Stove.*)

How I got the idea for *The Winter Blade*.

ADRIANNE. I read that.

    (THOMAS *starts to clear the plates.*)

THOMAS. (*Building.*) See Frank, I used to go up to the old house and I could have gone to the local dive bar, or into town and done whatever I wanted. I had published *The Chicago Stories*. I was young. But I stayed in. And I wrote. *That's* what I did. Okay?

FRANK. (*Matching him.*) Actually Tom, *doing that* is not what got you kicked out. And then you didn't have that old house anymore, and everyone forgot about the *The Chicago Stories*, you couldn't do whatever you wanted. Because you needed help.

THOMAS. Well I had my good friend didn't I? And he let me crash on his couch. And then I wrote *Alvin's Wish*. People were nice to me again. Very nice. And now here we are and my old buddy is saying awful things about me. Why, I'm not sure but here we are.

ADRIANNE. What are you guys talking about?

ELLEN. What does that mean?

FRANK. Neither of you need to worry about it.

ELLEN. What awful things?

(ADRIANNE, *now a bit drunk, stands up.*)

ADRIANNE. Could I have a cigarillo?

(THOMAS *gives* ADRIANNE *a cigarillo.*
She lights it and sits down.)

FRANK. It's time for you to go.

ADRIANNE. Why?

FRANK. Because I'd like to talk to Thomas alone. And you're drunk.

ADRIANNE. That doesn't make sense.

THOMAS. Tell her really why.

FRANK. (*To* THOMAS.) *Why* are you doing this?

THOMAS. You're being ridiculous.

FRANK. This is not fair. Not at all.

THOMAS. You sure about that?

FRANK. Don't start with me Tom.

THOMAS. I'm not scared of you Frank.

ELLEN. *Why* can't she stay?

ADRIANNE. Yeah, why?

THOMAS. Frank?

FRANK. You sure you want me to do this?

THOMAS. I have nothing to hide.

FRANK. Because I don't trust Thomas around my daughter.

(*Pause.*)

ADRIANNE. Jesus Dad. That's dark.

FRANK. He's known to be…

ELLEN. (*Fired up.*) Whoa Watch it.

THOMAS. Please stop what you're saying. It's embarrassing.

FRANK. You asked me to say, so here it is. Here it goes.

ELLEN. What makes you say that?

FRANK. I've known him for a long time.

THOMAS. That has nothing to do with it.

FRANK. Sometimes when you see or when you know—

ELLEN. (*Appalled.*) What did you see what did you know?

THOMAS. I forgot that this is how Frank is.

FRANK. COME ON.

ELLEN. Dad could you say something.

THOMAS. What should I say?

ADRIANNE. Aren't we going?

ELLEN. Whatta freak you are.

FRANK. It's my daughter.

ADRIANNE. (*Ending it.*) Okay, I want to go! See Ivan and his friends. Let's have whiskey sours or something!
Please. Now. Please.

> (ADRIANNE *takes a cracker.*)

ELLEN. You're eating now? You gonna be okay?

ADRIANNE. Can we please go?

> (*Pause.*)

ELLEN. I don't blame you for wanting out. Not at all.

FRANK. Hey thanks.

> (ELLEN *starts to walk towards the door. QUICKLY.*
> ADRIANNE *follows.*
> ELLEN *checks her phone.*
> *She stops.*)

ELLEN. Oh Fuck. Fuck.

> (*They look at her.*)

I fucking knew he'd do this. FUCK.

> (*She puts her phone away.*
> *Long Pause.*)

ADRIANNE. Not very nice of him.

ELLEN. You don't know him. So shut up.

ADRIANNE. You're the one who was saying he was—

ELLEN. A dick? I know. But only I can say it.

(THOMAS *offers wine to* ELLEN.)

THOMAS. Now you can see me beat Frank in the game.

FRANK. Now We can play.

ELLEN. Are you fucking kidding?

FRANK. We have four.

ELLEN. (*To* FRANK.) I didn't forget what you just said.

> (ELLEN *and* ADRIANNE *on one side of the room.*
> THOMAS *and* FRANK *on another.*)

THOMAS. We can call it a night.

ELLEN. Great.

THOMAS. Ellen—

ELLEN. I can't believe I came up here for this. No offense of course.

> (*Pause.*)

ADRIANNE. There's this kid at my school who would text girls asking them to meet him in like the library or under the arch, and then he wouldn't show up, but instead he would hide and film them on his phone. And then he'd post the clips online, just like girls waiting for him. In the rain, in the cold, just waiting.

ELLEN. So?

ADRIANNE. So to get back at him some girls put all the really specific things he does in bed on the bathroom walls all over school. You can imagine.

ELLEN. This isn't school and Ivan isn't *filming* me. He's flaking.

ADRIANNE. You could do something.

ELLEN. You think it'd be a good idea for me to put on the bathroom walls that Ivan likes it with the lights on? Something like that?

ADRIANNE. You could call him.

ELLEN. Desperate.

ADRIANNE. We can go to a bar ourselves.

ELLEN. Do you have an ID?

ADRIANNE. I could wait in the car. While you drink.

ELLEN. That would be so dark.

ADRIANNE. Really dark.

> (*They have a moment.*
> *Pause.*)

ELLEN. We could just talk about my father The Perv.

ADRIANNE. What about the game?

ELLEN. Fuck. No.

(ELLEN *starts to head upstairs.*)

THOMAS. You okay?

(ELLEN *doesn't answer, continues upstairs.*
ADRIANNE *stays in the room.*
Silence.)

ADRIANNE. We could talk about the Bolaño.

FRANK. You think?

THOMAS. If you go past the old barn, there's a remarkable view of the stars. One of the advantages of being so far from the City.

(ADRIANNE *stands there for a moment then exits.*
THOMAS *and* FRANK *sit in the room.*
There is silence.)

FRANK. Stars huh?

THOMAS. Aren't we friends? You knew me in school, when I first got published

FRANK. And published and published and published

THOMAS. That's what this is about? *Alvin's* was five years ago.

FRANK. And then the new one.

THOMAS. Okay, so.

FRANK. So then for you to walk around like it's all here for you
That everyone is here for the taking

THOMAS. I was trying to help your daughter.

FRANK. You sure about that?

THOMAS. I thought that's what I was doing. And then you wanted to talk about your book and now I don't know what to say, Frank.

FRANK. Really? Should I say something *for* you to use? Would that help? Tom?

(*Long Pause.*)

THOMAS. This isn't about a girl, or a book or Adrianne or *Esquire.*
You think I'm going to use your words? For a story?
That's what *this* is?

FRANK. Maybe you'd just use my entire story.

THOMAS. Sorry?

FRANK. *The Train in South Chicago.*

THOMAS. You think what? That I   what?

FRANK. *Chicago* was your breakout story.

(*Pause.*)

THOMAS. I never said you weren't an influence.

FRANK. I brought a story into workshop that was very similar.

THOMAS. It's not the *only* thing I ever wrote.

FRANK. Look at you now. Look at what you get.

THOMAS. Do you know how *many hours a day* I work?

FRANK. You know? I've been having this conversation in my head for so long and now, now, forget it.

THOMAS. There are *reasons* why I have what I have.

FRANK. You took my idea. You took my fucking idea.

THOMAS. Why didn't you say something 17 years ago when it happened? Why'd you let me crash on your couch?

FRANK. We were friends.

THOMAS. I was miserable.

FRANK. So was I.

THOMAS. I've been lucky, Frank.

FRANK. It's *not* luck. My daughter is obsessed with your work. She loves your writing.

> (*Pause.*)

THOMAS. This new book of yours could be the one that gets you back.

FRANK. Gets me back?

Tommy, I was never there.

And here you are—

After I called you a philanderer and a molester and saboteur and thief

Still here you are trying to make me feel better.

Whatta joke.

> (FRANK *stands up.*
> He *looks around.*
> He *pours himself a big drink.*)

I am so fucking fucked.

> (FRANK *exits.*
> THOMAS *drinks.*
> ADRIANNE *enters from outside.*
> She starts to go upstairs.*)

THOMAS. (*Exasperated.*) Why am I supposed to read a story of yours from *high school?*

ADRIANNE. I would have sent you something else.

THOMAS. Well it's your *job* as a writer, no as a *person*, to find out what it takes.

ADRIANNE. Okay, sure.

THOMAS. (*Staying on her.*) Don't do that.

ADRIANNE. Do what?

THOMAS. You really don't show your dad any of your new stories? He's a very good writer. He could help you.

ADRIANNE. If you don't think I'm good enough—

THOMAS. You're still not hearing me. Why should I have to read your Panda story?

ADRIANNE. Sorry.

THOMAS. If you want this you have to actually demonstrate that you can interact with me as a writer. As an adult.

ADRIANNE. How would that work?

THOMAS. If I have to tell you…

     (*Pause.*)

ADRIANNE. So *this* is the interview.

THOMAS. Do you want it to be?

ADRIANNE. I'd rather just have the job. Internship.

THOMAS. *Apprenticeship.*

ADRIANNE. That. Yes.

     (*They look at each other.*
     Pause.)

THOMAS. It's late.

ADRIANNE. Didn't you used to stay up late? You're not that old, are you?

THOMAS. I think you'd be surprised.

     (ADRIANNE *takes a sip of wine.*)

ADRIANNE. Let me ask you a question.

THOMAS. What kind of question?

ADRIANNE. It's literary. It's a game.

THOMAS. A Literary Game?

ADRIANNE. Your Favorite book is:

THOMAS. *Really?*

ADRIANNE. If you don't want to answer the question.

THOMAS. I'd rather throw around a baseball.

ADRIANNE. I don't play baseball anymore.

     (*A moment.*)

Favorite book?

THOMAS. *Don Quixote.*

ADRIANNE. *Really?*

THOMAS. What?

ADRIANNE. Nothing.

THOMAS. And Yours?

ADRIANNE. There's another question for you.

THOMAS. I see, a set up. Expectation.

ADRIANNE. What's the Best book?

THOMAS. What do you think?

ADRIANNE. *Harry Potter* is amazing.

THOMAS. Ha. *Anna Karenina.*

ADRIANNE. So, you have a problem. At least according to my teacher.

THOMAS. I have a lot of problems.

ADRIANNE. Do you want to know your problem?

THOMAS. I do.

ADRIANNE. If you think the best book and your favorite book are different then you don't trust your taste.

> (*Pause.*)

THOMAS. (*Not genuine.*) What a cute game.

ADRIANNE. Don't be patronizing

THOMAS. Okay, I won't be patronizing.

ADRIANNE. I really admire your work.

THOMAS. Thank you.

ADRIANNE. My favorite book is *The Virgin Suicides* But I always say the best book is *The Sun Also Rises*

THOMAS. Great book. The Hemingway.

ADRIANNE. We have some of the same problems. We don't trust our taste.

THOMAS. Well, I do actually trust my taste.

ADRIANNE. Oh. Sure.

> (THOMAS *gets up.*)

THOMAS. I have to get up early to finish a chapter.

ADRIANNE. I meant what I said about your work.

THOMAS. I expected a little more, Adrianne. To be honest.

> (ADRIANNE *gets up.*)

ADRIANNE. Where's my dad?

THOMAS. In his room.

(ADRIANNE *goes to get her dad.*
ELLEN *comes downstairs.*
She faces her father.)

ELLEN. He called you a pedophile basically.

THOMAS. He's having a tough time.

ELLEN. So you aren't allowed to say anything?

THOMAS. I'm not ever sure what he's talking about.

ELLEN. I know why you and Mom split.

THOMAS. Ellen, that was different.

ELLEN. Let's make them go.

THOMAS. We can't. You'll understand that later.

ELLEN. Why do people always say that to me, that I'll understand later when I won't?

Why don't people just say, you know what, here's the Big Fucked-Up Thing I'm going to do. Why do they have to break it up into little pieces of fucked up?

THOMAS. I don't know.

ELLEN. Well you don't ever know unless it's about you.

(*Pause.*)

Am I *ugly?*

THOMAS. *No.*

ELLEN. You said I was fat. You said I was pigging out.

THOMAS. When you have someone who really loves you.

ELLEN. You are so bad at this. No one really loves me

THOMAS. I do.

ELLEN. Where do I work?

THOMAS. Come on Ellen, I've tried.

ELLEN. Where do I work?

THOMAS. You work for a bank.

ELLEN. Which one?

THOMAS. Please don't tell me that after all I've done

ELLEN. Done? Done?

THOMAS. If you're going to be like this

ELLEN. You don't even know where I work.

THOMAS. YOU WORK AT A BANK, what's the difference

ELLEN. I'm not a teller Dad, I make six figures.

THOMAS. I'm sorry Ivan didn't come out here.

ELLEN. We've been going out for over six months and you never once met him. You never once had him up here. And now he's gone for good.

THOMAS. I would have invited him.

ELLEN. Instead you invited them. And look at them. Look at what they're doing here.

THOMAS. Adrianne's not bad.

ELLEN. She's got her underwear all over the bathroom.

THOMAS. I think she was probably feeling rushed.

ELLEN. Because she wanted to run down and talk to you. You think I don't see that? And you just sit there.

THOMAS. I'm sorry that I don't know the name of where you work

ELLEN. Yeah, I get it—

THOMAS. I am sorry that I'm drunk and that Adrianne is being like she is and Frank is here and it's weird.

(FRANK *and* ADRIANNE *have come out.*)

FRANK. It's weird that I'm here?

THOMAS. Yes, Frank, you made it weird.

FRANK. And what about you?

ADRIANNE. (*To* THOMAS.) You said I should talk like a writer. You said—

THOMAS. I was *trying.* With both of you.

FRANK. So no book game?

THOMAS. Maybe it's time for bed.

ELLEN. Or maybe you should just go home.

(*Pause.*)

THOMAS. It's not the worst idea.

ADRIANNE. Is this because of the game?

ELLEN. It's because it's weird.

FRANK. We just got here.

ELLEN. So you can pack up easily.

THOMAS. It is really uncomfortable.

FRANK. Where are we supposed to go?

ELLEN. Sleep at the lake. On the shore.

ADRIANNE. Are you *serious?*

THOMAS. I can't see how this gets better.

ELLEN. If you want to stay some place you're not wanted.

FRANK. We were invited here.

THOMAS. Well let's be honest.

ADRIANNE. I wanted to meet you.

ELLEN. You've met.

FRANK. Thanks for the great times.

ELLEN. Don't be such a child.

ADRIANNE. You're the one who is on the phone, texting.

THOMAS. There's nothing wrong with that.

ADRIANNE. Why are you doing this to us?

ELLEN. *We're* not doing anything.

ADRIANNE. Why are you being like this to us? What did we do?

ELLEN. What else can we do?

THOMAS. (*Taking charge.*) Okay look look look: Let's forget it. Stay.

FRANK. How can we do that??

ADRIANNE. What is going on?

THOMAS. Let's play the game. That will help.

ELLEN. What? How?

THOMAS. (*To* ELLEN.) It's not going to work, them leaving.

ELLEN. They started it.

FRANK. What are you doing?

THOMAS. This is no way to end the night. Ellen we can do better.

    (*Pause.*)

ELLEN. Fine. Let's just play.

FRANK. You were *just saying we should go.*

ADRIANNE. We should, we should go.

THOMAS. This is what happens at the summer house.

ELLEN. It's true, There's always a fight.

THOMAS. Every summer. It gets strained.

FRANK. Aren't we old friends? Didn't you stay on my couch?

THOMAS. And so here I am, saying THANK YOU.

ADRIANNE. CAN WE PLEASE GO?

ELLEN. I was upset. It's been a long night. Come on.

    (*Pause.*)

FRANK. Let's play then. Yes.

ADRIANNE. Really?

FRANK. (*Pissed.*) Hey! We'll bury the hatchet. Okay?

ADRIANNE. I'm not playing.

THOMAS. We'll even let you guys win.

FRANK. Go To Hell.

Adrianne, get a book from the shelf.

ADRIANNE. (*To* FRANK.) Why are you doing this?

THOMAS. Because Frank really wants to beat me in something.

FRANK. (*To* THOMAS.) You're minor. You write Airport fiction.

ELLEN. Your daughter doesn't think so. She loves it.

ADRIANNE. Fine. Let's play.

THOMAS. (*Taking charge.*) Okay, everyone go get a book from the shelf.

> (*A moment.*
> ADRIANNE, ELLEN, FRANK *and* THOMAS
> *all go to get a book from the shelf.*
> *They all sit on the couches.*
> *Drinks are poured.*)

THE GAME

THOMAS. Okay, so, the rules of the game. To review and for those who have not played.

FRANK. It's like Dictionary for Books.

THOMAS. We each have a book. One person shows everyone else their book.

Then we all write down what we imagine the first line of that book to be.

FRANK. While the person with the book writes down the actual first line.

He or she then reads the real first line as well as all of our first lines without saying what is what.

THOMAS. Then we vote. Your goal is to guess the actual first line.

FRANK. And also to fool people into thinking your line is the first line.

ADRIANNE. I'll figure it out.

THOMAS. For instance, if I pulled a book about the history of basketball, you might write:

"James Naismith was the Canadian physical education instructor *who invented basketball* in 1891."

FRANK. Or "Long ago, Mayans played sports with heads of their prisoners."

THOMAS. You wouldn't write that.

FRANK. You might write that.

THOMAS. And you would have to decide what line you thought was closer: mine or Frank's.

ELLEN. Scoring.

FRANK. You get a point if you correctly guess the first line.

THOMAS. You get a point if someone thinks that what you wrote is actually the first line.

ADRIANNE. So it's a game about deception.

THOMAS. Imagination.

FRANK. Reading people.

ADRIANNE. Let's go.

ELLEN. I'll start.

FRANK. Why do you start?

THOMAS. She's the quickest.

ELLEN. Thank you.

>   (ELLEN *picks up her book.*)

This is: *A Jest of God* by Margaret Laurence.

ADRIANNE. Wait a second. These are your books. You've read them.

THOMAS. We're on our honor. Ellen, have you read *A Jest of God* by Margaret Laurence?

ELLEN. I really wish I had but No Dad I haven't. Have you read *A Jest Of God*?

THOMAS. I have not.

ADRIANNE. So we just believe you?

THOMAS. Friends come up and leave books here all the time.

FRANK. (*A quip.*) Your better friends?

THOMAS. (*Also, light.*) Richer. Who truth be told, are not very good at this game. Glad we're playing with the everyman.

FRANK. The everyman is excellent at the book game.

THOMAS. Now, note the cover.

>   (ELLEN *holds up the book.*)

ELLEN. It's a young woman leaning against a tree.

ADRIANNE. She looks very unhappy.

FRANK. No chatting.

THOMAS. Everyone can think for themselves.

ADRIANNE. Can I see it?

>   (ELLEN *hands the book to* ADRIANNE.
>   ADRIANNE *studies it.*)

The full title of the book is *A Jest of God: A moving novel of a woman yearning for love.*

>   (*She hands it back to* ELLEN.)

ELLEN. Can she do that?

FRANK. It's important information.

THOMAS. Okay, let's go.

> (*Everyone writes.*
> *They pass the papers to* ELLEN.
> *She shuffles them.*
> *She looks at them.*)

Now we are voting on what we think is the actual first line.

ELLEN. Someone has really bad handwriting.

FRANK. So be sure you know what they all say before you start.

THOMAS. Try not to telegraph the real answer as you read through the choices. Everything should have equal value.

> (ELLEN *nods.*
> *She reads.*)

ELLEN. 1) That morning, walking to work, she realized there was no way around it: She was cursed with desire.

2) They are not actually chanting my name, of course.

3) Rachel, her heart pounding, walked quickly out of history class, stuffed her diary into her denim bag, pulled her thrift store overcoat tightly over her skinny, lovesick frame and went under the tree to smoke a cigarette in secret, thinking only of him.

4) There was a warm wind coming from the south, and that meant her father would be coming home soon and this time she was ready for him, this time she wouldn't be fooled.

THOMAS. Now Ellen re-reads the lines and we will raise our hand if we think it's the actual first line.

FRANK. *A Jest of God. A Jest of God.*

ELLEN. That's what the book is called.

1) "That morning, walking to work, she realized there was no way around it: She was cursed with desire."

THOMAS. If you think it's 1, raise your hand.

> (*No one raises a hand.*)

ADRIANNE. I don't really read these kinds of books.

THOMAS. What kind is that?

ADRIANNE. Romance novels.

THOMAS. Now we know what *your* line is.

ELLEN. 2) "They are not actually chanting my name, of course."

> (THOMAS *and* FRANK *raise their hands.*)

ELLEN. Should people have to close their eyes? So they don't copy votes.

ADRIANNE. We're on our honor.

THOMAS. (*Genuine.*) Frank is quite good at this game.

FRANK. Used to be.

THOMAS. Did I tell you how we had Franzen up? *Refused* to play. Probably scared.
And in the morning he wanted to use my cabin to write.

ELLEN. So you took him antiquing.

THOMAS. No one gets to use my Cabin.

FRANK. You went *antiquing* with Jonathan Franzen?

ADRIANNE. Are we still *playing?*

THOMAS. Just telling a story.

ADRIANNE. I'm just trying to actually demonstrate that I can interact with you as a writer. As an adult.

(*A moment.*)

ELLEN. (*Continuing.*) 3) "Rachel, her heart pounding, walked quickly out of history class, stuffed her diary into her denim bag, pulled her thrift store overcoat tightly over her skinny, lovesick frame and went under the tree to smoke a cigarette in secret, thinking only of him."

(*No one raises a hand.*)

FRANK. Jonathan Franzen? Wow.

ELLEN. (*Going over.*) 4) "There was a warm wind coming from the south, and that meant her father would be coming home soon and she was ready for him, this time she wouldn't be fooled."

(ADRIANNE *raises her hand.*
A moment.)

It really was the second one that Dad and Frank guessed.

(*They give each other a small high five.*)

FRANK. I knew that last line about blowing hot air had to be yours.

THOMAS. And is there any doubt *who* would write a line about being cursed?

ELLEN. You both got it, congrats.
And Adrianne you thought it was the line that Thomas wrote so that's 2 for Dad, 1 for Frank and 0 for Adrianne.

THOMAS. (*To* ADRIANNE.) That's an old trick you fell for.

ADRIANNE. What?

FRANK. Thomas' line. About a woman *not* being fooled. Power of suggestion.

ADRIANNE. Smart.

THOMAS. And of course the waiting for the father. But we won't get into that.

ADRIANNE. What?

FRANK. Don't let him get into your head.

ADRIANNE. You guys really love this game.

FRANK. (*To* ADRIANNE.) What was that line about Rachel and her diary?

ADRIANNE. The game *just* started.

THOMAS. Hey, any time you want a cigarillo, let me know. There's a great tree back there for smoking.

ELLEN. (*To* THOMAS.) You're being an asshole.

THOMAS. *This* is the game. *This* is how we play.

FRANK. I'll go.

THOMAS. No I'll go.

The next book is called: *The Man in The Closet* by Roch Carrier. And it was translated by Shelia Fischman. *Take note.*

> (THOMAS *shows the book*
> *They look at it.*)

FRANK. Can I see the cover?

THOMAS. Sorry Frank, There's no picture of a man in a closet. You'll have to imagine.

> (*They write.*
> THOMAS *finishes writing and reads:*)

Oh one last bit of very pertinent information. According to *The Globe and Mail* "Roch Carrier is a risk-taker...a lively and readable book."

FRANK. Sounds like someone else I know.

THOMAS. Lively?

FRANK. Readable.

THOMAS. (*Soft.*) Ouch.

> (FRANK *and* THOMAS *share a moment.*
> *They pass their pieces of paper to* THOMAS.)

You were right about the handwriting issue.

FRANK. Let's go.

THOMAS. 1) The sun is going down behind the pine trees.

2) John looked in his closet and realized that because he couldn't have the shoes he wanted as a child he compulsively bought Imported Italian Leather Loafers.

3) The air was impossible so I had no choice but to go to the Maple Street Inn and catch my breath.

4) Louise checked in under a fake name and, after scouring the room for bugs, told the hotel clerk her husband would be joining her shortly.

Okay, so again. This is for *The Man in The Closet.*

Remember there's only four rounds so pay attention.

The first line is: "The sun is going down behind the pine trees."

      (ADRIANNE *raises her hand.*)

The second line is: "John looked in his closet and realized that because he couldn't have the shoes he wanted as a child he compulsively bought Imported Italian Leather Loafers."

      (*No one raises a hand.*)

Anyone?

Third: "The air was impossible so I had no choice but to go to the Maple Street Inn and catch my breath."

      (*No one raises a hand.*)

No?

The fourth is: "Louise checked in under a fake name, and, after scouring the room for bugs, told the hotel clerk her husband would be joining her shortly."

      (FRANK *and* ELLEN *raise their hands.*)

The game is heating up. That's one point for Adrianne because she got the first line.

FRANK. The first line was terrible.

ADRIANNE. Process of elimination.

FRANK. You knew my line?

THOMAS. The "impossible air." How could she not?

FRANK. Thought it might throw some people.

THOMAS. Who wrote the line about the fake name?

ADRIANNE. Me.

THOMAS. (*Barely impressed.*) Uh-Oh, The rookie comes on. Very Jim Thompson.

ADRIANNE. Dashiell Hammett. And the power of suggestion. Fake Name, Fake Line.

THOMAS. Conniving.

ADRIANNE. You said it, not me.

ELLEN. Okay, okay.

THOMAS. Adrianne has three points because Ellen and Frank guessed her line. She is in the lead.

FRANK. Nicely done.

THOMAS. Ellen what is this? Did you think the man in the closet was looking at his Italian shoes?

FRANK. Why *else* would he be in the closet?

ELLEN. Fuck both of you?

ADRIANNE. I almost guessed that line actually.

THOMAS. That was actually a terrible story from Ellen's youth, right?

(*Pause.*)

ELLEN. What are you doing?

THOMAS. We're with friends.

ELLEN. Let's forget it. Okay?

(*Pause.*)

THOMAS. I never got Ellen nice shoes as a child because I thought she should know limits and now—

ELLEN. Would you *please stop it?*

THOMAS. It's one of my great failings as a parent. I feel terrible. I'm sure Frank can relate, his daughter won't even share her stories with him.

FRANK. I'll go.

ADRIANNE. No, Dad, let me do my book. So then I can beat Thomas in the last round.

THOMAS. You have three, I have two, Frank has one and Ellen has none. Let's go.

(ADRIANNE *picks up her book.*)

ADRIANNE. This book is called: *A Sense of an Ending* by Frank Kermode.

THOMAS. Non-fiction is hard.

ADRIANNE. How do you know that it's non-fiction?

THOMAS. You want to go get another book? Go ahead.

ADRIANNE. On the cover is an old-style painting of men, naked, with muscles, blowing horns.

(ADRIANNE *shows the cover.*)

THOMAS. It's the *Sistine Chapel.*

ADRIANNE. Oh, yeah.

ELLEN. Have you guys ever been? It's *amazing.*

(*A Beat.*)

ADRIANNE. Write.

(*They write.*
They pass.
She reads.)

1) The critic's job, more than the artist's, is to help one make sense of the world.

2) I'm bored.

> (*They look at* ELLEN.
> ADRIANNE *continues reading.*)

3) It is not as expected of critics as it is of poets that they should make sense of our lives.

FRANK. Whoa.

ADRIANNE. Yeah.

> (FRANK *and* ADRIANNE *look at each other.*)

FRANK. (*To* ADRIANNE.) You heard that?

THOMAS. What?

> (*A moment.*)

ADRIANNE. 4) Without the end of a story, there is nothing.

FRANK. What's the score?

ADRIANNE. I have three. Thomas has two, you have one and Ellen has none.

THOMAS. Big round for you Frank.

ADRIANNE. Okay. All in favor of 1? The line is: "The critic's job, more than the artist's, is to help one make sense of the world."

> (*A moment.*
> FRANK *raises his hand.*)

2) "I'm bored."

> (*No one raises a hand.*)

THOMAS. That makes it much easier for them.

ADRIANNE. 3) "It is not as expected of critics as it is of poets that they should make sense of our lives."

> (THOMAS *and* ELLEN *raise their hands.*)

FRANK. Fuck.

ADRIANNE. Dad.

FRANK. How did you both know it was that one?

ADRIANNE. And 4) "Without the end of a story, there is nothing."

> (*No one raises a hand.*
> *A moment.*)

THOMAS. Who won?

ADRIANNE. You don't know?

THOMAS. Did Frank make his comeback?

ADRIANNE. It was obviously 3, and Dad you guessed Thomas'. So that's four for Thomas, 3 for me, one for Ellen, and one for you Dad.

ELLEN. Hey Frank we're tied.

FRANK. (*To* THOMAS.) This is bullshit. You basically wrote down the exact first line of that book.

ADRIANNE. (*To* THOMAS.) Your line was a *lot* like the real one. They both had the word critic and were about making sense of the world.

THOMAS. Writing about critics in a book by Frank Kermode? That's shocking?

ADRIANNE. You said you hadn't read it.

THOMAS. I know the author.

ELLEN. I've never seen him read it.

FRANK. That doesn't mean he never picked it up.

THOMAS. I'm just *that good.*

ADRIANNE. You're admitting that you cheated.

FRANK. Unbelievable. Every time, every goddamn time you do this. Nothing's changed, has it?

THOMAS. You guys want out? Too much? We can just go to bed.

ADRIANNE. (*To* THOMAS.) How much do you want to bet that I win?

THOMAS. I've never gambled during the book game but I'm intrigued by the compulsive self-destructive behavior.

ADRIANNE. The baseball? Should we bet that?

THOMAS. You're not serious.

ADRIANNE. I am totally serious.

FRANK. Adrianne.

ADRIANNE. That's what I get if I win. Okay?

THOMAS. What do I get if you lose?

ADRIANNE. I'll work for you for free this summer.

FRANK. Adrianne, don't.

ELLEN. Let her do it.

THOMAS. How about this: If you lose, no apprenticeship?

(*A moment.*)

ADRIANNE. Fine, let's go.

FRANK. Adrianne.

ADRIANNE. We on?

ELLEN. Is this real?

THOMAS. Adrianne, I know that you're smart.
And you know that you're smart.

And I'm sure you'll be a good writer some day
But do you know who I am?

ADRIANNE. Shake?

> (THOMAS *and* ADRIANNE *shake hands.*)

ELLEN. (*To* ADRIANNE.) I'm kind of rooting for you.

> (*Pause.*)

THOMAS. Okay, let's go.

> (*Pause.*)

ADRIANNE. Dad. Let's go. Let's do it.

> (FRANK *Takes A Moment.*)

Frank.

> (FRANK *looks at his book.*
> *He puts it down.*)

THOMAS. What are you doing?

> (FRANK *goes to his bag.*
> *And pulls out his manuscript.*)

Frank.

FRANK. If I can't beat Thomas maybe you can.

ADRIANNE. Dad.

FRANK. Don't say that anymore.
"Dad"
We're here to win right?

ELLEN. It's just a book game.

FRANK. You're the ones who cheated. Okay?

THOMAS. I didn't cheat. That's the irony.

FRANK. Okay, then SO:
Here's the book.
Thomas, if *you* can identify the first line of my book
That you already read
That you already loved
That is going to get me back
Then it's over.
And you keep your ball.

THOMAS. Don't.

ADRIANNE. This isn't the way the game goes. These aren't the rules.

FRANK. Says who? The title of the book is *Remorse*

ADRIANNE. Wait—

ELLEN. *Remorse?* Okay, sure

(ELLEN *writes.*)

THOMAS. Even if I hadn't read it, you really think I couldn't identify your style?

FRANK. Call the bluff.

THOMAS. Just pick the line that sounds "important"
And there you go.

FRANK. I've always imagined the cover would be Silver Letters Against A Light Blue Background.
Remorse.

THOMAS. I'm really not sure why you're doing this.

ADRIANNE. Me neither.

FRANK. It's one book here I know you haven't read.
So now we have a fair shot.
We never have a fair shot and now we do.
Okay?

Ade, you can do this.

ADRIANNE. Not sure I want to anymore.

ELLEN. Frank were you some kind of crazy soccer dad?

ADRIANNE. No, he wasn't.

FRANK. Okay? Go.

> (*A Moment.*
>
> *They all write.*
> *And write.*
> *They pass up the paper.*
> FRANK *collects them.*
> *He reads.*)

It's too bad some people don't take the game seriously.

1) There was a sad man who lived on a hill with his sad books and spent his time with sad people and talked about sad subjects on sad Sundays.

2) Mr. Costello, covered in sweat, woke up with his heart racing in a bed with a young girl he couldn't love.

3) Bananas.

4) When we got the news we knew we would never find out what happened to him and that's why we went to talk to his mother.

Okay, here we go.

ADRIANNE. Hold on, I need to think.

THOMAS. It's not obvious to you?

ADRIANNE. Just making sure.

FRANK. 1) "There was a sad man who lived on a hill with his sad books and spent his time with sad people and talked about sad subjects on sad Sundays."

If you think it's one raise your hand.

(*No one raises their hand.*)

2) "Mr. Costello, covered in sweat, woke up with his heart racing in a bed with a young girl he couldn't love."

(THOMAS *raises a hand.*)

THOMAS. Now it all makes sense.

FRANK. Three: "Bananas."

(ELLEN *raises a hand.*)

THOMAS. I guess it's possible.

ELLEN. Fuck you Dad.

FRANK. Four: "When we got the news we knew we would never find out what happened to him and that's why we went to talk to his mother."

(ADRIANNE *raises their hand.*)

THOMAS. (*Quick.*) You're going to need another job this summer.

ADRIANNE. Really?

THOMAS. It was pretty easy to get you. Just make the narrator the first person plural—we, us—that's a big trick with your Josh Ferris and your Jeffrey Eugenides. We didn't know them. We went to the mall. We don't know who we are. We sleep a lot.

ADRIANNE. You're gloating. Congrats.

THOMAS. Well, sure, a little.

ADRIANNE. But you chose my line too Thomas.

THOMAS. I did?

ADRIANNE. Not that it matters but you're pretty easy too: Just write a line about an older guy wracked with guilt 'cause he's with a younger girl and there you go.

THOMAS. Very nice!

FRANK. Ellen got the right first line. Thomas wins on points.

ELLEN. I beat you Frank.

FRANK. Congrats.

ELLEN. No one likes to be last.

(*Long Pause.*)

THOMAS. Good game. Good game.

ADRIANNE. That's not fair.

THOMAS. Why not?

FRANK. Sorry, Ade.

THOMAS. Come on, it's just a game.

FRANK. I guess we can't talk about my book tomorrow.

> (*Pause.*)

THOMAS. I'll still write the blurb.

> (*Pause.*
>
> *No one Moves.*)

I'll see you in the morning.

> (THOMAS *leaves.*
>
> ELLEN *puts books away.*)

ADRIANNE. I think I might take a walk.

FRANK. It's really late.

ELLEN. Lotta bugs.

ADRIANNE. (*To* FRANK.) What are you going to do?

FRANK. I'm going to read. What are you going to do?

> (*Pause.*
>
> ADRIANNE *goes upstairs.*
>
> FRANK *and* ELLEN, *in the living room.*)

I wonder who's had a worse night, me or you?

ELLEN. You gonna blow your head off?

FRANK. That's too much work.

ELLEN. Adrianne gonna be okay?

FRANK. Hope so.

> (*Pause.*)

ELLEN. Do you want some food?

FRANK. Yes. Thank you.

> (*She is about to go to the kitchen.*)

Don't you know that's how people put on weight? By eating at night?

> (*She turns around to face* FRANK.)

ELLEN. You're a *guest* in our house.

FRANK. I just thought you might be concerned about those things.

ELLEN. You can't talk like that.

FRANK. I'm trying to be honest.

ELLEN. Really? Why?

FRANK. I don't know what to do.

ELLEN. We made a bed for you.

FRANK. You don't understand.

The City.
My life.
My daughter.
Thomas.

ELLEN. You're okay Frank. You're okay.

FRANK. Why do people look down when I walk into a room?

I put on this stupid shirt
I sent Thomas my book

What am I doing wrong?
Can you tell me that?

ELLEN. Well for one you shouldn't accuse the host of messing around with young girls.

FRANK. (*Softening.*) Okay, okay.

ELLEN. You shouldn't tell anyone, especially a woman, what to eat.

FRANK. I know *that.*

ELLEN. You shouldn't take the game so seriously.

FRANK. You don't believe that.

ELLEN. Get a shrink.

FRANK. Okay.

ELLEN. Get a friend.

FRANK. You've got nothing? Not one little ounce of compassion? Really?
　　　(*He's gotten a bit closer to her.*)

ELLEN. I'm 25 years old and you're 50. What do you want from me?
　　　(*She's still there.*)

FRANK. Can you touch me? Please?

ELLEN. Seriously?
　　　(*He stands there.*
　　　He does not move.
　　　They are pretty close.
　　　She looks him in the eye.)

No. I can't.

FRANK. I'm sorry.

ELLEN. I almost got some action. Ha.

FRANK. It hurts. It really hurts.

ELLEN. Hey. You think you're the only one?
　　　(FRANK *exits.*
　　　ELLEN *goes into the kitchen.*
　　　ADRIANNE *comes downstairs.*

She looks at the house.
She opens the glass case containing the baseball.
The reflection lights up her face.
ELLEN *enters from the kitchen.)*

ELLEN. It's 1 a.m.

ADRIANNE. I couldn't sleep.

ELLEN. You trying to pull a *Wonder Boys*?

ADRIANNE. You read that?

ELLEN. Saw the movie.

ADRIANNE. Just looking.

ELLEN. Are you fucking crazy?

ADRIANNE. No, I said, I'm not.

ELLEN. You know how much that cost?

ADRIANNE. Am I not allowed to look?

ELLEN. Is that all you're doing?

> *(Pause.)*

Your Dad.

ADRIANNE. He's an idiot sometimes. I know.

> *(A Moment.)*

ELLEN. Look, Adrianne only a few people get to do it.

ADRIANNE. I know.

ELLEN. And *This* is what it's like.

> *(A Beat.)*

ADRIANNE. I'm not doing very well.

ELLEN. You're still here.

ADRIANNE. Well.

> *(A Beat.)*

ELLEN. Ivan tries to write. I think the reason he was dating me was to talk to my dad.

ADRIANNE. Is he any good?

ELLEN. You think I care?

> *(Pause.)*

I once tried to write and it was *so* bad.

ADRIANNE. How did you know?

> *(Pause.)*

What? Why are you looking at me like that?

ELLEN. I'm sure he'll let you do the internship. You know that right?

ADRIANNE. Really?

ELLEN. Now can you close the case?

> (ADRIANNE *does so.*)

ADRIANNE. Sorry.

> (ADRIANNE *starts to walk upstairs.*)

ELLEN. What were you going to do with the ball?

ADRIANNE. I had had the thought
I had had the thought that maybe I should take it.

ELLEN. You *shouldn't.*

ADRIANNE. I don't want problems.

ELLEN. You left your underwear in the bathroom.

ADRIANNE. I did?

ELLEN. Can't be leaving your stained underwear around if you do get to work for my dad.

ADRIANNE. I know.

ELLEN. It's disgusting. Can't be like that.

ADRIANNE. Okay, I get it.

> (*They Exit.*
> *The Stage Is Empty.*
> *Darkness.*
> FRANK *enters. He's alone on stage.*
> *Time Passes.*
> THEN
> *The light of Dawn.*
>
> *Early Morning.*
> *It's sharp, grey.*
> FRANK *looks out at the window.*
> *At the sky and the lake.*
> THOMAS *comes in.*
> *He has on his jogging clothes. And he's sweating.*
> *The men say nothing.*
> *After a bit:*)

THOMAS. Look, Frank. Next time we can plan better.

FRANK. That would be nice.

THOMAS. But this was

FRANK. No good.

THOMAS. Maybe it's time.

FRANK. Adrianne is still upstairs.

(THOMAS *starts to prepare breakfast.*)

I am glad we got to come up here.

THOMAS. Well, no rush.

(*Silence.*)

FRANK. (*Towards upstairs.*) Adrianne! Hey! Adrianne! CAN WE GO?

She must still be asleep.

Glad I got to see the sunrise. You?

THOMAS. Yes, on my jog. New thing. Lean body, lean mind.

FRANK. Gotta stay fit

THOMAS. Yes.

FRANK. Or else, it's all over.

(*Pause.*

FRANK *walks to the foot of the stairs.*)

ADRIANNE!

THOMAS. Could you go upstairs? And not yell throughout the house?

(FRANK *takes this in.*

FRANK *goes up two stairs, stops, looks at* THOMAS.)

What?

(FRANK *goes all the way up the stairs.*

THOMAS *goes to the kitchen.*

He pours some coffee.

He sits down and looks out at the lovely vista of his country house.

He takes out a pad and starts writing, facing the upstage window.

FRANK *comes downstairs.*)

FRANK. She'll be down soon.

(FRANK *Pacing.*

THOMAS *Writing.*)

THOMAS. (*Head down, writing.*) I'll give your book to my editor.

The least I can do. Considering.

(*A moment.*)

FRANK. That's great. Thank you. Really, Thomas, that's very generous. Thanks so much.

THOMAS. And if you could just give me a moment.

(*Pause.*)

FRANK. Of course.

(THOMAS *goes back to writing.*

FRANK *walking around the room.*

He looks at the book titles et al.)

Some game last night. I'm not talking about our game of course.
I'm talking about the Mets.

(THOMAS *writing.*
FRANK *pacing.*)

Baseball.

(THOMAS *writing.*
FRANK *pacing.*)

Writing?

(THOMAS *keeps writing.*
FRANK *watches him write.*
For A While.)

I just have to wait.

(THOMAS *continues writing.*)

You're not the only one. Not the only one at all.

THOMAS. (*Imploring.*) Are you going to let me write or not? *Please Fuck Off
Already.*

(THOMAS *returns to writing.*
FRANK *goes to The Old Stove.*
He picks up a Cast Metal Iron Poker.
Holding the poker, FRANK *walks over to* THOMAS *who does not see him.*
He stares at THOMAS.
ELLEN *comes down the stairs.*)

ELLEN. What are you doing?

FRANK. What?

ELLEN. What are you doing with that?

(THOMAS *turns to see* FRANK.
He looks at him.)

FRANK. I just took it out.

ELLEN. It looks like you were going to hit someone.

FRANK. Who?

THOMAS. Me. Looks like you were going to hit me. Look how close you
are.

FRANK. Are you kidding?

(FRANK *puts the poker away.*
THOMAS *stands.*)

THOMAS. You were going to bash my head in.

FRANK. Both of you are being overdramatic.

ELLEN. We could have you arrested.

FRANK. I was just walking around, Holding it.

THOMAS. That makes NO sense.

FRANK. I wasn't going to do anything.

ELLEN. Oh my God. Oh my God.

FRANK. (*Exploding.*) What do you want me to say?

THOMAS. What has happened to you?

FRANK. Can I still have the blurb? Or are you going to make me beg for that too?

THOMAS. If you get out of here *this very moment.*

FRANK. I have to get Adrianne.

> (FRANK *heads upstairs.*
> THOMAS *sits down and starts to write again.*)

ELLEN. Dad, are you okay?

Dad?

Dad?

> (ELLEN *pours some more coffee.*)

THOMAS. It was a terrible idea to have them up here. I'm sorry.

> (*Pause.*)

ELLEN. How was your run?

> (*Pause.*)

You getting quiet now?

THOMAS. I didn't run. I was on the phone. I had to go up the hill to get reception.

> (ELLEN *continues to make breakfast.*)

I won't be coming out here anymore. Kristin is going to be staying here while I'm in the city.

ELLEN. But you love it here.

THOMAS. But it's her house. The Delling Summer Home. My last name is Wright.

ELLEN. So is mine.

> (*A Beat.*)

THOMAS. She was very clear that she still wants you to come out here. She cares a lot about you and still wants you to think of this as your home.

> (*Silence.*
> ELLEN *continues to make breakfast.*)

I can't really help you. You know that, right?

ELLEN. You *think* I don't know?

THOMAS. I do love you.

ELLEN. What did *you do?*

THOMAS. What do you think I did?

(*Long Pause.*)

ELLEN. Could you please pass the juice?

(THOMAS *hands* ELLEN *the juice.*
He picks up his pages.
FRANK *and* ADRIANNE *come downstairs.*
They have their bags.)

FRANK. I told Adrianne that we all thought it would be best if we started to head back.

ELLEN. It's been really great having you up here. So glad you made it.

ADRIANNE. (*To* THOMAS.) I didn't get to see your cabin.

THOMAS. Next time.

(*Pause.*)

FRANK. Ellen? Great luck with everything.

ELLEN. Thanks very much.

(FRANK *picks up his bag.*
ADRIANNE *does not move.*)

FRANK. Ade?

(*She does not pick up her bag.*)

THOMAS. I'm going back tomorrow myself.

ADRIANNE. (*To* THOMAS.) I need to know if there's any possible way that I can still be considered for the job. Apprenticeship.

THOMAS. It's not going to work out.

ADRIANNE. Why?

THOMAS. Things have changed.

ADRIANNE. Is this about that bet? Is that what this is?

THOMAS. If you need a recommendation—

ADRIANNE. I'm sorry I don't understand. I *really* don't understand.

(*Silence.*)

I wanted to work with you.

THOMAS. Maybe in the future something will come up.

(ADRIANNE *turns to* ELLEN.)

ELLEN. (*Gentle.*) Probably not.

ADRIANNE. I knew this would happen.

ELLEN. I have to get packed too. Have a great term, Ade. I'll see you in the city sometime.

> (ELLEN *walks upstairs, exits.*)

THOMAS. I can still show you my cabin.

> (ADRIANNE *laughs.*)

Is that funny?

It's just an old carriage house.

FRANK. Okay, Ade, It's time.

> (ADRIANNE *turns to* FRANK.)

ADRIANNE. What did you do?

FRANK. Nothing.

ADRIANNE. I'm not going. Not with you.

THOMAS. I have to go to my cabin. Please just let yourselves out. Frank.

FRANK. Tom.

> (THOMAS *leaves.*
>
> *The front door is open. Waiting.*
>
> ADRIANNE *does not pick up her bag.*)

Long ride Ade.

ADRIANNE. Really long.

FRANK. You still going to write when you get back to school?

ADRIANNE. Yes.

FRANK. I am really proud of you.

ADRIANNE. No, you're not.   ·

FRANK. Sometimes I do like to see you fall on your face—

ADRIANNE. Wow.

FRANK. What's wrong with me?

ADRIANNE. Does it matter?

> (*She sees the ball in the case.*)

Remember when we went to Thomas' old country house and played catch with a hardball. You threw it so hard that I stopped playing. Do you remember that?

FRANK. You were young.

> (*She picks up the ball.*)

That is *not* a ball to play with.

ADRIANNE. What's it like to be Bill Buckner? To have Blown The Whole Series?

FRANK. What are you trying to say?

ADRIANNE. You fucking worm.

FRANK. Sound like Ellen. Sound like your mother.

ADRIANNE. (*Quiet.*) I should be so lucky.

FRANK. You wanted to come.

ADRIANNE. You took it away.

> (*She holds the ball.*
>
> *Silence.*)

FRANK. Ade, come on,

ADRIANNE. Don't talk to me.

FRANK. I can't take it away.

> (*A Beat.*)

How could I do that?

ADRIANNE. WHY DO I HAVE TO WALK AROUND WITH THIS
WHY DO I HAVE TO HAVE THIS
WHY DO I HAVE TO HATE MYSELF AND GO CRAZY AND
THINK EVERYTHING IS GOING TO TURN TO SHIT
COULDN'T YOU ONCE JUST FUCKING ONCE HAVE DONE WELL
AND DONE RIGHT AND DONE GOOD
JUST ONCE
JUST ONE FUCKING TIME
WHY
WHY

> (*Silence.*)

FRANK. I could take you to a bus station. You could go back by yourself.

> (*She puts the ball back.*)

You used to have quite an arm.

> (*Silence.*)

I taught you how to throw, you know. I *did*.

> (*She waits.*)

Really? Ade?

> (*Silence.*
>
> *She picks up her bag.*
>
> *She looks at* FRANK.)

ADRIANNE. (*With hope.*) I'm ready.

End of Play

TWO CONVERSATIONS
OVERHEARD ON AIRPLANES
by Sarah Ruhl

BIOGRAPHY

Sarah Ruhl's plays include *Stage Kiss* (Goodman Theatre, Playwrights Horizons), *In the Next Room, or the vibrator play* (Broadway, Lincoln Center Theater, Pulitzer Prize Finalist, premiered at Berkeley Repertory Theatre, subsequently at Victory Gardens), *The Clean House* (Lincoln Center Theater, 2005 Pulitzer Prize Finalist, 2004 Susan Smith Blackburn Prize, premiered at Yale Repertory Theatre, also produced at the Goodman Theatre), *Passion Play, a cycle* (Pen American Award, The Fourth Freedom Forum Playwriting Award from the Kennedy Center, Helen Hayes Award nomination for best new play; premiered at Arena Stage, also produced by the Goodman Theatre, Yale Repertory Theatre and Epic Theatre in New York), *Dead Man's Cell Phone* (Playwrights Horizons, Steppenwolf Theatre, premiered at Woolly Mammoth Theatre), *Melancholy Play* (premiered at the Piven Theatre Workshop), *Eurydice* (premiered at Madison Repertory Theatre, then at Berkeley Repertory Theatre, Yale Repertory Theatre, Second Stage, and Victory Gardens), *Orlando* (premiered at Piven Theatre Workshop, subsequently at Classic Stage Company and Court Theatre), *Dear Elizabeth* (Yale Repertory Theatre, Berkeley Repertory Theatre), and *Late: a cowboy song* (Piven Theatre Workshop). Her plays have been produced across the country as well as internationally, and have been translated into Polish, Russian, Spanish, Norwegian, Korean, German, French, Swedish, and Arabic. Originally from Chicago, Ms. Ruhl received her M.F.A. from Brown University, where she studied with Paula Vogel. In 2003, she was the recipient of the Helen Merrill Emerging Playwrights Award and the Whiting Writers' Award. She is a member of 13P and New Dramatists and won the MacArthur Fellowship in 2006. She was a recent recipient of the PEN Center Award for a mid-career playwright in 2010. She lives in Brooklyn with her family.

ACKNOWLEDGMENTS

Two Conversations Overheard on Airplanes premiered at the Humana Festival of New American Plays in April 2013. It was directed by Les Waters with the following cast:

WOMAN	Linda Kimbrough
MAN	Edward Hajj
YOUNG MAN	Joseph Metcalfe
OLDER MAN	Harry Groener

and the following production staff:

Scenic Designer	Antje Ellermann
Costume Designer	Kristopher Castle
Lighting Designer	Seth Reiser
Sound Designer	Benjamin Marcum
Stage Manager	Paul Mills Holmes
Assistant Stage Manager	Lizzy Lee
Casting	Zan Sawyer-Dailey, Meg Fister
Directing Assistant	Kate Eminger
Assistant to the Set Designer	Jessica Mentis

CHARACTERS

WOMAN
MAN
YOUNG MAN
OLDER MAN

Linda Kimbrough, Edward Hajj, Joseph Metcalfe, and
Harry Groener
in *Two Conversations Overheard on Airplanes*

37th Humana Festival of New American Plays
Actors Theatre of Louisville, 2013
Photo by Bill Brymer

TWO CONVERSATIONS OVERHEARD ON AIRPLANES

4 strangers on a plane. Separated by an aisle.

1.

A man and woman, both around sixty years old, sit next to each other on an airplane.
The woman is unfashionable. The man wears a rumpled suit.
It is November.

WOMAN. I'm from England.

MAN. You don't sound English.

WOMAN. Well, I've lived in Texas.

MAN. Texas is strong. It takes you over.

WOMAN. Where are you from?

MAN. Pakistan.

WOMAN. My husband had a Pakistani oncologist—a real nice gentleman.

MAN. I'm a doctor. I also speak fluent German.

WOMAN. Oh? One of my best friends is German. She's a war bride. I'm a war bride too.

MAN. Where are you from in England?

WOMAN. Manchester.

MAN. The English countryside is beautiful, isn't it?

WOMAN. The English countryside changes all the time.

MAN. How long you been in the states?

WOMAN. 29 years.

MAN. I've lived in Germany and Providence, Rhode Island.

WOMAN. Well, you've seen lots of the world.

MAN. You have children?

WOMAN. Yes, I have two. A daughter and a son.

MAN. Who are you closer to, the daughter or the son?

WOMAN. It's hard to say. I love them both.

MAN. No, no, no. It's not hard to say. You're either closer to one or the other.

WOMAN. The daughter.

MAN. Mothers are always closest to daughters. You have grandchildren?

WOMAN. Yes—my daughter has two real ones and my son married a divorcee and inherited two. I think about all of my grandchildren, but there are different kinds of love—you understand.

    Pause.

MAN. This is a very busy airport.

WOMAN. Yes, I flew through here back in the fifties. On TWA.

MAN. They still have TWA. They were gone and they came back.

WOMAN. There's a lot of competition these days.

MAN. The only one gone is PAN AM.

WOMAN. Oh—I'd forgotten about PAN AM.

MAN. Time changes a lot of things.

    Pause.

The head of Virgin Airlines used to be a balloonist. He's founder and chairman of Virgin Airlines. He's a billionaire.

WOMAN. Oh, my heavens!

MAN. Yes, yes.

WOMAN. Do you have to be at the hospital early in the morning, or…

MAN. I can delay if I want. I follow no one. I follow only myself.

WOMAN. That's nice.

MAN. So, what do you think of the election?

WOMAN. Oh, I think, it's time for a change. He's very handsome too.

MAN. Who?

WOMAN. The handsome one…with the hair…

MAN. The handsome one always wins. Or the tall one. Was Nixon tall? I can't remember.

Bradley's father was a Republican, you know.

WOMAN. What?

MAN. Bradley's father was a Republican.

WOMAN. Oh!

MAN. But he's a Democrat.

WOMAN. Oh. Yes. That's why I miss my husband—he was interested in everything—he told me about politics—he retained—a lot of things. A lot of things were over my head—but he listened to me. He died two years ago. We had hospice at the end. They're wonderful people.

MAN. I have a very dear friend right now dying of cancer.

WOMAN. That must be—

MAN. Yes. He has two daughters and a young wife. He's a doctor. He had blood in his stools.

WOMAN. That's sad.

MAN. He was such a nice man—always said hello to everybody.

WOMAN. There's always somebody worse. No matter how bad you have it—there's always somebody worse.

MAN. Yes.

WOMAN. I lost my mother when she was 51. High blood pressure.

MAN. I have high blood pressure.

WOMAN. And my father died at 87.

MAN. Fifty is young.

WOMAN. Fifty is very young.

MAN. I got my citizenship in 1953.

WOMAN. Oh?

MAN. Yes, I did. My wife is much younger than me. She's a very dignified soft-spoken person. And she said in the seventies everyone was smoking marijuana—boys, girls, everyone. She says she tried it.

WOMAN. My husband had a drinking problem. He didn't realize until the seventies and then he went to AA.

MAN. Alcohol kills more people than marijuana.

WOMAN. Yes, yes, it does.

MAN. So many people drink alcohol.

WOMAN. Yes.

> *Pause.*

Do you have children?

MAN. Three children. One son, two daughters. My daughters are Republicans but the other one is a Democrat. I'm not happy about that. He has a Ph.D. in psychology. He's a bleeding heart liberal. And his girlfriend is the same. Bleeding heart liberals. Give give give to people who do nothing.

WOMAN. Well, we tried to raise our children to make their own decisions.

MAN. I also have a ten-year-old son. He will be a Republican.

WOMAN. Maybe you'll have some influence. I wonder when we'll get off the ground. It's raining.

MAN. Chicago is a busy airport. Chicago has Mexicans everywhere—in the restaurants, the airports—people I talk to say they're good workers.

WOMAN. Yes. Times have changed since I've traveled.

MAN. It's nice to talk to you.

WOMAN. Yes, it's nice to talk to you too.

MAN. I agree with you about most things.

WOMAN. Thank you.

> *They sip their drinks and eat peanuts and steal looks at each other through the following.*

2.

> *A young man and an older man.*
> *The young man takes a picture out of his wallet and shows it to the older man.*

YOUNG MAN. This is a picture of my best friend.

OLDER MAN. She's very pretty.

YOUNG MAN. Yes—she's like a sister to me. I know she'll always be part of my life. I love her more than I love myself.

OLDER MAN. So this isn't the one who ran off with another man?

YOUNG MAN. No—this is my best friend. I love her to death. She's like a sister to me.

OLDER MAN. Well, it's not up to me, but it seems to me that if you feel that way about her you should marry her.

YOUNG MAN. She's like a sister to me.

OLDER MAN. Well, marriage is different from love. Being married is not only about being in love with someone. It's about wanting to do good things for them. My wife and I have been married for 47 years. And we're very happy.

YOUNG MAN. That's good.

OLDER MAN. Yes—she's going to meet me in Eugene, Oregon in 4 to 5 days.

> *The young man takes out another picture from his wallet.*

YOUNG MAN. That's nice. This is a picture of the woman who left me and the guy she left me for. He's a marine. He's stationed in South Carolina. They're very happy. I'm happy for them.

OLDER MAN. Well—this is the thing about women. They like a man to earn a good living. They like for him to be a good person and do good things and to earn a good living. At some point you might think about owning a company, something like that.

YOUNG MAN. I've mostly been living paycheck to paycheck.

OLDER MAN. Do they pay you well?

YOUNG MAN. 11 dollars an hour.

OLDER MAN. 40 hours a week?

YOUNG MAN. No, 60, 6 days a week.

OLDER MAN. Ah, well that's good, good money…let's see…11 times 60, that's…

YOUNG MAN. It's all right. I'll save up all my money—direct deposit—and buy a new car in six months. I won't have any expenses—my father says I won't need to pay for food or anything—and my paychecks will all go direct deposit.

What I really want to do is write. I'm a writer.

OLDER MAN. Oh!

What do you write?

YOUNG MAN. Oh, everything pretty much. Poetry, science fiction, novels, horror, sci fi, comedy.

OLDER MAN. Oh, good, good.

YOUNG MAN. I keep starting stories. I get more ideas and then I'm in the middle of five stories and can't finish them.

OLDER MAN. Do you think you'll have any published soon?

YOUNG MAN. Maybe in the next year or so.

OLDER MAN. That's good. I've published some books.

Why don't you read me one of your poems—just recite a favorite—whatever's stuck in your head.

YOUNG MAN. Oh, I can do better than that.

    He pulls a poem out of his wallet.

OLDER MAN. Oh, good! Why don't you read it aloud?

YOUNG MAN.

The pain sliced through my head
Life goes round and round

OLDER MAN. Slower. Read slower and louder.

YOUNG MAN.

The pain sliced through my head
Life goes round and round

She left me
my wife
my life
you cannot love another
if you do not love yourself.

OLDER MAN. Well, that's a very nice poem. I like it very much. I suspect it reveals something about how you see yourself.

YOUNG MAN. Yeah, at the time. I was engaged to a woman. The one in the picture. She left me for someone she met on the internet. I didn't tell her I loved her until she was leaving. She was very confused.

OLDER MAN. People *are* confused.

YOUNG MAN. Yeah. She's happy with the new guy though. I met him.

OLDER MAN. Perhaps you should have told her earlier that you loved her.

> *Pause.*

Have you been to college?

YOUNG MAN. On and off.

OLDER MAN. What did you study?

YOUNG MAN. General studies.

OLDER MAN. Well. I teach political science. I'm an internationally known figure, actually.

YOUNG MAN. That's nice.

OLDER MAN. I'm reading this book by Stephen Hawking—have you heard of him?

YOUNG MAN. Yes—I think I saw something about him on the Disney Channel.

OLDER MAN. He's a very interesting figure. He has a disease, you know. He was giving a lecture at Brown University and I was at a restaurant—his nurse was there—she asked me to feed him a little bit so I actually fed Stephen Hawking. The other book is on a theory of mind—we don't really know much about the mind. One wishes that better work were written on the topic.

YOUNG MAN. I'm interested in books about the mind—knowledge—how we think—I'd like to read books like that. Just to expand my personal knowledge.

OLDER MAN. And then there's biology. That's interesting.

YOUNG MAN. Yeah, I'm interested in biology. I used to take some biology in college. I wasn't very good at it—I don't know why—I was interested in it—maybe it was my professor.

OLDER MAN. My son does biology in Eugene, Oregon. I'm going to see him in 4 to 5 days. He studies animal DNA and compares it to human DNA to find out how it's the same and how it's different.

YOUNG MAN. I'm going out to be with my father—he's the foreman of the company and my stepmother. I love my stepmother. I've never met her family but my father says they're all as nice as her. They're all from Illinois and Texas.

OLDER MAN. I've been to Illinois.

YOUNG MAN. Yeah—me too—I've been to Illinois—a town called DeKalb. It was a beautiful town. I used to go to a diner every night, talk to people, people from the university. People were nice. Where I'm from—Massachusetts—people can be rude. I liked Illinois.

OLDER MAN. Yes—I gave a lecture at a university in Illinois once—I can't remember the name of it.

YOUNG MAN. There was a university in DeKalb.

OLDER MAN. Where in Massachusetts are you from?

YOUNG MAN. Wareham. Between New Bedford and Cape Cod.

OLDER MAN. New Bedford's a real city.

YOUNG MAN. They have a lot of drugs and crime.
I like Providence, where I live.
I live on Blackstone Blvd. do you know of it?

OLDER MAN. I might have heard of it.

Providence is like a second home to me.

YOUNG MAN. But my family is no longer there.

OLDER MAN. Right. You're going out to see your father and your?

YOUNG MAN. Stepmother. I love my stepmother like my mother. I've never liked my stepfather. I don't know why.

OLDER MAN. Well, you have to love your mother before you can love another woman.

YOUNG MAN. My stepmother has a belt of solid gold. And she is not a small woman.

> *The older man laughs in disbelief.*

Really.

> *A sound.*

What is that sound?

OLDER MAN. I hope it's not a terrorist attack. Or a flock of birds.

> *The older man first has a look of carefully studied amusement, then he looks terrified.*
> *A strange sound.*
> *He grabs the young man's arm.*
> *The young man shields the old man.*
>
> *In the adjacent seats, the woman collapses into the man's arms.*
> *The man and woman kiss and kiss and kiss.*

Then they all die.
And go to a new planet.
Where they are forced to spend eternity with each other.
They gaze.
They shake hands.
They vote.
The end.

End of Play

HALFWAY
by Emily Schwend

BIOGRAPHY

Emily Schwend's plays include *Carthage, South of Settling, Splinters, Route One Off, Take Me Back,* and *Behind the Motel.* In 2012, her play *South of Settling* was produced in Steppenwolf Theatre Company's NEXT UP series. Her ten-minute play, *Halfway,* was the winner of the 2012 Heideman Award and was produced at the Humana Festival of New American Plays at Actors Theatre of Louisville. Her work has been developed at The New Group, Roundabout Theatre Company, ACT Theatre, Marin Theatre Company, Partial Comfort Productions, Ars Nova, the Alliance Theatre, the Source Festival in Washington, D.C., and the O'Neill National Playwrights Conference, among others. She is a frequent contributor to Christine Jones's Theatre for One booth. She is a two-time winner of Lincoln Center Theater's Lecomte du Nouy Prize, the recipient of a MacDowell Fellowship, the 2011 ACT New Play Award winner, the 2009 David Calicchio Emerging American Playwrights Prize winner, a finalist for the 2011 Steinberg/ATCA New Play Award, and a 2009 Kendeda Graduate Playwriting Competition finalist. She is a former Interstate 73 member and a current member of the America-in-Play three-year artists' cohort. She is a proud alumna of the playwriting programs at Juilliard and Tisch.

ACKNOWLEDGMENTS

Halfway was produced at the Humana Festival of New American Plays in April 2013. It was directed by Meredith McDonough with the following cast:

KAT ....Rebecca Hart

MELISSA.. Amy Lynn Stewart

and the following production staff:

Scenic Designer..Antje Ellermann

Costume Designer .... Kristopher Castle

Lighting Designer ....Seth Reiser

Sound Designer... Benjamin Marcum

Stage Manager ....Paul Mills Holmes

Dramaturg..Jessica Reese

Casting ....Zan Sawyer-Dailey, Meg Fister

Directing Assistant .... Kate Eminger

Assistant to the Set Designer...............................Jessica Mentis

CHARACTERS

KAT

MELISSA

SETTING

The kitchen of a halfway house in East Texas, summer.

Amy Lynn Stewart and Rebecca Hart
in *Halfway*

37th Humana Festival of New American Plays
Actors Theatre of Louisville, 2013
Photo by Bill Brymer

HALFWAY

A kitchen, the middle of the day, probably on the weekend. In Texas, in the summer.

KAT *and* MELISSA, *both in their mid-ish, late-ish 20s, sit at the scrubbed table. The kitchen is clean but completely charmless.*

A pan of pecan squares rests between them.

KAT. Oh my God. I am so sorry.

MELISSA. It's not a big deal.

KAT. It is a big deal. It's a huge deal because like. Like you could have died. Here. In the kitchen. You could have died here and it would have been my fault.

MELISSA. It wouldn't have been your fault. It would have been the pecans' fault.

KAT. But I should know. Because I did know, like, at one point, like when we were kids, I did know that you were allergic to pecans, and I should, you know, I should still know. So.

MELISSA. Yeah, okay, but you handed me a pecan square, and you said to me, like you literally said to me "have a pecan square!" So. So if I just went ahead and took the pecan square and then bit into the pecan square, and then died, in this kitchen, well. That is not your fault. That is knowing suicide.

KAT. Still. I should have remembered. I should have remembered that. About you.

MELISSA. Well. I carry an EpiPen.

KAT. I just thought I'd, you know. Make something. And I don't know how to make a whole lot of things, but I do know how to make pecan squares. They had a class—well, I guess it wasn't really a class because we just like, watched this woman cook but we didn't get to cook or anything. And she made pecan squares. And meatloaf and chutney, but I figured it'd just be real weird to hand you a plate of meatloaf or, ah, or chutney, so. So I made the pecan squares.

MELISSA. Well. I appreciate it. Even if I can't eat 'em.

KAT. There's supposed to be more cooking classes, like I don't know when, but. So maybe there's something else I can make next time, 'cause I don't know how to make a whole lot by myself. And they don't have cookbooks here or nothing like that.

(KAT takes the pecan squares far away.)

There's other stuff. Non-pecan stuff. Not a lot of stuff. I have Oreos, if you want Oreos. In my bedroom. Like, locked in my bedroom because someone'll steal 'em if I leave 'em in the kitchen or anywhere else. I had to keep all the stuff for the pecan squares in my bedroom—even like, stuff like, like canola oil! Like canola oil that's in my dresser drawer next to my socks and stuff. So. So, anyway, there's Oreos. And I guess there's also canola oil. And, ah. Whatever else. Baking powder.

MELISSA. Maybe an Oreo.

KAT. Sure, all right. I'll be right back.

> (KAT *goes.*
>
> MELISSA *takes a moment. She looks around the kitchen; it's grim. She walks to a tiny window above the sink, peers out.*
>
> *Outside the kitchen, there's an argument between two women. A loud argument.*
>
> KAT *returns, calling back after her.*)

It's there on the sheet and you can talk to Sandy yourself and she'll tell you the same thing!

> (*She closes the door. She's rattled and a little pissed off.*)

MELISSA. What was that?

KAT. Just—nothing. Just this bitch who's living here and she's like. Like she's a pain in my fucking ass.

MELISSA. I thought you were liking it here.

KAT. I mean. Yeah. Yeah, I am. But. Like, some of the women here are just. They're fucking crazy, that's what they are. So I reserved the kitchen for an hour and like. And like that means they can't come in here for an hour and if they want to come in they have to knock and ask me and if they like. Need something then they have to get it before or after and like. Like fuck it. She's just being a pain in my ass.

MELISSA. We can go outside if you want. Or up to your room if it's...

KAT. Can't go up in my room. It's not, well—and it's too hot. Outside. Anyway.

MELISSA. All right.

> (*A beat.*
>
> KAT *takes off a rubber band sealing the box of Oreos. Pushes them towards* MELISSA.)

Thanks, Kat.

KAT. Sure. I really wish they taught us some other kind of square.

> (*A beat.*)

MELISSA. So how was it?

KAT. It was good. It was real good. It was real hard.

MELISSA. I bet.

KAT. But I think I figured some stuff out. Like a lot of stuff. Like, a lot a lot. And so. So it was real good. For that.

MELISSA. Okay.

KAT. And, ah. And I don't want to go back there, like. Like never again. But I am real glad I did. Like, I am so glad I did. I just. I feel like I'm in a whole new—like everything feels new. Everything feels like. Like if I can just keep it all the way it is, I can work it out all right. Like I'm in a whole new place, like in my head. Like I have a whole new head. And I'm gonna keep it that way, Melissa, I swear it. I have like. A sponsor. And I go to meetings every week, and I have to do that, but I would do that anyway even if I didn't have to do it. And they said I can even go more than once a week if I want to, because there's like. There's always a meeting. That's what they said.

MELISSA. That's good.

KAT. Yeah.

MELISSA. That's real good to hear, Kat.

KAT. Yeah. Yeah. Hey, so.

(*Beat. She changes her mind.*)

Did you see the plants on the terrace?

MELISSA. Yeah, they're real pretty.

KAT. They give you one when you get here. It's like. Your plant. Sometimes it's just a seed, but I got a plant because someone left early and left her plant here and. And so I got her plant. And I gotta keep it alive while I'm here, and then when I leave, I can take it with me if I want to. Or I can leave it here for someone else. I haven't decided what I want to do yet.

MELISSA. Well. You don't have to worry about that yet.

KAT. No. I know. I'll probably end up killing it anyway. Never had a. You know. A knack. For plants. I even killed that cactus I got at that dude ranch in West Texas—remember that? Who kills a cactus?

MELISSA. Maybe it wasn't killed. Maybe it just died.

KAT. Maybe.

MELISSA. Or maybe it just looked like it was dead and so we got rid of it. That happens sometimes with flowers. They look like they're gone over to the other side, but then you give 'em a little water and they perk right back up. But I don't know if that's what a cactus does.

KAT. Well. I hope I don't kill the plant they gave me here, 'cause, you know, 'cause that would look just, real bad.

(*Beat.*)

Peter couldn't come?

MELISSA. Not today.

KAT. Busy, I guess.

MELISSA. He's been working a lot. Weekends. And he's working from home now.

KAT. Oh, right.

MELISSA. And it's been a lot for him. All of this.

KAT. Right. I know. I know it. How's Mom doing?

MELISSA. Good days and bad days. The physical therapy helps. I think.

KAT. That's good. That's real good.

MELISSA. She was asking about you this morning. When I went to see her.

KAT. Oh yeah?

MELISSA. She's worried. I mean, she doesn't know about—everything, but. She's worried about you. Like she always was.

KAT. Yeah.

MELISSA. You should go see her. Show her you're doing all right. She didn't believe me when I told her we found you again.

KAT. Yeah, well.

(*Beat.*)

I will. I mean, I want to, but I can't right now, 'cause it's out of the perimeter.

MELISSA. What do you mean?

KAT. I mean that for the first 30 days you're here, you can go two blocks in any direction, except north you can go three blocks because three blocks away is the Super Target and a while ago, like before I got here, some people complained about how there ain't really a whole lot in two blocks north and south and east and, you know, and there's this huge Super Target three blocks north and so they put together this whole, you know, like a presentation about it and they voted on it and now the perimeter is three blocks going north, but still two blocks everywhere else. And no matter where you're going, you have to go with at least two other people and a chaperone, and the chaperones don't really like going out that much, so no one really goes out that much. But if we wanted to, and if they go with us, we can go to the Super Target.

(*Beat.*)

Some people got jobs working there. Like a sort of deal they did—the people who run this place and the people who run the Super Target—and so some people here can get jobs working there. Like after 30 days, you can do that, 'cause you can go anywhere. Not anywhere, but. But you can go to the Super Target by yourself, so. So I was thinking about doing that. After 30 days are up.

MELISSA. I think that'd be great.

KAT. Yeah, 'cause. 'Cause I know it's costing you money—you and Peter—a lot of money to help me pay for this place and for the last place too, and I want you to know that I'm planning to pay you back. For all of it, however long it takes.

MELISSA. Well. We don't have to worry about that now.

KAT. Okay. Yeah. Okay. I just, I really have a real good feeling about it. About being here and about working on my steps and staying clean, and I have been, the whole time and like, and that wasn't easy either, but I did it and I'm doing it, and I swear to you, Melissa, I know I messed it up before, but it's different this time. It's real different.

MELISSA. I know. I know you feel that way.

(*A beat.*)

KAT. And, ah. And I thought maybe you could bring Hailey next time.

(*Beat.*)

Or like. Or I could see her after 30 days when I can go anywhere. Like outside the perimeter. You know?

MELISSA. We'll have to work something out. We'll have to see.

KAT. Because I was talking to my sponsor and she said that a lot of women can get custody of their kids again. After, you know, like I know it'll take time to like. To prove that I'm serious. And that I can do it. But she said that, like in my kind of situation, where there's family support and where there wasn't ever any kind of abuse or nothing like that, sometimes it can work out.

(*A beat.*)

MELISSA. I don't think we should think that far ahead, Kat.

KAT. I want to think that far ahead.

MELISSA. Let's just wait, okay? See how this goes and then take the next step.

KAT. Yeah. Yeah, all right.

MELISSA. She's doing real good though. She's talking a lot now, I think it was just a few words back when, ah. When you left. And she's just a little chatterbox now. Talks in these little half-sentences. Like her own language. Like, ah. What's the word. Shorthand. Like a shorthand language. It's real special. She's real special, Kat.

KAT. I know. I know it.

MELISSA. There's a daycare real close to the house, and they're great. The two ladies who run it are just great, and all of the daycare teachers are grad students studying, you know, children's education and one of 'em is studying child psychology and so. So they're great too. She just loves it there, I have to tear her away when I'm picking her up.

KAT. God. I can't—I just miss her. So much.

MELISSA. Yeah. Yeah I know you do.

(*Beat.*)

I, ah. I don't think she remembers you, Kat.

(*That cuts into* KAT *like a knife.*

A long beat.)

KAT. Right, ah. Do you, ah, do you want another Oreo? You can have one, I can't eat the whole box myself. Or I shouldn't, anyway.

MELISSA. All right.

(*She takes an Oreo.*)

KAT. I wish I could give you a glass of milk, you know? Like it almost feels stupid having this big bag of Oreos and then never having even a cup of milk to give you to eat 'em with, but. But milk barely lasts more'n a day in the fridge—someone uses it on her cereal or in her mac and cheese and so. Well. I guess I don't really like milk anyway, so even if no one was gonna drink my milk, maybe I still wouldn't have any in here to give you.

MELISSA. Well, you're lactose intolerant. Or you were, when we were kids.

KAT. Right. Well. I don't know if it's lactose intolerant, but I never did like it. Milk. Any kind of, ah. Milk product. You know, they make dinner here on Sundays, but no one eats it, or at least I don't eat it because it's always just some kind of casserole that's not so much a casserole as it is just a few potatoes or noodles or rice covered with melted processed cheese on the top. It's worse than family meal at the restaurant. Remember that? So godawful, and no one ate it, and then we had to serve burgers and fries all night long.

MELISSA. It got a little better once you left.

KAT. I just remember it was always cut-up hot dogs and rice.

MELISSA. Sometimes noodles. Cut-up hot dogs and noodles.

(*A beat.*)

KAT. I know you don't believe me, but I'm going to do it, Melissa, I swear.

MELISSA. All right.

KAT. I swear to God, Melissa.

MELISSA. All right.

(*And they sit in the kitchen together.*)

End of Play

SLEEP ROCK THY BRAIN
by Rinne Groff, Lucas Hnath
and Anne Washburn

ABOUT *SLEEP ROCK THY BRAIN*

This article first ran in the January/February 2013 issue of Inside Actors, *Actors Theatre of Louisville's subscriber newsletter, and is based on conversations with the playwrights before rehearsals for the Humana Festival production began.*

Though sleep takes up fully a third of our lives, its purpose has remained one of nature's most enduring mysteries. For centuries, writers, philosophers and scientists understood sleep as little more than the obliteration of consciousness ("the death of each day's life," as Shakespeare put it). But neuroscience has exploded that notion. Experts now understand sleep to be as active and productive a neural state as wakefulness, with a vital role to play in learning and the consolidation of memory. These days, interest in the brain science of sleep has spread beyond the research lab into mainstream cultural consciousness, with techno-jargon (think "circadian rhythm") making its way into common cocktail party parlance. Our fascination isn't hard to understand: sleep science illuminates what might be our most universal—but also fundamentally private—experience.

Every year, Actors Theatre commissions a group of playwrights to collaborate on a new piece for our resident Acting Apprentice Company, usually organized around a unifying topic. But the first generative impulse for *Sleep Rock Thy Brain* was not thematic, but formal: a desire to explore the boundaries of dramatic storytelling through aerial choreography. The sleeping mind, in all its mystery and complexity, seemed to offer fertile territory for such multidimensional exploration. This suite of three one-acts—*Comfort Inn* by Rinne Groff, *nightnight* by Lucas Hnath and *Dreamerwake* by Anne Washburn—was developed by Actors Theatre over three seasons, in partnership with University of Louisville, Lincoln Performing Arts School and ZFX Flying Effects. In a series of collaborative workshops, the playwrights met with University scientists, visited a sleep lab, spent time at ZFX's Louisville aerial effects studio, and even learned to fly. (Anne Washburn, it must be said, does a mean aerial flip.) The result of their exploration—equal parts science, story and spectacle—was on vivid display when *Sleep Rock Thy Brain* premiered at Lincoln's Owsley Brown II Theater in a production directed by Amy Attaway, starring the 2012-2013 Acting Apprentice Company.

Of her inspiration, playwright Rinne Groff explains, "I'm energized by how new the study of sleep is, as a field of scientific inquiry. The study of sleep sits at the intersection of such a specific set of medical specialties, and has only recently blossomed as a discipline. As I began this process, I found myself as interested in the scientists themselves—the doctors and the researchers and the sleep lab technicians—as I was in what they were attempting to understand." That interest found its expression in *Comfort Inn*, a moving, madcap tale that unfolds over the course of one eventful night in a sleep lab (which happens to be housed within the walls of a popular chain hotel). As the evening wears on, the destinies of the lab technicians, their patients and several hotel guests intertwine, to hilarious and transformative effect.

Lucas Hnath's *nightnight* takes us out of Earth's orbit and heavenward, where three astronauts' mission to repair the International Space Station is complicated by one's sudden inability to sleep. As he finds his ambition at odds with the limits of his physical ability, all three are caught in a triangle charged by mistrust, desire, and mutual need. "My immediate impulse was to link sleep and flight via space travel," says Hnath. "Space travel takes us to the edge of the world, to the edge of what we can experience—and in a way, so does sleep. Every night we settle into bed and lose consciousness. Sleep kind of dances on the edge of death, and so does space."

Anne Washburn's *Dreamerwake* began as an attempt to engage with an appealing contradiction. "I'm interested in what it is to talk publicly about sleep, our most private experience," the playwright explains, "and to talk about dreams, our most vivid and remarkable and incommunicable experience." Set primarily inside a sleeping brain, *Dreamerwake* explores the ways in which the human mind metabolizes experience—and, in the case of the play's troubled protagonist, trauma—through dreaming. Compelled by what she learned about sleep's cyclical, multi-stage structure, Washburn sought to imitate that logic in the construction of her play. And just as our dreaming minds assimilate raw material from the stimuli of waking life, recombining familiar images and sounds to fill the nightly theatres of our minds, so Washburn's dreamer pulls from the worlds of Groff's and Hnath's plays to build a new one.

For all involved, the project presented not only an enormous formal challenge, but also a rare creative opportunity. "I'm a playwright who typically only writes two-character scenes on bare stages," says Hnath. "*Sleep Rock Thy Brain* gave me the chance to take a risk and make something much bigger: many characters, all talking at once; people in the air, floating every which way; actors walking on walls." For the Apprentices, that challenge was also physical—the young actors trained for months to prepare for the production's athletic demands.

The annual Apprentice project also represents an opportunity for rigorous collaboration, as the playwrights work in concert with the Apprentice Company to build something together. *Sleep Rock Thy Brain* has been no exception. "The particular demands of collaborative work are really appealing," says Washburn. "I love the idea of creating a work for a specific group of people at a particular, and particularly intense, time in their lives." Groff agrees. "Having had two plays premiere at the Humana Festival in the past," she says, "I have become indebted to the heroism of the Apprentices. To write something for them feels just lovely."

—Sarah Lunnie

BIOGRAPHIES

Rinne Groff's plays and musicals, including *Schooner, Compulsion, Saved, The Ruby Sunrise, In the Bubble, Moliere Impromptu, Jimmy Carter was a Democrat, Orange Lemon Egg Canary, What Then, Inky*, and *The Five Hysterical Girls Theorem*, have been produced and commissioned by Playwrights Horizons, The Public Theater, Manhattan Theatre Club, Berkeley Repertory Theatre, Trinity Repertory Company, Actors Theatre of Louisville, the Women's Project, PS122, Clubbed Thumb, Target Margin, and Andy's Summer Playhouse, among others. Television: *Weeds* (Season Two). Groff is a recipient of a Whiting Writers' Award, a Guggenheim Fellowship, an Obie Award grant, and a NYSCA grant. Residencies: Cape Cod Theatre Project, the MacDowell Colony, the Orchard Project, the Sundance Theatre Lab, the Australian National Playwrights Conference, the Perry-Mansfield New Noises Festival, and Chautauqua Theater Company. She is a founding member of Elevator Repair Service, a New Dramatists alum, and a member of the Dramatists Guild. Groff teaches in the Department of Dramatic Writing at New York University's Tisch School of the Arts. She holds a B.A. from Yale University and an M.F.A. from NYU.

Lucas Hnath's plays include *The Christians* (2014 Humana Festival), *Red Speedo* (Studio Theatre, D.C.), *A Public Reading of an Unproduced Screenplay About the Death of Walt Disney* (Soho Rep.), *Isaac's Eye* (Ensemble Studio Theatre), *Death Tax* (2012 Humana Festival, Royal Court Theatre), and *The Courtship of Anna Nicole Smith* (Actors Theatre of Louisville). Hnath has been a resident playwright at New Dramatists since 2011. He is a proud member of Ensemble Studio Theatre and has enjoyed residencies with the Royal Court Theatre and 24Seven Lab. Hnath is a winner of the 2012 Whitfield Cook Award for *Isaac's Eye* and a 2013 Steinberg/ATCA New Play Award Citation for *Death Tax*, and twice won the Alfred P. Sloan Foundation Grant for screenwriting. He is also a recipient of commissions from the Ensemble Studio Theatre/Sloan Foundation Science & Technology Project, South Coast Repertory, Actors Theatre of Louisville, and New York University's Graduate Acting Program. Hnath received both his B.F.A. and M.F.A. from New York University's Department of Dramatic Writing and is a lecturer in NYU's Expository Writing Program.

Anne Washburn's plays include *Mr. Burns, The Internationalist, A Devil at Noon, Apparition, The Communist Dracula Pageant, I Have Loved Strangers, The Ladies, The Small* and a transadaptation of Euripides' *Orestes*. Her work has been produced by 13P, Actors Theatre of Louisville, American Repertory Theatre, Cherry Lane Theatre, Clubbed Thumb, The Civilians, Dixon Place, Ensemble Studio Theatre, The Folger, London's Gate Theatre, Playwrights

311

Horizons, Soho Rep., D.C.'s Studio Theatre, Two River Theater Company, Vineyard Theatre, and Woolly Mammoth Theatre Company. She has received a Guggenheim Fellowship, a New York Foundation for the Arts Fellowship and a Time Warner Fellowship, has been a finalist for the Susan Smith Blackburn Prize, has enjoyed residencies at The MacDowell Colony and Yaddo, and received an Artslink travel grant to Hungary to work with the playwright Peter Karpati. She is an associated artist with The Civilians, Clubbed Thumb and New Georges, and is an alumna of New Dramatists and 13P. She is currently commissioned by Manhattan Theatre Club, Playwrights Horizons, Soho Rep., and Yale Repertory Theatre.

ACKNOWLEDGMENTS

Sleep Rock Thy Brain premiered at the Humana Festival of New American Plays in March 2013. It was directed by Amy Attaway and co-conceived with Sarah Lunnie, with flying effects by ZFX, Inc. and lead choreographer Brian Owens. The production featured the following cast:

Comfort Inn

ANGELA	Tamara Del Rosso
DR. ABRAMOVITCH	Kim Fischer
TOMMY	Bobby Johnson
CAROL	Chalia La Tour
MARK	Joseph Metcalfe
KENNETH	Derek Nelson
JOE WHITE	Andy Reinhardt
ZELDA	Angeliea Stark
ISAAC LERNER	Ben Vigus
CHARLENE	Kimberly Weinkle
FAYE	Sarah Grace Welbourn
SYLVIE MYERS	Madison Welterlen
ELEPHANT-HEAD MAN	Ian Whitt

Dreamerwake

AMELIA	Noelia Antweiler
COLIN	Conor Eifler
TONY	Bobby Johnson
NICK	Joseph Metcalfe
LOU	Derek Nelson
DANI	Liz Ramos
ABBY	Angeliea Stark
JESSICA	Kimberly Weinkle

```
ELI .......................................................................... Ian Whitt
NICOLE................................................Christa Wroblewski
```

VOICEOVER:

```
RYAN THE WEATHER GUY........................... Conor Eifler
SLEEP LAB TECH................................................ Laura Engels
AMY.................................................................. Samantha Beach
SLEEPY WOMAN............................... Sarah Grace Welbourn
```

nightnight

THE ASTRONAUTS

```
SUE ...................................................................... Samantha Beach
ALEX......................................................................Ethan Dubin
TOM............................................................................ Jeff White
```

MISSION CONTROL

```
CONTROL................................................................ Laura Engels
FLIGHT DIRECTOR ............................................ Kim Fischer
FLIGHT SURGEON .........................................Chalia La Tour
RETRIEVAL ................................................................ Liz Ramos
GUIDANCE ...................................................... Andy Reinhardt
DICK.......................................................................... Ben Vigus
CLOCK .......................................................Christa Wroblewski
```

and the following production staff:

```
Scenic Designer.......................................................Karl Anderson
Costume Designer ............................... Kristopher Castle
Lighting Designer.......................................Seth Reiser
Sound Designer/Composer ................................Scott Anthony
Stage Manager .............................................. Katie Shade
Dramaturg.......................................................Sarah Lunnie
Directing Assistants...................... Kate Eminger, Rachel Karp
Assistant Lighting Designer..........................Christine Ferriter
Assistant Choreographer ..............................Robert McFarland
Production Assistant ................................................. Travis Harty
Assistant Dramaturgs............Naomi Shafer, Kathryn Zukaitis
```

The cast of *nightnight*
in *Sleep Rock Thy Brain*

37th Humana Festival of New American Plays
Actors Theatre of Louisville, 2013
Photo by Bill Brymer

Comfort Inn
by Rinne Groff

CHARACTERS

SYLVIE MEYERS

JOE WHITE, Patient #1

ISAAC LERNER, Patient #2

ANGELA

CAROL, Patient #3

KENNETH

FAYE

TOMMY

ELEPHANT-HEAD MAN

CHARLENE

ZELDA

MARK

DR. ABRAMOVITCH

SETTING

A sleep study lab, located in the Comfort Inn hotel. The present.

Comfort Inn

Eleven thirty at night. The "control room" of a sleep study lab, located on the top floor of the Comfort Inn hotel.

Two desks, each set up with a computer with attached speaker and a microphone for communicating with the sleep study rooms down the hall. Also on desks: a telephone and a call box with a buzzer button which opens the front door to the lab.

Each computer is set up to show live video feed for two of the sleep study rooms (four rooms total). The audience can see the live coverage of the rooms either on the computer monitors themselves, or on separate larger screens to provide easier viewing, or in some other ingenious way utilizing video or stagecraft! At rise, all four monitors, however they are represented, are dark, indicating that the screens are off.

SYLVIE, 24, a certified RPSGT (Registered Polysomnographic Technologist)— new on the job—enters the control room wearing scrubs and carrying a bin of extra electrical wires which she doesn't know quite where to put.

She sits at her desk, balancing the box of wires on her lap. She hits a button on her computer. The first of the four monitors blinks on, showing...

Patient #1, JOE WHITE, with electrodes hooked up via wires (a.k.a. leads) to his head, chest, fingers, and legs. It's a little Frankenstein-y: man wired up for a scientific experiment. JOE sits on the edge of his bed, nervous and wide-awake.

SYLVIE activates her microphone, allowing verbal contact with JOE's room.

SYLVIE. Hello, Mr. White.

(*Her voice startles JOE. His being startled startles SYLVIE.*)

Sorry. I didn't mean to scare you. It's Sylvie. Your registered polysomnographic technologist.

JOE. (*Heard through the speakers.*) Who?

SYLVIE. Sylvie? From before. I just hooked you up with the leads.

JOE. Where are you?

SYLVIE. I'm back in the control room now.

JOE. Where's the control room?

SYLVIE. Just down the hall from you.

JOE. But you're still in the hotel?

SYLVIE. Yes, Mr. White, the whole sleep lab is within the hotel.

JOE. Then why did it take you so long to get there?

SYLVIE. I had to hook up a couple other patients after I got you set.

JOE. Do they have nightmares, too?

SYLVIE. You don't have to worry about the other patients.

JOE. Who said anything about being worried?

SYLVIE. No one?

JOE. You can't see what it is that I'm dreaming about on that computer of yours, can you?

SYLVIE. All I can see is if you're asleep or not, if you're in REM or non-REM, how your oxygen levels…

JOE. No, I know. I was just joking. No one can see your dreams, right? That's impossible.

SYLVIE. Mr. White, why don't we go ahead and get started on those instructions real quick?

      (*A moment of concern.*)

Do the electrodes feel okay?

JOE. They still feel weird.

SYLVIE. But not like they're going to fall off?

JOE. You said they wouldn't fall off.

SYLVIE. So, good. Okay. So you need to close your eyes and keep them closed for six seconds, okay?

      (*He closes his eyes and then opens them four seconds later.* SYLVIE *monitors the computer.*)

Okay, that was four seconds. Could you do it again? I'll tell you when to open them. Close your eyes.

      (*He does; she types notation into the computer.*)

Open. Okay. Now without moving your head, just moving your eyes, look up and down twice.

      (*He follows instructions, she notates.*)

We're going to try that again, okay? Without moving your head. Up and down. Do not move your head.

      (*He's doing the best he can.*)

Now left and right. Just your eyes. Not your head, Mr. White. And now if you could move your jaw like you were chewing.

      (*Not good enough.*)

Like you were chewing?

      (*Not good enough.*)

Chewing meat.

JOE. Steak or chicken?

SYLVIE. I'm not sure.

(*He chews.*)

That was good.

JOE. It was chicken.

SYLVIE. And lastly I need you to take in a big breath and hold it for three seconds and then release it.

(*Three seconds pass, he keeps holding his breath.*)

Good, release it. Breathe, Mr. White.

(*He releases it.*)

Good. So it's time to lie down, okay?

(*As soon as he does…*)

Your sleep study is now started. Good luck and good night.

JOE. Wait. What if I need something; later on?

SYLVIE. Your microphone will always be on. If you call out, I'll be able to hear you.

JOE. But will I hear you?

SYLVIE. I'll turn my mic off for the night so you're not disturbed.

JOE. Could you maybe… Do you know any lullabies?

SYLVIE. Lullabies? I don't think the protocol…

JOE. No, I know. I was just joking. Nobody needs anybody to sing to them, right?

(*Beat.*)

I'm going to sleep now.

SYLVIE. Good night.

(SYLVIE *clicks off her microphone. She remotely turns off the lights in* JOE's *room. The video feed switches to infrared: hazier than before.*

SYLVIE *switches on the monitor for Patient #2.* ISAAC LERNER *is right in front of his camera: his face in extreme close-up.* ISAAC *looks terrible, with dark circles under his eyes. Something both disturbing and intimidating about him. He, too, has leads attached to his body.*

SYLVIE *presses the microphone button so she can communicate with Room #2.*)

SYLVIE. Hello, Mr. Lerner.

(ISAAC *doesn't even blink.*)

Mr. Lerner, can you hear me? It's Sylvie. Your registered polysomnographic technologist.

(*She fidgets with the button.*)

Is there something wrong with the microphone hook-up?

ISAAC. (*Through the speaker.*) No.

SYLVIE. Oh. So if you wouldn't mind backing away from the camera.

(*He doesn't move.*)

Mr. Lerner, we need to do a few biometric calibrations before you go to sleep.

ISAAC. I don't sleep.

SYLVIE. I know that you said that.

ISAAC. You don't believe me?

SYLVIE. (*Trying to indulge him.*) I believe that your *experience* is what you say your experience is. (*He's not satisfied.*)

And your *experience* is that you haven't slept for a single night in over five months.

ISAAC. Five months and eleven days.

SYLVIE. And that experience is something that Dr. Abramovitch will be able to help you with after he reads your sleep study in the morning.

ISAAC. Even if I don't sleep?

SYLVIE. Everyone sleeps, Mr. Lerner. Even elephants sleep.

ISAAC. What do elephants have to do with it?

SYLVIE. Nothing.

(*Embarrassed, she's a nerd.*)

Just, before I came in tonight, I was looking at a study about sleep patterns in large mammals.

ISAAC. You want to talk about elephants?

SYLVIE. No, it was just this sleep science journal I was reading.

ISAAC. You ever see a picture of a village in India after an elephant went nuts, smashing and killing everything? Stomping everyone to death until there was no one left alive. Just smeared blood and mangled bodies. Is that what you're hoping for?

SYLVIE. Ummm, no?

(*And then.*)

Mr. Lerner...

ISAAC. If we're going to spend the night together, shouldn't you call me Isaac?

SYLVIE. I know that falling asleep can sometimes be hard, Isaac.

ISAAC. (*Pointed.*) I bet you know, Sylvie. Why else would you be working the night shift?

(*This lands on SYLVIE, hard.*
A loud buzz startles her.)

SYLVIE. Can you give me a few minutes, Mr. Lerner, Isaac?

>(*Loud buzz again.*
>SYLVIE *presses a button on the call box.*)

University Sleep Lab, may I help you?

ANGELA. (*Unseen, through speaker.*) It's Angela. I forgot my keys.

SYLVIE. Ummm… I'll buzz you in.

>(SYLVIE *finds the door-open button and presses it.*
>
>On Monitor #1, JOE *lies very still in bed. On Monitor #2,* ISAAC *stares down at* SYLVIE; *it's creepy.*
>
>ANGELA *enters, also wearing scrubs, carrying three cans of Red Bull.*)

ANGELA. Hey. Who are you?

>(SYLVIE *stands. The box of wires which was on her lap falls to the floor.*)

SYLVIE. Oh. Sorry. I'm Sylvie.

>(*Picking up the wires.*)

I'm the new registered polysomnographic technologist.

ANGELA. But this is Frieda's shift.

SYLVIE. I think her sister's having a baby.

ANGELA. Uh huh.

SYLVIE. So they brought in the new hire.

ANGELA. I heard the new hire hadn't completed her training hours yet.

SYLVIE. I guess they were in a bind?

>(ANGELA *crosses to her desk. As* SYLVIE *puts the wires away,* ANGELA *switches on the video monitor for Room #3.* CAROL, *also wired up, sits in bed watching TV.*)

ANGELA. (*She expected this.*) Still watching TV.

SYLVIE. Terrible sleep hygiene, right? She told me her usual registered polysomnographic technologist…

ANGELA. You can just say "tech." Her tech.

SYLVIE. Her usual tech let her watch TV before all *three* of her previous sleep studies. I can't imagine what Dr. Abramovitch would say about that.

ANGELA. We'd better not tell him then.

SYLVIE. Why not?

ANGELA. Because I'm her usual tech.

>(ANGELA *turns up the volume on the computer speaker: faint sounds of a sporting event. She clicks on her microphone.*)

Hi, Carol; it's Angela. I'll give you ten more minutes and then the TV's got to go off even if the game's in overtime. Carol, say yes if you hear me.

CAROL. Yes.

(ANGELA *turns* CAROL's *volume down again. She opens a can of Red Bull. She notices* ISAAC's *monitor.*)

ANGELA. What's up with him?

SYLVIE. Poor guy says he hasn't slept a wink since the day his mother died.

ANGELA. Bullshit. Everyone sleeps. Even elephants sleep.

SYLVIE. That's so funny. Did you read that article in the latest issue of *Sleep Disorders and Therapies*?

ANGELA. (*She doesn't read journals.*) What?

SYLVIE. Nothing.

(*The phone rings.*)

University Sleep Lab, may I help you?

(*Looks at* ANGELA.)

Yes, she's here. Do you want to… [*talk to her*]?

(*Pause.*)

Oh. All right-ey, I'll tell her. Bye.

(*Hangs up the phone.*)

That was Tommy at the front desk?

ANGELA. Did he snag me some food?

SYLVIE. That's what he said. He said he'd bring it on up.

ANGELA. Awesome, I'm starving.

(*Re:* ISAAC *again.*)

Your patient number two looks pretty psycho. Did he say anything threatening?

SYLVIE. Threatening like what?

ANGELA. Like something that made you feel threatened. If he threatened you even the teeniest bit, you can call Dr. A, and get him discharged.

SYLVIE. I wouldn't want to bother Dr. Abramovitch with this.

ANGELA. I'm just saying, get him discharged, and we'd have one less patient to worry about.

SYLVIE. But then Mr. Lerner wouldn't get his sleep study.

ANGELA. Freida had a freak-o once who said a few just kind of hinting-at-violence things; and then when she went in to adjust his leads, he grabbed her by the neck and tried to strangle her to death. She finally broke free, and she went to press charges, and the dude was all like, I was sleeping.

SYLVIE. *Was* he sleeping? If his brain waves indicated REM during the time of the assault, it could have been a paradoxical sleep event.

ANGELA. Who gives a crap? If you're dead, you don't give a crap.

SYLVIE. Okay. But my patient didn't threaten.

ANGELA. Oh well. At least we only have three tonight.

SYLVIE. The fourth one isn't coming?

ANGELA. He canceled. His insurance wouldn't cover it.

SYLVIE. That's terrible.

ANGELA. Tragic.

> (ANGELA *lies down on the floor.*)

SYLVIE. Are you okay?

ANGELA. I'm just so friggin' tired. Truth is I'm not cut out for night work.

SYLVIE. So, ummm, why do you do it?

ANGELA. The time-and-a-half paycheck kicks ass. Plus it's nice not having a boss around.

SYLVIE. Yeah. For me, it's a little different, I guess. It might sound weird, but… Ever since I was a little girl, I was kind of afraid to go to sleep at night. It all started this one night when I was about seven years old…

ANGELA. (*Getting up.*) Hey, can we save the getting-to-know-you stuff until we're both bored out of our minds at three a.m.? No offense.

SYLVIE. None taken.

ANGELA. (*Re: Red Bull.*) I'm going to put these in the fridge.

> (ANGELA *exits.*
>
> SYLVIE *looks back at* ISAAC*'s monitor. Intently. He's still creeping her out.*)

ISAAC. (*Through speaker.*) Do you want to tell *me* your story?

> (*This totally startles* SYLVIE.)

I mean you're looking right at me, right?

SYLVIE. You cannot see me.

ISAAC. Can't I?

SYLVIE. How can you even hear me?

ISAAC. Because you left the microphone on.

> (*Panic! How could she make a mistake like that?*)

Why *don't* you call the doctor? You think he'll be mad if you wake him up?

SYLVIE. It's not that.

ISAAC. So what are you afraid of? You afraid his wife will answer the phone?

SYLVIE. No.

ISAAC. Did you have an affair with him?

SYLVIE. No.

ISAAC. You're blushing!

SYLVIE. How can you know that?

ISAAC. I can hear it in your voice.

SYLVIE. I never even met Dr. Abramovitch.

ISAAC. You love him.

SYLVIE. I admire him.

ISAAC. Did he know you were a former drug addict when he hired you?

> (*He nailed it.*)

Bingo! What was your poison? Downers, I bet. No, uppers. No, both! And then it got out of control.

> (*Loud buzz on the call box.*)

That's probably Tommy with Angela's food.

SYLVIE. You need to mind your own business, Isaac.

ISAAC. I like your business better. How messed up were you? Did you ever get arrested?

SYLVIE. I really need you to stop talking now.

ISAAC. Why don't you come to my room and make me? If there's nothing threatening about me, you can come back to my room and when you adjust my leads, I'll…

> (SYLVIE *yanks the plugs out of the speaker, silencing* ISAAC's *voice even as his threatening speech goes on unheard.*
>
> *The loud buzz again.*)

SYLVIE. (*Over call box.*) Come on back, Tommy.

> (SYLVIE *presses the door-open button on the call box.*
>
> KENNETH *and* FAYE *enter. He in a tuxedo, she in a wedding dress. They are pretty drunk.*)

KENNETH. Is this the sleep lab?

SYLVIE. Where'd you come from?

FAYE. I think you buzzed us in.

SYLVIE. You guys can't be in here.

KENNETH. You told us to come on back.

FAYE. And then you went, BUZZZZZZZZ.

SYLVIE. But who are you?

KENNETH. Presenting Mr. and Mrs. Kenneth Jones.

FAYE. Ken saw the sign for the sleep center.

KENNETH. We thought we'd come check it out.

SYLVIE. Oh, okay, no. You can't be here. This is a private floor. The hotel elevator shouldn't even let you up here.

KENNETH. We took the stairs.

SYLVIE. The stairs to this floor are locked.

FAYE. Obviously not.

(*Loud buzz on call box.*)

BUZZZZZZZZZ.

SYLVIE. Will you quiet down please?

(*Into call box.*)

University Sleep Center, may I help you?

TOMMY. (*Offstage.*) It's Tommy. Sorry it took me so long. Someone threw up in one of the elevators.

(*Buzz.* SYLVIE *buzzes* TOMMY *in.*

FAYE *sees* ISAAC'*s creepy face on the monitor.*)

FAYE. There's something wrong with that man.

SYLVIE. Don't look at that. At any of those. It's a violation of HIPAA Patient Privacy and Security.

(FAYE *still looking.*)

No, really.

(SYLVIE *switches off all the monitors.*)

You two have to go. The hotel rooms on this floor are hospital property, okay? I get it that it's confusing because it's within the walls of the Comfort Inn.

FAYE. We got married at the Comfort Inn. Isn't that sweet? The *Comfort* Inn? Is that why there's a sleep lab here?

SYLVIE. I'm not sure what you mean.

FAYE. (*Meaningfully.*) Comfort.

KENNETH. (*Even more meaningfully.*) Inn.

SYLVIE. The sleep lab is located here because Dr. Abramovitch...

KENNETH. Dr. Who?

FAYE. Dr. Abama-a-bubba.

SYLVIE. The founder of this center is Dr. Abramovitch.

FAYE. Oh my gosh, are you in love with him?

SYLVIE. Why would you say that?

FAYE. Is he so cute?

SYLVIE. I've never even met him face to face.

KENNETH. Kinky.

SYLVIE. Okay, you really need to leave. This room is strictly for authorized personnel.

(TOMMY, *dressed in the Comfort Inn uniform, bursts in the door, carrying a couple of plates heaped with wedding food.*)

TOMMY. Who's munchy?

(*He sees the bride and groom.*)

TOMMY. Oh, hey, mazel tov, guys.

FAYE. Is that our Beef Wellington?

TOMMY. I think it's your *Pot au Feu.*

KENNETH. (*Proud.*) Two kinds of beef.

TOMMY. What are you guys doing up here?

FAYE. Leaving, I guess. She said we had to go.

KENNETH. No, we're not giving up. We're not interlopers: We have a sleep problem.

TOMMY. What kind of problem?

SYLVIE. Okay, this isn't a walk-in clinic.

FAYE. It's stupid.

KENNETH. It's not stupid, baby.

FAYE. Thanks, baby. I'm just having, like, this weird fear thing about going back to our honeymoon suite.

KENNETH. Since we got together, we've always had roommates…

FAYE. So there was always someone down the hall…

KENNETH. Or coming home soon…

FAYE. Or probably maybe going to come home soon, and I just feel a little nervous about, like, will there really be no one there?

(ANGELA *returns, bearing popcorn.*)

ANGELA. Whoa. Party.

TOMMY. Par-tay!

ANGELA. Who're you guys?

SYLVIE. They're leaving.

KENNETH. Why are you refusing to help us?

SYLVIE. We have a *system* of patient admittance. If you feel you have an actual sleep disorder which Dr. Abramovitch can help you with, then you can call the office during working hours.

KENNETH. But we're here now. Don't be lazy.

ANGELA. She's not lazy. I'm lazy. She's just terrified of screwing everything up.

(CAROL *calls out over the speakers.*)

CAROL. (*Through speakers.*) Angela, are you there?

ANGELA. Who turned the video monitors off?

(ANGELA *turns on Monitor #3 and clicks on the microphone.*)

Hey, girl. Who won?

CAROL. They did.

ANGELA. Bummer.

CAROL. Major.

ANGELA. You ready for bed?

CAROL. Do you have my calibrations from last time? I'm not up for all that blink and chew for six seconds stuff.

ANGELA. We can skip it.

SYLVIE. What?

ANGELA. (*Off the mic.*) There's nothing wrong with her. She just likes sleep studies.

SYLVIE. We still need to follow Dr. Abramovitch's protocol and allow him to make his assessment in the morning.

ANGELA. What's your obsession with Dr. A?

SYLVIE. He's our boss.

ANGELA. Yeah; not our daddy. Carol pays for these things out of pocket. It's her business how she wants to spend her cash.

CAROL. Are we cool?

ANGELA. We're cool. Go to sleep, Carol. (*To* SYLVIE.) You want to get those monitors back on?

(SYLVIE *flips on the other two monitors.*)

SYLVIE. Don't any of you people look at these.

(*Monitor #1 shows* JOE. *Monitor #2 shows an empty room: no* ISAAC.)

ANGELA. Sylvie, where's your second patient?

SYLVIE. (*Turning to see.*) Holy steaming pile of crap. (*On her microphone.*) Isaac, where are you?

(ANGELA *finds the disconnected speaker.*)

ANGELA. What's up with the speaker?

SYLVIE. Oh my god. I lost a patient.

TOMMY. Lost like killed?

SYLVIE. What should I do?

ANGELA. I don't know. I never lost a patient.

TOMMY. Lost like killed? This is freaking—!

(SYLVIE *rushes to the door, but* ANGELA *blocks her.*)

ANGELA. Wait. This is the psycho guy?!

SYLVIE. He was a little psycho.

ANGELA. What if he's waiting to pounce? Remember what I told you about Freida's strangled neck?

SYLVIE. I thought you just made that up so we'd have less work to do.

ANGELA. I did. But it could happen.

(*A KNOCK, KNOCK, KNOCK on the door. Everyone quiets.*

SYLVIE *goes to the door. Tentative. Everyone else stands back.*

The door rattles: someone trying to get in.)

SYLVIE. Isaac?

(*No answer.*

A man wearing a large elephant head enters. He moves around the control room, maybe making elephant sounds.

SYLVIE *is in shock.*

ELEPHANT-HEAD MAN *is followed by a man and two women wearing evening clothes with football helmets covering their faces—*MARK, CHARLENE, *and* ZELDA.)

CHARLENE AND ZELDA. (*With cheerleader moves.*)

STAMPEDE

WILL STOMP ON YOU

STAMPEDE

WILL PUSH IT THROUGH

WE'RE ROUGH AND TOUGH AND THAT'S ENOUGH

STAMPEDE WILL STOMP ON YOU

(*Shocked pause, broken by…*)

FAYE. You guys are so full of shit.

CHARLENE. Found you!

FAYE. These are my maids of honors.

KENNETH. (*To* ELEPHANT-HEAD MAN.) You stole the mascot gear?

FAYE. That is so high school.

MARK. Stampede. We scared you bitches.

ANGELA. Bitches?

MARK. I meant *bitches*, not *bitches*. I'm Mark.

ANGELA. You play football, bitch?

SYLVIE. Angela, stay focused.

ANGELA. Right. I'm calling 9-1-1!

MARK. It was just a prank.

SYLVIE. Don't call 9-1-1.

ANGELA. Your patient could have gone anywhere. He could be anywhere. Typically, I could give a shit, but what if he actually is as sleep-deprived as he says he is? He'd be psychotic.

SYLVIE. If you call 9-1-1, and it's nothing, I'll be fired.

ANGELA. If I don't call, and it's something, you'll be dead.

SYLVIE. If I fail at this job, I'm dead.

ANGELA. It's just a job.

SYLVIE. For you. For me, it was the light at the end of the tunnel.

ELEPHANT-HEAD MAN. Were you in rehab?

(*Beat. Everyone's looking at her now.*)

SYLVIE. Yes, okay? Yes. And yes, I got arrested once.

TOMMY. Arrested?

SYLVIE. Ever since I was a little girl, I was afraid to go to sleep at night. It started this one night when I was about seven years old…

ANGELA. Okay, stop, fine, go. Go look for your patient.

SYLVIE. You have that much disdain for personal revelations?

ANGELA. It's just you're clearly so desperate to share your backstory. You'll stay alive just so you can bore us with it.

SYLVIE. You *want* me to stay alive?

ANGELA. I hate cleaning up blood.

SYLVIE. (*With tenderness.*) Lock the door behind me.

(SYLVIE *leaves.* ANGELA *locks the door.*)

CHARLENE. There's going to be blood?

MARK. Are we all going to die?

ANGELA. Not if we keep the door locked. Okay, who's sober here?

(*Only* ELEPHANT-HEAD MAN *raises his hand.*)

See that screen? If you see Patient Number One get up, like he hears something at his door, you tell me right away. Tommy, you shove these wires back in and get this speaker working again.

(ANGELA *gets on the mic to Room #3.*)

Carol. I want you to stay in your room and don't open the door if anyone knocks until after I tell you it's all right.

CAROL. (*Through speakers.*) Can I watch the post-game?

ANGELA. As long as you don't open the door.

CAROL. Like I would open the door during the post-game.

(CAROL *turns her TV back on.* SYLVIE *appears on Monitor #2, looking around.*)

KENNETH. She's in.

(SYLVIE *goes close to the camera and mouths, "Can you hear me?"*)

ANGELA. We can't hear you, but we're getting it fixed. He's not there?

(ISAAC *appears behind* SYLVIE.)

Sylvie, watch out!

(SYLVIE *turns, panics, and calls out for help.*)

SYLVIE. (*Voiceover.*) (*Heard through the speakers.*) Dr. Abramovitch!

> (*In the control room, the lights flash on and off. The monitors shut down. Everyone in the control room freezes.*
>
> *Time stands still.*
>
> *From on high, like a deus ex machina,* DR. ABRAMOVITCH *descends.*)

ABRAMOVITCH. What is it, Sylvie?

> (SYLVIE *looks up to* DR. ABRAMOVITCH *in the sky. He looks amazing. Maybe he, too, wears an Elephant Head. Maybe he's amazing in some other way.*)

SYLVIE. Dr. Abramovitch? You are not what I expected.

ABRAMOVITCH. Come on, I'm exactly what you expected. Exactly what you picture right at this moment in your mind's eye.

SYLVIE. Dr. Abramovitch. Ever since I was a little girl, I…

ABRAMOVITCH. Yeah, Sylvie, it's not just Angela who doesn't want to hear this story.

SYLVIE. But it's the reason I can't sleep at night. It led to my drug addiction, my self-destruction.

ABRAMOVITCH. I'd like to be sympathetic, but I think it's great that you can't sleep at night. If you could, you wouldn't be here, working your ass off for me.

SYLVIE. But I have a sickness.

ABRAMOVITCH. Why not think of it as a gift? Tell this story: When you were a little girl, you received a lasting gift. It changed you, shaped you, sent you on a journey, and made you adept at a very difficult job.

SYLVIE. Adept?! Right at this very moment, I'm failing miserably.

ABRAMOVITCH. You mean because that Isaac guy might kill you?

SYLVIE. Is he going to kill me?! God, I want something so bad right now. I know a guy who sold these little purple pills, I don't even know what they were, but these little purple pills; I still have the phone number. I could just walk out of here and call the guy with the little purple pills, and everyone would be better off.

ABRAMOVITCH. Sylvie, come here.

SYLVIE. I don't know how.

ABRAMOVITCH. I hired you because you do know how.

> (SYLVIE *flies to him. It's magic.*)

SYLVIE. What if I can't live up to what you need me to be?

ABRAMOVITCH. Have you noticed that you're flying?

SYLVIE. I am?

ABRAMOVITCH. You're doing it. You're already doing it.

(She and DR. ABRAMOVITCH *dance: a mentor/student pas de deux in the air.*

The graceful dance develops, and then devolves into a wrestling match on the ground.)

SYLVIE. (*V.O.*) (*Exact repeat of how she called out before.*) Dr. Abramovitch!

(Through the speakers, the sound of SYLVIE *and* ISAAC *in a tussle.)*

Get off of me.

ISAAC. (*V.O.*) You're on top of me.

SYLVIE. (*V.O.*) Because you grabbed me.

ISAAC. (*V.O.*) You grabbed me.

SYLVIE. (*V.O.*) Because you pushed me.

ISAAC. (*V.O.*) You fell on me.

SYLVIE. (*V.O.*) Because you disappeared on me.

ISAAC. (*V.O.*) I didn't disappear.

SYLVIE. (*V.O.*) Isaac.

ISAAC. (*V.O.*) What?

SYLVIE. (*V.O.*) Were you hiding under the bed?

ISAAC. (*V.O.*) So what?

(Lights flash on again, and the control room comes to life. DR. ABRAMOVITCH *and* SYLVIE *are no longer flying in the sky.*

The video monitor for Room #2 flashes on, showing ISAAC *and* SYLVIE, *post-kerfluffle in his room.*

The whole gang in the control room watches ISAAC *and* SYLVIE's *scene, rapt.)*

FAYE. Is she okay?

MARK. Ask her if she's okay.

ANGELA. She's okay. No interrupting.

(On the screen, through the speakers…)

SYLVIE. Why are you being such a total jerk?

ISAAC. I was hoping you'd kick me out.

SYLVIE. You want to get kicked out? Why would you want that?

ISAAC. Because maybe I don't want to be cured. If I get cured, it's like…

SYLVIE. It's like what?

ISAAC. It's like I don't love her anymore.

(Pause.)

SYLVIE. Sometimes it feels that way: Like your sickness is the only connection you have to the person who's gone away. But I don't think it's true. You can still love her. Even if you don't keep on doing all the things she used to do even before you understood what drugs even were but you knew something was weird about the way she behaved sometimes.

ISAAC. You lost me there.

SYLVIE. I'm saying your mother would want you to get some sleep, Isaac.

ISAAC. I've tried.

SYLVIE. Then stop trying.

ISAAC. Stop trying?

SYLVIE. Yeah. Stop trying so hard.

    (*Almost like she's coaching herself.*)

There's a reason you're here. Something led you to this place. Can you just be in this place?

    (*Her voice lulling.*)

Can you trust that? That you're in the right place. How lucky you are. To be here. Right here. Right now. In...this...place.

    (ISAAC *is asleep.*)

Isaac? Isaac. Ever since I was a little girl, I was afraid to go to sleep at night. It started this one night when I was about seven years old...

    (ANGELA *re-pulls the plug out of the speaker.*)

TOMMY. Hey, I just fixed that.

ANGELA. Her past is private. Show a little respect.

    (*On the monitor,* SYLVIE *keeps talking, without any volume: a moving tale of trauma. They all watch as she finishes the revelation, and then pulls herself together and exits.*)

Okay, dudes. Out of here. Party's elsewhere.

KENNETH. You don't seem lazy to me.

MARK. Me either.

ANGELA. Oh yeah, what do I seem?

MARK. Can I answer that later?

ANGELA. Like eight-thirty a.m. later?

MARK. In the lobby?

ANGELA. No, in your hotel room. Yes, in the lobby.

    (*The interlopers in the control room head towards the door. To* KENNETH *and* FAYE:)

You two, wait.

KENNETH. Are we in trouble?

ANGELA. Just wait.

    (SYLVIE *enters just as the* ELEPHANT-HEAD MAN *leads* TOMMY *and the* FOOTBALL PEOPLE *out the door.*

ELEPHANT-HEAD MAN *stops and has an intimate moment face-to-face with* SYLVIE.)

ELEPHANT-HEAD MAN. I had a dream like this once.

(SYLVIE *nods. The visitors exit, except for* FAYE *and* KENNETH.)

ANGELA. Is it okay if these two spend the night in the spare room? I know the protocol doesn't technically allow for it.

SYLVIE. No, sure. I was actually thinking the same thing. You guys want to set yourselves up in Room Four?

FAYE. And you'll watch over us?

SYLVIE. We'll be right down the hall. Just to get you over the hump. And then you'll be on your way into a brand new life.

ANGELA. I'll show you guys where to go.

(ANGELA *exits with* FAYE *and* KENNETH.

SYLVIE *alone in the control room.*

She consults the three video monitors that are on: CAROL *asleep in glow of TV,* ISAAC *asleep,* JOE *lying motionless, and soon* FAYE *and* KENNETH *snuggling together.*

SYLVIE *consults the computer readings and notices something.*)

SYLVIE. Joe, what are you still doing up?

JOE. (*Through speakers, still not moving.*) Still a little tense, I guess.

SYLVIE. Joe?

JOE. Yeah?

SYLVIE. (*Sings.*)
GO TO SLEEP, LITTLE CHILDREN.
YOU'RE SUCH GOOD LITTLE CHILDREN.
DOWN GOES THE SUN.
YOUR HARD WORK'S DONE.
GOOD LITTLE CHILDREN SLEEP.

(*Everybody sleeps.*

But not SYLVIE. *And that's okay.*)

End of Play

Dreamerwake
by Anne Washburn

CHARACTERS

NICK
AMELIA
NICOLE
DANI
ELI
JESSICA
ABBY
TONY
COLIN
JOE

Also:

X, Y, Z, P, Q, R, B, N, S, T, V, M

are all hapless Apprentices in Actors Theatre of Louisville's 2012-2013 company. The actors who play these characters will assume various other dramatical duties as well.

Including:

ANGELA, a sleep lab technician
RYAN, a weatherman on the TV
AMY, a director
SLEEPY WOMAN WHO HAS LOU'S PHONE NUMBER NOW, just that

SETTING

A sleep lab and a brain.

PLAYWRIGHT'S NOTES

ON PUNCTUATION

Sometimes there is a lack of punctuation. This lack does not necessarily imply speediness, although it suggests an internal momentum; it indicates a section where the actor must work the punctuation out for him/herself; in general these sections could probably be a bit slower than normal, but it's the kind of slow which comes from digging heels in while being tugged forward, or from thrusting forward while being pulled backwards, if that makes sense.

THE MAKING OF THE PLAY

The bewildering, pleasurable, distressing discovery of poking around in the science of sleep and dreaming is that it's crammed with mysteries. We spend around a third of our lives in a state that defines us, and shapes us, but which very few of us give much thought to, and about which very little is known.

Partly a quasi-scientific investigation, partly a way to get a better sense of the actors, and partly a way to explore my own feelings and theories about dreaming, I set up my own deeply arbitrary sleep study with the Acting Apprentice Company. When they had just begun the program with Actors Theatre, and before I had met them, I asked the actors to keep a dream diary and to fill out a dream questionnaire in which I asked them did they dream of flying, losing their teeth, wild animals—all the classics—did they have the dream where you're trying to run but your feet are glued to the pavement, where you're performing naked, where your living room is a swimming pool, etc. etc. etc.

A month or so later I had a chance to meet with them and to talk, more informally and widely, about their experience of dreaming. Their answers to the questionnaires had fallen somewhere in the realm of where you'd think they might fall—only half had flown in their sleep or murdered someone, almost everyone had lost their teeth or performed naked; the one dream they had in common—they had all dreamt of each other. What I didn't expect, and what the diaries and actual conversations revealed, was what different relationships they had to their dreams. Some think about them all the time, some almost never; some cherish their dreams, and their dreaming life; for others it's a torment, or a bore.

I used almost none of this material directly in the completed play, but gathering it allowed me to think a little more carefully about dream realities and logics, and about the very intense work- and hope-saturated life of an Actors Theatre Apprentice.

The play includes overheard conversation gathered surreptitiously during a flying rehearsal, and approved for use by the Apprentices overheard.

ATTRIBUTIONS AND RECOMMENDATIONS

This play was created specifically for, and in partial collaboration with, the 2012-2013 Acting Apprentice Company at Actors Theatre of Louisville. Anyone interested in producing this play with a smaller number of actors is welcome to consolidate the roles sensically. Anyone wishing to rejigger the play so that it is adapted to a different producing context is welcome to do so in consultation with the playwright.

Initial weather broadcast language courtesy of Ryan Hoke.

Dreamerwake

The stage is dark.

RYAN THE WEATHER GUY ON TV. And good evening I'm Ryan Hoke with your forecast update. We've got a pretty active week shaping up with warmer temperatures and the possibility of some strong storms on Wednesday

> (*In the dark we can hear the sleep lab technician, on an overhead mic, and* NICK's *replies, from the stage.*
>
> *The broadcast continues beneath.*)

SLEEP LAB TECH. Hey Nick, sorry about that, I'm back. You're not asleep already are you?

NICK. Nope.

SLEEP LAB TECH. Excellent-o. Alright so we did the eyes.

Now if you could just jiggle your legs. That's great.

Now if you could cough for me.

> (*He coughs.*)

Wonderful. Now grit your teeth please.

Thank you...you can open your eyes now, if you want.

NICK. I like them closed.

SLEEP LAB TECH. Great. Now please make with the Bubblicious.

> (*Tiny pause.*)

NICK. The what?

SLEEP LAB TECH. Where you chew. Like the gum. There's still Bubblicious, right? Do *not* tell me that's before your time.

NICK. Um, probably.

SLEEP LAB TECH. You mean you don't know Bubblicious??

NICK. I don't really chew gum.

SLEEP LAB TECH. That's a major, major brand

Okay, chew for me please.

Good. You are calibrated and ready to go Mister. Time to switch off the program.

> (*This whole time we've been hearing a weather report in the background. It amplifies.*)

RYAN THE WEATHER GUY. —you can see this on Doppler radar here—stretches from the Louisville area all the way back to Iowa

NICK. Can I leave it on for another just for another few minutes? I can't fall asleep without it

SLEEP LAB TECH. Five more, and then it's going off, asleep or no. M'kay?

NICK. Sure…

SLEEP LAB TECH. Night night.

RYAN THE WEATHER GUY. It looks like we're going to see some afternoon to evening storms on Monday with a high of 61

By Tuesday more rain rolls into the area with a high of 62 degrees—

I think we could hear a clap of thunder or two with that system coming through on Tuesday and then by Wednesday

Strong storms come into the forecast with a high of 67 degrees we could hit 70 here if we get some warmer air up from the south

And also I think there could be a risk of some severe weather here on Wednesday it's too early to tell right now but I think Thursday and Friday we could

> (*As* NICK *is falling asleep the sound is starting to fade out and to become a little tinnier.*)

Take a hit on temperatures—46 and 45 respectively under partly cloudy and cloudy skies there partly *tornado-y partly severe* I think we'll hear a clap of thunder or two *I think we'll hear some applause*

I think we'll see more rain by the weekend. *The skies are really churning out there. I think we're going to see some unexpected incidents.*

We have strong winds coming out from *the north and sweeping away and we have a hilarious I think we are going to have to ask the coach about the playoffs we have weather systems featured on the sound stage and he's recently had a whirlpool system installed in his home bathroom with very powerful jets and bubbles and cloud systems.*

SONG SNATCH (ONE VOICE). THE WINDS ARE FROM THE NORTH

RYAN THE WEATHER GUY. *There's a weapons complex at the base of the mountains. Certainly I didn't build that thing for speed I think if you look closer, you'll have to hesitate. Guys. Guys?*

SOMEONE ELSE. $6.50, right?/Or is it $6.75. A rip-off.

SOMEONE ELSE. I said he could put it down there.

LOU. Ha ha ha ha ha, put that down man.

SONG SNATCH (TWO VOICES). THE SKY IS SLIDING SOUTH LITTLE CHILDREN

ADD ANOTHER VOICE. YOU'RE SUCH GOOD, LITTLE CHILDREN

(*The lights begin to kindle.*

Rooms/images on set begin to glow

On the margin of the stage, almost unseeable, bodies are slowly falling, and whisking away.)

AMY. Okay you guys I'm going to need everyone to get in their places again. We're going to take it from the top of the scene.

SONG SURGE HALF BEHIND AMY. WE'VE BURST INTO A FLAME/WE'RE ASH AND SMOKE AGAIN

(*Which fades out a bit.*

The lights are fading and the images flicker out.

The sound is still audible, but fading, and a little dispassionate.)

AMY. Nick I'm going to need you to focus on this okay. Okay everybody, everybody. Take it from: Sylvie What? What are you doing here? Kenneth is this the sleep lab

SOMEONE ELSE, RIGHT IN OUR EAR, QUIET. T-minus, 50, 55, T-minus 22, 21, 20, T minus

ANOTHER SOMEONE ELSE—ALMOST INAUDIBLE. Roger that

SOMEONE ELSE, RIGHT IN OUR EAR, QUIET. Presenting Mr. and Mrs. Kenneth Jones.

ANOTHER SOMEONE ELSE—ALMOST INAUDIBLE. and we have lift-off

THE ACTRESS WHO PLAYS FAYE. (*All but absent.*) Ken saw the sign for the sleep center.

AMY. We have lift-off

THE ACTOR WHO PLAYS KENNETH. (*Absent.*) I missed the sign for the exit. I'll keep driving.

AMY. T minus 9, 8, 7

SOMEONES. (*Singing.*) GO TO SLEEP, LITTLE CHILDREN YOU'RE SUCH GOOD LITTLE CHILDREN

AMY. Lift-off confirmed.

We have lift-off.

(*Lights have faded off. The stage is black. It is completely silent.*

For, like, five seconds

There is a footfall

Maybe a tiny tiny glow kindles somewhere

We hear a voice.)

NICK. (*Very matter-of-fact, not very engaged.*) I remember that guy who would who was it was it Jason? Jason? Who would scoop the coffee in…with scoops…he was afraid to eyeball it…he was very insecure, he would scoop would measure would count the exact scoops

> (AMELIA *starts to fade in. As* AMELIA *starts to fade in,* NICK *starts to fade out.*)

as though once you start as though once the lid is shut and the water cascades into the chamber there's no, at that point there's no

AMELIA. Okay so this guy. This tourist. He's in the *Australian outback.*

> (*Lights are starting to fade up on* AMELIA *and a number of Apprentices at Freddie's, a bar.*)

And he has the hat…with the little string around the rim. And he has the vest with all the pockets on it. And a big air-conditioned Jeep.

And it's totally hot and dry and flat and he sees this sign for this little town. (*Teasingly.*) And the name of the little town…

JESSICA. What's the name of the town?

AMELIA. (*Sort of triumphantly.*) Wouldn't you like to know!

So this little town? It's totally famous. And what it's totally famous for is—

NICK. Wait where's Lou?

> (*Everyone turns to look at* NICK.)

NICOLE. Amelia's telling a joke, Nick.

NICK. Yeah but where's Lou? Shouldn't he be back from the can by now?

ELI & JESSICA. Nick. Amelia's telling a joke.

AMELIA. It's okay, so this little tiny town totally in the middle of nowhere is totally famous for its koala tea.

NICOLE. Koala tea?

AMELIA. Yes.

NICOLE. Made, from koalas?

AMELIA. *Yes.* So when he enters this little town

…whose name you shall not yet know…

he goes straight to the koala tea house.

NICOLE. That's disgusting. This is tea made with dead koalas?

JESSICA. It's a *joke*, Nicole.

AMELIA. It's just from the *hair*, Nicole.

NICOLE. Oh. The *hair.*

AMELIA. The fur. Whatever.

NICOLE. Not, like, haunches.

AMELIA. No.

NICOLE. Okay that's gross, but not immoral.

AMELIA. Thank you. So they seat him at this table with like this starched white table cloth, and there's flowers, and beautiful china, and a guy playing a violin.

NICK. No but Lou should really be back by now.

(*They turn and they stare at him.*)

ABBY. He ran into a girl.

NICOLE. He got into a fight.

JESSICA. He went outside for a cigarette and a friend drove by in a car and he got in.

ABBY. Amelia's telling a *joke.*

ELI. (*Suddenly remembering.*) He got that great part.

AMELIA. Oh that's right he got that great part

NICOLE. Lou got that *great* part.

ABBY. God it's amazing.

TONY. He's going to be famous. Right?!

ELI. He's going to be crazy crazy famous

NICK. He left town?

AMELIA. Yeah they were like: next flight out, buddy!

NICK. He just he just left?

ELI. He wanted to tell you but they were like: look, if you want the part you've got to go now because they have to make that suit, like, totally to measure

NICOLE. They have to absolutely make it super specifically for your exact body

ELI. They make it out of rubber and I think actual hog parts, for the joints

TONY. They make it out of rubber and I think actual hog parts for the pistons

AMELIA. The hogs are cut to measure, that's the dark secret about it, that's why it looks so good

NICK. You are shitting me

NICOLE. No I'm telling you the truth; Thursday bright and early in the morning Lou is going to be standing up to his ankles in gore in a special secret film factory slaughter house in Encino while they cut hogs to his measurement for that suit. *THIS* is why I'm a vegan Nick. Because all over the world people are doing fucked up things so that men can be superheroes

JESSICA. Can *look* like superheroes

NICOLE. Right can have that appearance because

AMELIA. The man doesn't have powers. Doesn't have real powers.

ELI. I love Lou, right? Love him. But the man can't really fly.

TONY. He's not a good flier.

ELI. He's not even a great *fake* flier, let's be honest.

JESSICA. Lou? He can't fly.

AMELIA. Omigod we're late.

JESSICA. We're late for rehearsal. Amy is going to kill us.

NICK. But it's midnight

ELI. You weren't drinking anything were you?

NICK. Yeah it's midnight

ELI. Fuck, well don't let anyone know

NICK. You're all drinking!

NICOLE. We're drinking ginger ale and O'Doul's because of the flying rehearsal Jesus what are you drinking?

> (*He has a moment where he actually doesn't know. He looks down at his Maker's.*)

Well don't let Amy or Brian know or they'll kill you it's fucking irresponsible.

> (*They all turn and stare at him.*)

ALL. C'mon we're late we're late we're late!

NICOLE. Brian is especially going to kill you. Well maybe Amy will kill you more. Maybe they'll work *together.*

> (*The Flying Rehearsal is forming around them. Clusters of Apprentices rehearsing or sitting on the floor in small groups chatting.*
>
> *In the background we should see characteristic moves from <u>nightnight</u> with the actors who play those parts.*
>
> *At some point* JESSICA *and* TONY *are dancing around with a great dance they're working on, which might or might not relate to a dance moment in* <u>Comfort Inn</u>, *and they may or may not continue it in a low trajectory in harness at some point.*)

AMELIA. (*Still telling her joke.*) And there are beautiful crystal bowls of honey, *great* Australian outback honey. And little fans of lemon on a gold plate. And the waiter—the waiter is very *formal.* Very *impressive.*

> (*In the foreground* DANI *is being strapped into a harness.*
>
> ELI *is helping her into the harness.*)

ELI. It's probably not worth it to wait for Brian, I feel like I've done this a million times already. (*He adjusts something.*) What about now, do those points feel right on the side?

DANI. They feel a little bit high.

ELI. What about…

DANI. It's digging! It's digging!

ELI. Okay toughen up a bit okay I'm going to adjust the back strap…

T. (*Helpfully, to* DANI.) Try bending your knees a little bit

ELI. Give her some slack. Better, right?

DANI. Should it feel this loose?

ELI. Yeah it's good to have options. Do *not* tell me you are worried about this.

DANI. Yes I'm worried about this. Why wouldn't I be worried? What's Not to be worried about? I'm about to be suspended in midair. That is *not normal*.

ELI. Not to be worried baby I've gotcha, I've gotcha, now I'm pretty sure we want to strap this thing over here…

T. Does it go there? I thought it went over by the left.

DANI. Maybe we *should* wait for Brian. I'm thinking maybe we should wait for Brian.

ELI. (*Absently.*) I don't know. It's pretty late. He's probably not coming after all. I'm going to say if we loop this, and hook *this*, we're fine. Right?

T. That looks right.

ELI. Ready?

DANI. No, I don't think so.

T. Wait, do we need to do that balance safety thingie check first.

ELI. Nah. (*To the people on rope:*) Ally Oop!

> (*She is slowly hoisted up.*
>
> *She emits a brief startled shriek.*
>
> *As she is being hoisted up a small group of Apprentices start singing.*)

SINGING. GROUND CONTROL TO MAJOR TOM
GROUND CONTROL TO MAJOR TOM
TAKE YOUR PROTEIN PILLS AND PUT YOUR HELMET ON…

> (*And are joined gradually by many more but not all of them:*)

JESSICA AND AMELIA AND DANI SINGING.
WELL YEAH I WANNA MAKE LOVE TO YOU
JUST THE WAY THE ASTRONAUTS DOOOO
I GOT AN ORBIT THAT'S ALL MY OWN
AND SOON YOU'LL CALL THIS NEW CRAFT YOUR HOME
GONNA OPEN UP MY AIRLOCK
THRUSTERS ON FULL AND YOU'RE READY TO DOCK
YEAH SOON YOU WILL DISCOVER
I'M YOUR ZERO GRAVITY LUUUUVER
YEAH I'M YOUR ZERO GRAVITY LUUUUVER

> (*Once she's high up—with the encouragement of* ELI *and* T—*she starts twirling—awkwardly at first and then more gracefully.*)

SINGING. THIS IS GROUND CONTROL TO MAJOR TOM, YOU'VE REALLY MADE THE GRADE
AND THE PAPERS WANT TO KNOW WHOSE SHIRTS YOU WEAR
NOW IT'S TIME TO LEAVE THE CAPSULE IF YOU DARE

(*Meanwhile, a small cluster:*)

COLIN. I have so much stuff to do in the scene changes, you don't understand

ABBY. Oh my God I have to move all those gravestones/back against the wall

COLIN. That curtain/that curtain that I hang up

ABBY. Put the curtains back, and then I have to go and open the door for Van Helsing, AND Sullivan

COLIN. The curtain that I hang up is the most stressful thing I've ever done in my life

X. No no, stressful, let me tell you about *stressful*—

COLIN. (*Doggedly continues.*) It never slots into the fucking track, it always gets caught, and I know that like Marc is about to come out and like be hilarious and I'm like holding him back. Uch. And every school matinee I have kids yelling at me. Every matinee, it never fails, as soon as I come out of the black they're all like "GAHH"

(*Someone laughs.*)

Y. They see you?

COLIN. Yeah they see me and they're afraid, they're like "there's a, there's a MAN there"

ABBY. Yeah. They're totally worried at first that he's Dracula.

COLIN. And I'm like "Please ignore me" "Please leave me alone" the moment I appear they start yelling: "There's someone moving the gate! There's someone moving the gate!" Like when I move that gate, yeah.

ABBY. They're totally into the glimpse. Of what goes on. Of like the

COLIN. "Pay no attention to that man behind the curtain"

ABBY. Yeah kids can't handle that man behind the curtain shit. They love it, but they can't handle it.

NICK. You know what you could do, if you really wanted to fuck them up, you bring one of those, like one of those sets of teeth, one of those cheap Halloween sets of glowing vampire fangs and you slip it in your mouth before you go on you charge it up with a flashlight and slip it in and when they're all, "there's a MAN" you turn around and you flash them a big fangy grin.

COLIN. And that does it.

ABBY. Yeah that's going to do it. After that point—they're never going to know what's fake and what's real. Just that it's ALL scary. Just great. Let's fuck them up.

COLIN. It's not funny, Nick. They're *little kids.*

NICK. They're in middle school. They're in high school.

ABBY. There's war. There's terrorism. There's kidnapping.

COLIN. There's sexual abusers.

Z. There's bullies.

ABBY. There's leaking nuclear plants

X. there's tornadoes

Z. and hurricanes

ABBY. and earthquakes.

COLIN. There's a lot. There's a lot they're going through. I'm not going to take away like the last shred of some little kid's security just because it's *funny.*

P. Jesus, Nick.

ABBY. There's snakes, there's zombies, there's creepy half-glimpsed things,

X. there's sections of the sidewalk which just suction onto your feet so you can't move no matter how hard you try to move

ABBY. and you open your mouth to scream and you can't scream

Q. You open your mouth to scream

Y. and nothing comes out but a little tiny raspy cry

X & Z. and no one hears it

ABBY. And then all of your teeth fall out and land on the ground.

Q & X &Y & Z. But no one hears *that.*

COLIN. No one hears it Nick, I mean fuck, do you ever *think*???

(*Another cluster.* AMELIA *is still telling the joke:*)

AMELIA. And he says waiter, waiter, come here!

And the waiter *glides* over.

And he says waiter! Waiter! Look! Look here!

There is a *hair,* in my koala tea!

And the waiter, is incredibly offended.

And he draws himself up. To his full, waiterly height. And he says:

Oh…fuck.

Fuck. Actually…

I messed it up. Actually you *did* need to know the name of the town.

You totally needed to know the name of the town. Damn.

Okay the name of the town: is Mercy, okay? Mercy.

Okay you totally needed to know that before.

I think I ruined the joke.

(*This whole time* NICK, *after his first conversational attempt, has been kind*)

*of in the middle of everything, or to the side, with it all swirling around him,
observing in a daze until somehow he is brought into the gravity of* LOU,
already hoisted in the air.)

LOU. Nick—where you been? You're my rope man, right?

NICK. Lou.

LOU. I'm gonna need my man on the rope

(*Whoever it is transfers the rope to* NICK.)

NICK. Lou I thought you were…

LOU. Thought I was what. Hang on tight there.

NICK. I thought you were…

LOU. Oh, hey, check out what we figured out, the last day we're here,

(*Someone laughs.*)

is my birthday. So we're all gonna get shit-faced!

(NICK *is still a bit distracted with the question of why it seems odd or wrong
to him to find* LOU *there.*)

NICK. I'm glad you're thinking this far ahead

V. Yeah

LOU. We were talking about it in the car and were like, "when's your
birthday" and I was like "it's the LAST DAY WE'RE HERE"

I'm buying—well the first couple of rounds

M. If you're buying, I'm drinking!

Z. So we're gonna go back into the real world, dead drunk.

Y. Which is probably the only way we'll be able to cope with it

LOU. Maker's on me at Freddie's!

(LOU *shudders and slips a few inches.*)

R. Nick!

COLIN. WHAT ARE YOU DOING?

ABBY. You're supposed to be holding the rope!

NICK. I'm holding the rope!

TONY. You're letting go of the rope

NICK. I'm not letting go of the rope!

(LOU *lets out a "yiiiii" as he drops, abruptly, a half-foot.*)

R. You're letting go of the rope

LOU. Hang on to that rope, man

COLIN. Oh my god you let go of the rope! You let go of the rope!

(LOU *screams, or something, falls, suspends a foot above the ground,
People are variously lurching forward, lurching back, frozen still*

He is suspended
Everyone is frozen
He falls, with a resounding thump, he is still
Everyone is frozen for a few seconds
There is a tiny lurch, and his body slowly begins to churn
People move towards him)

RAIN OF SWEARS. Oh shit dammit hell!

(*Simultaneous with:*)

OUTBURST OF RELIGIOSITY. Oh please god please no

JESSICA. Don't touch him! Don't touch him!/

Y. Don't touch him!

Q. (*Simultaneous.*) Do not touch him!

ABBY. Omigodomigodohmigodohmigodohmigodohmigod

JESSICA. Whatever you do, don't touch him!

ELI. Call 911, someone call 911

N. Someone call 911!

DANI. Lou, you're gonna be okay, okay, we're with you, you're gonna be fine

JESSICA. Dani get away from him!

Q. Don't touch him!

DANI. I am not touching him! We have to let him know we're with him! We're all here Lou, we're all with you

(*Already a few people have turned their attention from* LOU *to* NICK *who is standing, utterly frozen, at the very edge of the circle. They are only looking at him, he doesn't see them, as he is focused entirely on the slowly convulsing Lou.*)

TONY. I'm at the at that school at at…

M. Lincoln Elementary!

TONY. Lincoln Elementary in the back in the It's at Main, Main and uh… uh…

NICOLE. It's at, it's at…oh Hell

TONY. We're at the corner of Main and…

NICOLE. Wenzel!

TONY. Wenzel! We're in the back but you can come around the front we have a fallen person we need a paramedic we need an ambulance we need a doctor we have

ABBY. Omigodomigodohmigodohmigodohmigodohmigod

TONY. He's a fallen man we have he's still alive he's still moving he's still but we need but it doesn't look good so please send someone right away we're in the back it's hard to get to

NICOLE. There's a side door!

TONY. There's a side door we'll have someone standing by the side door we aren't moving him no one has touched him please send someone right away okay please send someone right

ABBY. Omigodomigodohmigodohmigodohmigodohmigod

NICOLE. Okay just shut up okay just shut up

ABBY. Omigodomigodohmigodohmigodohmigodohmigod

> (*The convulsing has been slowing and now it has stopped.*)

Z. Oh hell

JESSICA & Y. Don't touch him!

DANI. I'm not touching him shut up I'm not touching him I'm just trying to find out is he I'm not going to touch him

> (*Just a few more people have turned to look—in a steady, hard, cold manner— at* NICK *who doesn't see them he is still transfixed by the now-still* LOU.)

JESSICA. Is he?

> (*Someone is kneeling next to him, trying to*)

DANI. I can't tell

> (*Trying to find out if he's still breathing.*)

I don't...

> (*To* JESSICA:)

I'm touching his wrist. I'm touching his wrist. I can't break him if I

> (*Touching the wrist, her head right against his.*
>
> *Then very gently touching his neck.*)

I don't think so.

I don't think so.

COLIN. Here let me

> (*Action repeated.*)

No.

AMELIA. Oh. Oh.

> (*There is a certain amount of clutching and hugging*
>
> *A certain amount of standing there frozen*
>
> *And then slowly and not all at once people turn and stare at* NICK
>
> *Until everyone is staring at him, accusingly*
>
> *He finally feels the weight of all that staring*
>
> *He stares back*
>
> *Finally someone speaks up.*)

COLIN. You let go of the rope

(Beat.)

NICK. I didn't let go of the rope

COLIN. You let go of the rope

NICK. I didn't—

JESSICA. You weren't paying attention

DANI. You were texting with your girlfriend

ELI & AMELIA. You were daydreaming

ABBY & TONY. You were playing fantasy football

COLIN. You were drunk

NICK. I wasn't drunk

COLIN. You were drunk we all went to Freddie's and you

ELI & JESSICA & DANI & Z. Were jacking off, we all saw you you weren't paying attention you weren't holding on

TONY. To the rope

ELI & NICOLE & ABBY & AMELIA & Y. You were jacking off and you let the rope go and Lou fell and Lou died and

TONY & DANI & Y. We all saw you you were

NICK. Oh fuck I wasn't I wasn't I swear I wasn't I

NICOLE & ABBY & Z & N. You smoked a fuck-load of weed and you were jacking off and

NICK. I don't remember I

PRETTY MUCH BUT NOT QUITE EVERYONE. We saw you we all saw you

NICK. I don't I

> *(A small groan*
> *They all stop*
> *Another small groan*
> *They all turn, to look at* LOU
> *A hand twitches*
> *A coordinated burst of ohmigod don't touch him etc. sound*
> *A groan and a sort of half torso rise*
> *A coordinated burst of ohmigod don't touch him etc. sound with a different more hopeful pitch to it*
> LOU's *hand to head, hand feeling head*
> *A joyous coordinated babble*
> *He sits up, one hand still feeling head the other kind of patting at his body.)*

Lou!

Oh my God, Lou!

Oh dear God. Oh dear God. *Lou.*

> (NICK *is kneeling next to him.*)

LOU. Don't yell. For Christ's sake—don't yell.

NICK. Lou you're alive.

LOU. Yeah. Yeah I know.

NICK. I thought you were dead.

LOU. Nope. Don't think so.

> (*He's rising,* NICK *rises with him.*)

NICK. Man I thought you were dead. I thought I had killed you. I thought you were completely fucking dead! I thought I had absolutely fucking killed you!

God you're an asshole.

LOU. Me!?

NICK. You're a complete asshole

LOU. Who's the asshole who can't hold on to a rope?!

NICK. (*He is half clasping him by the elbows.*) I'm a *complete* asshole. I'm a complete asshole because you know what I was thinking I wasn't even thinking I wasn't thinking I was thinking I wasn't thinking about you, and dead you and your mom and your sister and you're never going to live and have kids and everyone is going to be sad I'm the asshole I was *strictly* thinking about me and about how deeply deeply deeply it was going to suck to have you dead how fucking inconvenient it was going to be I mean I was *outraged* I was already thinking I'm going to call you and you're *never* going to pick up which you *know* that pisses me off and I'm going to text you: nothing, and I'm going to be waiting at Freddie's and *that fuck is never going to show*—

Oh my gosh and this is how much of a complete asshole I am part of me is thinking: Lou almost dies, Lou's back, God loves me after all.

LOU. (*Initially super grand and theatrical.*) The Koala Tea of Mercy is not strained
It droppeth from heaven in gentle driblets
Like the drops of cum
Shaken from your limp dick
When your business is done

NICK. The fuck? You fucking *freak*!

> (*They punch and pound each other briefly then another clasp.*)

Y. Get a room!

S. Get a room!

> (*Siren coming closer.*)

TONY. Oh fuck it's 911.

V. (*Essentially lighthearted.*) We're in trouble now

NICOLE. No one called off 911!

COLIN. This is gonna piss off the paramedics

ELI. They're going to be all: we came for blood, we will not leave, without our blood!/

DANI. Someone's gotta fake a seizure or, a stomach ache or something.

TONY. (*In a high-pitched English accent.*) "Show us the body!"

ABBY. Lou you're gonna have to let them at least poke at you.

AMELIA. Can't we just lie?

JESSICA. We could just lie

Y. Yeah. Yeah.

JESSICA. We could say someone was wigged out because they didn't know

AMELIA. It was an acting exercise and someone didn't know

LOU. No it's cool, they should probably take a look at me anyway

ABBY. You feeling okay?

LOU. I'm feeling okay but probably, it was a long way down

NICOLE. How's the head?

LOU. The head's fine but my stomach—

DANI. Are you okay?

LOU. is not feeling completely hot to tell you the truth

     (*There's shushing and attention from the rest of the group.*)

NICK. Not hot not hot how what's wrong with it

LOU. It's probably just the like stress and there's just a little bit

NICOLE. What is it?

DANI. Can you describe it

LOU. There's a little bit of a headache just it's not

NICOLE. Tony would you go out there and make sure they know which door to come in?

LOU. It's just a little tender

ABBY. Is there, is there like, on a side?

LOU. I probably just need an aspirin and—

     (*He lifts up his hand and puts his other hand on his stomach.*)

NICK. Wait what, what

LOU. No I just felt a little nauseous for a moment it's—

     (*He has a moment.*)

Okay maybe…I may have to hurl

NICK. We need a wastebasket!

LOU. Oh…

> (*He sort of jolts, puts his hands to his head, people reach for him.*)

Okay nobody touch me. Nobody touch me for a moment okay just—get back get back

NICK. Just hang on.

Z. Get back everyone!

> (*A jolt-shudder passes through his body, it looks something like a wave of nausea and an electrical current.*
>
> *Another one.*)

DANI. I think maybe this is a seizure—Lou you should probably try to lie down

LOU. (*Something a little wild, a little desperate.*) Get away from me get away

M. Back off everyone, *Jesus.*

> (*Another wave of current and at the same time he thrashes out scattering the people around him a bit.*)

LOU. Augh

Augh

NICK. Oh Christ

R. Somebody get something for his tongue

> (*With an even more wrenching Augh he jolts upward a few inches from the ground.*
>
> *A cry of response from the onlookers.*
>
> *Another cry of rather primal pain and he's jolted up a few feet.*
>
> *Coordinated waves of overlapping response from the onlookers:*
>
> "*Don't touch him don't touch him*"
>
> "*Grab him grab him grab him*"
>
> "*Oh sweet horrible fuck*"
>
> "*Oh sweet Jesus oh no*"
>
> *He's suspended there for a moment in agony and then he's jerked up, screaming, as fast as he can go and as it were "flattened" against the ceiling.*
>
> NICK *watches below, rapt with horror.*
>
> *Blackout.*
>
> *Sound of* NICK *crying out.*
>
> *And thrashing.*
>
> TECHNICIAN *on microphone screaming at him.*)

SLEEP LAB TECH. Nick the leads! The leads! Leave the leads alone! You're tearing them—you're in the sleep—oh Jesus—you're in the sleep lab Nick! Remember? You're in the lab! Christ. *Nick!*

NICK. (*Overlapping.*) Where's my phone???
Where's my phone???

> (*Sound of rummaging in jeans? Belt buckle?*
> *Small blink of light illuminates his face from his phone.*
> *[Good if he has leads dangling from his face.]*
> *We hear the sound of the numbers*
> *the dial*
> *the pick-up, a woman's voice.*)

NICK. Traci? Traci? Put Lou on! This is Nick, can you put Lou on?

> (*A small pause.*)

Lou?

SLEEPY WOMAN WHO HAS LOU'S PHONE NUMBER NOW.
Listen. You've got to stop calling this number. There's no Lou here.

NICK. Traci?

SLEEPY WOMAN. No, I'm not Traci. There's no Lou here. This isn't his number any more. This is my new number.

NICK. Wait, let me check if I hit the right number.

SLEEPY WOMAN. This *is* the right number but it isn't Lou's number. I'm really really sorry for your loss but, the next time you call, I'm not going to pick up.
I'm not going to pick up the next time you call.
Okay?

> (*A small pause.*)

NICK. Right.

Okay.

Right.

SLEEPY WOMAN. Okay? I'm going to hang up now. Please don't call again.

> (*A small pause.*)

NICK. No. I won't.

SLEEPY WOMAN. Thank you.

> (*Phone off.*
> *Phone is shut, so that it's now dark.*
> *Sounds of* NICK's *sobs.*)

End of Play

ADDENDUM—COORDINATED SOUNDS

A coordinated burst of ohmigod don't touch him etc. sound

Ohmigod don't touch him
Don't touch him step away
Ohmigod he's alive
Ohgod is he alive?

A coordinated burst of ohmigod don't touch him etc. sound with a different more hopeful pitch to it

Ohmigod don't touch him
Don't touch him step away
Ohmigod he's alive
Ohgod is he alive?
Lou are you alive?

A joyous coordinated babble

Lou you're alive you're alive!
Ohmigod Ohmigod you're alive!
Lou you're okay you're okay!
Lou yay Lou yay Lou yay Lou!

nightnight
by Lucas Hnath

CHARACTERS

THE ASTRONAUTS
TOM, American
SUE, American
ALEX, Russian

MISSION CONTROL
DICK, the CAPCOM, primary communicator between astronauts and Mission Control.
FLIGHT DIRECTOR, oversees mission.
FLIGHT SURGEON, doctor overseeing the mission.
CONTROL, GUIDANCE & RETRIEVAL, additional support in Mission Control.
CLOCK, announces time. Also announces all scene titles.

SETTING

21st Century. Earth and space.

PLAYWRIGHT'S NOTE

Play the play swiftly. I mean fast—*very* fast.

Slashes indicate where the following line should begin. Parenthetical lines are spoken under non-parenthetical lines. [*] is an abrupt "jump cut" in time.

Once the astronauts make it to "outer space" they are in zero g. They float, they walk along the back wall, some are upside down, some are right side up, some are sideways. In each scene (or sub-scene), the astronauts assume a different tableau. Vary it up. Let there be times when they are hanging in a row facing the audience; let there be times when they are scattered about all over the place.

Everyone in Mission Control has a light Texan accent; Alex has a Russian accent.

Portions of this play are sampled from transcripts of the Apollo-Soyuz Test Project's Technical Air to Ground Recording. This source material is available at history.nasa.gov/astp.

Six hours sleep for a working man,
Seven hours for a scholar,
Eight hours sleep for a simpleton,
Or a knave not worth a dollar.
—Old English Proverb

nightnight

A long table on stage.
And three chairs mounted on the stage's back wall.

SCENE 1: BEFORE ASTRONAUTS GO INTO SPACE, THEY ARE HOOKED UP TO LOTS OF MONITORS THAT MONITOR THEIR BODIES WHILE THEY ARE FAR FROM THE EARTH

Three ASTRONAUTS, *upstage, near the back wall.*

They're being hooked up by the crew: mics placed, hooked up to the flying rig, and electrodes to record biomedical telemetry.

A soft electronic TONE [*] *sounds, and then a couple of* MISSION CONTROL TECHS *calibrate the equipment.*

TOM. (*To* SUE.) she says six months is a long time,
I say it's not that long,
she says you don't need to go,
and I say I do
she says why
I say to fix the space station
she says why
I say because it's broken
and she says "why is that important, why do you—?"

> [*]

I say, if I don't go they'll think I'm useless,
they'll think I'm—and someone else will get my slot on this mission,
and I won't get the slot I normally get, they'll give it to

> [*]

acts like this mission's no big deal, and I said you're wrong, it is a big deal,
and she said, I know you think it's a big deal but it's not a big deal,
not as big a deal as you think, because people don't care,
not as much as you think they do—no one cares about astronauts and what astronauts do,
she said, no one even knows the names of astronauts, no one knows who you are—
except for the first ones, the first ever astronauts and the ones who went to the moon
and the ones that get blown up in space shuttle explosions

SUE. no, that's not true, people don't remember the names of the ones who get blown up either

TOM. and I said they'll know who I am, and they'll know my name,
and they'll know because someday, if I keep going the way I'm going,
I'll be one of the first ones who goes to Mars—
when the time comes to—when we can to go to Mars, when we—and she says,
she tells me if I go on this mission, this six-month mission we're about to go on—
she says that if I go on this mission,
then when I come back she'll be gone and

                [*]

but it's my job, this is what I do,
this is—and she says

                [*]

and then the other girl, that other one

SUE. the redhead—?

TOM. no, the other one that I was seeing on the side

SUE. with the

TOM. yeah

SUE. and the

TOM. she said almost the same exact thing to me this morning, almost—
I mean come on, what is it with these

                [*]

SUE. are you sad—?

TOM. no

                [*]

SUE. are you sad—?

TOM. no, not really it's just really shitty timing is all

                [*]

SUE. are you—?

TOM. I'm gonna go to Mars someday and when that happens, that'll be

                [*]

ALEX. ...

TOM. ...

ALEX. ...

TOM. what are you looking at?

ALEX. …Nothing.

I am looking at nothing.

[*]

> (*Just as the crew finishes hooking them up, remainder of* MISSION
> CONTROL *enters, sits at a long table, and…*)

SCENE 2: THE LAUNCH

[*]

CLOCK. T-minus, 20, 19, 18, 17…

> (*And so on.*
>
> *And as the* CLOCK *counts down, the* ASTRONAUTS *walk up the wall*
> *about 20 feet or so*
> *to a row of three chairs*
> *placed tightly, side by side.*
>
> *The* ASTRONAUTS *sit in their chairs,*
> *countdown continues.*)

12, 11, 10

> (*The* ASTRONAUTS *strap in…*)

5, 4, 3, 2, 1

> **CONTROL.**
> Ignition

TOM.

and we have lift-off

> **DICK.**
> lift-off
> **DIRECTOR.**
> And the clock is started

[*]

> **CLOCK.**
> time zero seconds/ into launch
> **DICK.**
> roger

SUE.

and program 11

TOM.
roger

               CLOCK.
               we're at 12 seconds/ and

ALEX.
Roger
TOM.
Roger,/ we have
SUE.
Roger. Tower clear.

               DICK.
               Roger Tom—good thrust on all engines/ —right on the money.

TOM.
Roger
ALEX.
roll program started

               DICK.
               Roger, Alex.

TOM.
There she/ goes.
SUE.
Pitch program, a little shaky lift-off but, it's smooth as silk now, Dick.

               DICK.
               Okay.
               CLOCK.
               at 30 seconds

       [*]

               DIRECTOR.
               Stand by for Mode 1, Bravo.

                                      GUIDANCE.
                                      (Mode 1)
                                      CONTROL.
                                      (Mark 1, Bravo.)

               CLOCK.
               at 47 seconds

                                      GUIDANCE.
                                        (copy)

SUE.
Roger. 1 Bravo, 2 g's.

DICK.
Roger, cabin

GUIDANCE.
(stand by
checking on)

CONTROL.
cabin pressure's coming down

RETRIEVAL.
(copy)

SUE.
Roger.

DICK.
Your feet are wet and you are on your way

TOM.
Roger, feet are wet

GUIDANCE.
(still in Mode 1)
RETRIEVAL.
(stand by for
Mode 2)

ALEX.
real smooth launch, Dick

DICK.
roger
CLOCK.
1 minute,/ 3 seconds on the clock

TOM.
EDS Auto
SUE.
off
TOM.
2 Engine
SUE.
out

CONTROL.
(we need a check
on the EDS light)

TOM.
LV Rates

GUIDANCE.
(copy)
RETRIEVAL.
(roger, stand
by for)

ALEX.
copy

CLOCK.
1 minute, 38

[*]

we are at 2 minutes,/ 3 seconds
CONTROL.
and you are GO for staging.

TOM.
Roger, GO for staging
SUE.
4 g's

GUIDANCE.
(confirmed
GO for staging)

TOM.
Inboard
ALEX.
Outboard
TOM.
Staging

DIRECTOR.
(Control,   please
affirm standby)

ALEX.
Staging.

DICK.
Roger.
CONTROL.
confirmed, we have you staging

TOM.
roger

RETRIEVAL.
(Check that light
on the IVB)

CLOCK.
we are at 3 minutes, 32 seconds

[*]

TOM.
Roger, Dick

CLOCK.
we are 4 minutes, 47/ seconds into mission

SUE.
48, 49, 50

ALEX.
—jett it

TOM.
Tower jett—there she goes

CONTROL.
Tower jett

DICK.
Roger, confirm/ tower jett

RETRIEVAL.
Roger, tower jettison affirm

GUIDANCE.
(copy, and
ready for Mode 2)

TOM.
Adios

CONTROL.
and you're Mode 2

ALEX.
Roger, Mode 2 is

DICK.
ya' holdin up fine there Alex—?

ALEX.
roger, holdin up

GUIDANCE.
(preparing
for guidance)

CONTROL.
(guidance)

DIRECTOR.
Okay, and we got the steam
running with the water.

SUE.
guidance is initiated.

CONTROL.
Roger. Concur.

ALEX.
(onboard looks good, Tom)

TOM.
(copy, Alex)

SUE.
at 5-11

CLOCK.
5 minutes

[*]

6 minutes

[*]

7 minutes, 27 seconds

[*]

TOM.
Dick, confirm clear status

DICK.
Stand by, we are

GUIDANCE.
(We're gonna get
you that clear
status ASAP)

SUE.
Onboard lights are

RETRIEVAL.
Roger lights,
stand by for
pressure/ readout

TOM.
(back to 1-g/ acceleration and looking good, Dick)

SURGEON.
(please/ confirm we are getting readouts on biomedical telemetry on all/ three)

DIRECTOR.
(Roger Flight Surgeon, copy, we are getting clear readouts on biomedical telemetry)

DICK.
Roger, Tom

ALEX.
Pressure/ steady at 50.3

CONTROL.
Tom

TOM.
Roger

CONTROL.
at 8 minutes you're a GO.

DICK.
Roger, that is a beautiful trajectory and/ you are confirmed for clear status

CLOCK.
8 minutes, 0 seconds

CONTROL.
you are GO for final staging

CLOCK.
5,/ 4, 3, 2, 1

DICK.
GO for final staging

TOM.
final staging

RETRIEVAL.
(stand by
final staging)

SUE.
Roger that, final/ staging

DICK.
final staging

GUIDANCE.
roger, go for

DICK.
and

[*]

DICK.
confirm you are in zero g now

TOM.
roger, that's affirm

[*]

(MISSION CONTROL *crew applauds.*)

DICK.
an' I reckon you can unbuckle those seat belts
now and have a

[*]

SCENE 3: THE ASTRONAUTS ARE IN SPACE

[*]

(*Music plays, Chopin's Nocturne in F-minor.*
TOM *and* SUE *and* ALEX *unbuckle and leave their seats.*
They float in zero g.)

DICK. how's it look up there

TOM. Looks good onboard, Dick. And we've got a beautiful

SUE. view of the

TOM. see the Earth there—

SUE. those effects of zero g

DIRECTOR. How're ya hanging in there Al—?

SUE. roger, I am hanging in

TOM. see the Earth here and it's

DICK. roger

TOM. got a big blue ocean out there

DICK. must be somethin

TOM. wish you were here to see it, Dick

SUE. not sure if that's a star

DICK. wish I could see what you're seein'

TOM. make sure to take some pictures

DICK. ha ha ha ha—roger

TOM. ...Man, I tell you, this is worth all those hours in the vomit comet

DICK. roger, that really

TOM. and wish you were here, Dick

DICK. so do I, I'm really

TOM. next in line

DICK. that's what they tell me

TOM. roger, you'll get here

DICK. just a rickety ticker here, little heart problem got me grounded, but I'm doin my best to

[*]

(*Cut music.*)

SCENE 4: THE ASTRONAUTS DO THE WORK THAT ASTRONAUTS DO

[*]

DICK. Alright we have a pretty full schedule—we need you guys to

TOM. ready when/ you are

CLOCK. at 9-20

CONTROL. check the valve in section H

TOM. (copy)

SURGEON. Alex, I'd like to start you off with/ exercise, for

ALEX. (copy)

RETRIEVAL. Sue, get some photos on the upcoming/ ATS passes

SUE. (roger)

CONTROL. replace the H-valve and then/ test the H-valve

TOM. (roger)

SURGEON. need to get your heart rate up to at least 70

ALEX. (copy)

CLOCK. 12-46

GUIDANCE. there' s a faulty panel on the

TOM. (copy)

DIRECTOR. check the temperature on the fungal/ specimens

SUE. (roger)

RETRIEVAL. Those ATS passes are coming up/ in 10, 9, 8

SUE. (copy)

CLOCK. 2-oh-5

SURGEON. Alexsandr

ALEX. I am exercising/ now

DICK. gonna have you update the navigation/ coordinates on the

TOM. (roger)

CLOCK. 4-37

RETRIEVAL. Sue, your first target is Death Valley

SUE. (copy)

DIRECTOR. Tom, Control isn't happy with the readout we're getting/ on that H-valve

TOM. (roger)

GUIDANCE. Tom, we need you to adjust your trajectory by

TOM. (roger, standby)

RETRIEVAL. Sue your next target is the Grand Canyon

SUE. (copy)

SURGEON. Alexsandr

ALEX. I am still exercising

DIRECTOR. Tom, we need you to update those/ coordinates now

TOM. (Roger, I)

CLOCK. 5-oh-5/ o'clock

CONTROL. Tom, we're gonna need you to go a little faster/ than that

TOM. sorry I can't move that fast,/ I'm trying but

SURGEON. Al, you don't have a go-ahead to stop exercising, not yet

ALEX. (roger)

RETRIEVAL. Sue I think you missed Death Valley, those pictures aren't quite

SUE. (roger)

RETRIEVAL. this is your last chance to

SUE. (copy)

DIRECTOR. and if you don't

TOM. (roger)

CONTROL. on target for a collision if you

TOM. (copy)

ALEX. heart rate is at 75

CLOCK. 6-32

DICK. we're behind schedule, folks—we need to

[*]

SCENE 5: AFTER A LONG AND DIFFICULT DAY OF WORK, THE ASTRONAUTS SLEEP

[*]

(*The* ASTRONAUTS *sleep.*

And even though it's night, MISSION CONTROL *is still staffed, still busy, still monitoring the* ASTRONAUTS, *except that we don't hear them.*

Bright bright lights stay on ASTRONAUTS.

Sound of spacecraft, ambient sound, loud, disconcerting noises.

They are all sprawled in different directions akimbo, floating.

All astronaut eyes are closed, except for TOM; *his eyes are wide open.*)

[*]

(TOM *appears very much alone.*

Floating.)

[*]

(*In space.*

Miles and miles and miles away from home.

We stay in this moment for a while.)

[*]

SCENE 6: WHEN THE ASTRONAUTS WAKE UP IN THE MORNING, MISSION CONTROL MAKES THEM ANSWER A BUNCH OF QUESTIONS ABOUT HOW THEY'RE DOING

[*]

SURGEON. ready for morning reports go ahead—

CLOCK. Day 2, 8-11 o'clock

DICK. crew, do you copy

SUE. we copy

DIRECTOR. when you're ready

RETRIEVAL. (standby for dietary reports, and we're)

SURGEON. start with dietary reports

TOM. one chicken, one cream spinach, one

[*]

SURGEON. confirm heart rates

[*]

blood pressure

[*]

radiation levels at

[*]

approximate stress level

[*]

water consumption

[*]

urination

[*]

urine color

[*]

bowel movements if any

[*]

consistency of bowel

[*]

approximate size of

[*]

sleep, please report on the duration and quality of

[*]

Al we have you down for

RETRIEVAL. 7 hours 15/ minutes

DICK. please confirm whether

ALEX. affirm

GUIDANCE. (copy)

SURGEON. any interruptions, any

ALEX. no

GUIDANCE. (copy)

SURGEON. Sue

SUE. roger

GUIDANCE. 5 hours 30 minutes

SUE. that's affirm

SURGEON. any interruptions

SUE. affirm, woke up around 3a.m. Awake for approximately 30 minutes

RETRIEVAL. (copy)

SURGEON. and Tom

GUIDANCE. stand by

SURGEON. roger,/ stand by

GUIDANCE. our readouts

SURGEON. copy

GUIDANCE. we show only 45 minutes

SURGEON. Tom, can you

TOM. roger

SURGEON. is that affirm

TOM. ...

DICK. Tom, is that affirm

TOM. that's a negative

SURGEON. that's a negative—?

TOM. that's a negative

RETRIEVAL. (roger, we have negative on 45/ minutes of sleep)

CONTROL. (we're getting a negative on the sleep readout for Tom, get some follow-up on the)

SURGEON. do you, could you just

TOM. I slept for 7 hours last night

GUIDANCE. (copy, 7 hours)

SURGEON. roger

TOM. roger

SURGEON. you're sure/ that's a

TOM. pretty sure about that, roger

SURGEON. cuz we have you sleeping for/ only

TOM. I copy that, 45 minutes, that's not correct—definitely slept for 7/ hours

DICK. and Gail can you one more time confirm your readout

GUIDANCE. we have 45

RETRIEVAL. (copy 45)

CONTROL. roger, that's affirm

TOM. definitely/ 7 hours, 6 maybe, probably 7

CONTROL. why don't you check your connection there,/ maybe something's broken

DICK. Sue, maybe you can check that monitor, make/ sure everything is working the way it should be working

DIRECTOR. Sue do you copy

SUE. roger, stand by, checking the monitor

TOM. you're wrong, that's not—no, 7 hours definitely, I

                    [*]

SCENE 7: SUE AND TOM HAVE A SECRET CONVERSATION IN THE MIDDLE OF THE NIGHT WHILE ALEX SLEEPS

                    [*]

TOM. kinda seems like they're on my ass

SUE. you just

TOM. kinda

SUE. because you didn't sleep last night

TOM. so

SUE. you didn't sleep

TOM. I slept

SUE. very little

TOM. I

SUE. no, I know you're

                    [*]

for the past two days

                    [*]

the past three days

                    [*]

past four days, we've been in orbit for—for almost a week, you've barely slept, it's now

TOM. never had this problem before

SUE. are you having trouble sleeping because you're nervous—?

TOM. about

SUE. the extravehicular mission

TOM. no

SUE. because space walks are scary

TOM. not really

SUE. going out into space, into nothingness, just you and me

TOM. nah

SUE. fixing the space station, scared that you'll mess up

TOM. nah

SUE. it'll be fine nothing to worry about

      [*]

TOM. and they won't let me come back if they find out I'm not sleeping— grounded in Mission Control, I can't

      [*]

no more mission to Mars, no

      [*]

really want to go to Mars

      [*]

just like Dick. They found out he had some heart pains, here and there, a little pain, no big—so what—who cares—and now he's grounded, stuck in Mission Control, never coming to space, never

      [*]

replace with a

      [*]

that guy, that

      [*]

Russian, never trained with us, never part of our—not one of us

      [*]

gonna keep happenin'—if we—replacing us with Japanese and Russians and the

      [*]

used to be we were the leaders, and then—and what happened to—?

      [*]

slipping away, out of our

      [*]

and look at him—sleeping like a

      [*]

lazy

      [*]

turd

      [*]

gonna need your help here

      [*]

need your help

      [*]

SUE. what sort of—?

TOM. the monitor

SUE. what

TOM. this thing they got me hooked up to

SUE. yes, what about it

TOM. make it so they can't tell—make it so that—
tell them my monitor is broken, that they can't watch me,
can't listen to my body, can't tell when I'm

SUE. if I

TOM. tell them the monitor is broken, and

SUE. you want me to actually break the monitor

TOM. yes

SUE. break it

TOM. you know how to do it so it doesn't look like we broke it

SUE. that's a bad idea

TOM. it's a good idea

SUE. no

TOM. but you know how

SUE. I do, yes, I do, but

TOM. so

[*]

because really actually I feel fine, I feel really good, feel like I'm on top of the

SUE. you're going to crash

TOM. sharp as a—and drink coffee, stay hydrated

SUE. you crash, it affects me, it affects all of us

TOM. volunteered for extra exercise because that helps too, keep me alert and keep the blood running

SUE. that's not

TOM. just concentration, just about making my head focus, and it's all in your head

SUE. but

TOM. almost like I can push from the back of my head to make myself more awake, and feel more

[*]

TOM. biggest problem are the little sleeps

SUE. the little sleeps

TOM. they're harder to avoid in zero g—because with gravity, you drift off, your head falls, your neck muscles snap, and that wakes you up, and you're back

SUE. but

TOM. here, with no gravity, it's just too easy to drift off for a

     [*]

and ya' know

     [*]

I fought for you to be on this mission,

I told Dick, an' I told Bo, an' I told Vance,

I said she's the best, she's tops, she's a pro, she's a real—

SUE. I know

TOM. told them I couldn't do it without you

SUE. I know

TOM. if I hadn't put my neck on the line, then

     [*]

SUE. but what if

TOM. yes what

SUE. the problem doesn't go away

TOM. it will

SUE. and you get worse

     [*]

SCENE 8: THE NEXT MORNING

     [*]

TOM. I told you my biomedical monitor was broken

CLOCK. Day 6, we are at 8-10 o'clock and 27 days until extravehicular/ mission

SURGEON. roger, we

TOM. told you it was wrong about how much I was sleeping

SURGEON. roger

TOM. told you I was sleeping

DICK. any sort of workaround that we could try to get his biomedical monitor up and workin' again—?

TOM. no

DIRECTOR. Sue

SUE. …no workaround

DICK. you can't just

SUE. nope

CONTROL. and you couldn't

SUE. nope

SURGEON. so how do we—?

SUE. you can't

DIRECTOR. confirm that we are getting no biomedical data from Tom for this entire mission

SUE. roger, nothing we can

CONTROL. actually

SUE. nothing

CONTROL. actually, it seems like one possible solution would be to just switch back and forth between Tom and Sue—have one wear the monitor one day and the other the other day—they could share—doesn't that seem like a workable solution?

SURGEON. …

CONTROL. …

SURGEON. …no, I don't think

CONTROL. but

SUE. roger, that's a very bad idea

SURGEON. you'd just get half the data on two people instead all of the data on/ one person and

DICK. I agree that's a very bad idea

SURGEON. well shit then

TOM. roger, sorry to

SURGEON. well shit

DICK. copy, nothing we can do, we

[*]

SCENE 9: AFTER A LONG DAY OF WORK, THE ASTRONAUTS PLAY A GAME TO KEEP THEIR SPIRITS UP

[*]

TOM. okay, here I go

     (TOM *does two flips.*)

SUE. that's the most Tom can do

ALEX. I will try

(ALEX *does three flips.*)

SUE. is that the most you can do—?

ALEX. no, I can do five in a row

SUE. that was three, five is a lot harder than three

ALEX. I know but I can do five, that was three but at my best I can do five

TOM. so you're saying you're not at your best—?

ALEX. you're

TOM. clearly

ALEX. did five all the time on the Russian missions—on the Soyuz missions, we

TOM. you're not on the Soyuz anymore.

ALEX. What does that mean—?

TOM. just saying you do less here than you did on the Soyuz.

ALEX. …

TOM. …

ALEX. Five is very difficult, Sue. I bet you can't even do three

SUE. I bet I can do four in a row

ALEX. four is difficult, Tom can barely do two

SUE. Tom isn't very good at this

TOM. I could probably do three

ALEX. I can do five

SUE. if I can do four what will you give me

ALEX. I'll give you my strawberries

SUE. I don't want your strawberries

ALEX. that's what I

SUE. I do four, then I get to sleep where you sleep

ALEX. that's not, no, why

SUE. because I know why you sleep where you sleep, you sleep where you sleep,

because where you sleep is by the water tank, and when you sleep by the water tank

you get less radiation

ALEX. okay

SUE. you get less radiation there, I know that's why you don't let anyone else have that spot,

and that's why you're always the first to sleep, because you don't want to give up that spot, you

ALEX. okay

SUE. where I sleep, that's the spot where the radiation levels are highest, and I don't want that spot anymore

ALEX. I

SUE. don't want any more radiation than I already

ALEX. you

SUE. get all sorts of tumors

ALEX. if

SUE. I win, I get your spot for the next week,
if I win, we trade and

ALEX. no

SUE. then I won't play the game.

ALEX. …

SUE. …

ALEX. …five

SUE. …I have to do five—?

ALEX. you can't do five

SUE. okay, I can probably do five

TOM. I could probably do three

ALEX. okay, you will do five

SUE. how many tries do I—?

ALEX. One. One try

SUE. if I can do five, then I get the spot by the water tank for the remainder of the mission. And if I lose, then you get the spot for the remainder of the mission. Deal?

ALEX. …deal.

> (SUE *does one flip, followed by…*)

okay that's one, that's easy

> (*A second flip.*)

two is also easy, it will start to get harder on the third

> (*Followed by a third flip.*)

that's three, okay, so what, that's three

TOM. If I practiced I could probably do that many

ALEX. four is harder,

see—? you're having difficulty on the fourth

> (*Completes the fourth, and she's just starting to lose some momentum.*)

that's four, but you're not going to be able to do the fifth, I can tell

(*Making the fifth.*)

I can tell, you're not going to be able to do five

    (*Still going, barely, but still going.*)

nope

    (*Still going.*)

TOM. she's doing five

ALEX. nope

    (*And she just barely makes it to a fifth.*)

SUE. …

ALEX. …

SUE. five.

TOM. You're not on the Soyuz anymore, Alex.

    [*]

SCENE 10: ALEX HAS A PROBLEM

    [*]

ALEX. I have a problem

DICK. roger, Alex—what is your

ALEX. I am very unsatisfied by my assignments on this mission.

CLOCK. Day 17, 4-15 o'clock

DIRECTOR. roger, would you repeat that, Alex

CLOCK. 16 days until extravehicular/ mission

ALEX. I believe my talents are under-utilized. I was supposed to be doing things here. But all of things I was supposed to be doing, the experiments and the studies, I am not doing

DIRECTOR. roger, we copy we had to make some adjustments to the flight plan in order to

ALEX. all I have been doing

DICK. (roger)

ALEX. is reporting temperature, reporting cabin pressure, and exercising.

DICK. (roger)

ALEX. I have been exercising a lot

DIRECTOR. because we haven't been able to get biomed readings from Tom, we had to/ give you the bulk of the

ALEX. roger, I understand but

DIRECTOR. roger we appreciate your cooperation with those last minute changes

ALEX. Sue and Tom do everything, and they are going on the space walk

DIRECTOR. roger, that was the original plan—do not anticipate having to change/ that plan

ALEX. would like to propose that if a second extravehicular mission is necessary

DIRECTOR. roger Alex, we copy, but we do not anticipate needing a second/ space walk

ALEX. roger, but if a second one is needed, I would like to go on that mission.

DIRECTOR. …

ALEX. Flight Director, do you copy—?

DICK. Alex, we copy

ALEX. and

DIRECTOR. the answer is no

ALEX. no

DIRECTOR. roger, that's a negative

ALEX. explain why

DIRECTOR. several factors

ALEX. I have trained extensively for/ extravehicular activities

DICK. copy, we hear you. You trained.
We are aware of that.
The answer is no.

ALEX. why—?

DIRECTOR. you haven't trained in our suits

ALEX. it's close enough

DICK. you haven't trained with the other two

ALEX. are professionals, they are/ adaptable

DIRECTOR. and if there's a problem in/ the suit and

ALEX. there won't be a

DICK. but if

[*]

DIRECTOR. policies are

[*]

regulations are

[*]

strict, so we

[*]

have to understand the

[*]

the position we're in is

[*]

if a Russian cosmonaut died in an American suit, it would be a problem/ in
the

ALEX. oh come on

DIRECTOR. just the kind of

ALEX. oh come on

DIRECTOR. it's

ALEX. but

DIRECTOR. Roger—Alexsandr, we appreciate your understanding—your
compliance with our—thank you for

[*]

SCENE 11: IN THE MIDDLE OF THE NIGHT, ALEX AND SUE HAVE A SECRET CONVERSATION WHILE TOM PRETENDS HE IS SLEEPING

[*]

ALEX. I am sorry for waking you up, Sue, but

SUE. it's not

ALEX. speak with you about

SUE. it's very late

ALEX. sometimes I

[*]

don't think you like me

SUE. no, I

ALEX. like me better than he likes me—
he hates me.
You don't hate me,
but you don't like me

SUE. I'm neutral

ALEX. but if you're neutral with me
but better than neutral with him
then I might have a problem, I might

[*]

I know something,
I know something that you and him are trying to keep secret from

[*]

an' if I say something about it,
and if nobody believes me,
then I look like the bad guy,
I look like the difficult one,
but I know I'm right,
and if I tell them what I saw,
they would not believe

[*]

I am not difficult

[*]

I am not

[*]

I am very easy, and I

[*]

he's a mess

[*]

screwing up

[*]

and you know it

[*]

and I know you know it, he's not handling this mission well,
he's not—
I have seen him working,
then stop,
and for a long time
just stop, his eyes closed,
and you see him eyes closed,
and you nudge back, nudge him awake, and

[*]

down there, they do not know about this,
but I know,
and you know,
but you haven't told them

SUE. you

ALEX. know he cannot function

SUE. you think I

ALEX. should tell Mission Control what's really happening,
because if I tell they won't believe me,
and if you don't tell then
they will send you and him on the space walk
and he will screw it up, and who knows what will—

    [*]

SUE. there's nothing to tell

    [*]

there's nothing to

    [*]

ALEX. just answer me this, this is all I'm asking

SUE. what

ALEX. do you feel safe—?

SUE. safe

   (*She stares at* TOM, *"asleep"* TOM.)

ALEX. with him, do you feel safe going out there with him,
very soon you are going on an extravehicular mission,
and you will be out there,
with him,
alone with him.
Do you feel that if something went wrong,
he could react,
he could save you,
do you think if you needed—?

    [*]

I could, I am really

    [*]

but you

    [*]

and he

    [*]

and they all

    [*]

just so awkward sometimes

    [*]

your country, my country

    [*]

always in competition, even though
                    [*]
one thing that I learned from being a Buddhist is that
                    [*]
perspectives are
                    [*]
been away from Earth so long I
                    [*]
and all I want, more than anything
that moment, where I am out there,
in space
out there in space, floating,
and I can look down
and I can see the Earth
and I can say to myself,
there is the Earth, and there are my feet,
there is the Earth, and there are my—
there are my feet just—and there is the Earth beneath—
if I cannot have that moment,
then why was I even born, why
                    [*]
and if I do tell what I know
SUE. you won't
ALEX. seems I have got no other choice
SUE. you said they won't believe you
ALEX. but maybe they will
                    [*]
don't
                    [*]
don't say anything I
                    [*]
SUE. If you agree to say nothing, I'll give you your old spot,
the spot by the water tank—so you don't get so much radiation.
You can have that spot back if you agree that you'll
                    [*]
ALEX. no
SUE. but you like to sleep next to the water tank
                    [*]

ALEX. if you don't tell them, I will—I will tell and

[*]

SCENE 12: IT'S THE MIDDLE OF THE NIGHT AND ALEX IS ASLEEP AND TOM IS STILL NOT SLEEPING AND SUE CAN'T SLEEP BECAUSE TOM'S NOT SLEEPING AND BECAUSE SHE'S WORRIED THAT IF HE DOESN'T GET SOME SLEEP THEN SOMETHING REALLY BAD IS GOING TO—

[*]

SUE. so I made a list

[*]

I made a list

TOM. a list

SUE. of everything you could possibly do to make yourself sleep—I'm going to go through the list and

[*]

SUE. meditation

TOM. yes

SUE. you've tried

TOM. yes

SUE. breathing exercises

TOM. yes

SUE. melatonin

TOM. yes

SUE. triazolam

TOM. yes

SUE. doxepin

TOM. yes

SUE. temazepam

TOM. yes

SUE. doing math problems in your head

TOM. yes

SUE. crossword puzzles

TOM. yes

SUE. sudoku

TOM. yes

SUE. writing

TOM. yes

SUE. reading

TOM. yes

SUE. what about reading something really boring—?

TOM. yes

SUE. making lists—?

TOM. yes

SUE. listening to music

TOM. yes

SUE. relaxing music

TOM. yes

SUE. closing your eyes and refusing to open them

TOM. yes

SUE. watching movies

TOM. yep

SUE. praying

TOM. yes

SUE. masturbating

TOM. yes

SUE. like several times in a row

TOM. yes

SUE. chamomile tea

TOM. yes

SUE. or what about closing your eyes and just letting the thoughts go, just tell yourself that you can think anything you want, and you don't stop your head from thinking whatever it wants to think

TOM. no

SUE. should try it

TOM. no

SUE. because maybe that's the problem: you're trying to keep your head from thinking what it wants to think

TOM. no

SUE. why

TOM. scared to

SUE. but

TOM. no

      [*]

SUE. Tom.

      [*]

Tom

TOM. yes?

SUE. Next week

TOM. yes

SUE. we're going out there,
we're going to get into space suits,
we're going to be tethered by a cable
to the ship,
and we're going out into a vacuum
into space
into nothingness

TOM. yeah

SUE. and it's dangerous

TOM. roger, I

SUE. it's

TOM. roger that, I

SUE. and it's gonna be you and it's gonna be me,
and we're going to have to do work on the space station,
and we're going to fix a space station that's worth billions of dollars
that took years and thousands of people to get into orbit,
and if we screw it up,
then the whole thing breaks
and then it's my fault and it's your fault
and

      [*]

fact is—I know—if there's a problem, they'll say it's more my fault than your fault,
because they're like that with the women.
No one admits it, but it's true, they're always

      [*]

don't wanna be the one they all use as an example of

      [*]

TOM. ...

      [*]

SUE. you're keeping me up, I have to go to sleep

      [*]

TOM. maybe it would help me sleep if you hold me

SUE. hold you

TOM. as I close my eyes and

SUE. hold you—?

TOM. might help me fall asleep

SUE. ...

TOM. might help.

SUE. ...I think it would be a little awkward

TOM. yes

SUE. in zero g, to

TOM. yes, I guess, sure

      [*]

you're right

      [*]

SUE. I need/ to sleep

TOM. no yeah that's okay I

      [*]

SUE. ...

TOM. ...

      [*]

SUE. if you don't get some sleep Alex is going to tell Mission Control—said if I don't tell then he'll tell and

TOM. I know, I heard.

      [*]

SCENE 13: MISSION CONTROL RUNS THROUGH FINAL PLANS FOR THE SPACE WALK

      [*]

DIRECTOR. one last time—we're gonna run through the plans for

CLOCK. we're at 11-oh-6

DICK. please confirm that you

DIRECTOR. turn to page 187 of your

CLOCK. day 25, and 7 days until extravehicular mission

[*]

DICK. and after you suit up, you will exit the spacecraft

CONTROL. turn left, you will locate a 5-foot rod at

[*]

you will use this rod to climb up to east port of the

[*]

DICK. make sure you move at a rate of one foot per 20 seconds

[*]

CONTROL. remove the panel labeled HR-GG045

[*]

using a screwdriver you will

[*]

DIRECTOR. careful of any debris

[*]

possibility of debris that could puncture the suit, so you have to

[*]

CONTROL. once the panel is open

[*]

if you determine that there is wire damage

[*]

if you replace the wires running into the

[*]

DIRECTOR. but if you do

[*]

careful of the

[*]

CONTROL. could short the

[*]

set off the radiator

DIRECTOR. whole space station will incinerate if you

CONTROL. but also be careful to

[*]

and if you

[*]

RETRIEVAL. don't forget to

[*]

CONTROL. and make sure you pause at every 2-minute mark, and confirm oxygen tank levels

        [*]

or else

        [*]

and then

DIRECTOR. check to make sure that the cabin pressure levels are at

DICK. that's the outer cabin unit we're talking about, not the

        [*]

CONTROL. or else

        [*]

locked out of the space craft

DIRECTOR. nothing we can do if you

DICK. do you copy

SUE. roger, I copy

DICK. do you copy, Tom

TOM. roger all of that, copy

DICK. alright, are there any questions or concerns?

TOM. …

SUE. …

ALEX. …

DICK. no concerns? no questions?

ALEX. …

TOM. roger

DICK. Go ahead Tom

TOM. I'm going to recommend that Alex replace Sue on the mission

DICK. …roger

TOM. do you copy

DIRECTOR. you are requesting that Alex replace Sue on the space walk

TOM. roger that's affirm

DIRECTOR. Sue have you—?

SUE. negative

DIRECTOR. you

SUE. roger I am very surprised by what Tom has just said and am not sure why Tom said what Tom just said, I

TOM. observed Sue drift off on several occasions during the past couple of weeks

SUE. roger, that's a negative/ I have

TOM. Flight Surgeon can confirm that she's been sleeping 5, 4 hours a night

[*]

think it's taking a toll

DIRECTOR. stand by Tom, we

SUE. I haven't

DICK. get confirmation on

SUE. That's a negative, Tom is the one who has been having problems sleeping

DICK. down here in Mission Control we're under the impression that Tom has been sleeping 6 to 7 hours and the impression we had that he was not sleeping was due to the broken biomed monitor

SUE. yes, that's

[*]

yes, that's true I

SURGEON. are you telling us that Tom's monitor/ was not broken—?

DICK. Sue, are you telling us that Tom's monitor was not broken—because three weeks ago you said—?

SUE. roger, I

CONTROL. confirm for us whether or not

SUE. yes, I did report that Tom's monitor was/ broken

CONTROL. Tom's monitor is broken, but your monitor seems to be working fine

SURGEON. have data reporting that you've been sleeping 4 to 5 hours a night

SUE. roger, I

[*]

DIRECTOR. and Alex—?

ALEX. roger

DIRECTOR. Alex have you also observed Sue falling asleep mid-activity?

ALEX. …

DICK. do you copy, Alex—?

ALEX. yes

DIRECTOR. have you—?

ALEX. I have

DICK. is that affirm—?

ALEX. roger, that's affirm

RETRIEVAL. copy/ that's affirm I

ALEX. I have seen her drift off

DICK. and you

ALEX. do not think she should
go on this extravehicular mission, I

[*]

DICK. copy

[*]

DIRECTOR. stand by, while we

[*]

SUE. I do not affirm what they

DICK. Sue, stand by while we

[*]

stand by...

[*]

SCENE 14: TOM TRIES TO SAY HE'S SORRY

[*]

SUE. ...

TOM. ...

SUE. ...

[*]

TOM. I'm sorry I

[*]

not a bad guy

[*]

you were gonna tell them that I wasn't

SUE. wasn't going to tell

TOM. yes, you said

[*]

and so I

[*]

no choice

[*]

if you had

[*]

have to understand
SUE. no, I don't
                          [*]
won't ever come back, that's it for me—I'm
TOM. no, that's not necessarily
                          [*]
I needed to go on this mission, I couldn't just
                          [*]
and when I go home, there's nothing there,
I have nothing,
this is all I have,
I have nothing,
I'm all alone
SUE. and now I know why
                          [*]
TOM. ...
SUE. ...

                          [*]
TOM. someday you'll forgive me
                          [*]
didn't have a choice, I
                          [*]
someday
                          [*]
just gotta—someday—gonna go to Mars and
                          [*]
              (*Chopin returns.*)
                          [*]
TOM. ...
SUE. ...

                          [*]
TOM. I've been sleeping.
SUE. ...
TOM. I've been sleeping a lot now.
SUE. ...
TOM. like 7, 8 hours a night
SUE. ...

TOM. I sleep all night now, but when I sleep, it's all
                    [*]
nightmares
                    [*]
terrible nightmares,
nightmares about the space walk
that's happening in 3 days
                    [*]
2 days
                    [*]
that's happening tomorrow
                    [*]
every night, same nightmare
                    [*]
where I'm out there
in the suit
and the tether breaks.
In the dream, I never see how it breaks
or why it breaks,
but that's what happens,
every time: the tether breaks,
and I try to grab onto the edge of the ship
but I miss
                    [*]
and I just keep going
farther and farther away from the spacecraft.
And my suit is equipped with a nitrogen blast.
And I fire it and hope that it sends me back in the direction of the spacecraft.
But every time it either doesn't fire
or it misfires
or it fires but it fires in the wrong direction.
And so I keep floating because there's nothing to stop me.
But I have my radio,
and I have about 45 minutes of oxygen left in my primary tank,
and I can hear Mission Control and they can hear me.
And the people on Earth, in Mission Control,
they can patch me through to
maybe a girlfriend or something.
And I try calling but she doesn't pick up.
So I try calling one of the other girlfriends,

but she's not home.
And I ask Mission Control to play me a song or something,
but in the dream, they don't have any of the music that I like,
and so I sit in silence and look around
and I can see the stars,
and the stars look different because
all I have is a thin visor between me and the stars
and I can see what starlight really looks like
and real starlight is all sorts of colors like red and purple and blue.
And when my 45 minutes of oxygen run out,
I have a choice: I can let them run out
or I can switch to my secondary tank,
and that will give me another 2 hours
and I can use that extra time to call my mother and say goodbye
or I could just keep drifting off and looking at the stars,
but whether or not I switch to those secondary tanks,
either way,
eventually, the oxygen will run out.
And when it runs out, it runs out gradually.
And when it runs out, I start to feel myself fading,
my vision becomes hazy,
and the one sun looks like two blurry suns.
And I look at our spacecraft,
and the spacecraft now looks like a tiny white speck,
a small point of light, way far away,
but a "far away" that seems sort of close
and easy to get to,
except I'm too tired to try,
and that feels good,
because that's how the brain tells you to feel
in moments like this,
that's how—and I feel sleepy,
and I feel slow,
and I feel hazy,
and I feel nice.
And then my brain shuts off.
And soon after,
so do I.

[*]

and then
that's when I wake up.
SUE. ...

TOM. …

[*]

CLOCK. End of Play.

[*]

(*Blackout.*)